THE GREAT IRISH POTATO FAMINE

THE GREAT IRISH POTATO FAMINE

JAMES S. DONNELLY, JR

SUTTON PUBLISHING

First published in the United Kingdom in 2001 by
Sutton Publishing Limited · Phoenix Mill
Thrupp · Stroud · Gloucestershire · GL5 2BU

Paperback edition first published in 2002

Reprinted in 2002, 2004

British Library Cataloguing in Publication Data
A catalogue record for this book is available from the British Library.

ISBN 0-7509-2928-6

Typeset in 11.5/15pt Garamond.
Typesetting and origination by
Sutton Publishing Limited.
Printed and bound in England by
J.H. Haynes & Co. Ltd, Sparkford.

For Joan

'While still I may, I write for you
The love I lived, the dream I knew.'

(*From Yeats's poem 'To Ireland in the coming times'*)

Contents

Preface

The central core of this book stems from a set of chapters on the great Irish potato famine that first appeared in 1989 as part of *A new history of Ireland* (volume v, part 1), published by Oxford University Press. This massive volume of almost 850 pages, like the others in that remarkable scholarly enterprise, had a limited circulation outside academic circles and university libraries, even though the contributors often took an approach that would have made their work accessible to a wider audience. Since those chapters were written, the amount of scholarly attention devoted to the great famine has expanded enormously, mostly as a result of the impetus given by the official sesquicentennial commemoration of the famine in the years 1995–7. Along with numerous other scholars, I made contributions to the extraordinary surge of publication associated with the commemoration. As I argue in the introduction to this book, the flowering of famine scholarship during the 1990s has given academic respectability to certain key nationalist perspectives on the famine, and on the issue of British government responsibility, that were previously out of fashion among professional historians, especially those working in Ireland itself. At the same time that interpretations have altered, our knowledge of the complexities of the famine experience and the British response to it has been greatly enriched by the new work. It seemed to me that useful purposes would be served by attempting to encourage a wider awareness among students and the interested lay public of the new knowledge and new understandings of the famine among professional historians.

My *New history of Ireland* chapters are republished here with only slight changes because the interpretations that they offer are firmly consistent with what turned out to be the general scholarly consensus that emerged during the 1990s. (Had they not been consistent, I hope that I would have had the good sense at least to reconsider my earlier views.) To this central core I have added the fruits of my own post-1989 thinking and writing on the famine and on the way in which it came to be remembered. Included in the largely historiographical introduction is a consideration of 'old' (nationalist) and 'new' (revisionist) interpretations of the famine that first appeared in *History Ireland* in the autumn of 1993. In what is now Chapter 4, I have drawn heavily on my essay published in the 1996 collection *'Fearful realities'* dealing with the poor law amendment act of June 1847, a law which enshrined the principle enthusiastically endorsed in Britain that 'Irish property must pay for Irish poverty'. To Chapter 6, dealing with landlords and tenants, I have added previously unpublished material on the mass evictions in County Clare and portions of my essay on the clearances which appeared in the 1995 collection of the Thomas Davis lectures entitled *The great Irish famine*. This chapter and the introduction also draw on the new work of other scholars who have recently written about the mass evictions of the late 1840s and early 1850s. Chapter 7 includes new material on epidemic disease and on the 'coffin ships' which synthesises some of the results of recent scholarship on these topics as part of a wider consideration of famine mortality and emigration. Chapter 9, which deals with the construction of the memory of the famine in Ireland and the Irish diaspora between 1850 and 1900, is essentially a republication of my essay on this subject that appeared in the journal *Éire-Ireland* in 1996. I am grateful to the editors of these publications for their kind permission to make further use of work which originally appeared in their pages.

In the introduction to this book I have tried to be especially mindful of the needs of students and general readers to know why the great famine struck Ireland with such ferocious intensity, why it affected certain social groups and regions so disproportionately, and why nationalist perspectives on the catastrophe enjoyed such longevity and (after a period when they became unfashionable among professional historians) have made a decided comeback in the last decade or so. All historical writing, and especially history aimed at a wide audience as this book certainly is, can be enhanced by visual representation. The struggles of numerous contemporaries to create and transmit visual images representing the disaster, however inadequately, are made abundantly manifest in the many illustrations reproduced in this book. The lengthy bibliography at the end, which heavily emphasises scholarly and occasionally more popular work published since about 1990, is a testimony to how much has been added to the literature on the famine in the very recent past. If this book opens doors for my readers to that now ample literature, I will feel well satisfied.

Acknowledgements

The primary debt of the author of a work of synthesis, such as this one is, must be to his fellow labourers in the vineyard of Irish famine studies. Their numbers and the quality of their output have grown remarkably in the last decade or so, to the point that the great famine has passed from being a strangely neglected byway in the historiography of modern Ireland to being deservedly one of its most heavily trafficked thoroughfares. My indebtedness to the work of these other scholars should be evident in various ways from the introduction, the notes, and the bibliography. Even when I have found myself in strong disagreement with some of them, they have provided the stimulation and intellectual nourishment on which scholarly discourse thrives.

Because much of this book first appeared as part of a large collective volume published by Oxford University Press, I am grateful for its permission to incorporate this earlier material in the expanded form presented here. I am particularly indebted to Dr Richard Hawkins, the secretary of *A new history of Ireland*, and to Dr W.E. Vaughan of Trinity College, Dublin, the editor of the particular volume in question, for all that they did to facilitate the realisation of a long-standing ambition to bring my famine chapters before a wider audience. Besides making significant editorial improvements at the outset, Dr Vaughan has made other valuable contributions to this book as well. I owe thanks of special magnitude to my good friend Dr Laurence Geary of University College, Cork. Words of his spoken in the right place really set in motion the events that led to the publication of this book. He also contributed generously from his own rich fund of knowledge about the medical history of the famine. For vital encouragement, sound criticism, and special acts of friendship at critical stages, I will always be enormously grateful to my dear friend Professor Líam Kennedy of the Queen's University of Belfast.

In the acquisition of the illustrations that enliven this book I received generous assistance from Síghle Bhreathnach-Lynch of the National Gallery of Ireland, who answered every anguished cry for help as soon as it was uttered, and from Noel Kissane of the National Library of Ireland, who showed the way in his own fine work and freely shared his resources with me. I also benefited greatly in this endeavour from the expert knowledge and kind assistance of my graduate student Michael de Nie and my friends Jim Baughman, Ruth Dudley Edwards, Larry Geary, Bill Maguire, James McGuire, and Betty Steinberg. The professional services that I received from Sandra Paske and her colleagues in the

Micro-imaging Laboratory of Memorial Library at the University of Wisconsin-Madison were magnificent in every respect. I would like to thank John O'Driscoll, manager of the Famine Museum at Strokestown Park, for the image of Major Mahon used in this book. Interested readers can access the museum's website (www.strokestownpark.ie), or e-mail info@strokestownpark.ie.

I must also acknowledge with deep gratitude the sabbatical leave granted for the writing of this book by the University of Wisconsin-Madison and the support received from Jane Crompton, senior editor at Sutton, whose personal interest in this work has been critical to its appearance in this accessible form. For the preparation of the electronic version of the typescript, a task requiring many skills and much patience with a very finicky and yet technically challenged author, I am extremely grateful to Scott Martin. The unpayable debts that I owe to my wife Joan, which include her gratuitous labours on this book in her professional capacity as a graphic designer, are recognised all too briefly in the dedication, and our daughters Jennifer, Eileen, and Elizabeth have made their own distinctive contributions to shaping their father's preoccupation with these immensely tragic years of the Irish past.

Lastly, interested readers should know that the bibliographical abbreviations and numerous short titles used in the notes section of the book are those prescribed in 'Rules for contributors to *Irish Historical Studies*', revised edition, by T.W. Moody, in *Irish Historical Studies*, supplement I (January 1968).

James S. Donnelly, Jr

Introduction

Pre-Famine Poverty

It was above all the poverty of such a large segment of the Irish population that made the great famine so destructive of human life. People with the scantiest resources were the most likely to succumb to starvation or disease when the potato crop failed repeatedly in the late 1840s. The dimensions and regional distribution of poverty on the eve of the famine can be gauged in a variety of ways. Contemporaries considered those who were exclusively or heavily dependent on the potato for their food to be poor, and historians today would strongly agree. Such people constantly struggled to keep their heads barely above water and were plunged below it whenever bad weather or crop disease or their own personal misfortunes struck without warning. Nowhere else in Europe did so high a proportion of the population come to rely on the potato for its food. P.M.A. Bourke, who did more than any other recent scholar to enlighten us on the central role of the potato in pre-famine Ireland, estimated that in 1845 as many as 4.7 million people, out of a total of about 8.5 million, depended on this root as the predominant item in their diet. Of these 4.7 million, some 3.3 million had a diet consisting more or less exclusively of potatoes, with milk or buttermilk and fish as the only other important sources of nourishment.[1] Dominating the ranks of the potato-eaters – and the poor – were landless agricultural labourers, cottiers (the smallest landholders), and other tenants with less than 20 acres of land. These groups made up that huge portion of the Irish population for whom the potato was either the very staff of life or, even in the northern 'oatmeal zone', still the predominant item in their diet. In those years before 1845 when the potato was in usual abundance, the average adult male of the labourer, cottier, or smallholder class consumed 12 to 14 lb of potatoes every day. This prodigious quantity of food, though stodgy and monotonous, generally maintained health when taken in conjunction with sufficient milk, since the milk supplied the nutriments missing in the potato. Though middling and larger farmers also included some potatoes with their more varied diets, their average daily consumption was only about one-half or one-quarter respectively of that of the poorest social groups.[2] The poorest together consumed perhaps 75 per cent of all the potatoes eaten by humans in Ireland on the eve of the famine, and they fed their pigs on a large additional fraction of the animal portion of the crop.[3]

When potatoes were in good supply before 1845, the average adult male of the labourer, cottier, or smallholder class consumed as much as a stone (14 lb) of potatoes a day. Even farmers with 20 to 50 acres of land, whose diet was much more varied, ate about half as much on average. Thus large quantities of potatoes were kept near at hand, such as in the loft over the fireplace of Pat Brennan, a 'small farmer' on Daniel O'Connell's estate in south Kerry, whose house is depicted in this sketch of February 1846. (*Pictorial Times*/The Trustees of the National Library of Scotland)

Pre-famine poverty was thus very much a matter of class, and famine mortality would be too.

Pre-famine poverty also exhibited strong regional dimensions, which can be seen in relation to the distinctly inferior quality of rural housing and the prevalence of illiteracy in the countryside. Though some observers maintained that farmers of real substance often disguised their wealth by living in houses of the meaner sort, this claim has been effectively refuted by recent research, and there is every reason to believe that the quality of housing occupied by different segments of the population is a reasonably good proxy for relative income and its regional distribution. The commissioners responsible for the 1841 census distinguished four different types of house. Those in the fourth or lowest class were 'all mud cabins having only one room', while those in the third class were 'a better description of cottage, still built of mud, but varying from 2 to 4 rooms and windows'. In Ireland as a whole, more than three-quarters of all houses fell into one or the other of these two lowest categories, and nearly two-fifths consisted of one-room mud cabins. The south-western and western counties from Cork to Donegal had the highest concentrations of fourth-class housing. In virtually every barony west of a line drawn from Derry to Cork, at least 40 per cent of the houses were in this category, and in some western baronies the proportion exceeded 60 per cent. By contrast, counties in Leinster and Ulster generally had substantially lower concentrations of one-room mud cabins and higher proportions of better houses.[4] A similar regional pattern emerges from an analysis of the 1841 data on literacy, which has commonly been employed as another proxy for poverty.[5] Illiteracy was greatest along the western seaboard on the eve of the famine. Male illiteracy topped 60 per cent in 1841 in Mayo, Sligo, Galway, and Kerry, with Cork, Clare, Roscommon, and Donegal not far behind. Somewhat lower levels of male illiteracy prevailed in an intermediate zone comprising most of Munster and the north midlands, whereas male literacy was highest in the north-east and the south-east as well as in Dublin.[6]

Confirming this picture of regional variation in the extent of pre-famine poverty is a recently published analysis of data from the mid-1830s on the daily wages and annual income of male labourers. Landless agricultural labourers constituted a substantial fraction of the population on the eve of the great famine. Together with their dependants, they numbered nearly 2.3 million in 1841, or more than a quarter of the total.[7] Many of them were 'bound' labourers, contracted to work for a particular farmer for a certain number of days per year in return for a cabin, a small plot of ground, and other 'privileges'. Other agricultural workers were 'unbound' and took work where they could find it, earning a wage that often included their diet or food, but sometimes did not. Underemployment was an especially severe problem among unbound labourers, many of whom had to migrate seasonally to other parts of Ireland or even to Britain in order to eke out a meagre living. Taking these and other complexities into account, the authors of the aforementioned study have enhanced our understanding of pre-famine poverty by mapping the income of Irish male labourers by county in 1835. Their map of the mean daily wage makes it possible to distinguish three broad areas: an eastern seaboard region of relatively high wages, an intermediate area of lower wages extending down through the centre of the country from Donegal to Cork, and a western band of counties (Kerry, Clare, Galway, and Mayo) where daily wages were lowest. Their companion map and analysis of average annual income demonstrates that labourers in the west were the recipients of even lower *annual* incomes, as compared with their eastern counterparts, than suggested by the map of *daily* wages alone.[8] Indeed, by another calculation the average yearly income of labouring families in Connacht in the mid-1830s was less than three-fifths of that in Leinster, the province with the highest wages.[9] These figures are of the utmost significance for the catastrophe that was about to happen. Confronted by the failure of their potatoes in the late 1840s, western labouring families lacked the means to buy food. They 'stood penniless in the face of doom'.[10]

POPULATION EXPLOSION

If poverty was widespread in pre-famine Ireland, and if it was especially acute in the west and much of the south, what had made it so, and was the problem actually worsening in the decades immediately before the famine? Pre-famine

Ireland was notorious for the rapidity of its population growth, and in the absence of sufficient economic expansion (there was certainly expansion but not enough) the swift pace of demographic increase firmly depressed the general material welfare of at least half the population. The great spurt in the population of Ireland began in the mid-eighteenth century and continued strongly, though with substantial regional variations, until the end of the Napoleonic wars in 1815. Only in the immediate aftermath of the wars did there finally occur a definite slackening in the national rate of growth, which persisted until the famine. Even so, the overall magnitude of the increase was enormous. Between 1750 and 1845 the total population of the country mushroomed from about 2.6 million to 8.5 million, or by some 225 per cent in a century.[11] Ireland was hardly alone in experiencing rapid population growth in the late eighteenth and early nineteenth centuries. What was distinctive about the Irish case were two things: the rate of expansion, which was exceptional even by contemporary European standards (perhaps the fastest of 'any society in Europe in the century before the famine'),[12] and the relative weakness of the accompanying industrialisation. The initial spread of the domestic system of rural industry between 1750 and 1815 was reversed in the three decades before the famine, when much of the Irish countryside was deindustrialised under the impact of the industrial revolution in Britain and around Belfast.[13]

Historians are not in agreement on the reasons for the Irish population explosion, and there has been much debate about the exact role of the potato in the demographic upsurge. Some historians have assigned to the potato a primary role in initiating and sustaining the spurt, suggesting that it significantly lowered the age of marriage by making it much easier to establish new families on very small plots of often marginal land.[14] Other scholars have been inclined to see the growing dominance of the potato in the Irish diet more as a relatively late response (mostly after 1800) to the pressures of an already rapidly expanding population on available resources of land and employment.[15] Some fall in the death rate also contributed to the swelling population, though the extent of its contribution is disputed. Improved diet and better transport no doubt helped considerably and make much more comprehensible the almost century-long gap between the last major famine of 1740–1 and the great famine. But about the consequences of the population explosion there is considerably less disagreement. Greatly increased demand for land, especially during the long period of almost continuous warfare in Europe and further afield between the early 1790s and 1815, meant that tenants of all kinds had to pay much higher rents. Even when farm prices tumbled after 1815, landlords were slow to adjust rents, and population growth exerted upward pressure on all land values. This affected adversely not only farmers but also landless agricultural labourers, who were compelled to hire land on a seasonal basis, usually from farmers, in order to grow potatoes. Such was the keenness of the competition for this kind of potato ground (generally called conacre) that it was a leading cause of agrarian violence in the late eighteenth and early nineteenth

This 'bog village' in County Roscommon probably came into existence between 1780 and 1845, when land-hungry tenants invested extraordinary effort in reclaiming bogs, mountainsides, and other waste land. Much of this land was devoted to potato cultivation in 'lazy beds', as in this sketch of 1880. Access to waste land initially came cheaply, as landlords charged little or no rent at first in order to promote reclamation on their estates. The combination of an excess supply of labour, cheap and abundant waste land, and the nutritious potato stimulated rapid population growth – from an estimated 4.4 million in 1791 to 8.5 million in 1845. But by the 1840s this style of estate development was out of fashion with most landlords. (*Illustrated London News*)

centuries. Besides pushing rents higher, the population explosion also helped materially to keep the average income of agricultural and rural textile workers at relatively low levels. Using the voluminous data collected by the poor inquiry commission in the mid-1830s, Joel Mokyr has estimated that the average annual income of Irish labourers and their dependants was only barely more than £13, a figure that includes their income from pigs as well as other sources. Though he places per capita income in Ireland in 1841 slightly higher than this, the figure for Ireland is only a little more than 60 per cent of the corresponding number for Britain.[16]

The population explosion was also responsible for some of the already observed regional variations in the levels of wages and income, the quality of rural housing, and the degrees of literacy – in other words, for regional differences in poverty. The demographic upsurge was not evenly spread across the island. From the early 1750s to the early 1790s Ulster experienced the fastest demographic growth of the four provinces, a ranking consistent with the lusty development of rural textile industry and rising real wages for linen weavers and other workers in that province during the same period. The slowest growth was in Leinster, with Munster and Connacht occupying an intermediate position. But over the next thirty years (1791–1821) the rankings changed dramatically, with Ulster's growth being even slower than that of third-place Leinster, and with Connacht and Munster moving into the first and second positions respectively. Ulster's rate of expansion in this later period was curtailed by relatively heavy emigration and probably 'the fact that earnings for most weavers in Ulster's staple industry were no longer rising in real terms after the 1790s'.[17] On the other hand, the wartime boom in farm prices brought unprecedented benefits not only to large dairy farmers and graziers but even to smallholders involved in tillage and pig production. It is difficult not to think that the unusually swift pace of population growth in Connacht and Munster in this period was mostly the result of the disproportionate effects of the wartime boom on small farmers and cottiers in these two provinces, though in the case of Connacht the expansion of the domestic system in textiles (especially among women) no doubt also played a role of some significance.[18]

As already mentioned, the end of the wartime boom initiated a general demographic adjustment in Ireland, with population growth slowing down quite sharply in the decades before the famine. All four provinces were affected by this deceleration in the rate of expansion. But as in the period 1791–1821, so now too in the years 1821–41 Connacht and Munster again headed the provincial list. In other words, population was still growing fastest in those regions – the west and the south-west – with the highest degrees of poverty. One way of interpreting this pattern, as Joel Mokyr indicates, is to say that 'population grew unrestrained, continuously exacerbating poverty, thus making the resolution of the problem by a catastrophe ultimately inevitable'.[19] But the matter is not so simple. As Cormac Ó Gráda has pointed out, the deceleration in the rate of growth seems to have been greater than average in the west and the south-west between 1821 and 1841, and 'presumably, the adjustment would have continued in that might-have-been Ireland without the potato blight in the late 1840s'.[20] But the general economic conditions of the three decades before the famine were not nearly as favourable to cottiers and smallholders as those which had prevailed during the French revolutionary and Napoleonic wars, and it is difficult to resist the conclusion that the exposure of the poor of the west and south-west in the event of some catastrophe was rising in tandem with increasing population. As Ó Gráda concedes, growth in these regions was still fairly vigorous, even if slower.

TOWARDS THE ABYSS?

Whether Ireland was sliding towards the abyss in the decades before the famine is a question on which historians' views have shifted considerably over the last twenty or thirty years. Where once the tendency would have been to say that the condition of the great majority was clearly worsening, now the tendency is to say that the general lot of a large minority was improving, and that even the majority were not going downhill fast. It has long been firmly established that, considered as a national unit, the Irish economy was much larger, and Irish society much wealthier (or much less poor), on the eve of the great famine than it had been in 1750 or even in 1815. The decline of hand manufacture in the countryside and in many southern provincial towns after 1800, and even more rapidly after 1825, was counterbalanced by the vigorous growth of textile mills and factories in Belfast and the surrounding Lagan valley. Cotton was very important in this region throughout the first quarter of the nineteenth century, but in the second quarter it was overtaken and then completely eclipsed by the linen industry. By 1850 Belfast and the Lagan valley were well on the way towards seizing industrial leadership in linens among all urban centres of the industry in the United Kingdom.[21] But if the rise of Belfast was hard to miss, perhaps even more noticeable were the adverse social consequences of progressive rural deindustrialisation between 1800 and 1845. Machine production in mills and factories hurt hand spinners first and handloom weavers eventually. Technological change of this kind heavily contributed to pre-famine rural impoverishment in certain regions of the country, especially west Ulster, north Leinster, and north Connacht. The counties worst affected were Mayo and Sligo in Connacht, Donegal and Tyrone in Ulster, and Longford and Louth in Leinster.[22] Still, it would be misleading to connect this development too closely with suffering during the great famine, since of these six counties, only Mayo and Sligo were to experience very high levels of excess mortality in the late 1840s.[23]

More important than these industrial developments, however, were the changes working their way through the agricultural economy. Two-thirds of the population lived on the land, according to the 1841 census, and agriculture was by far the most important sector of the economy. Cormac Ó Gráda has estimated that on the eve of the famine the value of Irish agricultural output amounted to about £45 million. Given the impressive increases that had taken place in Irish exports of grain and pigmeat just since 1815, this figure must represent a very substantial increase over the corresponding number thirty years earlier. Admittedly, on the pastoral side after 1815 the weakness of demand in Britain for Irish meat (apart from bacon and ham) and for dairy products meant that output in these sectors was expanding only slowly in the three decades before the famine. But under the British protective umbrella provided by the corn laws, Irish grain production leaped upwards, partly on the strength of expanded acreage but also as a result of very respectable increases in crop yields. By the mid-1830s Ireland provided as much as 80 per cent of British corn imports, in contrast to less than 20 per cent in the mid-1790s.[24] Farm prices were not at all buoyant during these decades, and there were several severe price depressions, but to a very considerable extent the lower prices were offset by rapidly rising tillage and pig production. Under almost any set of reasonable assumptions the bulk of middling and large farmers must have been at least mildly prospering if the period is considered as a whole.[25]

If pre-famine Irish agriculture was not nearly so backward as has often been claimed, it was still far behind the pace of improvement in England.

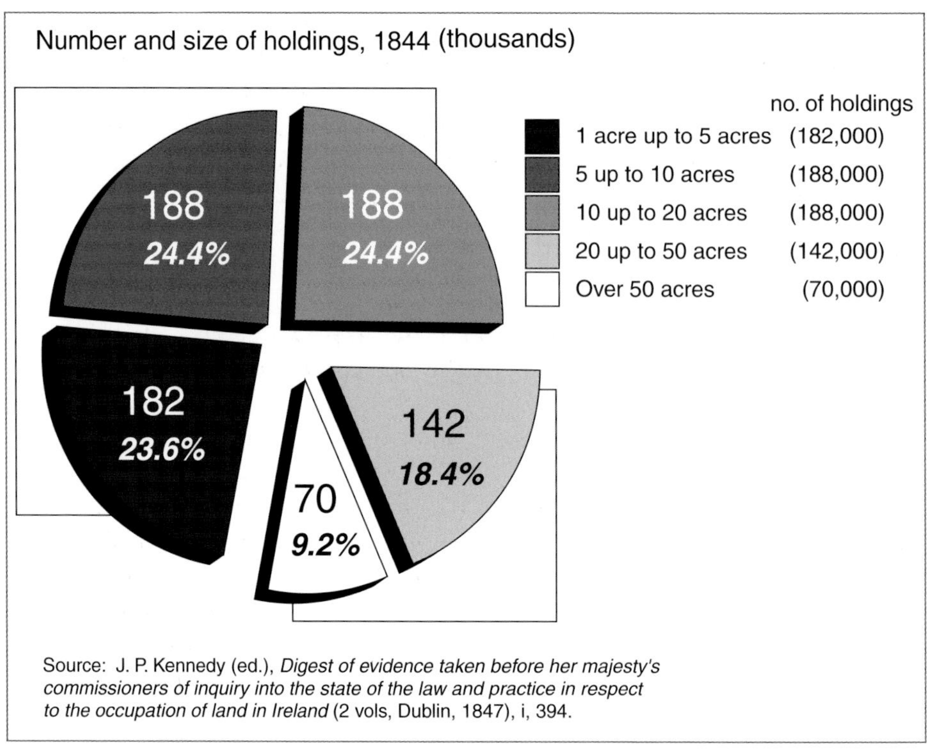

The most comprehensive parliamentary examination of the Irish land question before the famine was that carried out by the Devon commission, which was appointed in late 1843 and produced a report and three stout volumes of evidence in 1845. Many of the witnesses before this body drew attention to the severity of the problems of subdivision and subletting. This pie chart of the number and size of holdings in Ireland in 1844 vividly demonstrates that critics had a huge target at which to shoot. Only a little more than a quarter of all holdings of at least an acre reached or exceeded 20 acres. Research on the famine has shown that there existed a strong correlation between excess mortality and the occupation of holdings of less than 20 acres. (Joan Murphy Donnelly)

Agriculture in England and large parts of Scotland was the most advanced in the world, and the educated élites on both sides of the Irish Sea were increasingly conscious of the disparities and increasingly anxious to see the gap reduced. At the top of almost every Irish landowner's list of Irish agrarian problems was the fragmentation of holdings, and this view was also an integral part of the highly negative image of Irish rural society in Britain. Widely canvassed in Britain was the extreme idea of converting 'the cottier, who is nicknamed a farmer and who starves on a *cow's grass*, into a labourer subsisting on competent wages'.[26] Under the acute pressure of the population explosion the subdivision of holdings had been carried to extraordinary lengths by the eve of the famine. Aside altogether from the 135,000 holdings of less than 1 acre in 1844, almost half of the other 770,000 holdings did not exceed 10 acres, while another quarter were between 10 and 20 acres. Barely more than a quarter of the total number of holdings above 1 acre exceeded 20 acres.[27]

As a result, labour productivity in Irish agriculture was very low by British standards. According to Ó Gráda, 'the most generous comparison suggests that British output per worker [in agriculture] was about double that of the Irish'.[28] Élite observers were quite convinced of the potential scope for large economies of scale within Irish agriculture, if only the 'surplus population' could somehow be removed, and there was also a growing desire to expand pastoral farming, perhaps encouraged by price trends that favoured pasture over tillage from the 1830s.[29]

But if labour productivity was low by hard-to-match British standards, output per acre was relatively high and 'could well have reached British levels on the eve of the famine'.[30] A large part of the reason was the potato, always a heavily manured crop, which replaced the need for fallow in preparation for the cultivation of oats, wheat, or barley, the cereals that usually followed it in rotation. The potato also furnished food for livestock and above all for pigs, and their manure, heaped in front of the dwellings of almost every landholder, was soon returned to the soil, along with enormous quantities of seaweed and sea sand in regions within reach of the coasts. Lastly, 'as a sturdy pioneer for breaking new ground and clearing land, [the potato] was far more suited to Irish conditions than the less vigorous turnip, which needed a well prepared seed-bed'.[31] Along with these inherent advantages of the potato in boosting yields went the intense labour associated with the sowing and management of the crop, a by-product of the abundance of the available work-force and the indispensability of the root. One contemporary observer testified to the unflagging energy which cultivators devoted to the potato:

> I have never seen any field cultivation in England, except perhaps hops, where more diligence is discovered [than in growing potatoes in Ireland]. Every ounce of manure is carefully husbanded, and every weed is destroyed. The drainage is made complete; and the hoe, or rather the apology for that instrument [the spade], is constantly going.[32]

This lavish expenditure of labour power paid dividends in the relatively high nutritional levels and comparative health of the Irish population. Research into the height of Irishmen both before and after 1815 indicates that adult Irish males 'were taller than their English peers and by implication [were] reared on a healthier diet'.[33] These findings also point to the general reliability of the potato as a food source in the pre-famine period. There were undoubtedly some episodes of serious deficiency in the potato crop during the three decades before the famine, with the worst ones occurring in the years 1815–17, 1821–2, 1830–1, and 1839–40, but both the extent of these scarcities and the resulting excess mortality were limited and should not be viewed as the harbingers of an approaching doom. Some contemporary observers saw dietary deterioration in the rapidly spreading use of the 'lumper' variety of the potato following its introduction from Scotland soon after 1800. Though the lumper was deficient

Most Irish potato growers used the 'lazy bed' system in which the potatoes were planted by hand in broad raised ridges. These ridges were separated by narrow trenches, which allowed the cultivators space to tend the plants and permitted water to drain off. Agricultural improvers of the upper classes, who preferred to sow in neat drills with a plough, often criticised lazy beds, and the name of this popular method gave them added ammunition. But the irony was that growing potatoes in this way required a great deal of labour. The system was well suited to the damp soil and wet climate so common in Ireland and to cultivating coarse land, hilly fields, and mountainsides. The photograph here shows two young women setting seed potatoes in lazy beds and breaking clods with their spades at Glenshesk, Co. Antrim. (Photograph reproduced with the kind permission of the Trustees of the National Museums & Galleries of Northern Ireland)

in taste (it was watery) and in keeping quality, the poor especially favoured it because of its suitability in inferior soils, its higher yields, and its general reliability. Until the appearance of *phytophthora infestans* in 1845 this preference seemed amply justified by results. Recent scientific research has also confirmed that while the lumper is inferior to premium varieties of the potato, it ranks well among modern supermarket varieties.[34]

Besides benefiting from relatively high nutritional levels, Irish society displayed definite signs of improvement in certain other areas of material welfare in the early nineteenth century. Consumption of tea, sugar, and tobacco was increasing between the end of the Napoleonic wars and the famine, a trend that could indicate at least some improvement in the average standard of living during that period. The limited number of studies of the cost of living between

1815 and 1845 also point emphatically in this direction. Admittedly, these studies indicate that the decline in living costs was concentrated in the years before 1830, with a sharp drop of perhaps as much as 25 to 30 per cent, but stability in subsistence costs apparently characterised the 1830s and early 1840s.[35] Also militating against any notion of advancing immiseration before 1845 is the substantial evidence of improvement in rural literacy. School attendance was increasing modestly – according to one calculation, from 5.5 per thousand people in 1824 to 6.1 per thousand in 1841. Illiteracy was falling after 1815 in all four provinces, though the most impressive declines were concentrated in the wealthier provinces of Leinster and Ulster.[36]

Nevertheless, these signs of an improvement in *average* living standards almost certainly mask a deterioration in the position of the poor, who constituted at least half of the population on the eve of the famine. Many rural dwellers must have felt the pain of the 'scissors effect' of rising money rents and falling money wages between 1815 and 1845.[37] Nutrition levels, though still making adult Irishmen taller than their English counterparts, seem to have been dropping, to judge from the narrowing of the gap in this period between Irish and English male height.[38] Rural deindustrialisation, as previously noted, was greatly exacerbating the already severe problem of underemployment. Most telling of all perhaps, there were very few educated contemporaries who believed in the years before the famine that the preceding decades had witnessed improvement in the living conditions of the poor. A massive amount of impressionistic evidence was given on precisely this issue to the poor inquiry commission of the mid-1830s, and Joel Mokyr has systematically analysed the usable replies of the 1,590 witnesses from counties throughout Ireland. The rating of the thirty-two counties on a five-point scale from 'much deteriorated' to 'much improved' allows Mokyr to construct what has been called a 'subjective impoverishment index'. In only two counties in the whole of Ireland – Wicklow and Wexford – 'does the index take on a positive value'.[39] Altogether, then, it seems reasonable to conclude that though Ireland was certainly not careering towards economic and social disaster in the decades before 1845, about half of the population were victims of some degree of immiseration and stood dangerously exposed to a foreign and devastating plant disease. The fact that the arrival of this fungus could not have been predicted only made matters worse.

HISTORIOGRAPHY

Long after historical writing about pre-famine Ireland had gathered pace in the 1960s and 1970s, writing about the great famine itself lagged badly behind. For decades, in fact, professional historians carried on the important task of revising our understanding of the Irish past without paying much heed to the most cataclysmic event in the modern history of the country. The professionalisation of Irish history in the twentieth century was closely identified with the journal *Irish Historical Studies*, founded in 1938. Little was heard of the famine in its pages. In the first half-century

The two historians in this photograph of *c.* 1947 – Theodore William Moody (1907–84) on the right and Robert Dudley Edwards (1909–88) – were the joint editors of the journal *Irish Historical Studies* at its foundation in 1938. Along with other leading Irish scholars of their generation, such as T.D. Williams, they wished to raise the standards of historical writing on Ireland and to professionalise the discipline, a task in which they were highly successful. They saw themselves as revisionists, ready to encourage challenges to received wisdom, as in the the special category of articles entitled 'historical revisions' in their journal. Among the main targets of this revisionism were a variety of nationalist myths about the history of Ireland and Anglo-Irish relations. Perhaps partly because they had usually received their graduate training in British universities, professional Irish historians like Moody, Edwards, and Williams were out of sympathy with traditional nationalist interpretations of the Irish past. (Photograph reproduced with the kind permission of Dr Ruth Dudley Edwards and Dr James McGuire)

of its existence, through a hundred issues, this journal carried a scant five articles on topics related to the famine, and the record of *Irish Economic and Social History*, founded in 1974, was equally barren in this area.[40] The scholars who established and supported *Irish Historical Studies*, and those who followed in their wake, came to be substantially concerned with debunking nationalist interpretations of the Irish past. Rightly for the most part, they busied themselves with correcting those often very simplistic and emotional accounts in which Ireland and the Catholic Irish were portrayed as victims of British imperialism or Protestant sectarianism, or both together. In general, what came to be called 'revisionism' had a triumphal march, slaying one dragon of nationalist historiography after another.

Eventually, however, there emerged such a discrepancy between what 'revisionist' historians professed and what many Irish people believed that in certain quarters the revisionist enterprise was subjected to ridicule. Some of this ridicule concerned treatment of the great famine and was directed at historians associated with Trinity College, Dublin, viewed by certain non-professional critics as a bastion of revisionism. In December 1984 a notorious and uproariously funny lampoon of revisionism, as allegedly practised by certain Trinity College historians, appeared in the satirical weekly magazine *In Dublin*. In what purported to be a flattering review of a supposedly new book entitled *The famine revisited* by one Roger Proctor, the reviewer, whose name is given as Professor Hugh T. Lyons, tells us with a straight face that Proctor has turned the accepted interpretation of the famine on its head:

> Proctor produces an array of evidence to show that most of those who died in the famine years were neither small farmers nor cottiers, but were in fact landlords, their families, and their agents.
>
> The details recounted are harrowing. Richard Mortimer, a landlord in east Kerry, kept a diary for the years 1846 to 1847. He records how, after giving away all his family goods to his tenants (whom he assumed to be starving), he watched powerlessly while his aged father, his wife, and seven children died, one by one, of hunger in the dark winter of 1847. What makes the Mortimer case particularly shocking is that it now emerges from a study of the London money market accounts that two of the Mortimer tenants, Tadhg O'Sullivan and Páidín Ferriter, actually invested considerable sums of money in London in those very years.[41]

But since such jibes generally came from beyond the redoubts of Irish historians, they could be largely ignored as uninformed or misguided or both.

Bradshaw's Attack on Revisionism

It proved much harder to ignore the far more serious challenge mounted to the whole revisionist enterprise by Brendan Bradshaw, a formidable and respected historian of early modern Ireland who, though born and bred in Ireland, had made his career in the University of Cambridge in England. In November 1989 Bradshaw published a now famous 'anti-revisionist' article in *Irish Historical Studies*, of all places. In this article, entitled 'Nationalism and historical scholarship in modern Ireland', he took the whole revisionist school to task for its pursuit of a kind of scientific, objective, value-free examination of the Irish past. In this approach, Bradshaw charged, the revisionists had employed a variety of interpretive strategies in order to filter out the trauma in the really catastrophic episodes of Irish history, such as the English conquest of the sixteenth century, the great rebellion of the 1640s, and the great famine itself.[42] In fact, the famine provided Bradshaw with the best evidence for his case, revealing what he considered 'perhaps more tellingly than any other episode of Irish history the inability of practitioners of value-free history to cope with the catastrophic dimensions of the Irish past'. In the fifty years since the emergence of their school of history in the mid-1930s, he asserted, they had managed to produce 'only one academic study of the famine', and when the revisionist Mary Daly published a brief but significant account in 1986, she too, according to

Bradshaw, sought to distance herself and her readers 'from the stark reality'. Seconding criticisms of Daly's book made by Cormac Ó Gráda, Bradshaw asserted that she did this 'by assuming an austerely clinical tone, and by resorting to sociological euphemism and cliometric excursi, thus cerebralising and thereby de-sensitising the trauma'.[43]

Bradshaw's views aroused heated controversy, even *ad hominem* attacks, and spawned a lively and generally useful debate among scholars and a wider audience.[44] The echoes of the early clashes can still be heard. It seemed to me at the time, in the early 1990s, as it still does now, that Bradshaw was largely correct in his insistence that professional historians of Ireland had often failed to confront squarely and honestly what he termed 'the catastrophic dimensions of the Irish past'. His criticisms appeared to be especially relevant to the general scholarly approach to the great famine. That approach had long been almost entirely dismissive of the traditional nationalist interpretation, which laid responsibility for mass death and mass emigration at the door of the British government, accusing it of what amounted to genocide. The problem can be highlighted by considering briefly what were, until the mid-1990s, the only two major book-length studies of the famine – studies which differed markedly in character, interpretation, and audience.

For revisionists, the publication in 1962 of *The great hunger: Ireland, 1845–1849* by Cecil Woodham-Smith was not an altogether welcome event.[45] These academic historians no doubt envied the commercial success of the book. *The great hunger* was immediately a bestseller on two continents, and its premier status as the most widely read Irish history book of all time has only grown with the years. But far more troubling to the revisionists was the 'ungoverned passion' to which numerous reviewers of the book succumbed. Vigorously protesting against 'this torrent of muddled thinking', the late and great historian F.S.L. Lyons called attention in *Irish Historical Studies* to a striking aspect of the popular response:

> Ugly words were used in many reviews – 'race murder' and 'genocide', for example – to describe the British government's attitude to the Irish peasantry at the time of the famine, and Sir Charles Trevelyan's handling of the situation was compared by some excited writers to Hitler's 'final solution' for the Jewish problem. This response to Mrs Woodham-Smith's work was not confined to Irish reviewers, nor even to imaginative authors like Mr Frank O'Connor, but cropped up repeatedly in English periodicals also, occasionally in articles by reputable historians.[46]

Among such reputable scholars, Lyons must have had in mind A.J.P. Taylor, the distinguished, if controversial, historian of modern Germany, whose review of *The great hunger* appeared in the *New Statesman* and was later reprinted under the title 'Genocide' in his *Essays in English history*. At times Taylor sounded just like the famous Irish revolutionary nationalist John Mitchel, whose genocide

Cecil Woodham-Smith already enjoyed an international literary and historical reputation by 1962, when she published *The great hunger*, her classic on the Irish potato famine. Two of her previous books – *The reason why* (about the Crimean war) and *Florence Nightingale* – had become bestsellers. She spent almost a decade researching *The great hunger*, and she generously acknowledged the assistance of such leading Irish historians as R.B. McDowell, Kevin Nowlan, and T.P. O'Neill, as well as her gratitude to the contributors to that revisionist classic, *The great famine* of 1956. But professional historians in Ireland gave her book on the famine an unenthusiastic reception. In their view it veered too closely to the traditional nationalist interpretation in which the British government had been accused of genocide. (Special Collections, Cleveland State University Library)

interpretation of the famine revisionists had long pointedly neglected. In the late 1840s, declared Taylor with a sweeping reference to the notorious German extermination camp, 'all Ireland was a Belsen'. He then proceeded to insist that 'the English governing class' had the blood of 'two million Irish people' on its hands. That the death toll was not higher, Taylor savagely remarked, 'was not from want of trying'. As evidence, he offered the recollection of Benjamin Jowett, the master of Balliol: 'I have always felt a certain horror of political economists since I heard one of them say that the famine in Ireland would not kill more than a million people, and that would scarcely be enough to do much good.'[47]

Woodham-Smith herself was reasonably restrained in her conclusions, and Lyons absolved her of responsibility for what he saw as the emotionalism and the wholly inappropriate comparisons of the reviewers.[48] But at the same time he accused her of other serious faults: vilifying Charles Trevelyan, the key administrator of famine relief, and exaggerating his importance; failing to place the economic doctrine of *laissez-faire* firmly in its contemporary context and glibly using it as an explanatory device without acknowledging the looseness of this body of ideas; and in general committing the cardinal sin of the populariser – choosing narrative and description over analysis. Admittedly, her merits as a

Charles Edward Trevelyan (1807–86) was permanent head of the treasury throughout the famine years, with far-reaching control over government relief policy. Though in theory subject to ministerial direction, in practice he exercised wide discretionary power, especially while serving the badly divided Whig cabinet of 1846–52. A tireless worker and an evangelical Protestant, he was insensitive and uncompromising. About Ireland he was ill-informed. The former Irish chief secretary under Peel said of Trevelyan in late 1846 that he 'knew as much about Ireland as his baby, if he has one'. His name is synonymous with *laissez-faire* economics, but that did not prevent him or his political masters from wanting to see the Irish agrarian economy transformed on the British model. He was knighted for his famine-related work in April 1848. (By courtesy of the National Portrait Gallery, London)

populariser were great. 'No one else', conceded Lyons, 'has conveyed so hauntingly the horrors of starvation and disease, of eviction, of the emigrant ships, of arrival in Canada or the United States, of the terrible slums on both sides of the Atlantic to which the survivors so often found themselves condemned.' And if all that students wanted to know was 'what happened in the starving time and how it happened', then *The great hunger* would supply the answers. But they would simply have to turn elsewhere if they wanted 'to know the reasons why' – a rather unkind ironic word-play with the title of Woodham-Smith's famous book about the British role in the Crimean war.[49] Apparently, Lyons's stinging criticisms of Woodham-Smith were widely shared by other members of the Dublin historical establishment. In University College, Dublin, in 1963 history students encountered as the essay topic of a final exam the dismissive proposition, '*The great hunger* is a great novel'.[50]

The Revisionist Classic

In saying that students of the famine who wanted to know the reason why would have to turn elsewhere, Lyons had in mind the academically acclaimed but much less famous book entitled *The great famine: studies in Irish history,*

1845–52. Edited by R. Dudley Edwards and T. Desmond Williams, two of the founding leaders of modern Irish historiography, this book was published in Dublin in 1956 (and in New York in 1957) after rather extraordinary editorial delays. Thanks to the detective work of Cormac Ó Gráda and the open-handedness of Ruth Dudley Edwards, the fascinating internal history of this collective and poorly managed but still highly important enterprise has recently been laid bare.[51] Ironically, given the academic and revisionist halo that eventually came to surround it, this project had its origin in a suggestion made in the early 1940s by Eamon de Valera, then the taoiseach, to James Delargy (Séamus Ó Duilearga), the director of the Irish Folklore Commission. Offering modest government financial assistance, de Valera proposed the production of a commemorative volume in time for the centenary of the great famine in 1945 or 1946.[52] If de Valera expected such a volume to have a nationalist and populist bias, he was to be sadly disappointed. It is not at all surprising to learn that de Valera, who liked to tax the British with seven or eight centuries of oppression, greatly preferred Woodham-Smith's book, with its sustained attack on British policies and administrators, to the much more scholarly and restrained work edited by Edwards and Williams.[53]

The editors of and contributors to *The great famine*, whose work continues to be of lasting value in spite of its faults, could not be accused of emotionalism or of politicising their tragic subject. They appear to have been quite anxious to avoid reigniting old controversies or giving any countenance to the traditional nationalist-populist view of the famine. The overall tone was set in the foreword, where Kevin B. Nowlan soothingly observed:

> In folklore and political writings the failure of the British government to act in a generous manner is quite understandably seen in a sinister light, but the private papers and the labours of genuinely good men tell an additional story. There was no conspiracy to destroy the Irish nation. The scale of the actual outlay to meet the famine and the expansion of the public relief system are in themselves impressive evidence that the state was by no means always indifferent to Irish needs. But the way in which Irish social problems so frequently overshadowed all else in the correspondence of statesmen testified in a still more striking manner to the extent to which the British government was preoccupied with the famine and distress in Ireland.[54]

The worst sins attributed by Nowlan to the British government were its 'excessive tenderness' for the rights of private property, its 'different (and limited) view of its positive responsibilities to the community', and its inevitable habit of acting 'in conformity with the conventions of (the larger) society'.[55] High politicians and administrators were not to be blamed; they were in fact innocent of any 'great and deliberately imposed evil'. Instead, insisted Nowlan, 'the really great evil lay in the totality of that social order which made such a famine possible and which could tolerate, to the extent it did, the sufferings and hardship caused by the failure of the potato crop'.[56] In other words, no one was really to blame because everyone was.

That their collective volume essentially failed to answer the basic question of British responsibility was recognised by at least one of the editors at that time. Very soon after the book was published at the end of 1956, Dudley Edwards confided to his diary, 'If it is [called] studies in the history of the famine, it is because they [the contributors?] are not sure all questions are answered. There are still the fundamental matters whether its occurrence was not due to the failure of the sophisticated to be alert.'[57] By 'the sophisticated' I assume that at a minimum he means the political élite in Britain. Indeed, Edwards was aware much earlier, in 1952, that a merely mechanical yoking together of a series of specialist contributions on such subjects as politics, relief, agriculture, emigration, and folklore would 'fail to convey the unity of what was clearly a cataclysm in the Butterfield sense'. The need to comprehend and to portray the disaster as a whole was, he felt, inescapable. If this were done, it would 'also answer the question of responsibility, so unhesitatingly laid at England's door by John Mitchel'.[58] But in the end, when the book was published, no comprehensive narrative was provided, and partly as a result the powerful Mitchel's most fully developed indictment – *The last conquest of Ireland (perhaps)*, first published in 1860 – does not even appear in the bibliography. Given the bias already discussed, this omission was entirely appropriate.

MITCHEL'S CASE

Clearly, one reason why Mitchel repels modern revisionist historians is that his language in *Last conquest* is so vehement in tone and so extreme in the substance of its accusations. Occasionally, these accusations were personalised, as against Trevelyan. The famished children whom Mitchel viewed as he travelled from Dublin across the midlands to Galway in the winter of 1847 prompted the vitriolic remark: 'I saw Trevelyan's claw in the vitals of those children; his red tape would draw them to death; in his government laboratory he had prepared for them the typhus poison.'[59] But usually Mitchel cast blame much more widely over British politicians and officials, employing bitterly ironic language that swept aside all restraint.[60] In his view the aim and result of British 'relief' measures ('contrivances for slaughter', he called them) was really nothing else but mass death: 'A million and a half of men, women, and children were carefully, prudently, and peacefully slain by the English government. They died of hunger in the midst of abundance which their own hands created. . . .'[61] Mitchel was incensed by the government's refusal to close the ports to the outward shipment of grain and livestock, and he skilfully exploited the issue – so skilfully that, as the last chapter of this book will show, he did more than any other nationalist writer to make the notion of an artificial famine a central part of the public memory of the disaster in Ireland and the Irish diaspora.[62]

John Mitchel (1815–75) was to do more than anyone else, mainly through his writings after 1850, to promote the view that the British government committed genocide against the Irish people during the famine. The son of a northern Presbyterian minister, Mitchel's special gifts were those of a journalist and writer driven by a passionate hatred of British misrule in Ireland. Soon after the premature death of Thomas Davis in September 1845, Mitchel in effect took Davis's place at the *Nation*, serving as its chief political contributor at the invitation of Charles Gavan Duffy, now its controlling editor. After the split with the O'Connellites in July 1846, Mitchel became a leading member of the Irish Confederation, but his disillusionment with Duffy's moderation and editorial restrictions led him to leave the *Nation* and set up in February 1848 his own paper, the *United Irishman*, which was soon savaging the British government and raising the cry for Irish revolution. (National Gallery of Ireland)

Understandably, modern professional historians of Ireland have invariably found this aspect of the nationalist interpretation to be almost completely without merit, though at the popular level it has long persisted as an article of faith with a multitude of people. But the force of Mitchel's case against the British government was (and remains) much stronger when he turned to consider the cost and character of those relief measures that he branded 'contrivances for slaughter'. Repeatedly, he condemned the utter inadequacy of the government's financial contribution and the gross unfairness in a supposedly 'United Kingdom' of throwing nearly the entire fiscal burden (after mid-1847) on Ireland alone. 'Instead of ten millions in three years [1845–8], if twenty millions', insisted Mitchel, 'had been advanced in the first year and expended on useful labour . . . , the whole famine slaughter might have been averted, and the whole advance would have been easily repaid to the treasury.'[63] Mitchel detected the genocidal intent of the British government not only in its refusal to accept the essential degree of fiscal responsibility but also in the relief machinery itself and in the way in which it was calculated to work. In his view the bureaucratic structures of 'relief' were murderous above all because of the goals they were intended to serve. Whatever relief was made available to the hungry and the starving, whether in the form of employment or of soup or of a place in the workhouses, was ultimately designed to break the grip of the Irish small farmer and cottier on his house and land, as a prelude to death at home or emigration and exile abroad. Mitchel was perfectly convinced – and convinced many others – that the consequences of British policy were not unintended but rather deliberately pursued, and he said so forcefully and repeatedly.[64]

Even though some of Mitchel's accusations were far-fetched or wildly erroneous, others contained a core of truth or an important aspect of the truth. In this category, as later chapters of this book will demonstrate, were the murderous effects of allowing the grain harvest of 1846 to be exported, the refusal to make the cost of fighting the famine a United Kingdom charge, and the legislative decree of June 1847 that Irish ratepayers (landlords and tenants) must bear all the expense of relieving the destitute. The harsh words which Mitchel had for Charles Trevelyan, who effectively headed the treasury in London, do not seem – to me, at any rate – to have been undeserved, even if the professional historian would choose different language.[65] After all, in the closing paragraph of his book *The Irish crisis* (1848), Trevelyan was so insensitive as to describe the famine as 'a direct stroke of an all-wise and all-merciful Providence', one which laid bare 'the deep and inveterate root of social evil'. The famine, he declared, was 'the sharp but effectual remedy by which the cure is likely to be effected. . . . God grant that the generation to which this opportunity has been offered may rightly perform its part. . . '.[66] These were hardly isolated musings. Thanks to the research of Peter Gray, we now appreciate how pervasive providentialist thinking was among the British political élite at the time of the famine, and how closely it was linked to central aspects of government policy towards Ireland during the crisis.[67] According to the strand of providentialism espoused by Trevelyan and other British policy-makers of the time, the workings of divine providence were disclosed in the unfettered operations of the market economy, and it was therefore positively evil to interfere with its proper functioning.

The suggestion has often been made by revisionist historians that Trevelyan's importance has been vastly exaggerated. This notion, however, is itself wide of the mark. Rarely has treasury influence and control been in greater ascendancy.[68] As Gray observes, Trevelyan's 'control over Irish policy grew as the famine continued, and he imposed his own rigid moralistic agenda with ruthless enthusiasm'.[69] What is true is that Trevelyan had a great deal of ideological company. As Gray hints here, Trevelyan was identified not only with providentialism and *laissez-faire* but also with what has come to be called 'moralism' – the set of ideas in which Irish problems were seen to arise mainly from moral defects in the Irish character. When many Britons of the middle and upper classes tried to take the measure of what was fundamentally wrong with Ireland before and during the famine, they strongly tended to ascribe to most Irish people flaws that they regularly attributed to the poor in Britain. In the case of the Irish, however, the intensity and scope of these flaws appeared to amount to national traits. Thus, notoriously, *The Times* of London was to declare early in 1847 that Britain faced in Ireland 'a nation of beggars', and that among their leading defects were 'indolence, improvidence, disorder, and consequent destitution'.[70] Trevelyan and other 'moralists', who were legion, believed passionately that slavish dependence on others was a striking feature of the Irish national character, and that British policy during the famine must aim at educating the Irish people in sturdy self-reliance.

In this *Punch* cartoon of October 1846 entitled 'Union is strength', John Bull offers food and a spade to a distressed Irish labouring family and promises to put them soon 'in a way to earn your own living'. Generosity and sympathy did mark the response of British public opinion at first, but there was a gradual shift towards tightfistedness and hardheartedness as the famine persisted, in spite of what was regarded in Britain as lavish public and private expenditure on relief. The cartoon title came to mock the bitter reality: Ireland from late 1847 was left to fend for itself financially in spite of the 1800 act of union between the two countries. (*Punch* Archive)

Even John Mitchel's insistence on the perpetration of genocide becomes more understandable when certain crucial facts and their interrelationship are kept in mind. Among the lessons that 'the most frightful calamities' of 1846–7 had driven home, according to the incorrigibly blinkered Trevelyan, was that 'the proper business of a government is to enable private individuals of every rank and profession in life to carry on their several occupations with freedom and safety, and not itself to undertake the business of the landowner, merchant, money-lender, or any other function of social life'.[71] Admittedly, the massive public works and the ubiquitous government-sponsored soup kitchens had violated the doctrinaire *laissez-faire* views thus espoused by Trevelyan, but that is precisely the point: they were gross violations which very recent experience, as interpreted by Trevelyan (and Whig ministers) in late 1847, had shown should never be repeated. And of course they weren't, even though the greater part of famine mortality was yet to come.[72]

THE AMENDED POOR LAW

As if to atone for its misguided profligacy through the summer of 1847, Russell's Whig government then moved to fix almost the entire fiscal burden on Ireland by amending the poor law in June 1847. The 130 poor law unions into which Ireland was divided were each self-contained raisers and spenders of their own tax revenue; the poorest unions in the country were to go it alone, even though their ratepayers might well sink under the accumulating weight of the levies needed to support a growing mass of pauperism. It mattered not in the eyes of the British government whether this weak fiscal structure was really capable of keeping mass death at bay. What mattered was the supposedly universal and timeless validity of a then cherished economic doctrine. 'There is', declared Trevelyan in late 1847, 'only one way in which the relief of the destitute ever has been or ever will be conducted consistently with the general welfare, and that is by making it a local charge.'[73] It was on this principle that British policy rested from mid-1847 onwards, with the result that, as Trevelyan himself said (and said proudly), 'The struggle now is to keep the poor off the rates'.[74]

Mitchel correctly emphasised the connections between the workings of the Irish poor law (as amended in June 1847) and the mass evictions, mass death, and mass emigration that marked the famine. Those connections will be thoroughly explored in a later chapter of this book. Here only a few points need be made. The amended poor law, the centrepiece of government 'relief' policy from September 1847 onwards, encouraged and facilitated wholesale clearances of tenants from many estates and greatly raised mortality rates in those districts of the south and west where mass evictions were concentrated. Numerous contemporaries drew attention to the ways in which clearances contributed materially to mass death. The prime minister himself, Lord John Russell, was in no doubt about at least some of the links between clearances and death.[75] In fact, many educated people in Britain became aware, in varying degrees, of the pitiless severities in the working of the poor law system. But British cabinet ministers, politicians, and officials, along with Irish landlords, mentally insulated themselves against the gross inhumanity and often murderous consequences of evictions by taking the view that clearances were now inevitable, and that they were essential to Irish economic progress.[76] The failure of the potato had simply deprived conacre tenants and cottiers of any future in their current status. 'The position occupied by these classes', proclaimed Trevelyan in *The Irish crisis*, 'is no longer tenable, and it is necessary for them to become substantial farmers or to live by the wages of their labour.'[77] But what if they could do neither?

Although a towering mass of human misery lay behind the twin processes of clearance and consolidation, Trevelyan (and many others) could minimise the human tragedy and concentrate on what they regarded as the economic miracle in the making. Among the signs that 'we are advancing by sure steps towards the desired end', remarked Trevelyan laconically in *The Irish crisis*, was the prominent fact that 'the small holdings, which have become deserted owing to death or emigration or the mere inability of the holders to obtain a subsistence from them in the absence of the potato, have, to a considerable extent, been consolidated with the adjoining farms; and the middlemen, whose occupation depends on the existence of a numerous small tenantry, have begun to disappear'.[78] Is it not remarkable that in this passage describing the huge disruption of clearance and consolidation, the whole question of agency is pleasantly evaded? Tenants are not dispossessed by anyone; rather, small holdings 'become deserted', and the reasons assigned for that do not include eviction. But whatever the reasons, the transformation is warmly applauded.

Thus there is no cause to think that Trevelyan would have disagreed with the Kerry landlord who affirmed privately in October 1852 that the destruction of the potato was 'a blessing to Ireland'.[79] This was by then the common view among the landed élite. Lord Lansdowne's agent William Steuart Trench put the same point somewhat differently in September of the same year: 'Nothing but the successive failures of the potato . . . could have produced the emigration which will, I trust, give us room to become civilised.'[80] But the connecting line that ran from the blight to mass eviction, mass death, and mass emigration embraced the poor law system imposed by Britain. This is not to say that the amended poor law did not save many lives; it is to say that it caused many deaths, incalculable suffering, and a substantial part of the huge exodus. As the economist Nassau Senior was told in 1852 by his brother, himself an Irish poor law commissioner, 'The great instrument which is clearing Ireland is the poor law. It supplies both the motive and the means. . . .'[81] From the vantage point of the early 1850s, then, the famine experience and the British response seemed to make accusations of genocide rather plausible among many Irish nationalists, and the next half-century was to witness the consolidation and elaboration of the Mitchelite case.

PUBLISHING BOOM

If Mitchel's full-blown genocide accusation is unsustainable, variants of what might fairly be called a nationalist or anti-revisionist interpretation have experienced a revival at the hands of professional historians during the unprecedented surge of research and writing about the great famine over the last decade. This surge has stemmed mostly from the official sesquicentennial commemoration of the famine which began in 1995 and concluded in 1997 – to make way for another commemoration of an earlier seismic episode in Irish history, the bicentenary of the 1798 rebellion. Academics have joined lustily in a variety of historical commemorations in recent decades, holding conferences and symposia, venturing into the public arena as lecturers and advisers to governments and private bodies, and publishing sudden torrents of books and articles. The sesquicentennial commemoration of the famine exhibited all the usual features of such clusters of events and some new ones besides ('famine walks', the rediscovery of famine graveyards, memorial plaques, pop concerts, and even a campaign for the beatification of the 'famine martyrs').[82] The outpouring of publications was especially remarkable in contrast to the extraordinary paucity of professional writing on the famine since the 1930s, to go back no earlier. As one of the principal contributors to this great flurry of academic publication has rightly said, 'more has been written to commemorate the 150th anniversary of the great famine than was written in the whole period since 1850'.[83] And the river is still in flood, with some of the most significant contributions appearing well after the close of the commemoration, including Peter Gray's *Famine, land, and politics*, Cormac Ó Gráda's *Black '47 and beyond*, and the multi-authored *Mapping the great Irish famine*, all published in 1999. The select bibliography at the end of this book emphasises the massive amount of historical writing about the famine during the past decade.

In passing from neglect to what some have seen as overweening attention, scholars of the great famine have frequently found merit in significant aspects of the nationalist interpretation. Admittedly, genocide allegedly arising from the 'forced exportation' of Irish food is not one of them. Christine Kinealy's anti-revisionist efforts to breathe some life into this particular Mitchelite and nationalist view have not been seconded by other historians.[84] Mary Daly, who still harbours certain definite 'revisionist' inclinations, was no doubt quite correct to insist in 1996: 'Many facts are clear: the Irish famine was real, not artificial, food was extremely scarce; it could not have been solved by closing the ports; the charges of genocide cannot be sustained.'[85] But this, of course, is hardly the end of the discussion, only a beginning. The very same research which has established the full dimensions of the great famine as an extraordinary subsistence crisis, with a colossal initial gap in the food supply beyond redemption by closing the ports to the export of Irish grain, has also established that heavy grain and meal *imports* went far towards closing that gap after 1847. According to Peter Solar's laborious and invaluable calculations, overall Irish food consumption between 1846 and 1850 was only about 12 per cent less than in the years 1840–5.[86]

Could government action have closed this gap? The shortfall was admittedly much greater in 1846 and 1847 than it was later. Ó Gráda has estimated that the retention of all the grain exported in 1846 and 1847 'would still have filled only about one-seventh of the gap left by [the loss of] the potatoes in Ireland in these two crucial years'. But he also acknowledges that 'a temporary embargo on grain exports coupled with restrictions or prohibitions on brewing and distilling – a time-honoured stratagem – or else a more vigorous public commitment to buying up and redistributing Irish and foreign grain in late 1846 and early 1847, might have alleviated starvation in these critical months'. Ó Gráda seriously doubts that a simple export embargo would have been politically feasible for several years in succession in the face of the likely resistance from Irish middling and large farmers who, riding above the disaster, were after all the ultimate exporters of the great bulk of the grain that left the country during the famine years. But this view, while reasonable enough, assumes what was undeniably the source of the problem: the refusal of the British government to treat Ireland as part of the United Kingdom and its famine as an imperial responsibility. After 1847 it would not even have required an embargo for the government to address the continuing crisis effectively, for that crisis was now not the outcome of an absolute shortage of food but a matter of maldistribution, or (in the language of the distinguished economist Amartya Sen) of the weak 'entitlements' of the destitute to the greatly increased availability of Indian corn and meal. Thus Ó Gráda is surely right to conclude that 'the persistence of destitution and famine throughout much of the west of Ireland during 1849 and 1850, despite plentiful supplies of food, would seem to fit the entitlements approach well enough'.[87]

The research of Christine Kinealy and others on the administration of relief, and especially on the operation of the amended poor law, has also helped to rehabilitate important parts of the nationalist interpretation. Her overall assessment at the conclusion of *The great calamity* (1994) amounts to a fairly scathing indictment of the whole approach of the British government to the Irish famine:

> By implementing a policy which insisted that local resources must be exhausted before an external agency would intervene, and [by] pursuing this policy vigorously despite local advice to the contrary, the government made suffering an unavoidable consequence of the various relief systems which it introduced. The suffering was exacerbated by the frequent delays in the provision of relief even after it had been granted, and by the small quantity of relief provided, which was also of low nutritional value. By treating the famine as in essence a local problem requiring a local response, the government was in fact penalising those areas which had the fewest resources to meet the distress.[88]

This summation, quite consistent with the wealth of detail provided earlier in the volume, makes rather inexplicable the assertion of Mary Daly about the poor law in her 1996 examination of 'revisionism' in relation to the great famine: 'Kinealy's work does much to rehabilitate its overall reputation given the strictures of Woodham-Smith and others.'[89] If Kinealy can be embraced as a revisionist, then the nationalist interpretation has really triumphed! What Kinealy's book does bring out clearly is that some British poor law officials in Ireland, both in Dublin and at the local level, became increasingly critical of the policies pursued by civil servants (Trevelyan above all), cabinet ministers, and other politicians in London.[90] Though they dissented, few of these officials resigned, but one who did – Edward Twistleton, the chief Irish poor law commissioner – left a searing record of the depth of his revulsion. He maintained in 1849 that though many were then 'dying or wasting away' in the

Evictions occurred on a massive scale during the famine and in the early 1850s, with the formal dispossession of some 250,000 persons from 1849 to 1854 alone. The rate of eviction varied greatly from one part of the country to another, with the western counties in the van. Clare and Mayo had the highest rates. Because the famine undermined or shattered the usual networks of community action and bonds of social solidarity, there was little violent resistance. This illustration of a single tenant vainly pleading against eviction in late 1848 may stand for the fate of hundreds of thousands. The sketch shows the tenant, his wife, and his daughter begging the landlord or agent for a reprieve, while bailiffs seize the tenant's goods and soldiers overawe possible resisters. (*Illustrated London News*)

acutely distressed western districts, 'it is quite possible for this country [Britain] to prevent the occurrence there of any death from starvation by the advance of a few hundred pounds, say a small part of the expense of the Coffre war'.[91] His resignation in March of that year was based on the grounds that 'the destitution here [in Ireland] is so horrible, and the indifference of the House of Commons to it so manifest, that he is an unfit agent of a policy that must be one of extermination'.[92]

Also helping to rehabilitate central features of the nationalist interpretation has been the re-examination of the whole issue of the mass evictions, or clearances, at the centre of the famine experience. The clearances in two of the worst-affected counties – Clare and Mayo – have been the subjects of studies by Donald Jordan, Ignatius Murphy, Ciarán Ó Murchadha, and Tom Yager, though more research is still needed on these and other counties.[93] In his magisterial account of landlord–tenant relations between the famine and the land war, William Vaughan emphasises how uniquely intense was the soaring rate of evictions in the late 1840s and early 1850s. He estimates that 70,000 evictions (of families) occurred between 1846 and 1853, and that almost half of these consisted of large clearances of tenants (over 400 clearances altogether), with 'each one on average involving the removal of eighty families'. This enumeration, however, deals only with formal evictions and makes no allowance for the extraordinary number of informal evictions and involuntary surrenders which, as shown in Chapters 5 and 6 of this book, also marked these years, and it probably underestimates even the formal evictions of 1846–8 (before statistics began to be kept). Vaughan is right to stress that the incidence of dispossession was very uneven geographically, with formal evictions in Tipperary being almost twenty times more numerous in 1849–53 than in Fermanagh, the county with the fewest removals. But it does seem a little bloodless to conclude, as he does, that the estimated 70,000 formal evictions of 1846–53 'would not have threatened or even seriously modified the structure of rural society if they had been evenly spread throughout the whole country'.[94]

What is now clear is that extraordinary rates of eviction – formal and informal – in a few counties, and high rates in a half-dozen more, helped to solidify the idea of genocide in the Irish popular consciousness and especially among active, vocal nationalists. Voices of opposition to the clearances were not lacking in Ireland. In fact, what made it all the more necessary for landlords and government ministers to excuse, rationalise, or justify clearances were the persistent linkages made in the Irish press between mass evictions and mass death. Typical of many such comments was the *Limerick and Clare Examiner*, whose special correspondent was chronicling the depopulation in that part of the country. In May 1848 the paper protested vehemently that 'nothing, absolutely nothing, is done to save the lives of the people – they are swept out of their holdings, swept out of life, without an effort on the part of our rulers to stay the violent progress of human destruction'. Significantly, the most active members of the anti-clearance lobby were Catholic priests and prelates. When their own parishioners were being evicted in droves, it is scarcely surprising that local priests felt compelled to denounce the 'exterminating' landlords whom they held responsible. A great deal of what we know about clearances in particular localities comes to us from the often detailed lists of evicted persons and accompanying commentaries supplied to the national or provincial press by parish priests and curates.[95]

It is also clear that in numerous cases evictions stimulated or strengthened specifically nationalist responses from the Catholic clergy. This tendency was generalised in a rather spectacular way by the British political reaction to the notorious assassination of the estate-clearing Roscommon landowner Major Denis Mahon in late 1847. As Donal Kerr has demonstrated in *'A nation of beggars'?* (1994), one of the most important books to be published on the famine in the past decade, this highly charged political episode was of great significance in the growing alienation of the Catholic priesthood and hierarchy from the British government and the British political world in general in the late 1840s

Major Denis Mahon of Strokestown Park House was shot to death in November 1847 after presiding over a huge clearance of tenants from his Roscommon property. Other Roscommon landlords were soon targeted and a local Protestant clergyman was also murdered, leading to rumours of 'an extensive conspiracy for exterminating Protestant landlords'. The Catholic parish priest of Strokestown was accused in the British House of Lords and in the British press of helping to incite the murder of Major Mahon by denouncing him from the pulpit on the previous Sunday. The local bishop cleared the priest of this charge and published a list of some 3,000 tenants evicted from Mahon's estate. The furious public controversy arising from the assassination of Mahon and the charges of incitement elicited a strong nationalist reaction from Catholic bishops and priests in Ireland. By a twist of fate what were once the stable yards of Strokestown House now contain the National Irish Famine Museum, a historical facility of real distinction, exhibiting many interesting documents and artefacts relating to the disaster. (Famine Museum, Strokestown Park, Co. Roscommon)

and early 1850s. Charges in England following Mahon's murder that Irish Catholic priests were conniving at assassination prompted seventeen of the bishops to protest with a 'fierce anger' against the absurdity and iniquity of these accusations in a common statement to Pope Pius IX in March 1848. 'So bitter was the resentment revealed in the bishops' protest', declares Kerr, 'that it was difficult to see how trust could be restored between them and the British governing class.'[96] Priests throughout Ireland, regardless of their political hue, were equally appalled at this reaction in Britain to the clerical denunciation of evictions.

So much of what happened in Ireland in the late 1840s was the result of policy failures in London that the nationalist interpretation was bound to benefit from close study both of high politics there and of the general British political context. Indeed, for many years this was one of the most glaring lacunae in the entire historiography of the famine. Though Woodham-Smith had paid some attention to policy-making at the highest levels, the narrowness of her preoccupation with Trevelyan cast doubt over the general applicability of her conclusions and the validity of her severe strictures. Even as late as 1994 Christine Kinealy, a scholar who is not in any sense an apologist for British policies in famine Ireland, could suggest that there was almost a conspiracy organised by Trevelyan and a handful of other British civil servants – 'a group of officials and their non-elected advisors. This relatively small group of people, taking advantage of a passive establishment, and public opinion which was opposed to further financial aid for Ireland, were able to manipulate a theory of free enterprise, thus allowing a massive social injustice to be perpetrated within a part of the United Kingdom.'[97] In fact, as Peter Gray has shown in his magnificent recent book *Famine, land, and politics* and in a series of important recent articles, the views of Trevelyan and other leading civil servants in London were widely shared, and his domination of policy was the outcome partly of divisions within the cabinet and partly of the congruence of many of his attitudes with those of both some key cabinet ministers and a wide section of the educated British public.

BRITISH POLITICS AND THE FAMINE

Gray's main achievement in *Famine, land, and politics* is to uncover as never before the workings of the British political system at its different levels, the interrelationships and frictions between the levels, and the attitudes that prompted action and inaction in the mid- and late 1840s. He shows that Trevelyan was allied with other 'moralists' within the cabinet, including Sir Charles Wood, the chancellor of the exchequer, and Sir George Grey, the home secretary, but that this faction was sometimes at odds with the 'moderate liberals' and the 'Foxites', with Lord John Russell, the prime minister, belonging to this last group.[98] The 'moderate liberals', however, included the marquises of Clanricarde and Lansdowne and Viscount Palmerston, all three being great Irish landowners with hard-line views on the need for drastic consolidation of holdings. Even though Russell denounced clearances and supported various proposals for government intervention in Ireland, cabinet divisions often thwarted him and made a shambles of his ineffective attempts at leadership. Given the comprehensiveness and carefulness of his whole approach, Gray's overall judgement on the Whigs' stewardship from the autumn of 1847 through the end of the famine carries all the more authority:

> The charge of culpable neglect of the consequences of policies leading to mass starvation is indisputable. That a conscious choice to pursue moral or economic objectives at the expense of human life was made by several ministers is also demonstrable. Russell's government can thus be held responsible for the failure to honour its own pledge to use 'the whole credit of the treasury and the means of the country . . . , as is our bounden duty to use them . . . , to avert famine and to maintain the people of Ireland'.[99]

Besides disclosing the inner workings of Russell's government, Gray's other principal achievement is to explore the main currents of public opinion in Britain in the late 1840s and to show how these currents constrained or forwarded the Irish policy prescriptions of ministers, civil servants, and politicians in general. He lays particular emphasis on the outcome of the general

Lord John Russell (1792–1878), a leading British politician for much of the nineteenth century, headed the Whig government that took office when Peel and the Tories fell from power in June 1846. His government was split into several factions that disagreed on many questions of Irish policy. Unfortunately, its members did agree to allow Irish grain exports to continue, to scuttle the soup kitchens after just a single season, to permit landlords to engage in clearances without hindrance, and to rely on the poor law as the main instrument of relief after September 1847. The son of a duke, Russell displayed an aristocratic hauteur that was aggravated by his need to compensate for his very short height, a feature often savagely caricatured. (By courtesy of the National Portrait Gallery, London)

election of July 1847, which greatly increased the number of independently inclined radical MPs (to a total of eighty or ninety) in the House of Commons, giving them, at least potentially, the balance of power there. The radicals' success in this election largely reflected middle-class industrial and commercial hostility towards large government expenditures on Irish relief and perceived government favouritism towards Irish landowners.[100] The conclusion drawn by Russell from this electoral result spelled retrenchment in government outlays for relief: 'We have in the opinion of Great Britain done too much for Ireland and have lost elections for doing so. In Ireland the reverse [i.e., losses there too, but for doing too little].'[101] Gray also stresses the dampening effects on British generosity of both the British economic downturn of 1847–8 and the abortive Irish 'rebellion' of July 1848.[102] But it is in his close examination of the ideological underpinnings of British politics that Gray is most original. He finds that 'the ideas of moralism' (which located the source of Irish problems in the moral deficiencies of the Irish character), 'supported by providentialism and a Manchester-school reading of classical economics, proved the most potent of British interpretations of the Irish famine'. 'What these ideas led to', Gray forcefully concludes,

> was not a policy of deliberate genocide, but a dogmatic refusal to recognise that measures intended 'to encourage industry, to do battle with sloth and despair, to awake a manly feeling of inward confidence and reliance on the justice of heaven', were based on false premises, and in the Irish conditions of the later 1840s amounted to a sentence of death on many thousands.[103]

British 'moralism' was deadly in another way. The strenuous objections of 'moralists' within and without Russell's cabinet explain in part why the enthusiasm of some Whig ministers and many Tory protectionists for state-assisted emigration on a large scale was never translated into action in the late

This sketch of a priest giving his blessing to a group of departing emigrants in 1851 should not be considered universally valid. At first, the greatly increased scale of emigration during the famine was accepted by the Catholic clergy, but gradually nationalist attitudes, clerical and lay, began to shift. The initial acceptance gave way to reservations, then to strong criticism of government policy and landlord action, and finally to full-blown condemnation of emigration as 'forced exile'. By the early 1850s there were relatively few priests who would have challenged the assertion that emigration was 'a devilish plot to exile the bone and sinew of the country'. (*Illustrated London News*)

1840s.[104] 'Moralists' stoutly resisted public funding of emigration because, as Trevelyan put it in August 1849, 'it would do much real mischief by encouraging the Irish to rely upon the government for emigration which is now going on at a great rate from private funds'.[105] Here resided another grievous misfortune for famine Ireland. The study of Irish emigration has been one of the great 'growth industries' of recent Irish historical scholarship, and though the expansion was already much in evidence before the 1990s (the prize-winning *Emigrants and exiles* of 1985 by Kerby Miller was a special landmark), growth has continued at an impressive rate in the past decade, as many of the titles in the select bibliography at the end of this book testify. Much of this scholarship has been concerned in whole or substantial part with the famine period. Although the traditional nationalist interpretation of the famine depicted emigration as a plot concocted by Ireland's 'hereditary oppressors . . . who have made the most beautiful island under the sun a land of skulls or of ghastly spectres',[106] some recent students of both emigration and the famine have rightly emphasised that it was a reasonably effective form of disaster relief, and that if the government and Irish landlords had both made it financially possible for many more to leave Ireland for foreign shores, the famine death toll might have been very considerably reduced.[107]

EMIGRATION: NOT ENOUGH?

Though more than a million people emigrated during the famine itself, the problem was that an extremely high proportion of those at greatest risk – labourers, smallholders, and their families – lacked the means to emigrate on their own. This was recognised at the time even by some government ministers, such as the Irish viceroy Lord Clarendon, who wanted to 'sweep Connaught clean' of the smallest tenants (he mentioned a figure of 400,000 people) in the late 1840s through state-aided emigration, knowing that most of them could not depart on their own.[108] Some proponents of assisted emigration pointed to what they regarded as the success of one government body – the commissioners of woods and forests – in sending about 225 people from a crown estate at Ballykilcline, County Roscommon, to New York in 1847–8.[109] This case has been the focus of one of the best known emigration studies of recent years – Robert Scally's *The end of hidden Ireland* (1995). Tracking these emigrants as closely as possible, Scally found that a substantial number of the 400 persons on the estate at last count fell victim to death, sickness, or other serious misadventure before ever setting foot on the emigrant ship in Liverpool, in spite of above-average expenditure per capita and much planning.[110] But some readers of Scally's fine study have objected that on the whole these emigrants were better off than many of those financed at lower rates by landlords, and that in any case assisted emigration on a much larger and well-financed scale, such as that which occurred in the Scottish Highlands in the 1840s with wealthy landlord backing, offered the possibility, never actualised, of escape for tens of thousands from the mass death imposed by the poverty trap.[111]

Other recent studies of emigration, by contrast, have made more comprehensible the reasons why the extraordinary famine exodus provoked such jaundiced and embittered nationalist responses and why the 'forced exile' motif lodged itself so deeply in the nationalist consciousness and so early in nationalist historiography. Re-examinations of the gruesome story of the 'coffin ships' and the horrors of the notorious quarantine station at Grosse Île in the St Lawrence river near Quebec City have disclosed the full details of this episode in a remarkably professional way.[112] But if anything, they have only increased the surviving emotional force of this tragedy, which proved itself capable of arousing a great public outcry among the Canadian Irish in the 1990s over the inadequate permanent safeguards initially offered by the Canadian government for the mass burial site of the famine dead at Grosse Île. Similarly, recent studies of the experience of Irish famine migrants in Liverpool, especially those by Frank Neal and Robert Scally, have painted a necessarily dark picture of the victimisation of the Irish who passed through that city on the Mersey, or who – much worse – perished there or found themselves permanently mired in the abject poverty of its worst slums.[113] Ó Gráda has reasonably estimated that 'some tens of thousands of famine refugees' perished in Britain as a whole during the late 1840s, and the victims of the 'coffin ships' are likely to have totalled about 50,000 in Canada and the United States or at sea.[114]

Against this understandably dark picture, however, must be set certain other highly important considerations. One is simply the ardent desire of so many destitute people in Ireland in the late 1840s and early 1850s to escape from their immiserated conditions at home, often to the point of making their destination a distinctly secondary matter. Perhaps too much emphasis can be laid on the involuntary or forced nature of the famine and immediate post-famine exodus, a distinct possibility emerging forcefully from David Fitzpatrick's painstaking examination of surviving letters to and from Irish emigrants to Australia in his ground-breaking book *Oceans of consolation* (1994) and his other work.[115] As Margaret Crawford has well said in reflecting on a portion of this correspondence, 'To the writers of these letters emigration appeared more as an escape from difficulties than as an infliction imposed on a suffering society.'[116] No doubt, as many recent studies of the emigrant Irish in mid-nineteenth-century urban America have emphasised, the newly arrived Irish refugees from famine encountered not only squalid living and working conditions but deep and venomous American nativist hostility.[117] Assessing the political side of this recent scholarly work, Ó Gráda says with force, 'No modern anti-emigrant movement in the developed world matches the Know Nothings at their peak [in the 1850s].' But he is quick to make an even more biting point, namely, that the assisted emigration of 100,000 'destitute famine victims' could have been accomplished by the government for about £1 million, and to have done so 'would almost certainly have saved thousands of lives in Ireland itself'.[118] Urban America at mid-century may have been especially brutish physically and politically for new Irish immigrants, but at least it was famine-free.

This sketch of emigrants dancing below decks on their voyage to America in 1850 no doubt captures part of the reality of famine emigration. It is a needed reminder that the 'coffin ships' of 1847 must not be taken to signify the general experience, and it also underlines the fact that many emigrants had positive feelings about setting out for the New World – relief perhaps to be escaping the grim circumstances at home, along with high and often exaggerated expectations of what awaited them across the ocean. But even positive feelings usually existed alongside a deep sense of loss about family, friends, and familiar places left behind, together with a conviction that the decision to leave was far from voluntary. (*Illustrated London News*)

COMPARATIVE PERSPECTIVES

The application of comparative perspectives to the great Irish famine has also lent support to significant elements of the nationalist interpretation. In the recent efflorescence of Irish famine scholarship no one has done more to take comparative dimensions into account than Cormac Ó Gráda. His recent book *Black '47 and beyond* is studded with illuminating comparative treatment of a wide array of issues.[119] He has taken advantage of the relatively abundant and ever-growing research on famines elsewhere in past time and in the contemporary world, and he has also applied to an understanding of the Irish experience of the late 1840s the techniques of economics and demography. Comparison is useful precisely because it often allows crucial differences to be isolated, and these differences frequently have substantial explanatory power. Comparison with other modern and contemporary famines establishes beyond any doubt that the Irish famine of the late 1840s, which killed nearly one-eighth of the entire population, was *proportionally* much more destructive of human life than the vast majority of famines in modern times.[120] Indeed, in another comparative foray involving the great famine, Peter Gray has declared, 'No peacetime European social crisis since the seventeenth century, with the possible exception of the Ukrainian famine of the early 1930s, has equalled it in intensity or scale.'[121] In most famines in the contemporary world only a small fraction of the population of a given country or region is exposed to the dangers of death from nutrition-deficiency or infectious diseases, and then typically for only one or two seasons, whereas in the Irish famine of the late 1840s successive blasts of potato blight 'deprived one-third of the population of virtually their only means of subsistence for several years'.[122]

Other comparisons with contemporary famines bring out differences that should or could have permitted the great Irish famine to be contained with far less loss of life. In many contemporary famines a variety of adverse conditions, including warfare and brigandage, remoteness from centres of wealth and relief, poor communications, and weak or corrupt administrative structures, make difficult or impossible the delivery of adequate supplies of food to those in greatest need. But famine Ireland was not generally afflicted with such adversities. Though it had a rich history of agrarian violence, the country was at peace, its system of communications (roads and canals) had vastly improved in the previous half-century, the Victorian state had a substantial and growing bureaucracy, reasonably efficient and honest (it generated an army of 12,000 officials in Ireland for a short time in 1847), and Ireland lay at the doorstep of what was then the world's wealthiest nation. Why, then, was not Ireland better able to counteract the consequences of the destruction of most of its traditional food supply? Again, comparison with contemporary famines elsewhere points strongly in the direction of ideology. Whereas today wealthier countries and international organisations provide disaster assistance (though often not enough) as a matter of humanitarian conviction and perceived self-interest, attitudes in Britain in the late 1840s among the political élite and the middle classes heavily militated against sustained and heavy relief. Deliberately oversimplifying in order to make his point more effectively, Ó Gráda observes, 'Today the famine problem is more one of agency than ideology. In Ireland in the 1840s it was the other way around. Ireland then was not Somalia now.'[123] John Mitchel bitterly remarked that Ireland died of 'political economy'. If he had added the companion ideologies of providentialism and 'moralism', of which he and other nationalists were quite aware, he would have been just about right.[124]

Both Ó Gráda and Gray have taken a comparative approach to the question of the relative effectiveness of the actions and inactions of different governments, including that of the Whigs in the late 1840s, when confronted by famine in their dominions. Giving added point to the significance of this approach are the results of the careful and wide-ranging research of the historian John D. Post, who has closely examined the great European subsistence crises of the early 1740s and 1815–17 and concluded that 'the success or failure of public welfare and relief measures, more than any other variable, influenced the relative severity of the national mortality peaks'.[125] Gray focuses on the responses of a range of European governments in the late 1840s to the threat of famine or serious food scarcity resulting from what was a general economic crisis compounded of potato blight, crop failure, technological change in industry, and other problems. Though Ireland was unique in the scale of its shortage and in the proportion of its exposed population, the crises in the Netherlands and in Belgium were severe and led to substantial excess mortality. Gray finds a sharp contrast in the liberality of the relief measures of the Dutch and Belgian governments and a striking difference as well in their respective levels of mortality. Whereas Belgian governments expended considerable sums on a variety of employment-giving public works in 1846–8, the Dutch government generally pursued a non-interventionist policy in a wider effort to restrain government expenditure. This contrast in fiscal approaches was mirrored by a contrast in mortality. Dutch excess deaths of about 60,000 in 1846–7 in a total population of 3 million were substantially higher than the Belgian figure of 48,000, especially in view of the much larger Belgian population of 4.3 million. Although there were other variables that affected the contrast in mortality, 'the highly different state responses cannot be discounted as a contributory factor in this discrepancy'.[126]

Ó Gráda's comparativism underscores in a different way the gap between Irish popular needs and British willingness to divert financial resources. While admitting the difficulties of putting a fair market value on the lost Irish potatoes of the late 1840s, he has conservatively estimated the shortfall in money at about £50 million and contrasted this huge sum with the less than £10 million spent or loaned by the British exchequer for Irish famine relief from 1846 to 1852. He quite properly acknowledges that even if the British political élite had been more generously disposed towards relieving the Irish famine, completely closing the gap would have seriously strained government fiscal resources. Still, he maintains that, after taking into account the differences in wealth between the United Kingdom during the 1840s and tsarist Russia in the 1890s, British outlays on the great famine 'compare poorly with the 150 million rubles . . . spent by the tsarist authorities during the much less threatening Russian famine of 1891–92'.[127] With such comparisons in mind Ó Gráda finds 'a strong resonance' for famine Ireland in the general proposition of the economist Amartya Sen that 'modern famines reflect a severe indifference on the part of the government in those countries where they occur'.[128] Ó Gráda's application of Sen's 'entitlements' analysis of modern famines to the great Irish famine shows, as previously noted, that British indifference (to put it no more strongly) was at its least excusable after 1847 or 1848, when government intervention could have accomplished more, at less cost, now that food imports had so greatly increased.[129]

ORAL TRADITION AND THE FAMINE

Nationalist viewpoints on the great famine, however, have not derived as much support as might have been expected from the increased concern of professional historians in the 1990s with the 'memory' of the famine, or at least with private, individual, and local 'memories' as these were passed down, across two or three generations, through a continuing, if steadily weakening oral tradition, especially in the Irish language. The greatest single repository of such 'memories' is the huge body of material gathered by the Irish Folklore Commission in the mid-1940s, partly in response to its centenary questionnaire entitled 'The great famine, 1845–52' and partly in related reports from its own collectors. This material joined other oral traditions about the famine gathered by the commission in the 1930s. The later material formed the basis of the important essay on famine folklore by Roger McHugh that appeared in that classic of revisionism, *The great famine* of 1956. Much more recently this material has been reassessed by Niall Ó Ciosáin, Carmel Quinlan, and above all Cormac Ó Gráda.[130]

In varying ways all three of these recent investigators have stressed the relative absence of Mitchelite and nationalist excoriations of the British government. Dealing specifically with the replies to the centenary questionnaire of 1944–5 (amounting to some 3,500 pages of material from more than 500 informants), Quinlan has observed:

> Indignation about the famine did not burn as deeply as one would expect into the folk memories of the survivors. While instances of cruelty and profiteering are vividly portrayed in the questionnaire replies, there is frequently a perceptible 'othering' of the victims by depicting them as 'strangers' or people who died in 'other places'. A sense of detachment may well be the result of the inability of survivors to articulate the magnitude of the disaster.[131]

Ó Gráda too has noted how striking is the 'rather muted' resentment 'against high-ranking politicians in Dublin and Westminster. Political leaders and administrators such as Peel, Russell, and Clarendon, or even the notorious Sir Charles Trevelyan, almost never feature.'[132] Other 'silences' have also been observed in these archives of oral tradition. Rarely do the narrators of this famine folklore refer to their own ancestors as having been employed on the public works of 1846–7, or as having been obliged by destitution to enter a workhouse, or as having been forced to engage in thievery in an attempt to stay alive.[133] Indeed, during the sesquicentennial commemoration of the famine in 1995–7 there was a great deal of muddled thinking and loose rhetoric about an alleged generalised silence among famine survivors and their descendants in Ireland persisting into the 1990s.[134]

Clearly, the trauma of the great famine, like other social cataclysms, caused personal memories to be selective and partial in numerous ways. This Irish famine, in common with all others elsewhere, gave rise to many sorts of anti-social behaviour – within families, between close relatives, among neighbours. This kind of conduct would later have been very painful for those affected to speak about, and it must usually have been avoided as a result. In addition, famine survivors and their descendants were also apparently reluctant to admit that they or their forebears had been reduced to the necessity of toiling on the public works, or waiting in line every day at a soup kitchen, or spending months in a workhouse, or stealing food – all actions that in post-famine Ireland might have detracted from their standing in the community or from the way in which they wished their status to be perceived. Perhaps at least partly because of the tendency in protracted social disasters for memories to emphasise earlier rather than later events, heavy food imports after 1847 were not recollected nearly as well as earlier food exports.[135]

On the other hand, there is much less silence in famine folklore about food leaving the country in the faces of the starving masses, or about the evictions of 'exterminating' landlords and agents (it was no disgrace to have been evicted). The humiliations imposed by the receipt of official relief, whether in the form of required work or food, persisted vividly in folk memories, as did the glorification of acts of private charity (even those by indulgent or generous landlords).[136] And, perhaps inevitably, the gruesome and unusual details of death and burial firmly attached themselves to popular memories. Informants of the Irish Folklore Commission throughout the country in the mid-1940s 'could still name local families who went to bed to await death, people who gave food to starving strangers only to see them swell and die before their eyes, men and women who found corpses by the roadside or in lonely places, and the location of stray famine graves'.[137] Also undying in popular memories was the sheer difficulty of burying dead loved ones decently or at all, with a great many stories 'of mothers carrying children's corpses in sacks or sheets, of boys wheeling their dead parents in barrows, of old men lamenting, as they brought their dead children for burial, that there would be no one to do the same for them on the morrow'.[138]

The muted antagonism expressed in famine folklore against specific British politicians probably reflected in part the still highly restricted electorate for parliamentary contests. The total Irish electorate, only 122,000 at the start of the famine, had dropped to about 45,000 by 1850 – a tiny fraction of the adult male population at both points.[139] And illiteracy was, as already emphasised, extremely widespread in those areas of Ireland hardest hit by the famine. Under these conditions knowledge of the identities of high-ranking British politicians should probably not be expected. Lack of such knowledge, however, and the relative rarity of specific denunciations of the British government in famine folklore, should not be interpreted to mean that victims and survivors of the famine had little or no grasp of hostile forces beyond those that they could see at close hand. Long before the famine the Irish popular ballad tradition in both Irish and English had identified England and Protestantism as fertile sources of

Normally before the famine the body of the deceased would have rested in the wake house until the funeral procession to the graveyard commenced. But now famine victims were often taken from their cabins immediately after death if other family members could secure a cart for the purpose, as depicted in this illustration of 1847. These were lonely removals, stimulated in many cases by the dread of 'famine fever'. Some victims fared worse: 'Uncoffin'd, unshrouded, his bleak corpse they bore, / From the spot where he died on the cabin's wet floor, / To a hole which they dug in the garden close by; / Thus a brother hath died – thus a Christian must lie!' (National Library of Ireland)

Irish woes, and O'Connell's mass movement for repeal of the act of union on the very eve of the famine intensified these long-standing political sentiments not only among the urban middle classes but also throughout most of the countryside.[140] Ó Gráda has carefully explored the relatively scant remains of famine songs in Irish, and though he stresses that 'it would be wrong to force them into a common thematic straitjacket', he also remarks that some 'have a Mitchelite ring to them'. Other songs discussed by Ó Gráda complain of a full workhouse and fever hospital, segregation of mothers even from their dying children in the poorhouse, starvation wages on the relief schemes, the exclusion of destitute people from public charity, and the severities of local poor law guardians.[141] During the famine it must have been difficult for even illiterate labourers and cottiers to miss the political implications of the soldiers and police who guarded movements of grain and meal against popular attacks, suppressed food rioting in the towns, combated agrarian violence in the countryside, and assisted in the clearances. Such 'silences' as there were in famine folklore are thus mostly explicable in psychological or concrete historical terms, or in terms of the processes used at a late stage – almost a century after the event – in gathering this mass of material.[142]

Furthermore, the heavily localised 'memories' found in famine folklore have been usefully distinguished by Niall Ó Ciosáin from what he calls 'national or state memory' – the kind of memory that, 'for the most part, is institutionalised and transmitted through the educational system'.[143] This 'national' memory is closely related to what I prefer to call the 'public memory' of the famine (the subject of the final chapter of this book), which was a matter of active construction by Irish nationalists at home and abroad in the half-century after the catastrophe. As Ó Ciosáin suggests, the growing strength of this public memory from the time of the famine itself essentially explains why localised 'memories' and the 'national' memory would not neatly dovetail with one another in their concerns, including the central issue of the responsibility of the British government for mass death and mass emigration in the late 1840s. Just as people usually don't bother to explain to each other what they already know, so too 'societies and cultures do not always articulate ideas which are basic to them and which are not in dispute'.[144] It was one of the many signs of the previous ascendancy of the Mitchelite case that his book *The last conquest of Ireland (perhaps)* was among those recommended for use in Irish national schools after independence in 1921. And it was no less significant that the veteran republican nationalist and prolific writer P.S. O'Hegarty opened the famine chapter of his *History of Ireland under the union, 1801 to 1922* (1952) with this flat assertion: 'The facts about the calamity which overtook Ireland in 1845 and the following years are fully established and are not disputed.'[145] Professional historians of Ireland would not agree that 'the facts' of the great famine have all been gathered, or that they will ever be, even though the past decade has been the most illustrious in famine scholarship yet. But they might well agree that the areas of dispute have narrowed remarkably. We need to bring these new and richer understandings to a wider audience, and this book is offered in that spirit.

CHAPTER 1

Famine and Government Response, 1845–6

The great accident of nature that struck Ireland in 1845 was a raging epidemic of the fungal disease *phytophthora infestans*, commonly known as potato blight or potato murrain. Prior to the sudden advent of blight early in September of that year, there had of course been potato shortages, some of which were serious enough to be classed by contemporaries as failures. These shortages or failures were attributable either to bad weather or to plant diseases much less destructive than *phytophthora infestans*. In exceptionally wet years potatoes became waterlogged and rotted in the ground; in seasons of drought the lack of moisture stunted their growth. Before blight appeared in Ireland (or elsewhere in Europe), there were only two major plant diseases that attacked the potato periodically: one was a virus popularly known as 'curl', while the other was a fungus that non-scientists called 'dry rot' or 'taint'.

Exactly when and how the new disease – a minute fungus of the genus *botrytis* – entered Europe are matters not surprisingly shrouded in some obscurity. Into these dark corners P.M.A. Bourke shed some valuable light.[1] Almost certainly, potato blight was not present anywhere in Europe prior to 1842, and it probably did not gain entry until 1844. The source (or at least one source) of the infection may have been the northern Andes region of South America, particularly Peru, from which potatoes were carried to Europe on ships laden with guano, the seafowl excrement so much in demand as a fertiliser on British and continental European farms during the 1840s. An even likelier source of the deadly infection was the eastern United States, where blight largely destroyed the potato crops of 1843 and 1844. Vessels from Baltimore, Philadelphia, or New York could easily have brought diseased potatoes to European ports.

Once blight had been introduced from the new world into the old, its diffusion among the potatoes was extremely rapid, indeed even faster than the spread of the dreaded cholera among humans. This was essentially a function of the nature of the disease. The mould fungus that grew on the undersurface of blighted potato leaves consisted of multitudes of extremely fine, branching filaments, at the tips of which were spores. When mature, these spores broke away and, wafted by the air, settled on other plants, restarting the process of destruction. Rain was, like the wind, a vector of the disease, since water-borne

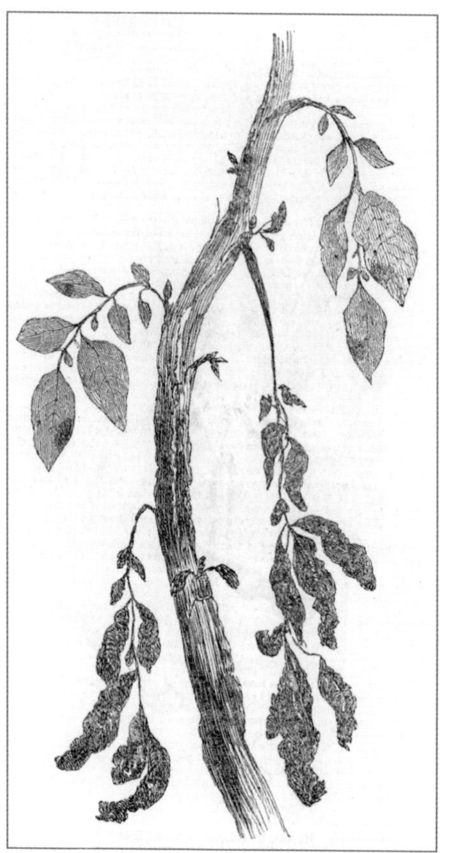

Never before 1845 had Ireland, Britain, or continental Europe been visited by an epidemic of the fungal disease *phytophthora infestans*. Diseased potatoes from the northern Andes region of South America or from the eastern United States, carried by ship to Europe, were probably the source of the destructive fungus, which was endemic in the Andes and had very recently found its way to the east coast of America. This sketch of July 1847 shows the stem, or haulm, of a potato plant ravaged by blight. The fungus grew on the underside of blighted potato leaves and generated spores which, carried by wind and rain, promptly attacked the leaves, haulms, and tubers of other potato plants. (*Illustrated London News*)

spores from the leaves and haulms penetrated to the tubers below ground. The blight's conquest of European potato fields was apparently the work of a single season or perhaps a little more. By the late summer and early autumn of 1845 it had spread throughout the greater part of northern and central Europe. The area of infection stretched from Switzerland to Scandinavia and southern Scotland, and from Poland to the west coast of Ireland. The ravages of the disease, however, were not the same everywhere. In regions stricken by blight early in the summer of 1845, crop losses were severe, whereas in areas not affected before mid-September, the damage was generally much less extensive, unless the harvest season was unusually wet. Thus Belgium, Holland, northern France, and southern England, all stricken by mid-August, were heavy sufferers, while Bavaria and Prussia among the German states, touched later and enjoying a dry harvest season, escaped with only slight damage. Ireland occupied an intermediate position in this spectrum of loss. On the one hand, blight did not make its first reported appearance until early in September, more than two months after the disease had originally been spotted near Courtrai in Belgium. On the other hand, much of the harvest season in Ireland was exceptionally wet, and the rains materially aided the progress of the disease.

For several reasons the early public reaction in Ireland to reports of blight was restrained. Everyone agreed that the oat crop had been unusually abundant – 'the best crop, in quality and quantity, we have had for ten years past', declared one northern observer at the end of September.[2] It was also apparent that a larger acreage had been sown with potatoes in 1845 than in the previous year, and this increase was initially rated as considerable. Lastly, no reliable calculations of the deficiency could even begin to be made until after general digging of the 'late' crop commenced in the second and third weeks of October.

But the absence of alarm at the outset rapidly gave way to deepening gloom and even panic in the last ten weeks of the year. Day after day, letters testifying to the ravages of the blight poured in from anxious, frightened gentlemen and clergymen in the countryside, and general estimates of the destruction naturally swelled. The Mansion House Committee in Dublin, to which hundreds of such letters were directed from all over Ireland, claimed on 19 November to 'have ascertained beyond the shadow of doubt that considerably more than one-third of the entire of the potato crop . . . has been already destroyed'.[3] At the beginning of December the *Freeman's Journal* asserted in an editorial that as

Hardest hit by the blight were agricultural labourers and cottiers, who typically rented potato ground (called conacre) each year. Their numbers had greatly multiplied since the 1760s, and so had their reliance on the potato. For an estimated 4.7 million people in 1845, the potato was the predominant item in their diet. Well over 3 million depended on it more or less exclusively, with milk, buttermilk, and fish providing the only other significant sources of nourishment. This illustration of August 1846 shows a group of distraught people standing over a pile of rotting potatoes. (*Pictorial Times*/By permission of the British Library)

much as 'one-half of the potato crop has been already lost as human food'.[4] What was so discouraging, and lent credibility to even the most despondent reports, was that potatoes which appeared sound and free of disease when dug became blighted soon after they had been pitted or housed. To many, it seemed that there was no stopping the rot. Typical of this despair was a Dublin market report at the end of October: 'The general impression now is that with the greatest care the crop will be all out by the end of January, be prices what they may, as the tendency to decay, even in the best, is evident.'[5]

Scientific Investigation

There was no shortage of putative remedies for staying the progress of the disease. As E.C. Large has remarked sardonically, 'The potatoes were to be dried in lime or spread with salt; they were to be cut up in slices and desiccated in ovens; and cottagers were even to provide themselves with oil of vitriol, manganese oxide, and salt, and treat their potatoes with chlorine gas, which could be obtained by mixing these materials together.'[6] The most prominent and widely publicised remedies were those offered by a scientific commission that Peel's government appointed in October.[7] Among its three members were Dr Lyon Playfair, an undistinguished chemist with good political connections, and Dr John Lindley, an accomplished botanist with both commercial experience and high academic standing (as professor of botany in University College, London), as well as the editor of the *Gardener's Chronicle and Agricultural Gazette*. These two Englishmen were joined by Professor Robert Kane of Queen's College, Cork, whose recent book on Irish industrial resources had attracted wide attention, and who already headed a subcommittee of the Royal Agricultural Improvement Society of Ireland that was investigating the blight.

The three commissioners had the triple task of recommending what should be done (a) to preserve seemingly healthy potatoes from infection; (b) to convert diseased potatoes to at least some useful purposes; and (c) to procure seed for the 1846 crop. In addressing the seed question, the commissioners could not ignore the fundamental issue of what had caused the blight in the first place. Here they went badly astray. Without pretending to certainty in the matter, they strongly inclined to the view that since the minute *botrytis* fungus must have existed as long as the potato itself, the root cause of the epidemic of blight was not the fungus but rather the cold, cloudy, and above all wet weather that had so visibly accompanied its progress. Without endorsing it, the commissioners did acknowledge the conflicting opinion of the Revd M.J. Berkeley, 'a gentleman eminent above all other naturalists of the United Kingdom in his knowledge of the habits of fungi', who believed that this particular fungus was itself the basic cause of the epidemic.[8] Berkeley's 'fungal hypothesis', though generally rejected when he elaborated it in 1846, was eventually proved correct. Yet even Berkeley admitted that wet weather greatly promoted the growth of fungi.

The commissioners therefore felt it safe to recommend that healthy potatoes from the blight-affected 1845 crop could be used for seed, since even if the germs of the disease were still present, they would be activated and spread only if the country had the great misfortune to be visited in 1846 by the same combination of bad weather that had prevailed in the current year. Any deficiency in home-grown sets of sound potato seed could be met, said the commissioners, by importing supplies from southern Europe (generally disease-free) on private commercial account. No active role as a direct purchaser was contemplated for the government.[9] In this aspect of their work the commissioners greatly underestimated both the shortage of seed that would exist in 1846 and the difficulty of ensuring that no slightly diseased potatoes from the 1845 crop would be planted through accident or ignorance in the following year.

In an earlier report the commissioners had grappled with the other two main parts of their charge. What could usefully be done with blighted potatoes depended on the extent of the decay. Potatoes only slightly diseased – with up to a quarter-inch of discoloration – could be eaten by humans without risk, said the commissioners, provided that the diseased parts were cut away before the potatoes were boiled. No time should be lost in consuming such potatoes, they urged, because the advance of the rot would soon render them useless for food. But if the discoloration went deeper and the potatoes gave off a telltale stench, there was nothing to be done but to break them up into starch. Though not food by itself, the starch could be used to make a wholesome bread after being mixed with meal or flour.[10] (Since the commissioners were concerned to maximise the amount of food that would be available for humans, they abstained from pointing out that diseased potatoes could also be fed to livestock, and farmers did this on a considerable scale.)[11]

What everyone wanted to know, however, was not so much what to do with potatoes going or gone bad, but how to keep good potatoes sound. Besides insisting that the bad potatoes should be segregated from the good, the commissioners' basic message was that the crop must above all be kept dry. In place of the traditional method of pitting the potatoes, which would bring 'certain destruction to them', the commissioners strongly advocated the adoption of a system of ventilation. Their plan called for shallow trenches in which the potatoes were to be placed in layered rows; the potatoes were to be separated from each other by a mixture of lime and dry clay, or of earth and the ashes of turf or sawdust, and the rows of potatoes were to be divided by sods of turf, which would provide the ventilation. Crowning the heap was to be a little roof of thatch.[12] These recommendations, which were actually based on a plethora of pit ventilation schemes already in circulation, were given extremely wide publicity. Of the 70,000 copies of the instructions printed by the government, each parish priest in the country received a set of thirty copies, and the Royal Agricultural Improvement Society distributed 10,000 copies to local agricultural bodies.[13]

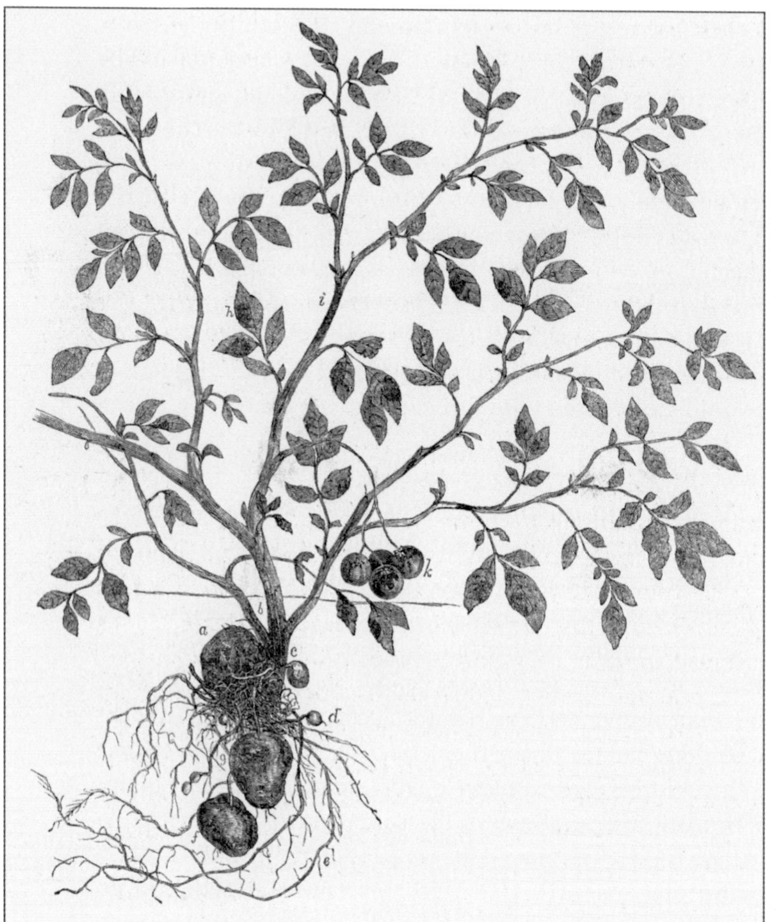

While the potato blight affected most of northern and central Europe by the autumn of 1845, Ireland escaped relatively lightly in that year, with the loss of one-quarter to one-third of the total crop. But the customary Irish climate, with frequent rains and strong winds, eventually favoured the spread of the fungus. This sketch of August 1846 sought to show how the disease attacked the potato plant, but scientists did not know its cause. The alarmed response indicated acute awareness of the extreme degree of popular dependence on this food source. (*Illustrated London News*)

To this avalanche of paper little attention was paid, and rightly so. The rot advanced in spite of ventilation, where that was tried. The commissioners further undermined their already shaken credibility when they publicly suggested that the steeping of diseased potatoes in bogwater might arrest the progress of decay – this less than a week after a report in which they insisted that the greatest desideratum was to keep the tubers absolutely dry! Understandably, the *Freeman's Journal* dismissed the whole exercise: 'The present commissioners have satisfactorily proved that they know nothing whatever about the causes of or remedies for the disease.'[14]

Privately, the commissioners seemed to have as gloomy a view of the impending food crisis as their worst Irish critics. In their report of 15 November to Sir James Graham, the home secretary, Lindley and Playfair concluded that 'one-half of the actual potato crop of Ireland is either destroyed or remains in a state unfit for the food of man'. As if this assessment were not sombre enough, they also remarked that theirs was 'a low estimate', that the most recent rains had 'in all probability' extended the destruction, and that not all of what now remained sound could be accounted safe because Irish circumstances would prevent their proposals for preservation from being fully implemented. Lastly, the two scientists pointed out that since at least one-eighth of the 1845 crop would be required in 1846 for seed (on the assumption of a constant acreage), only three-eighths of the 1845 crop could 'at this moment' be considered available as food.[15] Whatever else might be said about the commissioners and their work, they certainly did not underestimate the extent of the potato deficiency in 1845; indeed, unknowingly, they exaggerated it. This readiness to paint a pessimistic scenario, P.M.A. Bourke argued, helped to elicit government relief on a larger scale than if greater optimism had prevailed.[16]

EARLY CRITICISM OF PEEL'S GOVERNMENT

Historians have generally credited Peel's government with reacting promptly to the partial potato failure of 1845. A strong case can be marshalled in favour of this view. Most of the important policy decisions were taken in London before 1845 was over, but these did not pay dividends immediately. In the closing months of the year it seemed to many people in Ireland, and not to nationalists alone, that the Dublin Castle administration headed by Lord Heytesbury, the viceroy, was so dilatory as to be guilty of criminal neglect.[17] Castle officials appeared to believe that alarmists were exaggerating the ravages of the blight, and that even if the shortage of potatoes turned out to be serious, the food gap would at least partly be filled by the abundant harvest of oats. The Irish constabulary had been instructed to gauge the extent of the loss in every county, and its returns for December were somewhat reassuring; they showed that the damage was less extensive than many had claimed. According to these returns, the proportion of the 1845 crop deemed 'lost' in the country as a whole was somewhere between a quarter and a third. Deficiencies of more than a third of the crop were reported for only six counties: Kilkenny, Limerick, Louth, Queen's, Roscommon, and Wexford. The counties along the west coast from Kerry up to Donegal generally suffered less than the national average, and the lowest proportional losses occurred in Ulster, especially in Fermanagh, Londonderry, and Tyrone, where less than one-seventh of the crop had been destroyed. Furthermore, the constabulary returns indicated that the total potato acreage was about 6 per cent greater in 1845 than in the previous year.[18]

If Dublin Castle was inclined to cautious optimism, deep pessimism was characteristic of a broad spectrum of Irish public opinion. It struck many as scandalous that while the potato crop was melting away, the abundant oat crop, widely touted as a partial substitute, was rapidly being depleted through export, which the government refused to stop. For those with no choice but to buy their food, prices had escalated steeply. By early December retail potato prices had more than doubled, and grain prices had reached a level at least a third higher than the averages for 1843 and 1844.[19] Within just a few more months at most, there would be, if not actual famine, then acute and widespread distress. Action now to meet the developing crisis was insistently demanded of the government. At public meetings held in Dublin at the end of October, Peel's ministry was urged to allow the duty-free importation of foreign grain (i.e., to repeal or suspend the corn laws); to forbid the export of oats from Ireland; to raise a loan of £1 million for the relief of distress; to establish public granaries; and to provide employment for the destitute.[20] This was a great deal to ask of Peel's administration, though many of those doing the asking professed not to think so. With some elaboration and addition, these proposals were forcefully recommended to Peel on 7 November by Lord Cloncurry as chairman of the Dublin Mansion House Committee. Cloncurry urged that the loan (at least £1.5 million was now specified) be applied 'in the first instance' to raising the quantity and lowering the price of food in Ireland. It was also essential to set 'the people to work without any delay', and Cloncurry suggested that to accomplish this the government should promote and assist railway construction, drainage schemes, and 'other works of general or local utility'.[21]

Sir Robert Peel (1788–1850) was largely responsible for reviving the Conservative party after its disastrous defeat in the 1832 election. He led the Tories back into office in 1841. His successful effort to repeal the corn laws, against the wishes of a majority of his own party, led to his fall from power in June 1846. He handled the Irish crisis of 1845–6 quite well, but his general attitudes towards Ireland suggest that he might not have managed the later and far greater crisis much better than the Whig leader Lord John Russell. (By courtesy of the National Portrait Gallery, London)

The final Irish verdict on Peel's relief programme was to be highly positive, but since the government's approach to the crisis involved large elements of secrecy and delay, applause remained a scarce commodity for quite some time. Among the earliest measures was the secret purchase of £100,000 worth of Indian corn and meal in the United States through the agency of Baring Bros & Co., one of the great London international trading houses. This clandestine purchase Peel himself initiated early in November 1845, and the public remained perfectly ignorant of the transaction for about three months. The arrival of these supplies from America was a protracted affair, extending from February to June 1846. Additional quantities of maize and some oatmeal were bought in Britain at a cost of £46,000 and also shipped to Ireland. Altogether, the British treasury calculated that it had spent £185,000 by August 1846, a sum that covered not only the food itself, but also the costs of water freight, kiln-drying, and grinding. (The full outlay must have been considerably higher because this account excluded the expense of conveyance within Ireland and the wages of officials involved in the enterprise.) This expenditure made possible the official importation of an estimated 44 million lb (almost 20,000 tons) of Indian corn and oatmeal, a quantity said to be sufficient, at a rate of 1 lb a day per head, to feed 490,000 persons for three months.[22]

The efficient distribution of this food was the joint responsibility of a central relief commission (set up by Peel's government in November 1845) and of the hundreds of local relief committees that came into existence during the spring and summer of 1846. (Almost 650 local committees were at work by 10 August 1846.) The most important member of the central commission was undoubtedly Sir Randolph Routh, the head of the commissariat branch of the army in Ireland. Beginning in February 1846, the commissariat established a network of food depots. The west was to be served by stores at Galway, Kilrush, Limerick, Sligo, and Westport; the south and east by depots at Clonmel, Cork, Dublin, Dundalk, and Waterford; and the midlands by stores at Athy, Banagher, Longford, and Tullamore.[23]

It was not the government's intention, except under extraordinary circumstances, to become engaged in the distribution of free food from its depots or to sell food directly to those in want. Rather, the main burden of providing for the destitute was to be borne by the local committees, with the government selling food to them at cost price. The committees were to secure the means to purchase by raising subscriptions, chiefly among local landowners, and were in turn to sell at cost to the poor. Provision was made, however, for the lord lieutenant to supplement monies raised locally if, despite vigorous efforts, these proved inadequate. Eventually, government donations totalling nearly £68,000 (up to 7 August 1846) were made to local committees in aid of subscriptions collected for the purchase of food. It was also recognised that there would be districts where local relief committees could not be established or where their resources would be woefully inadequate, and in such areas the central relief commission promised to set up stores for the sale of food at cost

The loss of the potato made desperate the situation of many small tenants like Tom Sullivan of County Kerry. Their food was gone (the potatoes shown in this sketch of January 1846 were said to be rotting), they could not feed their pigs or pay their rents as usual, and they were thus in serious danger of eviction. With wages earned on the public works promoted by Peel's government, such smallholders could at least buy Indian meal – often at reduced prices – to feed themselves and their families. (*Pictorial Times*/The Trustees of the National Library of Scotland)

price. (Gratuitous distribution was contemplated only when the ability to pay was 'absolutely wanting'.) In the event, the need for such stores – designated subdepots – was much greater than officials had anticipated: the coastguard opened as many as seventy-six subdepots along the south and west coasts, and the constabulary operated twenty-nine more, mostly in the interior parts of Connacht and Munster.[24]

Relief officials engaged in a concerted effort to delay the opening of the depots as long as possible while at the same time meeting truly urgent cases of extreme distress. By exercising this policy of severe restraint, they sought to conserve their own limited supplies for the three-month period of greatest pressure between mid-May, when spring planting operations ceased, and mid-August, when the 'early' potatoes normally became available. By the same strategy they hoped to force Irish landlords, regarded in official circles as a slothful, negligent crowd, to be more zealous in furnishing relief; lastly, they wanted to check 'over-speculation', that is, the withholding of food supplies from the springtime market by private dealers greedily waiting for prices to rise still further in the summer. Routh told Charles Trevelyan on 4 April, when pressures for the general release of government stocks were already mounting, 'I . . . preach economy and reserve to all the [commissariat] department, so that nothing may be premature or done without reflection. If I were to throw open our depots now, there is not an effort nor a landlord that we could enlist through any other channel.'[25] A few depots initiated sales in restricted quantities before the end of March, but most of the government stores kept their doors shut until sometime in April or May. By the beginning of June nearly all the depots were open for business.[26]

'PEEL'S BRIMSTONE'

Government officials and relief committees promoting the use of Indian meal at first encountered considerable opposition to what was contemptuously decried as 'Peel's brimstone'. (Because of its bright yellow colour it was likened to sulphur.) A large part of this popular resistance could be traced to the physical discomfort associated with the switch from a habitual diet of potatoes (over 10 lb daily for adult males) to one of meal (a daily ration of about 1 lb). As Routh put it, the Irish 'are accustomed to potatoes, which satisfy by repletion, and a more nourishing substance, which does not fill the stomach, leaves a craving sensation, a want of support and strength, as if they had not eaten enough'.[27] Another important reason for popular opposition, and a far more serious problem, was that much of the Indian corn that entered Ireland early in 1846, having been imported in the grain, was not sufficiently ground by private millers. When it was sold in a coarse, lumpy condition and then eaten without being boiled long enough, such meal was liable to cause severe bowel complaints. Some of the maize from America also arrived in an unmerchantable condition, and unlike official imports found to be in this state, was treacherously unloaded upon a hungry populace. Circumstances such as these help to explain why, for example, the paupers in the workhouse at Limerick refused to eat Indian meal, and why, at Waterford workhouse, reports circulated that people who had eaten it became ill and died.[28]

But the resistance was short-lived: the Indian meal was 'much too good a thing to be long rejected by starving people'.[29] The government assisted in eroding opposition by publishing a cheap half-penny pamphlet containing simple cooking instructions. The little tract was extremely popular; demand for it was 'beyond credibility' by early April.[30] Steps were taken as well to instruct the milling trade in the special grinding requirements for Indian corn. It was also officially urged that oatmeal be added to Indian meal in a ratio of one part to three, and this mixture was widely found to be more palatable and hence more acceptable.[31] Very quickly, resistance melted away, to be replaced by an almost insatiable demand. Routh declared in mid-April that he 'could not have believed that the Indian corn meal would have become so popular',[32] and two months later, after virtually all the depots had been opened, Deputy Commissary-General Hewetson observed, 'The people everywhere have eagerly

Indian meal was not an altogether new relief food when the potato failed throughout the late 1840s. It had been used in some earlier periods of distress, but never on anything like the scale associated with the great famine. Its cheapness compared with other grains was a big point in its favour, and the government worked hard to popularise it as part of a general effort to overthrow a potato-based economy. The 'yellow male' continued to serve as relief food in later agrarian crises, such as that of 1879–80 depicted here. In this illustration of 1880 two women near Headford, Co. Galway, are shown carrying home sacks of meal obtained from a relief committee. (*Illustrated London News*)

taken to its use, but they all want ours, with the queen's mark, it being so very superior to that imported and manufactured by the trade.'[33]

The original choice of Indian corn as a substitute food had largely been dictated by its cheapness. For a government reluctant to interfere with private commerce, maize possessed the added advantage that it had not previously been a substantial item in Irish trade. Admittedly, Indian meal was not an entirely novel component of Irish lower-class diets in 1846, but only limited quantities had been imported in earlier years of the century.[34] The government could therefore argue that since there was no large established trade in this commodity, its interference with private commerce was minimal. What increasingly weakened this argument was that unofficial imports of maize swelled enormously in the first three quarters of 1846, and that the government's agents ostentatiously employed official imports to curtail private profiteering and to lower the price of alternative food. Relief officials were in no doubt that their efforts had been quite successful, and historians have generally believed that official imports were on a scale sufficient to give the government the leverage over food prices which it desired. 'The entry of the government into the market', commented T.P. O'Neill, 'was a spectacular example' of Peel's willingness to defy current economic orthodoxy, and 'it gave him an effective means of price control so as to defeat monopolists'.[35] Yet Bourke propounded a much less heroic view: 'The extent of "government interference" with the grain trade was trifling in comparison with the overall figures [of imports]; Routh was not exaggerating when he described the official imports as "almost only a mouthful".'[36]

Can these two apparently conflicting interpretations be reconciled? In the first eleven months of 1846 total Irish imports of maize and maize meal amounted to almost 122,000 tons, whereas official imports of food through August 1846 did not exceed 20,000 tons.[37] If these official imports had been released into the market gradually during the course of the year, the downward pressure which they could have exerted on prices would have been quite limited. But as already indicated, the government threw the bulk of its supplies on to the market in a concentrated period of three months (15 May–15 August), with June and July accounting for most of its sales. In this period government issues of meal constituted a sizeable fraction of the total amount of food available for consumption. As a result, they did have the effect of curtailing profiteering and dampening prices significantly. It should also be stressed that the impact of the government's food relief operations was greatest in the west and the south-west, where private wholesaling and retailing facilities were at their weakest. Lastly, and not least important, the government's 'interference' with the grain trade, together with its famous decision to repeal the corn laws, helped to transform what had been a minor trade in maize before 1846 into a major international commercial enterprise. It is no doubt true that the forced retention in Ireland of the entire grain harvest of 1845, or even the prohibition of the export of oats and oatmeal alone, would have been sufficient to offset the partial loss of the potato, but only if the government had been prepared to subsidise the purchase of higher-priced native produce. Thus oatmeal, costing around £15 a ton in the spring and summer of 1846, was about 50 per cent more expensive than Indian meal. But strong arguments could be and were made against such a policy, and in retrospect relief officials could only praise the decisions reached by the government. Deputy Commissary-General Hewetson informed Trevelyan early in June:

> I am assured from the best authority that in all the localities where our meal is in use, the general health of the people has wonderfully improved, and that where at this season gastric complaints were numerous, there are scarcely any; such is the wholesome and nutritious quality of the meal, so superior in every point of view to the potato. . . . I know not what horrors and misery would have ensued had not these precautionary measures been taken when they were; and I often think of the vile abuse heaped upon the ministers, at the very time they were deeply considering all these arrangements, for their callous neglect, as they were pleased to call it.[38]

OFFICIAL UNHAPPINESS WITH PUBLIC WORKS

Relief officials may have been enthused about the results of their food distribution programme, but they were much less happy with the public works undertaken to provide employment and thus to furnish the money that the destitute needed to buy food. In part, the dissatisfaction stemmed from the character of the public works. Peel's government had clearly hoped that many of the works would be of a reproductive or regenerative nature, permanently strengthening the Irish economy while furnishing temporary relief. Thus one of the four relevant bills that the prime minister presented to parliament in January 1846 was aimed at promoting the development of piers and harbours; a second measure sought to give increased encouragement to thorough drainage and other permanent improvements on landed estates. But under neither of these statutes was much money spent or much employment furnished. Pier and harbour projects consumed slightly less than £10,000, and the new land improvement legislation was practically a dead letter, mainly because it offered no increased financial incentives. Instead of reproductive works, road improvements became the chief vehicle for providing employment. These were carried out under the direction of either the county grand juries or the Board of Works. When grand juries sponsored the schemes, the entire cost was to be borne ultimately by the county, although in the first instance the British treasury advanced the full amount by way of a loan. Nearly £134,000 was thus advanced. On the other hand, when the Board of Works undertook the schemes, only half of the cost was liable to be repaid to the treasury, while the other half was treated as a grant chargeable to the consolidated fund. Inevitably, these more generous terms meant that the expenditures of the Board of Works (£453,000, with half recoverable) far exceeded those of the grand juries.[39]

Government officials soon came to regard 'the half-grant system' as a major legislative blunder. Trevelyan bitterly complained in mid-April that this system offered 'such advantages to the landlords as to have led to a general demand for it, whether relief *for the people* was required or not; so that instead of a *test of real distress*, we have a *bounty on interested exaggeration*'. Rather than dig into their private pockets, landed proprietors, it was said, spoke openly and unashamedly of getting 'their share' of the public grants. The treasury did what it could to 'resist the torrent' of allegedly premature and ill-considered applications by demanding proof of distress and asking for contributions from proprietors. But these efforts were in the end largely ineffectual. As Trevelyan painfully realised, delays in granting requests placed the government 'in the awkward and invidious position of hesitating to apply a remedy which it has itself devised, and withholding the relief which it had itself previously been supposed to offer'.[40] Even when works were initiated under grand jury presentments, with the whole expense falling on the county, government officials were convinced that the landowners who sat on grand juries often approved schemes more from fear of courting intense unpopularity than from an honest belief that such works were essential for relieving acute distress.

These complaints by no means exhausted official dissatisfaction with the operation of the system of public works. Payment of wages by the day rather than by the task led, it was claimed, to widespread indolence, and the rates of pay (usually 9d. or 10d., but sometimes as much as 1s.) were high enough to entice labourers away from farmers and other private employers. The harshest criticism, however, was reserved for the manner in which individuals were chosen for employment on the schemes of the Board of Works. The actual task of selection belonged to the local relief committees, which were supposed to issue tickets only to destitute persons and only in accordance with prescribed procedures. But many tickets were dispersed by individual committee members 'in the most irregular manner'; some tickets were 'sold and distributed by persons unconnected with committees'; and often tickets were issued in much larger numbers than the works could possibly accommodate efficiently.[41] Above all, the relief committees generally neglected to scrutinise the means of applicants and allowed many who were not destitute to secure a place on the rolls.

Lacking direct control over the recruitment of labourers for its schemes, the Board of Works could do little to restrain the dramatic escalation in the scope of its responsibilities in the summer of 1846. From a daily average of about 21,000 persons during the month of June, the number employed soared to 71,000 by mid-July and reached a peak of almost 98,000 in the first week of August. It has been estimated that another 30,000 persons obtained work on schemes supervised by the county grand juries or on pier and harbour projects, and that perhaps 10,000 more received employment on schemes undertaken directly by local relief committees. If these estimates are correct, then approximately 140,000 people were given work at one time or another by the various agencies which Peel's government had set in motion. To assign four dependants to each of these 140,000 labourers would raise the total number of beneficiaries to 700,000.[42]

Clearly, government officials believed that the public purse had been opened much too widely in these operations, a view epitomised in the lament that 'every labouring man in the country was directed to look to the Board of Works for employment'.[43] As the number of workers on its schemes was nearing 100,000 early in August, the board flatly asserted that the figures were 'not an index to the state of distress or of the amount of employment necessary to be given to afford relief'.[44] Statistics showing the distribution of employment by county lend much support to this conclusion. Five-sixths of all those who worked on roads under the board's control in July were concentrated in only seven counties. Ranked in descending order, these were Clare, Limerick, Galway, Tipperary, Kerry, Mayo, and Roscommon. What is even more remarkable is that slightly over 40 per cent of such employment was confined to only two counties, with Clare accounting for 26 per cent and Limerick for 15 per cent.[45] In most of the seven counties with the highest proportions of public works employment, the deficiency in the 1845 potato crop did not exceed the national average, and in three (Clare, Kerry, and Mayo) the shortage was actually below the average. Obviously, to gauge the level of distress from the extent of the potato deficiency alone would be short-sighted, but it is clear from these statistics on public employment, and especially from the dramatic case of Clare, that the Board of

Works was right to complain that the numbers employed on its relief schemes in different counties were no fair guide to the geographical distribution of distress. Even if one rejects the official view that the government seriously overspent in relation to the country-wide level of distress, it is difficult to resist the conclusion that there was a substantial misallocation of public resources.

But what appeared to be unnecessary extravagance from the perspective of officials wore an entirely different aspect for its beneficiaries. The employment provided, and especially the food distributed, by the government prompted an extraordinary outpouring of popular gratitude. Commissariat officers took delight in quoting the effusive comments of the poor in reference to relief measures. Said one labourer, 'This is the sort of repeal for Ireland, and may the Almighty bless our queen.' Another remarked, 'After all, Peel is a true man to old Ireland, and the right sort.'[46] The country people, observed Assistant Commissary-General Edward Pine Coffin, readily declared that they had 'been rescued from a state of frightful misery, or to use their own strong but common expression, that "only for the government meal, thousands would have been now dying by the roadside"'.[47] These golden opinions were not confined to the peasantry. As Routh gleefully told Trevelyan in mid-June, 'Even the radical papers have ceased to speak of us in any other way than praise.'[48]

But if governments can cover themselves with glory when their actions are perceived as having overcome a major crisis, they can also cover themselves with infamy when their inaction is perceived as having turned a crisis into a catastrophe. The record of Peel's government in responding effectively to the partial potato failure of 1845 embedded the expectation that in the face of some far worse crisis in the future, relief fully equal to the vast needs of the people would be delivered, and delivered promptly. The total failure of the potato crop in 1846 meant that infinitely more was expected of Peel's Whig successors, and the infamy that they earned in Ireland had a great deal to do with the perception of how far short they fell of the high standards established by their distinguished predecessor.

CHAPTER 2

Production, Prices, and Exports, 1846–51

In 1846 blight attacked the potato much earlier and far more destructively than in the previous season. Reports of the havoc made by the disease now began to appear in mid-July. 'God help the poor people who paid in advance for their gardens', exclaimed one observer in the Fermoy district of Cork.[1] Under blackened stalks and leaves the tubers lay completely rotten or were as small as marbles; fields affected by the blight gave off an intolerable stench. With these sights and smells in the summer of 1846, the great famine began. The speed with which the devastation occurred etched itself deeply into the national consciousness. Writing on 7 August, Fr Theobald Mathew, the celebrated 'apostle of temperance', conveyed to Charles Trevelyan a vivid picture of what a vast difference a week had made:

> On the 27th of last month I passed from Cork to Dublin, and this doomed plant bloomed in all the luxuriance of an abundant harvest. Returning on the 3rd instant, I beheld with sorrow one wide waste of putrifying vegetation. In many places the wretched people were seated on the fences of their decaying gardens, wringing their hands and wailing bitterly [at] the destruction that had left them foodless.[2]

Even before the 'late' potatoes could be lifted, government officials believed that the loss would amount to three-quarters of that crop.[3] When the constabulary tabulated the results of its county-by-county survey in late October, it was painfully obvious that the earlier estimates had not been nearly gloomy enough. According to the constabulary figures, the average yield per acre in recent years had been almost eight tons, whereas in 1846 it was barely more than one-third of a ton. Though there was wide geographical variation in yields, in no county did the average exceed one ton per acre.[4] Almost certainly, potato yields in the early 1840s were lower than the constabulary figures indicated (say, six tons in a normal year), and the actual yield in 1846 may have been higher than the constabulary estimates. P.M.A. Bourke suggested a 'highly speculative' yield of 1.5 tons per acre.[5] But quite obviously, to use the adjectives 'total' and 'universal' in reference to the failure of 1846 is to exaggerate hardly at all. As if it were possible to darken a picture already pitch black, the disruption of the conacre system and the

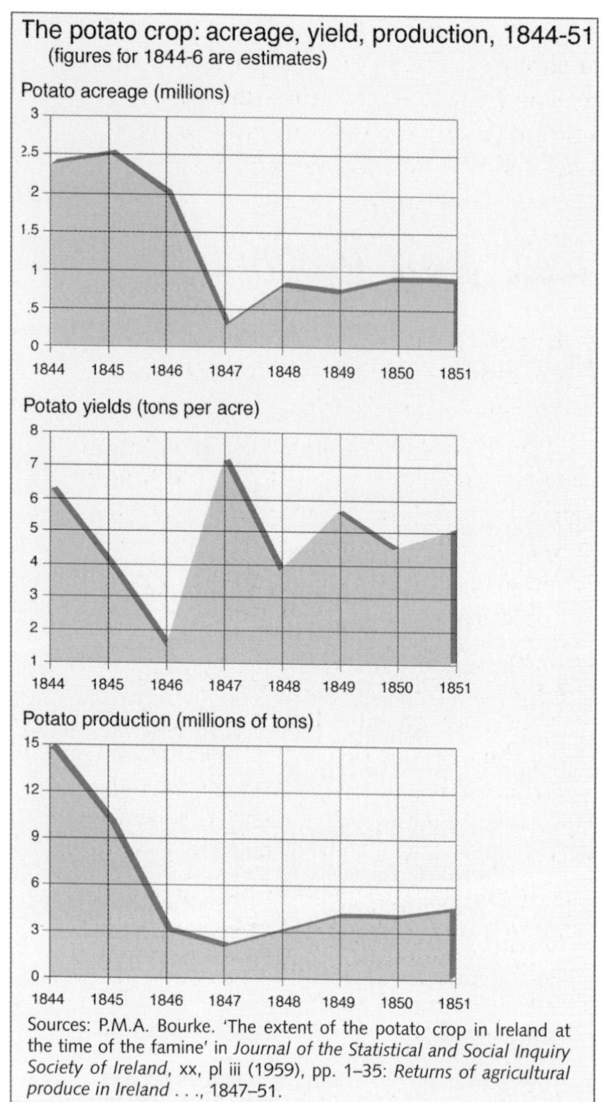

Sources: P.M.A. Bourke. 'The extent of the potato crop in Ireland at the time of the famine' in *Journal of the Statistical and Social Inquiry Society of Ireland*, xx, pl iii (1959), pp. 1–35: *Returns of agricultural produce in Ireland . . .*, 1847–51.

Blight destroyed the potato crop of 1846 almost completely. The shift from the appearance of luxuriance to universal rottenness and stench was dramatically swift. The disease was largely absent in 1847, but seed was so scarce that only a relatively small acreage was planted with potatoes, and the resulting harvest was only a fraction of normal. Blight returned in 1848 and 1849. Indeed, the potato only very rarely reached its pre-famine yield of about 6 tons per acre after 1850. These graphs illustrate the catastrophic decline in potato production over the years 1844–51. (Joan Murphy Donnelly)

shortage of seed after the partial failure of 1845 led to an estimated decline of 21 per cent in the acreage planted in 1846.[6] To say, as Fr Mathew did to Trevelyan, that 'the food of a whole nation has perished' was excessive, but under the circumstances his assertion was understandable and excusable.[7]

In several crucial respects the virtually total failure of the potato in 1846 paved the way for an equally great catastrophe in 1847. First, the traditional relationship between farmers and their bound labourers was thoroughly disrupted. Under the customary system such labourers had been willing to give work and to receive in exchange a patch of potato ground, a cabin, and a few so-called privileges. But as soon as blight blasted their potato gardens, money wages (at higher rates than usual) became absolutely essential if these labourers were to avoid starvation. The widespread refusal of farmers to make cash payments compelled the labourers to surrender their plots and to flee to the public works or, as a last resort, to the workhouses. Second, the failure of 1846 deranged the conacre system. Conacre lettings were even less extensive in 1847 than they had been a year earlier. Massive default by unbound labourers in the payment of conacre rents in the autumn of 1846 had taught farmers to insist that these rents must be paid in advance, but this demand was never more difficult to meet than in the spring of 1847, after the labourers' cash reserves had been totally exhausted.

To these two causes of the neglect of potato cultivation in 1847 must be added a third, which was indeed the most important – the enormous deficiency of seed, which dwarfed the shortages of 1846. Though urged to buy and distribute seed, the government refused to do so for a variety of reasons, the most myopic of which was that people would thereby be discouraged from preserving their own. In fact, with Indian meal selling at famine prices in the winter of 1846/7 and the subsequent spring, labourers and smallholders had no choice but to consume their seed potatoes if they wanted to stay alive. When they should have planted, they could not. 'I have asked them [i.e., the parishioners of Templecrone, County Donegal] why, instead of being idle, they do not dig their land', reported a commissariat officer in February 1847, 'and get but one answer – they have neither food to eat while working [for themselves], nor seed to put in, which is the case, for they have no person to help them.'[8] The combined effect of these adverse circumstances was an enormous decline in the potato acreage, which amounted in 1847 to a mere one-seventh of what it had been a year earlier, and to only one-ninth of the estimated acreage in 1845. The cruel irony of this situation was that the warm, dry weather of the spring and summer of 1847 had kept the destructive blight at bay. The national average yield of 7.2 tons per acre (this was the first year of official agricultural statistics) was excellent. But because of minimal planting, the total output was no larger and perhaps even smaller than in the catastrophic season of 1846.[9]

The general absence of blight in 1847 led to an extraordinary effort early in 1848 to bring the potato back from near-oblivion. This valiant attempt was made in the face of great obstacles, the chief of which was the continuing scarcity of seed. Reporting from the Rosscarbery district in Cork in April, a Quaker remarked, 'I know of a great many instances of the poor people fasting for eight and forty hours, trying to save the little remnant of their potatoes for seed.'[10] Such sacrifices helped to boost the acreage sown to a level three times higher than that of 1847 (810,000 acres compared with only 284,000). But in contrast to the previous season, the summer of 1848 was exceptionally wet, and blight again raged all over the country, sharply cutting the average yield to only about half of the 1847 figure. The net result was that total output in 1848 remained a mere fraction of production in pre-famine years.[11]

OTHER SERIOUS PROBLEMS

The drastic fall in potato production was the worst but not the only problem that beset Irish agriculture in the late 1840s and early 1850s. Some of these additional problems stemmed from the famine crisis itself, while others arose independently. To the former category belong the enormous decline in the number of pigs and the substantial, though less serious, contraction in the number of sheep. From a total of 2.1 million in 1841, sheep fell to a low of 1.8 million in 1849, though by 1851 they had regained the level of a decade earlier and stood on the verge of a remarkable advance. Pig numbers were cut by more than half between 1841 and 1847, declining from 1,400,000 to 622,000 over that period, and they still had not fully recovered by 1851, when the total fell short of 1,100,000.[12] As the export figures strongly suggest, the reaction of labourers and smallholders to the succession of potato failures was to dispose of their pigs and sheep without being able to restock. The shipment of pigs from Ireland to Britain plunged from 481,000 in 1846 to only 68,000 in 1849, while the export of sheep dropped from 324,000 in 1847 to fewer than 152,000 in 1851.[13] For the sharp contraction in

Before the famine the saying was that 'the pig paid the rent'. This was no mere piece of folk wisdom. It was the literal truth for most cottiers and labourers. They fattened pigs on the same food – abundant potatoes – that they ate. Pig fairs were normally crowded and boisterous, as depicted in this illustration of 1870. Without the potato, pig-raising steeply declined, and pig fairs went into eclipse temporarily in the late 1840s. (*Illustrated London News*)

sheep numbers there were other causes in addition to forced export without replacement. Farmers thinned their flocks because they could not protect them from nocturnal plunder and slaughter by famished labourers and cottiers. Flocks were also reduced by a widespread epidemic of liver-fluke disease spawned by heavy rains in the spring and summer of 1848.

The bad weather of 1848 also led to what was the worst grain harvest of the late 1840s. Wheat was hit especially hard, the average yield per acre declining to 4.5 barrels in contrast to 6.6 barrels in 1847. Despite the substantial fall in output, there was no compensating rise in price. On the contrary, wheat prices began to slump badly in 1848, and by 1851 they were as much as one-third lower than they had been as recently as 1847. This contracting demand, combined with another poor wheat harvest in 1850, prompted a large-scale abandonment of wheat farming throughout the country. Between 1847 and 1852 the area planted with wheat plummeted from 744,000 to less than 354,000 acres, or by 52 per cent.[14]

The other grain crops fared much better than wheat in the late 1840s and early 1850s. The yields of oats and barley were steadier, and their acreage underwent no serious decline. The production of oats did fall modestly in 1848 and 1849, but by 1852 it had risen slightly above the 1847 level. Oats were of course by far the most important grain crop, with an acreage in 1847 over twice as large, and in 1852 almost four times as large, as that of wheat and barley combined.[15] Thus the maintenance of oat production and prices at reasonably good levels over these years provided a significant element of stability in the otherwise dislocated tillage sector of the economy.

Yet even though the output of oats and barley did not falter seriously, tillage farmers were unable to convert these crops into income-earning exports at the usual rate of former years. The din of contemporary protest over the continuing flow of food out of the famine-stricken country has often been allowed to conceal the large-scale diversion of Irish grain from export to home consumption. Table 1, showing Irish exports of corn, meal, and flour to Britain from 1843 to 1849, highlights the extent of this diversion.[16]

Table 1
Exports of corn, meal, and flour from Ireland to Great Britain, 1843–9
(thousands of tons)

Year	Oats	Oatmeal	Wheat	Wheatmeal & Flour	Barley	Total
1843	218	152	40	48	20	478
1844	211	103	42	52	16	424
1845	235	95	78	89	17	514
1846	134	50	39	45	17	285
1847	69	30	26	13	9	147
1848	133	84	30	32	14	293
1849	93	64	21	29	8	215

One major reason for this diversion was the need of Irish livestock producers to secure a substitute for the fodder that plentiful potatoes had once furnished. On the eve of the famine as much as 5 million tons of potatoes, or about one-third of the total annual production, were fed to livestock. Almost 56 per cent of this was allotted to pigs, and another 40 per cent was consigned to cattle over the winter and early spring.[17] Largely because of the enormous deficiencies in the potato crop after 1845, the breeding of pigs went into eclipse until the early 1850s. But the raising of cattle increased substantially, and this expansion, together with the potato losses, made it necessary for farmers to feed a much higher proportion of their oat crop to their cattle.

What lowered grain exports even more, of course, were the appallingly large needs of humans. Insofar as grain retained in Ireland was marketed there to feed the starving, farmers' incomes benefited. Indeed, before 1848 the strength of domestic demand was such that fat profits (in 1846, obscene profits) accrued to that minority of farmers with large surpluses of grain to dispose of. But for the majority of tillage farmers, greatly increased subsistence needs cut deeply into the grain supplies that they could offer for sale. In County Cork even 'respectable farmers' holding 30 acres or more were said early in 1847 to be suffering acutely on this account: 'They are obliged to consume in their families and in their stables the corn which in former years procured clothes and other comforts for them.'[18] If this was true of the bigger farmers, smaller landholders must have had even less corn to place on the market. Thus, although the diversion of grain away from export was partly a matter of off-farm sales within Ireland, the scale of on-farm consumption rose so sharply in the late 1840s that this factor must be ranked among the leading causes of the serious erosion in tillage farmers' incomes.

NOT ALL GLOOM

Amid this general picture of crisis and malaise, however, there were some bright spots. Among the sectors of Irish agriculture that advanced in the late 1840s was dairying, a pursuit concentrated in the south-east and the south-west. In the absence of separate figures on the number of milch cattle before 1854, we must turn to the data available on butter exports for indirect information about the course of dairy output. What statistics we possess are not national in scope, but since they pertain to the Cork Butter Exchange, which was the largest single market in the country and drew its supplies from a wide area of Munster, it can be said with assurance that these regional data accurately reflect the general Irish trend. The rise in receipts of butter at the Cork exchange, illustrated in Table 2, strongly suggests that production increased moderately in the late 1840s.[19]

There is some reason to believe that a portion of the enlarged receipts in the years 1846–51 (about 15 per cent higher than in the previous five seasons) resulted from a decline in on-farm consumption, as the pressure of both rents

Table 2
Receipts of butter at Cork exchange, 1841–51
(thousands of cwt)

Year	Cwt	Year	Cwt
1841/2	134	1846/7	148
1842/3	155	1847/8	162
1843/4	168	1848/9	192
1844/5	149	1849/50	201
1845/6	159	1850/1	180
Average, 1841–6	153	Average, 1846–51	177

and poor rates drove dairy producers to maximise their marketed output. But the effect of this factor on the level of receipts seems to have been relatively small.

If most of the increase in supplies sent to Cork market was the result of a rise in production of similar magnitude, the reason for growing output was not a greater demand for Irish butter in Britain. The price of first-quality Cork butter in the years 1846–50 was virtually the same, on average, as in the previous quinquennium.[20] What made dairying attractive in the late 1840s was the high price of store cattle, of which dairy farmers were the chief suppliers. In 1847 and 1848 young stores (less than two years old) were about 50 per cent higher in price than in 1845, and older stores had risen even more in value, indeed, by as much as 80 or 90 per cent.[21] In the aftermath of the repeal of the corn laws, the long-term prospects of tillage in Ireland appeared bleak, whereas the future of pastoral farming seemed bright, given the country's natural advantages of soil and climate as well as the potential expansion of British demand for meat and butter. Even after the prices of butter and young stock declined sharply beginning in 1849, landlords considered it an unmistakable sign of lasting improvement when tenants enlarged their dairying operations. As Sir John Benn-Walsh recorded in his journal in August 1851 while visiting his estate in north Kerry,

> The great criterion in these times is to watch whether the farmers are increasing their cow and dairy stock. If they are reducing their cattle and ploughing up their lands, depend upon it, they are going to the bad, but if they are adding a collop [portion] or two to their stock, the productiveness of their farm and the security for their rent are both increasing.[22]

Indeed, the Irish cattle enterprise as a whole was growing in the late 1840s and early 1850s. This expansion represented a continuation of the rising trend of the early 1840s. The official statistics, however, need to be treated with caution. As P.M.A. Bourke pointed out, the number of cattle reported in the 1841 census – a total of 1,863,000 – did not include 'calves of the current year', with the result that the enumeration was deficient by some 16 to 20 per cent. A comparison of the higher corrected total for 1841 (2,233,000 cattle) with the figure for 1847 (2,591,000) reveals an increase of at least 16 per cent during the interval.[23] But if the effect of this correction is to reduce the extent of the growth in cattle numbers between 1841 and 1847, a countervailing consideration must be kept in mind. The impact of the partial potato failure of 1845 and the nearly total loss of 1846 forced cottiers and small farmers to dispose of their cattle in large numbers before agricultural statistics were collected in 1847. Had this crisis not occurred, the rise since 1841 would have been appreciably greater. In the four years following 1847, the national cattle herd increased by another 15 per cent, to a total of 2,967,000 in 1851. This latter rise, however, was anything but evenly distributed among the different categories of farm size. On holdings of 15 acres or less, the number of cattle actually decreased, and it was stationary on farms of 15 to 30 acres; the whole of the increase was thus confined to large farms exceeding 30 acres.[24] This is a striking illustration of a general phenomenon of the late 1840s – a drastic widening of the gap between rich and poor in Irish rural society.

Even well-to-do farmers, however, were hammered by the general depression in agricultural prices that started in 1849. The price declines were smaller for grain crops, which (apart from the exceptional year of 1846, when corn soared in value) had already shown a tendency to fall even before 1849; the decreases were much larger for store cattle, which had risen in price to great heights between 1845 and 1848. Graziers, together with dairy farmers who reared young stock, were hit especially hard. The great October fair at Ballinasloe in 1849 was sorely disappointing to the sellers of both cattle and sheep. 'I have been attending the fair of Ballinasloe for the last twelve or thirteen years', remarked the special correspondent of the *Freeman's Journal*, 'and never witnessed such indifferent prospects nor heard such general complaints on the part of breeders of stock.'[25] The cattle fair in particular was 'characterised by a dulness [*sic*] hitherto unknown'; indeed, it was 'admitted by all to have been the worst cattle fair ever experienced in Ballinasloe'.[26] By 1850 younger stores had declined in value by 43 per cent since the peak attained in 1847, and over the same period the price of older stores fell by 32 per cent. In addition, the value of both butter and beef tumbled, the first by 30 per cent between 1846 and 1850, and the second by 26 per cent between 1848 and 1850.[27] Although the worst was nearly over by the end of 1851, there was no real recovery in prices until the outbreak of the Crimean war.

CHAPTER 3

The Administration of 'Relief', 1846–7

'"We know your honour will help us again" is the consoling remark with which [the poor] wind up their tale of disappointment and prospective want, and this seems to them, after their late experience [of government intervention in the grain trade], a sufficient security against the risk of famine.' So Charles Trevelyan was told on 18 August 1846 by Sir Edward Pine Coffin, the commissariat officer in charge of the Limerick depot. Coffin knew that the relief operations of 1846–7 would be conducted very differently from those of the current season, and as if to justify the change, he said of the attitude of the poor: 'It is a characteristic feeling, but one replete with mischief to themselves and to the community. . . .'[1] Before the new relief system could be installed, the old one needed to be terminated, and this could safely be done, it was felt, because the harvest season was about to start. Employment on the public works was gradually reduced beginning in the second week of August. By the end of that month the number of persons earning wages from the Board of Works had fallen to a daily average of 38,000, and it continued to decline for several weeks thereafter.[2] (The corresponding figure for the week ending on 26 September was slightly below 15,000.) The food depots also reined back their sales, with a view to a complete cessation of operations at the close of August.

The relief policies of the new Whig administration had been disclosed to parliament by Lord John Russell, the prime minister, in mid-August, when all the available evidence already pointed to a calamitous failure of the potato crop. Russell announced that he and his colleagues were opposed to any general interference by the government with the grain trade. The primary emphasis in any new crisis would be placed less on the sale of food and more on the provision of employment through a revamped system of public works. In adopting these policies, the cabinet was basically accepting the proposals made by Charles Trevelyan. In an important memorandum submitted to the cabinet on 1 August, Trevelyan insisted that 'the supply of the home market may safely be left to the foresight of private merchants', and that if it became necessary for the government to interfere at all, its purchases should be restricted to the home market in order to encourage the private importation of food. As anxious as Trevelyan was to allow full scope to private enterprise, he recognised (though not sufficiently) that in parts of Ireland grain

POLITICAL ECONOMY; OR, LORD JOHN IN PEEL'S CLOTHES.

THE QUEEN (*loq.*) – "WELL! IT IS NOT THE BEST FIT IN THE WORLD, BUT WE'LL SEE HOW

This *Punch* cartoon of July 1846 – 'Political economy; or, Lord John in Peel's clothes' – shows Queen Victoria whispering in the background, 'Well! It is not the best fit in the world, but we'll see how he goes on!' While poking fun at Russell's small physical stature as compared with Peel's, the cartoonist was also expressing the widespread doubt that the new prime minister would be the political equal of his predecessor. This doubt was more than justified, especially in relation to Ireland. (*Punch* Archive) importers and retail traders either did not exist or were too few in number to provide adequate supplies in a period of extreme scarcity. Even so, he proposed minimal intervention: government food depots should be set up on the west coast alone, but not even there should they issue food while supplies could be purchased from dealers or obtained from other private sources. In essence, then, the government committed itself to acting as a supplier of last resort west of the Shannon. Everywhere else (around the north, east, and south coasts from Derry to Dublin and Cork, as well as east of the Shannon generally), ministers and relief officials considered themselves bound to a policy of non-intervention, and pledges to that effect were actually given to merchants.[3]

The partial potato failure of 1845 had allowed the government a period of six or seven months to prepare its relief machinery before having to set it in motion. But the new crisis was utterly different. The almost total failure of 1846 permitted virtually no breathing space before the destitute masses sought to throw themselves on government resources. With respect to food, those resources were shockingly inadequate, even for the west alone. By the end of August all but a few of the depots had closed, and the stocks remaining had dwindled to less than 2,100 tons of Indian meal and about 240 tons of oatmeal.[4] When the prospect of a total potato failure became all but certain in August, Trevelyan scrambled to increase official stocks by employing as corn factor the London merchant Eric Erichsen. His initial purchases were quite small, and on 19 September Routh protested to Trevelyan: 'It would require a thousand tons to make an impression, and that only a temporary one. Our salvation of the depot system is in the importation of a large supply. These small shipments are only drops in the ocean.'[5] The problem, as Trevelyan explained a few days later, was that 'the London and Liverpool markets are at present so completely bare of this article [i.e., maize] that we have been obliged to have recourse to the plan of purchasing supplies of Indian corn which had been already exported from London to neighbouring continental ports'.[6] Partly through such expedients Erichsen was able during August and September to buy about 7,300 tons of maize, along with 200 tons of barley and 100 tons of Indian meal.[7]

These imports, however, did little to raise commissariat reserves because the depots could not be kept shut altogether. The largest issues were made from the store at Sligo, which served the north-west, where acute distress became evident as early as mid-August. Over 650 tons of maize meal and oatmeal were distributed from here alone between 10 August and 19 September. Heavy pressure persisted for many weeks thereafter, and it was not until early November, after the first local arrival of private imports, that relief officials were able to close the Sligo store.[8] The combination of small government imports and unavoidable issues from some of the depots caused the total stocks in government stores to long remain well below the minimum level of 8,000 tons that Routh considered necessary before there could be any general opening of the depots in the west. Official stocks did not surpass 4,000 tons until the end of November, and a month later they barely exceeded 6,000 tons.[9] Even so, at the end of December the treasury finally consented to throwing open the western depots 'for the sale of food as far as may be prudent and necessary'.[10]

Could the government, by prompt action, have secured enough food from Britain or foreign countries to open its depots in the west of Ireland much sooner? It has been suggested that if Trevelyan had been willing to move decisively into the grain market as soon as he received the first reports of the reappearance of blight in mid-July, adequate supplies could have been accumulated. The late T.P. O'Neill pointed out that Trevelyan was urged by Assistant Commissary-General Hewetson in late July to purchase 4,500 tons of Indian meal immediately. 'This warning had been ignored,' O'Neill observed, 'and purchases began too late in the season to ensure the arrival of sufficient quantities before Christmas.'[11] But the matter is more complicated. Hewetson clearly did not anticipate issuing the meal until the spring of 1847.[12] On the other hand, it is true that Erichsen's purchases for the government did not begin until 26 August, and that of the 22,600 tons of maize bought through his agency up to mid-January 1847, only about 6,800 tons had actually arrived by that time in Ireland or Britain.[13] The government, in fact, had to contend with two serious obstacles. The first was the unavoidable delay of one to three months between the date of purchase and the date of delivery, and the second was that after such heavy imports in the first six or seven months of 1846, Indian corn was in short supply in the London and Liverpool markets as well as on the continent. Trevelyan had ruled out direct government orders to the United States, but even if he had not done so, American maize was not quickly accessible. As Routh noted of the requests forwarded by Irish merchants to America in September, 'These orders cannot be executed so as to arrive in the United Kingdom before the end of November, and then only the old corn of last year [1845], for the new corn of this year will not be ready for shipment before January.'[14] This much may be conceded: if Erichsen had been authorised to begin his purchases in late July instead of late August, there would have been considerably more food in the western depots before the end of 1846; perhaps the stores would have opened a month or so earlier than they did. But this would not have been enough to avert the onset of famine and epidemic disease.

Grain Exports Allowed

Since relief officials did not expect large supplies of foreign corn to begin to reach Irish ports before December, they were especially anxious to see the domestic harvest brought to market as rapidly as possible. One excuse offered for keeping the western depots generally closed and for not establishing stores outside the west was that this policy would accelerate the process of converting the grain harvest of 1846 into food. It soon became apparent, however, that in spite of steeply rising grain prices at home, exportation on a large, though diminished, scale was once again taking place. Routh was alarmed and more than once hinted at the desirability of stopping it. 'The exports of oats have amounted since the harvest to 300,000 quarters', he told Trevelyan at the end of September. 'I know there is a great and serious objection to any interference with these exports, yet it is a most serious evil. . . .'[15] As he remarked in another letter, 'The people, deprived of this resource, call out on the government for Indian corn, which requires time for its importation.'[16] But Trevelyan promptly and brusquely turned Routh's suggestion aside. 'We beg of you', said Trevelyan, 'not to countenance in any way the idea of prohibiting exportation. The discouragement and feeling of insecurity to the [grain] trade from such a proceeding would prevent its doing even any *immediate* good; and there cannot be a doubt that it would inflict a permanent injury on the country.'[17] Trevelyan's decision, never questioned by his political masters, seems to have been based more on his rigid adherence to *laissez-faire* economic doctrines than on a careful assessment of its practical short-term consequences. To have forbidden exports from the 1846 grain harvest might well have led to some reduction in food imports late in 1846 or early in 1847, but it would hardly have paralysed the trade, and it would have helped materially to fill the huge gap in domestic food supplies that persisted until long after the maize ordered from America began to reach Irish shores in December.[18] Most scholars would agree that this refusal to prohibit exports, even for a limited period, was one of Trevelyan's worst mistakes, although the blame was of course not his alone. More than any other single decision, it provided some substance to the later nationalist charge that the British government had been prepared to see a large proportion of the Irish people starve.

Allowing unhindered exportation certainly contributed significantly to the remorseless rise of Irish food prices between September and the end of the year. As long as the wholesale price of Indian meal remained at £10 or less per ton, as it did through August, there was little risk of famine, but as each succeeding month brought higher prices, malnourishment increased, eventually to the point of starvation, and along with it susceptibility to infectious diseases, the greatest scourge of all. At Cork the price of Indian meal rose from £11 a ton at the beginning of September to £16 in the first week of October, and before the end of that month it stood as high as £17 to £18; only slight reductions (to £16 or £17) were recorded in November and December.[19] When food was sold from the depots, as happened periodically before late December, the prices were purposely regulated by those prevailing in the nearest market town or by the current trade prices. This was justified on the grounds that private traders had to be allowed to earn reasonable profits, and that if they were undersold, there would be such a rush to the depots that the limited supplies would quickly be exhausted.

The latter argument contained some truth, but the former displayed, to say the least, undue tenderness for grain importers and dealers, whose profits swelled. Even commissariat officers conceded the point. As Hewetson told

Trevelyan in late October, 'The corn dealers and millers are everywhere making large profits, but I trust [that] Christmas will see prices much lower.'[20] Among the biggest beneficiaries were G.W. & J.N. Russell, 'the great corn factors and millers of Limerick', who at this time were grinding over 500 tons a week.[21] Their prices tended to regulate the cost of food not only in Limerick but also in north Kerry, Clare, and Tipperary. In mid-November Hewetson pressed this firm to reduce its prices and extracted a promise that the charges for Indian meal and oatmeal would at once be lowered to £16 and £20 a ton respectively. Yet 'even this is too high a figure for any length of time', and though the firm deserved what Hewetson called encouragement, he feared that if the matter were 'left altogether to the few houses in the city (theirs giving the tone), reductions will be very gradual in operation'.[22] And so they were, without effective government intervention and with ever more doleful consequences. Indeed, the depots actually made substantial profits on their sales: in mid-January 1847 the commissariat was charging £19 a ton (as high as £22 or even £24 'in some situations') for Indian meal that it had purchased a few months earlier for about £13.[23] This situation reflected Trevelyan's inflexible view that unless prices were allowed to attain the full market rate, Ireland would be even worse placed to attract foreign supplies to its ports and to retain within the country what food had been produced there. Or as he said in a little lecture to Routh late in September 1846, 'Imports could not take place into a country where prices are artificially depressed, but, on the contrary, the food already in the country would be exported to quarters where a fair market price could be obtained.'[24] This, needless to say, was to make a religion of the market and to herald its cruel dictates as blessings in disguise.

Massive Public Works

Against this pattern of non-intervention and general passivity with respect to the food supply in late 1846 must be set the burst of activity in the field of public works. It will be recalled that there had been intense dissatisfaction among relief officials with many aspects of the system of public works during the previous season of distress. The new system, devised mainly by Trevelyan in August 1846, was intended to avoid the inefficiency, waste, and extravagance which in the official view had characterised earlier operations. Instead of allowing the county grand juries to initiate and direct a significant proportion of the employment projects, it was decided that the Board of Works should assume complete responsibility for all public schemes. And rather than continue the practice under which the treasury paid half the cost of projects controlled by the Board of Works, it was ordained that in future all charges should ultimately be met out of local taxation. Though the treasury would advance the money for public works in the first instance, the proceeds of county cess were to be used to repay these loans in full. Irish property must support Irish poverty: much was to be heard of this maxim, a favourite of English politicians and civil servants, during the famine

Road-making was a central focus of the public works. Little of real economic benefit was accomplished. Indeed, two general complaints were that travelling the main roads became extremely difficult, and that many small new roads went nowhere in particular. By bringing large bodies of malnourished and infected people together for work on the roads, especially in the rigours of an unusually harsh winter, the authorities succeeded in spreading epidemic diseases. Worst of all, the wages paid on the public works fell far short of what was needed to procure sufficient food. Scenes like the one depicted in this later photograph were commonplace in late 1846 and early 1847. The picture shows women carrying stones which the sitting men had broken on relief works at Carraroe, Co. Galway, in 1898. (National Library of Ireland)

years. In sum, then, the government created a system that combined local financial responsibility with thoroughgoing centralised control of employment projects. By design the schemes were not to be 'reproductive', since Trevelyan wanted to restrict applications from landowners. This policy was soon modified under pressure from Irish landlords, but the practical results of the alteration were meagre and, in the new season of distress as in the old, the building or repair of roads and bridges was the most common activity. Cutting hills and filling hollows were the main tasks.[25]

With the assumption of complete control by the Board of Works came the imposition of time-consuming bureaucratic procedures. (The board itself was on the verge of becoming a mammoth bureaucracy, with 12,000 subordinate officials.) Only the viceroy himself could authorise the holding of an extraordinary presentment sessions, and the relief schemes proposed at the sessions had first to be scrutinised by the board's officials, who then might request the treasury to sanction them. Adherence to these procedures caused agonising delays in starting public works, not only when the new system was inaugurated but also, to some degree, throughout its whole duration, since at any given time, while some works were being closed, others were being opened. Delays, however, were particularly numerous at the outset. The viceroy had ordered public works to be restarted early in September, but it was not until October that the new schemes began.

Even though the problem of delay was never eliminated, the sheer pace and scale of operations soon became quite extraordinary. Indeed, the extension of the bureaucratic apparatus could hardly keep pace with the headlong expansion of employment. Between the first and the last week of October the average daily number of persons employed by the Board of Works soared from 26,000 to 114,000; throughout November the figure climbed steadily, reaching 286,000 in the fourth week. Though the rate of increase slowed somewhat during December, 441,000 persons had crowded on to the public works by the end of the year. The peak was reached in March 1847, when during one week as many as 714,390 persons were employed daily. Naturally, the expenditure was great. By the time that the system of public works was terminated in the spring of 1847 and replaced by the distribution of free food (in a terribly belated confession of failure), the accumulated costs of these relief schemes amounted to the staggering sum of almost £4,850,000. It could now be said that Irish property was paying, or rather was beginning to pay, for Irish poverty.[26]

FATAL INADEQUACY OF WAGES

Enormous as the expenditures were, they had not been nearly sufficient to bring enough food within the financial reach of the rapidly increasing masses of destitute people. The fundamental problem was the inadequacy of the wages paid on the public works. Beginning in September 1846, the Board of Works tried to substitute a system of task labour for the daily wages that had prevailed previously. The main reason for this drastic change in policy was to eliminate or at least to reduce the general indolence that had allegedly prevailed among labourers during the past season of relief operations. The board instructed its

Opposite: Local relief committees, such as that in County Cavan headed by Lord Farnham, played a vital role in administering the rapidly escalating scheme of public works in the winter of 1846/7. These committees were supposed to ensure that employment on the public works was confined to the destitute and that more fortunate souls were stricken from the relief rolls. But sorting out the 'deserving' from the 'undeserving' under famine conditions was impossible. Despite various stratagems to limit numbers and expense, over 700,000 people streamed on to the public works by March 1847. (National Archives of Ireland)

NOTICE.

CAVAN RELIEF COMMITTEE.

The Relief Committee have received numerous complaints of persons having obtained employment in the Public Works in this district, who do not come within the description laid down in the instructions issued by Government to the Relief Committees, that is "persons who are destitute of means of support, or for whose support such employment is actually necessary."

It is obvious that Pensioners at a shilling a day, Farmers (or their sons) possessing a cart and horse, and several cows, with stacks of oats in their haggard, cannot be included in this description; and yet many such, it is stated to the Committee, are at present employed.

When such persons once take into consideration that, as employment obviously cannot be afforded to all, their obtaining it throws out of the work poor destitute and starving people, the Committee confidently trust they will voluntarily with draw and give up their tickets.

The Committee, however, will continue to receive complaints; and if the party complained of does not withdraw of his own accord, he will be called upon to shew upon what grounds he claims to be employed on the Public Works.

The Committee will not recommend for employment Servants or Labourers who are actually engaged, or those who leave their employers without consent.

When any Gentleman or Farmer requires Labourers, to be paid at the same rate adopted in the Public Works, if he will notify to the Committee the names of those he wishes to hire, they shall be immediately struck off their Lists so long as they are thus required; the Committee being authorised to afford employment to those alone who cannot obtain it elsewhere.

The Commitee are informed that Carts and Horses belonging to wealthy farmers are employed at the Public Works. This they consider quite unjustifiable.—There are persons holding little or no land, who keep a Cart and Horse entirely for hire, and actually live by it. Of such, a list might, without much difficulty, be made; and the Committee think that such might fairly obtain employment at the usual wages, of 2s. 6d. per day, under the Board of Works, provided they cannot procure it elsewhere. But if it shall be found necessary to employ the Carts of persons not in want, the Committee recommend that they shall receive three men from the Public Works in exchange, or if they prefer it, two men, and the wages of the third in cash; but that in no case, shall the wages of 2s. 6d. a day for man, cart, and horse be paid, unless to those included in the list before mentioned.

The Committee are of opinion that, for the future, Overseers and Check Clerks, as far as may be found practicable, should be selected from persons at present in the Public Works; their merit might be judged from their conduct while employed, and if any should be found deserving of promotion, it would be a great incentive to others, and would also be a saving of the Public Money.

FARNHAM, *Chairman.*

November 10, 1846.

JOHNSTON, PRINTER, CAVAN,

officials that 'the sum to be paid for each portion of [task] work should be sufficient to enable an ordinary labourer to earn from 10d. to 1s. per day, and a good labourer who exerted himself, from 1s. 4d. to 1s. 6d. per day'.[27] As a punitive incentive designed to win acceptance for task work, those labourers who were unwilling (or unable) to do it were to be paid no more than 8d. per day.[28] This was from one-fifth to one-third less than previous daily rates for customary unmeasured work, even though food prices were already rising when the reduction was ordered.

The introduction of task labour was fiercely resisted by the workers, often to the point of violence, and many projects had to be stopped, at least temporarily, before popular opposition could be overcome. Officials tended to attribute the resistance they encountered to the labourers' unfamiliarity with task work or to their unreasonable fears of unfair treatment if they consented to do it. But there were serious practical problems, only too evident to the labourers, which the higher officers of the board were inclined to minimise or overlook. Any delay in the setting out of task work, and delays were unavoidable in view of the rapidly growing scale of operations, meant (or was supposed to mean) that wages had to be paid at the low daily rate of 8d. On the other hand, when task work was set out but not measured immediately, as was usually the case, the labourers were paid on account, the rule being that they were to receive three-quarters of the agreed value of the assigned work, for example 9d. on account for a task worth 1s. Delays in conducting measurements, occasioned by the shortage of qualified staff and by other factors, frequently caused severe hardship, and there were complaints that payments on account fell short of the stipulated three-quarters.[29]

Another reason for popular opposition to task work was that the scarcity of implements had the effect of seriously reducing wages. Many labourers assigned to task work in the closing months of 1846 were unable to earn even half the 'ordinary' rate of 10d. to 1s. because they lacked the proper tools. Among one gang of seventy-five men in the Cong district of Mayo there were only two wheelbarrows, two crowbars, and a wooden lever. The few possessing these implements received up to 10d. a day while the rest earned as little as 3½d. to 4d. Labourers whose task work once entitled them to 1s. a day but whose health declined were later unable to claim more than 6d. while toiling at the same job.[30] Indeed, the system of task labour operated to the general detriment not only of the sick or infirm but also of the old, women, and adolescents. Some labour gangs excluded individuals in these categories from their ranks because the presence of such people would have lowered the rates of wages that physically strong and healthy adult males could earn.

To judge from the reports of the inspecting officers of the Board of Works, however, a majority of workers in many districts eventually came to accept and even to approve of task labour. To many, it offered or seemed to offer the possibility of adjusting their wages to keep pace with the rapid advance of food prices; it was particularly attractive to younger adult males in sound health,

Many thousands of those employed on the public works in the winter of 1846/7 gradually starved or fell prey to epidemic disease. Malnourished or sick, they were frequently unable to earn enough at measured task labour to buy sufficient food to stay alive. By early 1847, and even earlier in some places, a high proportion of those employed on the public works must have worn the emaciated appearance of the woman in this later photograph, a potato picker named McCaffrey working near Tempo, Co. Fermanagh, in November 1899. (Photograph reproduced with the kind permission of the Trustees of the National Museums & Galleries of Northern Ireland)

who could thrive under this system or at least avoid being engulfed in the rising sea of misery around them. Another reason for acceptance or approval was that workers were often able to turn the system more to their advantage. Local overseers of the public schemes in numerous districts were subjected to great pressure by the labourers to exact less work for a given rate of wages than the application of strict standards would have required. Harsh overseers risked being beaten, and the fear of assault (along with humanitarian feeling, in many cases) inclined overseers to leniency in enforcing standards. Higher officials of the Board of Works complained that there was widespread collusion to raise wages between their subordinates and workers engaged in task labour. Early in December the head of the Board of Works, Lieutenant-Colonel Harry David Jones, told Trevelyan: 'I am quite convinced from reading our last week's reports and from other sources that our task system is not working as it ought to do; the men are receiving much larger sums than they ought to do. . . . I believe everybody considers the government fair game to pluck as much as they can.'[31]

Yet the sad truth was not that too many earned too much, but that too many earned too little to enable them to ward off starvation and disease. A signal defect of the task work regime was the growing physical debility of many labourers suffering from malnutrition, a condition which made it impossible for them to earn the sums of which 'ordinary' workers were considered capable. In west Clare, for example, debilitated labourers were seen to stagger on the public works at the outset of 1847, and 'the stewards state that hundreds of them are never seen to taste food from the time they come upon the works in the morning until they depart at nightfall . . .'.[32] Barely more than a month after telling Trevelyan that task work wages were too high, Lieutenant-Colonel Jones had to admit that the opposite was often true: 'In some districts the men who come to the works are so reduced in their physical powers as to be unable to earn above 4d. or 5d. per diem.'[33]

In many parts of the country where public works had been opened, task labour had not been introduced at all, or had been only partially adopted, or had been abandoned after a period of trial. In numerous instances the nature of the work to be performed or the character of the terrain was considered unsuitable for the adoption of task labour. In other cases the subordinate officials of the Board of Works were incapable of shouldering the additional technical and supervisory burdens associated with task labour. 'It is extremely difficult to carry out the board's wish respecting task work,' remarked the inspecting officer for north Kilkenny in late December, 'the nature of the soil being so different in various places that nothing like a fixed list of prices can be established, and the overseers are not capable, in most instances, of measuring and valuing excavations, &c., were the staff of the engineers sufficient to overlook the works properly.'[34] The board itself pointed out in mid-January 1847 'the impossibility of finding overseers qualified to estimate and measure tasks for 10,000 separate working parties'.[35] In the many localities where day labour remained the dominant or exclusive form of public employment, wages were even more likely to be inadequate to sustain health than in areas where task work prevailed. It is true that the rule limiting payment by the day to 8d. was not always scrupulously observed, but the wage for this type of work rarely exceeded 10d., and such sums condemned the recipients and their families to malnutrition and disease.

This became a common complaint in the weekly reports of the inspecting officers beginning in December 1846, though other commentators had called attention to the general insufficiency of earnings much earlier. From one inspecting officer in County Leitrim came the report that 'the miserable condition of the half-famished people is greatly increased by the exorbitant . . . price of meal and provisions, insomuch that the wages gained by them on the works are quite inadequate to purchase a sufficiency to feed many large families'.[36] Another inspector in County Limerick declared, 'I greatly fear that unless some fall shortly takes place in the rate of provisions, a great proportion of the families now receiving relief on the public works will require additional support, and that without it they will not long exist.'[37] Because the retail price of meal in County Limerick was as high as 2s. 8d. per stone, one labourer from a family of six or more could no longer furnish himself and them with enough food, obliging the inspecting officer to allow a second member of such families to be placed on the public works. (From other counties there were reports at this time of even higher retail prices for maize meal: 2s. 10d. per stone in Galway, 3s. in Meath, and up to 3s. 4d. in Roscommon.)[38] A month earlier (at the end of November), the inspector of north Tipperary, where Indian meal was much cheaper (2s. 2d. a stone), remarked, 'The country people are generally in the greatest distress. Tenpence a day will, I believe, only give *one* meal a day to a family of six persons. . . .'[39] A west Cork observer made a similar calculation early in January 1847: 'Indian and wheaten meal are both selling at 2s. 6d. per 14 lb; at this rate a family consisting of five persons cannot, out of the wages of one person, say 6s. per week, have even two meals per diem for more than four days in the week.'[40] Almost everywhere 8d. a day was literally a starvation wage for the typical labouring family, and so too, in most places, was 10d. Yet a high proportion of the labourers on the public works throughout the country earned no more than these sums, and many earned less. No wonder, then, that work gangs so often engaged in strikes, demanding at least 1s. a day, that overseers and check clerks were so frequently threatened or assaulted, and that in the winter of 1846/7 labourers on the works commonly collapsed from exhaustion.

Two other serious deficiencies exacerbated the general inadequacy of wage rates. One was frequent delay in the payment of wages. To this chronic problem several factors contributed: dishonesty or lack of zeal on the part of the pay clerks, who numbered 548 at the beginning of March 1847 (some of them were also robbed); shortages of silver; breakdowns in the elaborate system of paperwork; and the failure or inability of the overseers to measure task work promptly. Delays of one to two weeks were not unusual, and in some districts interruptions lasting as long as five weeks occurred occasionally. When in late October 1846 a labourer named Denis McKennedy dropped dead by the roadside in the Skibbereen district of Cork, with his wages two weeks in arrears, a coroner's jury declared that he had 'died of starvation due to the gross negligence of the Board of Works'.[41] This was the first in a string of similar verdicts, though not all of them involved alleged interruptions in the payment of wages. Persistent efforts were made to overcome this problem, and delays were reduced in duration, but they could not be eliminated altogether.

The other serious defect was the government's unwillingness to pay normal wages whenever work had to be curtailed because of bad weather during the winter of 1846/7. When the issue was first discussed in September 1846, the viceroy directed that if labourers were prevented from working by inclement weather, they should be 'sent home and paid [for] half-a-day's work'.[42] After frost arrived in early December, Trevelyan observed to Lieutenant-Colonel Jones: 'Now that the hard weather is come, you will, I presume, act upon the rule long ago settled by you with the lord lieutenant, that on days when the weather will not permit the people to work, they will receive a proportion of what they would otherwise earn; this is clearly the right way of meeting the exigency.'[43] To pay only half of what was already in many cases a starvation wage was scarcely right, but at least it was straightforward. Yet the Board of Works apparently never gave a clear instruction in this matter to its local officials. Some of them adopted a half-pay standard, but others – indeed, the vast majority – simply allowed the works to proceed. For obvious reasons, labourers in general did not wish to stop working if it meant the interruption of their pay. But in bad weather they were rarely able to earn much. When heavy snow fell in County Donegal in mid-December, 'the people continued work during the whole time, but could do nothing but break stones' for low wages.[44] At the same stage in King's County an inspecting officer declared that 'earnings this week, after measurement, are much reduced owing to the frost'.[45] Extremely bad weather in the second week of February 1847 brought about the first reduction in public works employment since the previous October. Because of a heavy snowfall, the number at work fell from a daily average of 615,000 to slightly less than 608,000. But in the third and fourth weeks of that month alone another 100,000 persons crowded on to the works in spite of the cold and the inadequate wages.[46]

Confession of Failure

Already, however, those responsible for relief policy had reluctantly concluded that the mammoth system of public works must soon cease to be the centrepiece of the battered strategy for warding off starvation and disease. By January 1847 mass death had begun in some localities, and inspecting officers of the Board of

Works anticipated heavy mortality 'within a very short period' in the counties of Clare, Cork, Galway, Kerry, Leitrim, Mayo, Roscommon, Tipperary, and Wicklow.[47] In mid-January the board confessed itself to be near the end of its powers and resources. Its officers, having already fought a losing battle to keep off the works small farmers with holdings valued at £6 or more, could now do almost nothing to limit the constantly swelling mass of claimants for employment. For their inability they castigated the local relief committees, whose only object, declared Lieutenant-Colonel Jones, echoing innumerable complaints by his subordinates, 'is to get as many persons employed as possible, instead of anxiously endeavouring to keep the numbers as low as the existing calamity will permit'. In rejecting 'undeserving' applicants designated as destitute by the committees, the inspecting officers drew 'down upon themselves and the board all the odium and vindictive feelings of the poorer classes'.[48] It was not unknown for inspectors to be denounced to their faces as the authors of starvation.

Even if those deemed undeserving could have been thrown back on their own resources, supposing they had some, the undeniably destitute would more than have filled their places. 'The number employed is nearly 500,000', Jones and his colleagues told the viceroy on 17 January, 'and 300,000 or 400,000 in addition will shortly require it.'[49] As many as one-third of those listed as destitute by the local relief committees were still not on the public labour rolls. Even for those currently employed, work to do on the roads was almost exhausted. Indeed, the main roads had been made much worse, not better. Landed proprietors, who had 'voted thousands and thousands of pounds' for such schemes, 'cry out that the great communications of the country are destroyed', Jones acidly remarked, 'and I have no doubt that for this season they are all more or less severely injured and many nearly impassable, but whose fault is that? Not ours.'[50] His board, he insisted to Trevelyan, could not possibly accommodate the additional multitudes likely to be driven to the public schemes in the coming months by want of food: 'We have neither staff nor work upon which we can employ them.'[51] Even if there were scope for a wide extension of the road projects, the system of task labour could not be retained. 'The fact is', Jones finally admitted, 'that the system . . . is no longer beneficial employment to many; their bodily strength being gone, and spirits depressed, they have not power to exert themselves sufficiently to earn the ordinary day's wages.'[52] Task labour had lost its original purpose, he and his colleagues declared, because 'the idleness of the idle' could no longer 'be distinguished from the feebleness of the weak and infirm'.[53] Taking all these circumstances into account, Jones was led to what for him was the distasteful conclusion that 'it would be better in many cases to give food than to be paying money away, as we are now obliged to do'. Like many others, he had been deeply impressed by the results of the distribution of soup to the starving by private groups such as the Quakers. 'You will perceive the great benefits derived from the soup establishments,' he told Trevelyan, 'and how very cheap is the preparation.'[54] Economy in public expenditure being one

With a long tradition of practical philanthropy behind them, Quakers in England and Ireland responded quickly to the need for direct food relief. The fifty giant soup boilers donated at the outset of 1847 by the famous Quaker ironmasters Abraham and Albert Darby of Coalbrookdale, along with boilers from other sources, allowed the Society of Friends to establish numerous soup houses, such as the one in Cork city depicted in this sketch of January 1847. Altogether, the Friends distributed almost 300 boilers during the famine. Quakers shared many of the reigning economic ideas of the day but were much less likely than others to cling to them in the face of crying human needs. (*Illustrated London News*)

of the gods that Trevelyan worshipped, the head of the treasury had not missed the significance of soup. Indeed, he was even ready to displace temporarily another of his idols – the general sanctity of the private food market – to exploit its enormous potential. The distribution of free food by agencies of government in virtually all parts of the country was soon to begin. Needless to say, it was too long in coming, and for thousands too late.

CHAPTER 4

Soup Kitchens and Amending the Poor Law

Once the government recognised at the very end of 1846 that its schemes of public works were failing disastrously to hold starvation and disease in check, a new system of relief designed to deliver cheap food directly and gratuitously to the destitute masses was gradually put into place. The government always intended that its new initiative would be temporary, lasting only until the harvest season of 1847, when a revised poor law system would begin to function. In the short term, soup was supposed to bring salvation. Even before the necessary legislation – popularly known as the soup kitchen act[1] – was hurried through parliament in late January and February 1847, relief officials in Ireland were busily promoting the installation of boilers for the making of soup. Their efforts had been anticipated by numerous individuals and groups during the closing months of 1846. The soup kitchens operated by the Society of Friends in Cork city (from November 1846) and elsewhere had won deserved acclaim, and these were matched by the generally unheralded enterprises of many other private philanthropists. Their collective success (in limited geographical areas and within the severe restraints imposed by their restricted resources) was largely responsible for the enthusiasm with which government agents belatedly embraced the new policy. To adopt a new policy was one thing, but to implement it rapidly, as the deteriorating situation required, was another matter. The first necessity was to erect new administrative machinery. Supervisory responsibility for implementing the scheme was entrusted to a relief commission. Among its six members were representatives of the Board of Works (Harry Jones), the commissariat (Sir Randolph Routh), the constabulary (Duncan McGregor), and the poor law commission (Edward Twistleton). The chairman of the new body was Sir John Fox Burgoyne, previously the inspector-general of fortifications in Ireland, and joining these five men was Thomas Redington, the under-secretary at Dublin Castle. The central staff of the relief commission was drawn from the commissariat department, and the inspecting officers, who served as agents of the commission in the localities, were selected from either the Board of Works or the commissariat, thus assuring an experienced contingent of central officials. To regulate expenditure and the distribution of food at the local level, two types of committee were established:

a small finance committee of two to four persons in each poor law union (there were then 130 unions altogether), and district relief committees, with a much larger membership, whose area of responsibility generally coincided with the boundaries of the electoral divisions of the poor law administration (there were 2,049 electoral divisions in the country).

Slow Implementation

Because the relief commission was firmly determined to impose administrative order and strict financial accountability on this extended bureaucracy, the machinery was not activated as quickly as the doleful circumstances demanded. The mere preparation, printing, and distribution of the forms and documents considered necessary – over 10,000 account books, 80,000 sheets, and 3,000,000 ration tickets – constituted a vast undertaking in itself, consuming invaluable time.[2] It was not until 4 March that the viceroy's order specifying the membership of the district relief committees was promulgated. This was followed within a matter of days by the issuance of detailed regulations for the inspecting officers, finance committees, and district relief committees. The actual distribution of food rations was authorised to begin on 15 March in those districts where the relief committees were willing and able to comply with the regulations.[3]

But weeks elapsed in many areas before the new regime was instituted. As late as 15 May only about 1,250 electoral divisions had come under the operation of the soup kitchen act (almost 2,000 would eventually do so). And in their report of the same date the relief commissioners themselves expressed 'considerable disappointment that this progress should have been so slow, seeing no good reason why the measure might not by this time have been in full activity all over the country'. The fault, insisted the commissioners, rested with the local relief committees. Some of them merely wanted to exhaust their own financial resources before adhering to the new scheme, but many others wished to see the public works system of relief extended as long as possible.[4] In spite of all their defects, the public works were a known quantity; they required labour in return for assistance and thus were not 'demoralising' like gratuitous aid; and they were less vexatious to the local committees than soup kitchens.

This foot-dragging the relief commissioners were unwilling to tolerate. The cost of the public works was fearsome, and so were starvation and disease – in spite of them. In conjunction with the Board of Works, the commissioners had already directed that from 20 March the number of labourers on the public works was to be cut by at least 20 per cent, beginning with landholders occupying 10 acres or more; even those with less land had to be discharged until the quota was reached. Further reductions were to take place in stages as the new system of relief was brought into operation.[5] Only by such pressure, the commissioners believed, could the recalcitrant local committees be compelled to inaugurate the soup kitchen scheme. A second cut of 10 per cent was ordered to

The Quakers' success in providing nourishing soup economically to large numbers helped to prompt the government to create a national system of soup kitchens. The model soup kitchen shown here was installed in Dublin in April 1847 at government invitation by Alexis Soyer, the famous French chef at London's Reform Club. London and Dublin society expressed delight with Soyer's soup recipes, but his ingredients have been compared very unfavourably with the 'minimum' Quaker recipe, which called for six times as much beef. Despite its shortcomings 'government soup' fed over three million people on a single day early in July 1847. (*Illustrated London News*)

be implemented as of 24 April, and in a dangerous move (it appeared reckless even to Trevelyan), all engineers in the service of the Board of Works were commanded to close the works in their districts entirely on 1 May unless they received specific instructions to the contrary before then.[6] Yet the destitution was so overwhelming, and the prescribed alternative to the public works was still so often absent, that this deadline simply could not be met. Although 209,000 labourers had been dismissed by the end of April (a reduction of 29 per cent from the peak of 714,000 in March), only another 106,000 (15 per cent) were dismissed during the whole month of May. The respite for most of the remainder, however, was indecently brief. By the last week of June 1847 all but 28,000 (4 per cent) had been discharged.[7]

Even though the pace of dismissals from the public works was less rapid than the relief commissioners had originally wanted, it was still too fast to be fully

Attacks on grain or meal travelling by road or canal were a common occurrence during the great famine, especially in its earlier years. The first sketch here depicts 'Irish armed peasants waiting for the approach of a meal cart' in October 1847. Armed escorts of soldiers, such as the one in the second sketch shown operating near a relief depot in Clonmel, were increasingly provided to prevent such assaults, but not even these precautions could guarantee that hungry people would abstain from violence. Popular feeling had always been against removing food from any particular locality in times of general scarcity. (*Pictorial Times*/The Trustees of the National Library of Scotland)

The completeness of the destruction of the potato crop of 1846 by blight suddenly put a dagger to the breast of half the nation. Scientific ignorance about the cause of the disease – only later identified as the fungus *phytophthora infestans* – accentuated the universal sense of doom. The great 'apostle of temperance' Fr Theobald Mathew wrote in August 1846 of having seen 'one wide waste of putrifying vegetation' between Dublin and Cork, and of how 'in many places the wretched people were seated on the fences of their decaying gardens, wringing their hands and wailing bitterly [at] the destruction that had left them foodless'. This awful reality is represented by the artist Daniel McDonald (1821–53) in his painting *The discovery of potato blight in Ireland* of *c.* 1847. (Courtesy of The Department of Irish Folklore, University College Dublin)

Itinerant labourers – usually called spalpeens from the Irish word *spailpíní* – were an increasingly numerous category of the rural poor in the decades before the famine. Tens of thousands migrated annually to England and Scotland to work as harvesters for three or four months. But many thousands more also migrated shorter distances within Ireland. The internal movement tended to occur from poor upland areas of small farms to better-endowed lowland areas of larger farms devoted heavily to producing grain and potatoes. The internal migrants were especially numerous in Leinster and Munster, the external ones were overwhelmingly from Connacht and west Ulster. The artist Sampson Towgood Roche painted this watercolour of three itinerant labourers with their spades, or 'loys', at a hiring fair in the 1830s. (Ulster Folk and Transport Museum)

Even though potatoes were so widely grown as a subsistence crop before 1845, there were significant groups in the population who frequented markets in order to buy them. Besides the urban poor, landless rural labourers who could not hire sufficient potato ground (usually called conacre) for the season needed to enter the market for potatoes. This was especially the case during the 'hungry months' of the summer, the period in between the exhaustion of the inadequate old crop and the harvesting of the new one. Distress associated with the 'hungry months' was increasing before 1845, as more and more people came up short. For those whose own stock of potatoes had run out, markets were essential. This watercolour of a potato market in County Waterford in the 1820s was painted by Sampson Towgood Roche. (Ulster Folk and Transport Museum)

Left: Few foreign travellers in Ireland between 1800 and 1845 failed to notice the swarms of beggars. They were particularly numerous wherever crowds congregated for commercial, religious, or recreational purposes, such as fairs, patterns, and race-meetings. Beggars were also prominent among the poor of the cities and large towns, where the concentration of wealthier citizens offered special opportunities. Many beggars were so engaged only seasonally, such as the wives and children of numerous migratory male labourers, but others depended on begging the year round. Rapid population growth after 1780 and the collapse of the domestic system of textile production after 1815 no doubt increased the scale of begging in pre-famine Ireland. This trio of beggars was painted by Sampson Towgood Roche in the 1830s. (Harland & Wolff Photographic Collection, © National Museums and Galleries of Northern Ireland, Ulster Folk & Transport Museum)

The coastal regions of much of the west and south-west before 1845 had very high population densities. In fact, the coastal fringe of Galway and west Mayo was just about the most densely settled part of Ireland. Landholding was often combined with fishing in these areas, and seaweed and sand were used as fertilisers in cultivating potatoes. Another source of revenue was kelp burning, which required much strenuous labour in gathering and then burning big stacks of seaweed weighing several tons each in order to produce kelp. From this seaweed ash came the soda used in making glass and soap as well as in bleaching linen. The discovery of iodine in 1812, another derivative from kelp, with numerous medicinal and industrial uses, gave the enterprise a century or more of added life. The artist Samuel Lover (1797–1868) painted this Connemara scene, *The kelp gatherers*, probably in the 1830s. The great famine struck hard at these densely settled coastal regions. (Courtesy of the Department of Irish Folklore, University College Dublin)

The domestic production of textiles provided an important source of rural income before 1815, especially in Ulster, the north midlands, and north Connacht. Women usually did the spinning and men the weaving. But in just two or three decades before the famine rural Ulster and indeed the Irish countryside as a whole were largely deindustrialised as a result of the expanding use of machinery in urban mills. The change-over from hand to machine, and from countryside to town, was delayed in the earliest decades of the century by the availability of cheap female labour, such as that of the women cottage workers depicted in this watercolour of the 1840s by William Kirwin (National Library of Ireland). But the invention of the wet-spinning process in 1825 led to the disintegration of the domestic hand-spinning of linen in the Ulster countryside by the eve of the famine.

Rebellion by agrarian secret societies was a recurrent and widespread feature of rural life before the famine. The major rebellions coincided with or were prompted by sharp economic downturns that aggravated tensions at all levels of rural society. Labourers and cottiers gave violent expression to their grievances against the larger farmers, and at the same time tenants of differing means pursued their own disputes with landowners. The rebels displayed much organisation and sophistication. This contemporary lithograph depicts rebels known as Rockites (followers of a mythical Captain Rock) swearing in a new member of their organisation in County Westmeath in 1824. During the great famine landowners took advantage of the collapse of the social bonds that had sustained agrarian secret societies before 1845. (Nicholas Robinson Collection/The Board of Trinity College, Dublin)

The very widespread practice of unroofing the houses of evicted tenants is captured by Lady Butler (1846–1933) in this painting – *Evicted* – of 1890. The wholesale destruction of houses in the Kilrush clearances of 1847–50 horrified many observers at the time. Some of them sent a public address to Queen Victoria during her visit to Ireland in 1849: 'Madam, in no other region of the habitable globe would it be permitted to two or three satraps, however specious the pretences of law or custom which they might allege, to unroof and demolish at their pleasure the homes of fifteen thousand human beings, and to turn out that multitude, in itself a nation, to die by the slow wasting of famine and disease.' The senders of this address told her bluntly that 'thy royal name must be connected in future history with the astounding record of the extermination of our unhappy race'. (Courtesy of the Department of Irish Folklore, University College Dublin)

In this painting *The Irish famine*, one of a series of four works in 1849–50 by the artist George Frederic Watts (1817–1904), an infant seems to be dying in the arms of its helpless parents. Witnesses to the horrors of the famine struggled to find appropriate words or images to convey what they had seen. The fate of mothers and their children was a recurrent image. In February 1847 an English midshipman sent to his family a letter describing the ghastly nightmare of the famine in the Schull district: 'Babes are found lifeless, lying on their mothers' bosoms. I will tell you one thing that struck me as peculiarly horrible; a dead woman was found lying on the road with a dead infant on her breast, the child having bitten the nipple of the mother's breast right through in trying to derive nourishment from the wretched body. . . . Instead of following us, beggars throw themselves on their knees before us, holding up their dead infants to our sight.' (Trustees of the Watts Gallery, Compton, Surrey, UK/Bridgeman Art Library)

Table 3
Scale of relief under the soup kitchen act, May–September 1847

Date	Electoral Divisions (No.)	Rations (No.)	Persons Relieved (No.)
8 May	1,063	826,325	944,372
5 June	1,989	2,388,475	2,729,684
3 July	1,989	2,643,128	3,020,712
31 July	1,990	2,205,329	2,520,376
28 August	1,098	967,575	1,105,800
11 September	623	442,739	505,984

accommodated by the slow extension of the new scheme of assistance. As Table 3 indicates,[8] at the beginning of May the number of rations issued daily in the 1,063 electoral divisions then covered by the soup kitchen act had reached 826,000; because children received less than a full ration, the total number of persons relieved was about 994,000. But this scale of distribution was almost certainly insufficient to reach all of the 209,000 labourers who had by that time been discharged and who, together with their dependants, probably numbered 1,045,000 (if we calculate the average family size at five persons). And this problem persisted. By the first week of June the daily ration count had soared to 2,388,000, and the total number of persons relieved with soup or other food was then estimated at 2,730,000. The continuing inadequacy of this vastly increased distribution can partly be judged from the fact that through the first week of June the number of discharged labourers amounted to 633,000. The addition of their dependants raises the total to 3,165,000 persons (again on the assumption that the average family contained five members). This means that even on the most sanguine view almost 15 per cent of the population directly affected by the dismissals were still excluded from the relief furnished under the soup kitchen act. To these should be added the destitute who had been unable to obtain employment on the public works before the discharges started in late March. Even at the point of its widest extension during the first week of July, when rations were distributed to as many as 3,021,000 people a day, there is good reason to believe that the provision remained insufficient. For by the end of June the population directly affected by the closure of public works had grown to perhaps 3,530,000, and this figure again takes no account of the destitute who had never found employment on such schemes.

Assessing the System

In assessing the defects and benefits of the system after its termination early in September, however, the relief commissioners did not fault themselves, nor, in general, the local committees for failing to throw open the gates more widely. If anything, they were convinced that the scale of assistance had been excessive, though not wildly so. That some abuses did exist can hardly be denied. In a small proportion of electoral divisions the number of persons appearing on the relief lists actually exceeded the total population of those divisions as recorded in the 1841 census, and in others popular intimidation, deceit, illegitimate influence, or simply the liberality of committee members secured places on the lists for persons who were not utterly destitute or (in a few cases) not even poor. The most serious problem of this kind concerned able-bodied labourers who were in receipt of wages. In contrast to the three categories of the poor who were now entitled to gratuitous relief (the non-able-bodied, destitute unemployed labourers, and destitute landholders), working labourers were barred from obtaining free food. If their wages were insufficient to enable them to feed their families, they were allowed only to purchase food, paying at least the cost price. The relief commissioners were adamant that there must be no gratuitous assistance that would supplement wages, however inadequate. The inevitable result of this policy was that unemployed labourers often obtained more food without having to pay for it than employed workers who were charged for it. In such cases there was obviously a disincentive for those in work to remain so, and many of them abandoned their employers in order to qualify for gratuitous relief. Farmers also entered into collusive arrangements under which they formally discharged their regular labourers, thus entitling them and their dependants to free food, but still employed them 'at odd times'. Relief committees not infrequently tolerated this practice. In particular, they did not strictly enforce the rule requiring the attendance of all able-bodied members of a family at the soup kitchen before rations could be issued to any of them.[9]

But if the system was open to abuse, it was increasingly operated in such a way as to exclude or discourage many more people who would have benefited from a less stringent and demeaning regime. The controversy over whether food should be distributed in an uncooked or a cooked form highlights this problem. The relief commissioners were generally opposed to the issuance of uncooked rations, and the central Board of Health strongly supported their position.[10] The medical arguments against the distribution of uncooked food by local committees were quite sound. Either through popular ignorance or more often because adequate cooking facilities were lacking, the practice led to the consumption especially of Indian meal in a raw or badly cooked state, thus aggravating the diarrhoea and dysentery which were already so widespread. In addition to the medical case against it, the distribution of uncooked meal or flour also led to fraud, as when it was subsequently sold in order to raise money for tea, tobacco, or whiskey. Nevertheless, many local committees long persisted in dispensing uncooked food. This was less troublesome than erecting, staffing, and supervising soup kitchens; it was somewhat cheaper in terms of unit costs; and it was the method which most of the poor, at least at the outset, heavily preferred.[11]

But the relief commissioners and their inspecting officers were convinced that besides the other evils which attended it, the issuance of uncooked food attracted to the public trough many people who were undeserving of assistance.

As one inspecting officer insisted in May 1847, 'The issue of raw meal or flour must lead to great imposition; I have heard hundreds say they would go for meal, when they would reject the cooked food.'[12] Thus, although cooking the rations raised unit costs, this increase was more than offset by the decline in the number of claimants for relief. 'The introduction of cooked food', declared an inspecting officer, 'has reduced the numbers of applicants wonderfully, and it is generally liked by the really destitute, and immeasurably better than the uncooked Indian meal.'[13] Another inspecting officer also observed that cooked food served as a fitting test of destitution: 'In consequence of cooked food being issued, not more than two-thirds of the usual numbers attended for rations, and many of those who did [attend] indignantly refused the cooked food, which was really of better quality and as well cooked as that which I daily breakfast upon.'[14]

The main reason for the popular resistance was plain enough, though it was not sufficiently appreciated by the relief authorities. The demeaning business of requiring the whole family to troop every day to the soup kitchen, each member carrying a bowl, pot, or can, and waiting in a long queue until one's number was called, painfully violated the popular sense of dignity. Among many similar incidents, one crowd at Templetouhy, County Tipperary, collected around the kitchen, yelled that they would not accept soup and 'ill treated a female who had been engaged to attend to the soup kitchen'; another crowd at Miltown Malbay, County Clare, burst into the kitchen and destroyed the boiler.[15] Under the unrelenting pressure of the central relief authorities, the great majority of local committees eventually fell into line with the policy of restricting rations to cooked food alone, though only after the inspecting officers in some districts had been subjected to 'threats of personal violence and conflict with members of committees in urging its adoption'.[16]

For many local committees the most telling argument in favour of the soup kitchen regime was its economy. With individual rations costing 2½d. and eventually only 2d. on average, it was much less expensive than the public works had been. Indeed, many committees claimed that 'in their respective districts it only cost one-third of the expense' of the discarded system.[17] The substitution of cooked for uncooked food was also a considerable economising factor through its effect in reducing the relief lists. The overall impact of this effect is impossible to measure precisely, but there is no doubt that it was substantial. The relief commissioners adduced the example of two electoral divisions that were reputedly alike in all respects except that in one division uncooked food was issued while in the other cooked food was distributed. In the former the proportion of the population receiving relief was as high as 58.5 per cent, whereas in the latter the corresponding figure was only 36 per cent.[18]

The ever-present desire to restrain costs had also been evident in the early administrative decision about the size of the daily ration. This could hardly be described as generous. The relief commissioners stipulated in their original instructions to local committees that the soup or other food was to include

This food riot in Dungarvan, Co. Waterford, in the autumn of 1846 exemplified a common form of popular protest against scarcity and high prices in the earliest years of the great famine, when the bonds of solidarity among the poor were still strong enough to sustain large-scale collective action. The riot was part of a wider attempt in and around Dungarvan to prevent food from being shipped from the port there and to lower the prices of local bakers and other provision merchants. As the famine intensified, the old bonds of solidarity weakened or snapped, and collective action degenerated into furtive food-stealing by individuals or small bands. (*Pictorial Times*/By permission of the British Library)

either 1 lb of meal or flour (of any grain), or 1 lb of biscuit, or 1½ lb of bread for all persons over nine years of age, with those under nine receiving a half-ration.[19] Sharply criticised for the inadequacy of this scale, the commissioners replied that the ration 'must be reduced to what is strictly necessary', and they endlessly invoked the authority of the central Board of Health for its reasonableness.[20] In practice the raw ration usually consisted of two-thirds Indian meal and one-third rice (when obtainable). This mixture, when cooked with water as 'stirabout' or porridge, swelled into a ration weighing 3 to 5 lb. Some local committees, however, took it upon themselves to reduce the raw ration below the 1 lb stipulated by the commissioners, and others 'issued only two pounds weight of cooked food instead of the full weight produced by the

The local poor, especially women and children, besieged the houses of the resident gentry in their quest for soup, bread, or other food in 'black '47'. Observers could detect the dramatic deterioration in their physical appearance, even in just a few months. These two sketches by an unknown artist depict two groups of the poor assembling for soup at Poulacurra House, one group in February 1847 and the other in the following May. Famine conditions multiplied by many times the crowds of beggars for which pre-famine Ireland had already been notorious. (National Library of Ireland)

pound of meal'.[21] Especially at the outset of the scheme much of the soup was very thin; instead of soup for the poor, it was a case, as has been said, of poor soup. The commissioners conceded as much: 'The soup originally issued, before the "stirabout" was brought into use, is reported to have been highly obnoxious to the people; and in Clare [and not only there] it was found necessary to discontinue it.'[22] Even when the approved ration was not diminished by local parsimony even greater than that of the central authorities, there were other problems to which the Board of Health drew attention. One was the lack of solidity (too much liquid) in the ration, which intensified the normal relaxation of the bowels coincident with the onset of warm weather, and another – far more serious – was the absence of variability in the food portion of the soup, which gave rise to scurvy.[23]

The varied efforts to practise and enforce economy produced financial results which the relief commissioners deemed to be more than satisfactory. Like the public works system, the soup kitchen scheme had been designed to place the heaviest fiscal burden on local ratepayers, with supplementation of the rates through private subscriptions from local landowners and others. The government's fiscal responsibility was limited to advancing loans to the finance committees (to be repaid out of the poor rates) and to making grants or donations, normally to be in an amount equal to the combined proceeds of rates and private subscriptions, although larger donations could be given in extremely urgent cases. In practice, however, the government had to shoulder by far the greater part of the burden. Private subscriptions or voluntary assessments did not exceed £46,000, and the government donated an equivalent sum, without reference to the rates collected locally. Much more important, the loans advanced by the treasury on the security of the rates were almost never repaid. Even so, the cost of the soup kitchen scheme to the government was not considered excessively heavy by the relief commissioners, who brought the scheme to a close in September 1847 without spending £530,000 that had been voted for loans and grants under the act. Total government outlays amounted to £1,725,000, consisting of £953,000 in loans, £717,000 in grants and donations (including £118,000 for fever hospitals), and £55,000 in staff salaries and expenses.[24] Substantial savings were effected by both the treasury and the local relief committees when the arrival of massive quantities of foreign grain and meal led to a drastic fall in prices. The cost of Indian corn declined from as much as £19 a ton in mid-February 1847 to £13 at the end of March and to only £7 10s. by the end of August.[25]

By contrast, total expenditures for the relief works carried out from October 1846 to June 1847 had amounted to £4,848,000. Although this entire sum was supposed to be repaid to the government out of the poor rates and county cess, prospects for the recovery of the money from this source were dismal. In the nine months during which the public works were in operation, slightly less than £450,000 of rates could be collected, and the gap between what was owed and actual receipts was widening in 1847 with almost every passing month.[26] In the likelihood that only a small portion of public works outlays would be recouped by the treasury, the alternative system of soup kitchens was considerably less expensive.

FINAL VERDICT

For all its shortcomings the soup kitchen scheme must be judged more than a qualified success. As one relief worker remarked, 'However easy it may be to find fault, it is not so easy to feed more than three millions of souls.'[27] Though many additional thousands should have been fed, and though all should have been fed more generously, the scheme was by far the most effective of all the methods adopted by the government to deal with starvation and disease between late 1846

Notoriously, Sir Charles Trevelyan once thought that the famine in Ireland was essentially over by the summer of 1847, and he was not alone. In this *Punch* cartoon of September 1847 entitled 'Consolation for the million – the loaf and the potato', the cartoonist depicts the potato restored to health and conversing amiably with cheap bread, in a reflection of the complacency which then prevailed in Britain about the food situation in both countries. The British upper and middle classes were now beginning to display what today is often termed 'famine fatigue' – a weariness with endless accounts of suffering and a diversion of focus towards less painful experiences. (*Punch* Archive)

and 1851. Indeed, the most profound regrets that might be voiced are that the system was not introduced much earlier, and that it was not continued after September 1847. While it lasted, and for those whom it reached, starvation was generally averted and disease considerably lessened. The distribution of cooked food in particular greatly reduced the incidence of diarrhoea and dysentery, and where proper care was taken to vary the rations and to include vegetables in the mixture, scurvy was diminished as well. Even the awful scourge of typhus, which had already taken hold in many districts before the scheme was instituted, and which was undoubtedly spread by the gathering of crowds around the kitchens, was reportedly less often fatal among food recipients. The members of one relief committee in the Macroom district of Cork expressed the general view when they declared at the end of the scheme that 'had they not witnessed it themselves, they could scarcely have conceived it possible that such a change for the better could have been brought about in the health and appearance of the poor in so short a time and at comparatively so small an expense'.[28] The relief commissioners understandably took pride in having accomplished so much under the soup kitchen act, but with an ineradicable dogmatism they insisted that because of 'its many dangers and evils', the measure 'could only be justified by such an extreme occasion, including a combination of circumstances that can hardly be expected to occur again'.[29] Yet history did repeat itself, and more than once, and now the official responses to extreme occasions were murderous in their consequences, though not in their intentions.

AMENDING THE POOR LAW

While soup kitchens were gradually replacing the failed public works in the early months of 1847, the Whig government was preparing the legislation which became the poor law amendment act, a measure eventually passed in June, whose antecedents are not sufficiently understood. This law would radically shift the burden of providing relief away from the British treasury, placing it instead squarely on the shoulders of Irish landlords and tenants. It was also this same law which would drastically increase the weight of that burden by authorising relief outside the workhouses in a broad array of circumstances. In so doing, the amendment act of June powerfully contributed to the famine clearances, which were specifically facilitated by one of its provisions – the notorious Gregory, or quarter-acre, clause.[30]

IRISH LANDLORDS VILIFIED IN BRITAIN

It is generally recognised that the act embodied the principle popular in Britain that Irish property must support Irish poverty. But not adequately appreciated are the vehemence and scope of the attacks made in Britain on Irish landlords and the Irish land system before, during, and after the passage of this legislation. According to their many British critics, Irish landed proprietors had been so neglectful of their duties and so oppressive over many generations that they had created the conditions that led to the famine. The cruel evictions long practised by Irish landlords, declared the *Illustrated London News* in March 1847, 'have hardened Englishmen against those who have for centuries held the fate of Ireland in their hands. The plain fact is before us, too dreadfully evident to be overlooked: with the possession of the property of the island, an absolute monopoly of political power, patronage, and place . . . , the dominant class in Ireland have reduced both England and Ireland to this.'[31]

The predatory character of Irish landlordism was widely attributed in England to the deep financial indebtedness of many Irish landowners. 'As a body it appears in a thousand ways that the curse of need and embarrassment is upon

PEEL'S PANACEA FOR IRELAND

Russell. "OH! THIS DREADFUL IRISH TOOTHACHE!"
Peel. "WELL, HERE IS SOMETHING THAT WILL CURE YOU IN AN INSTANT."

The British political élite shifted much of the blame for the famine on to Irish landlords, whose alleged irresponsible behaviour and spendthrift ways long before 1845 had supposedly paved the way for the famine catastrophe. In Britain exaggerated notions about the insolvency of Irish landlords and their incapacity to improve their estates inspired a widespread belief that the prime solution to Irish problems lay in the sale of heavily indebted Irish estates to a new race of landlords who would transform their properties into well-managed economic enterprises. Early in 1849 *Punch* published this cartoon – 'Peel's panacea for Ireland' – in which the former prime minister suggests to a pained Lord John Russell that the cure for 'this dreadful Irish toothache' lies in such sales. (*Punch* Archive)

them: they are obliged', commented the *Illustrated London News* in February 1847, 'to screw and extort the utmost farthing that can be got in any possible way from anybody. . . .'[32] *The Times* sneered at the Irish landlord in March as 'the old original pauper of Ireland' and as 'the grandfather of all destitute persons'. Among 'the things which disgrace Ireland and disgust Christendom', the paper declared, were 'the squalid destitution of the many and the unscrupulous necessities of their needy masters'.[33] But the very condition that made Irish landlords predators in their own country turned them into greedy, clamouring supplicants at Westminster. John Arthur Roebuck, the independent Radical MP for Bath and one of their fiercest critics there, proclaimed in January of the same year that 'he had no sympathy whatever for Irish landlords, whom he designated as beggars'.[34] Another Radical, Archibald Hastie, MP for Paisley, contemptuously dismissed Irish landlords in February as a body of men who 'had done nothing but sit down and howl for English money'.[35] In the press as well, the Irish landed élite was pictured with a begging bowl in its hands. However much Irish proprietors might differ in other respects, acidly remarked the *Illustrated London News*, they 'are ready alike to hold out their hands for loans and grants' from the government.[36] 'Give, give', was their constant cry to others. *The Times* posed as the protector of British working-class interests against the outright robbery 'deliberately planned' by Irish landlords – 'those shameless and importunate mendicants', 'the spoilt pets of the state'.[37]

Among the crimes charged against Irish landlords, none perhaps aroused more resentment in Britain early in 1847 than what was seen as their dumping of evicted pauper tenants on the shores of England, Scotland, and Wales. In the British press and in parliament a strong connection was drawn between Irish evictions and the swelling tide of Irish immigrants into Britain, most of them very poor and many of them diseased. Liverpool took the brunt of this so-called Irish 'invasion', with as many as 50,000 pouring into that port city during the month of March alone, and with many of the new arrivals dying in the streets or crowding into its hospitals and workhouses.[38] In driving their pauper tenants across the Irish Sea to Britain, Irish landlords were widely held to be capitalising on the knowledge that in extremities these destitute people would be supported there under the English poor law. Thus Irish immunity from a poor law which would recognise at least a limited right to outdoor relief became in English eyes another means by which Irish proprietors evaded their social responsibilities and shifted a burden which properly belonged to them on to the shoulders of British taxpayers. As *The Times* complained in April, 'Liverpool, Manchester, and Bristol pay with vicarious infliction the penalty of English indifference [to the inadequacies of the Irish poor law] and Irish immunity.'[39] And the paper warned that unless the Irish poor law were amended to provide for substantial outdoor relief, 'every port, every city in this island, will atone for its political negligence by the actual presence of that Irish poverty' which it had not insisted that parliament order to be relieved in Ireland.[40] It was not only a question of money, but also one of threatened physical and cultural degradation. 'No argument that pen ever writ or heart ever indited [about maintaining the Irish poor at home in Ireland] can match with the spectacle', declared *The Times*, 'of England positively invaded, overrun, devoured, infested, poisoned, and desolated by Irish pauperism.' Maliciously, the paper suggested that the classical economist Nassau Senior should try to proclaim the virtues of the workhouse test and the evils of outdoor relief at the doors of the Liverpool Exchange.[41] It was assumed that he would be about as popular there as evicting Irish landowners.

PARLIAMENTARY DEBATES

It was this badly soiled reputation that Irish landlord MPs and their parliamentary allies took into the lengthy debates that surrounded the relief policies of Russell's Whig government in the early months of 1847. What the

The system of 130 union workhouses built in Ireland under an 1838 law were capable of accommodating barely more than 100,000 people at the start of the famine. Overcrowding was generally at its worst, and most lethal, in the first half of 1847, but severe congestion still afflicted some western and southern workhouses in winter and spring after 1847. Despite the horrors of Irish workhouses, crowds of the destitute, many of them near death already, often clamoured for admission, as in this sketch by a later artist with an anachronistic gaslight over the gate. (National Library of Ireland)

parliamentary spokesmen for Irish landlords wished above all to avoid was any change in the Irish poor law which would result in the general or widespread extension of outdoor relief. It is not difficult to understand why. The existing workhouses, even if filled to capacity, were capable of accommodating only a small fraction of the three million or more people who were destitute in the spring and summer of 1847. The prospect of having to extend outdoor relief to these millions, or even to just a substantial portion of them, filled Irish landlords with dread. They claimed to be 'willing to submit to any charge' necessary to further extend workhouse accommodation, but they loudly clamoured for the retention of the workhouse test of destitution for the able-bodied poor. A petition to this effect was signed and presented to parliament by forty-three MPs and sixty-four peers who were said to have residences in both Ireland and Britain.[42] But public opinion in Britain was horrified at the apparent consequences of conceding what Irish landlords were seeking. They were pilloried and ridiculed for resisting the principle of outdoor relief at the very time, in March 1847, when over 700,000 Irish labourers and cottiers were in effect receiving it on the public works and would mostly have perished without it. When Irish landlord MPs cited the arguments of such classical economists as Nassau Senior and George Cornewall Lewis against outdoor relief, *The Times* answered them dismissively by saying that they were citing 'names which, to all public purposes, not only are dead but stink'; the paper flatly labelled these economists' opinions as 'putrid'.[43]

Very much in line with the weight of middle-class public opinion in Britain, Russell's government had resolved to amend the Irish poor law in such a way as to allow outdoor relief in the form of food to be given not only to those disabled from labour but also to the able-bodied if the workhouse was full or otherwise incapable of receiving them. The cost of any relief given outside the workhouse was to be charged on the poor rates of the union as a whole, with the landlords paying all the rates for holdings valued at £4 or less, and about half the rates for holdings valued at more than £4. Union rating and the £4 rating clause were bound to be contentious issues. Landlords and their spokesmen tended to favour the use of administrative divisions smaller than the union for the assessment of rates. But the government worried that if rates were charged not on the union as a whole but rather on those chunks of it called electoral divisions, many landlords would behave irresponsibly. They would be strongly tempted, it was thought, to evict pauper tenants from their own estates in the hope that these destitute people would take refuge in some other electoral division, on someone else's property, thus freeing the evicting proprietor from claims for their poor relief. As *The Times* was to put it with characteristic pungency, if rating by electoral division were conceded, it would permit estate-clearing landlords to create a multitude of 'traps for human vermin', a Skibbereen in every poor law union, or '130 vast almshouses maintained from the public exchequer'.[44] Union rating, by contrast, would equalise burdens by removing the premium on dumping, and in theory it would provide an incentive for proprietors to create employment without their having to fear the imposition of a double burden – the relief of one's own tenants and someone else's besides. But whatever the exact distribution, the general landlord burden, especially with the £4 rating clause included, would be great. Indeed, taken together, these proposals appeared to spell a staggering load of new taxation for the Irish landed interest.

In terror at this prospect, Irish landlord MPs tried to persuade their British colleagues that the Irish landed interest would be ruined by the proposed legislation. 'In fact,' declared William Gregory, the Galway landowner and Tory MP for Dublin city, 'the whole rental of Ireland would not suffice for the relief which must be required under this bill.' Apart altogether from demoralising much of the rural population, Gregory argued, the bill would absorb the capital of the country, diminish wages, reduce labourers to paupers, and thus in the end 'would be more prejudicial to the poor than the rich'.[45] Thomas Bateson, a Conservative MP for County Londonderry, employed essentially the same reasoning to draw an even more alarming picture. 'If once the right of outdoor relief to able-bodied paupers were established by law,' he declaimed, 'pauperism would be encouraged, the whole property of the country absorbed, and the population demoralised. Having brought the country into this state of insolvency and ruin, the whole of Ireland would be one monster union, and the prime minister of England the head relieving officer.'[46]

But in spite of their dramatic and anguished portrayals of looming financial disaster, Irish landlords and their parliamentary spokesmen failed to elicit much sympathy from English or Scottish MPs or from the British press. *The Times* doubted that an amended poor law would 'swamp the landowners', as their friends alleged. But even if it did, 'we are not sure that the price is too great to pay for the regeneration of the people. . . .'[47] The worst enemies of Irish landlords almost hoped for their destruction. Proclaimed Roebuck with implacable bitterness: 'He would apply the English poor law [with provision for limited outdoor relief] to Ireland, which, though it might sweep away two-thirds of the Irish landlords, he cared not for [them].'[48] Apparently Roebuck was not alone. The Irish MP William Gregory openly admitted in the House of Commons that it would not be enough for him to show that 'all the property in many parts of Ireland would be entirely swallowed up' by granting outdoor relief to the able-bodied poor, for 'he feared that, with many members of the house, that would be the chief recommendation of the measure'.[49] At least one British newspaper, the Catholic *Tablet*, happily embraced this extraordinary reasoning: 'When, therefore, we hear it urged as an objection to the poor laws that a compulsory system of outdoor relief will ruin the landlords, we answer that this is its best possible recommendation.'[50] Even much less hostile commentators ridiculed the 'lamentable stories' of landlord partisans, heard especially in the House of Lords, about the 'black and hideous ruin before them'. If Irish landlords 'could be believed', declared the *Illustrated London News*, 'one would think they were the class to be pitied, not the famine-stricken peasantry'. This paper was certain that the predicted doom of Irish landlords was premature: 'Some remaining thousands [of pounds] will still flow in even after the rates are paid; and on the whole the affliction of an estate, even an Irish estate, may continue to be endured.'[51]

Given the extreme unpopularity of Irish landlords at this juncture among middle-class Britons, the Whig government had no difficulty in turning back efforts by protectionist Tories and Irish landlord MPs to throw the entire burden of the poor rates on the occupying tenants. The attempt to do so only intensified middle-class revulsion for what was considered the almost criminal avoidance of their social responsibilities by Irish landlords. Even British peers generally failed to support them on this issue. Sensing his isolation, the protectionist leader Lord Stanley 'did not venture even to divide' the House of Lords on his amendment for tenant payment of the rates. 'Never', crowed the *Illustrated London News*, 'did a long-threatened and rather dreaded opposition end so innocently; it was a most lame and impotent conclusion.' Had the effort succeeded, its critics argued, it 'would have made the collection of any rate impossible', so great would have been the outrage among Irish tenants.[52]

These were among the first of a series of now famous illustrations of 1847 by the Cork artist James Mahony (1810–79), who was commissioned by the *Illustrated London News* to visit the Skibbereen district 'with the object of ascertaining the accuracy of the frightful statements received from the west, and of placing them in unexaggerated fidelity before our readers'. His artistic work uniquely brought home the grim reality of the famine to middle-class doorsteps in Britain and helped to elicit an initial – but unsustained – outpouring of private philanthropy. In the three scenes of February 1847 depicted here a starving boy and girl at Caheragh turn up the ground with only their hands searching for potatoes; fever prostrates the village of Minanes, where dogs gnaw at the bodies of the unburied dead; and a doctor attends a dying man in a cabin at Schull while the man's children huddle around the turf fire. (*Illustrated London News*)

ASSERTED JUSTICE AND BENEVOLENCE

Thus British government ministers, many British MPs and a wide section of the British press and public were able to project the poor law amendment act of June 1847 as a long overdue measure of popular justice and as a distinctive exercise of genuine benevolence towards Ireland on the part of parliament. The absence of such a measure since the beginning of the famine, loosely claimed *The Times*, had cost England £10 million and Ireland 'probably a hundred thousand lives, not to mention the sufferings of the survivors'.[53] Almost all of the leading press organs would have agreed with Roebuck's description of the proposed law as 'a great act of justice due to the Irish people . . . by England'.[54] For *The Times* the government's bill was 'the just extension to the Irish poor of the rights long guaranteed to the English poor'; it was 'the chief and most desiderated fruit of the union [of 1800]'.[55] In their justifications for a revamped Irish poor law British newspapers easily mixed arguments based on economic self-interest with others based on the injunctions of Christian charity. Property, the *Illustrated London News* told its readers, was not 'a citadel to be defended against the attacks of pauperism'; instead, Christians must recognise 'the duty of sharing our good things with our poorer brethren, to which "the scripture moveth us in sundry places"'.[56] Of course, British financial self-interest would be well served

by the new law, and with varying degrees of frankness this critical point was made frequently: Irish poverty, massive in its dimensions, could not permanently be allowed to siphon off English wealth. 'Pauperism in Ireland', moaned the *Illustrated London News*,

> is now draining ten million [pounds] a year from the English exchequer; to that the Irish legislators make no objection; it is quite according to 'sound principles'. Englishmen think the drain can be stopped, and [want to] fix Irish property with a rate, as they themselves were saddled with one between two and three centuries ago.[57]

What is most remarkable, then, about the discussion of the great famine in Britain in early and mid-1847 is the extremely harsh and almost unanimous verdict given against Irish landlords, to the point of holding them primarily responsible for having allowed the country 'to sink to its present awful state'.[58] The poor law amendment act was partly intended as a heavy punishment for their grievous derelictions of duty in the past, and it was also designed to ensure that they met their responsibilities in the future. This British fixation on the delinquencies of the Irish landed élite helped to blind much of the educated British public as to how the amended poor law would operate in practice. To judge from the scarcity of comment in the British press at the time of its adoption, the significance of the Gregory clause (to be discussed in the next chapter) was missed almost completely. If it was correct to say that melancholy tales of Irish evictions had hardened English hearts against the objections of Irish landlords to a 'real' poor law, it is bitterly ironic that such a poor law was itself so deeply implicated in the clearances and other horrors that followed its enactment. In the later course of the famine the attitudes of middle-class and upper-class Britons towards the clearances by Irish landlords were to undergo a significant shift.

CHAPTER 5

The Amended Poor Law and Mass Death, 1847–51

When the soup kitchen scheme was terminated early in September 1847, the government resorted to the poor law system as the principal means of affording relief to the destitute. The adoption of this approach was one gauge of the rising impatience of the governing élite in Britain with the intractability of the famine crisis in Ireland. It was also a measure of the government's unwillingness to allow what it considered the enormous dead weight of Irish poverty to drain – endlessly, it seemed – the financial resources of the British treasury. The legislation which defined the general conditions of public relief for the rest of the famine years was enacted in June and July 1847, that is, before anyone could know if the vast potato deficiencies of 1846 would be perpetuated or if typhus, relapsing fever, dysentery, and diarrhoea would continue their appalling ravages of the recent past. Admittedly, with foreign grain and meal pouring into the country, food prices had fallen drastically by the late summer and autumn of 1847. But the private labour market had sharply contracted and was incapable by itself of providing employment and wages on a scale sufficient to ensure a general absence of mass death.

Government ministers recognised the nature of this problem. As the prime minister, Lord John Russell, told the chancellor of the exchequer, Sir Charles Wood, in March 1847, 'It is more than ever necessary that between this time and the harvest of 1848 as much employment as possible should be given. Otherwise we shall see our poor law utterly fail from not getting a wind to take it out of harbour.'[1] But to raise the necessary wind the government was mainly relying on its loans to Irish proprietors for agricultural improvements. The stimulation given to private employment by means of these loans was not insignificant. But the near-insolvency or utter bankruptcy of a substantial section of the Irish landed élite was so apparent by 1848 that the government had devised a measure – the incumbered estates bill – that it hoped would rid Ireland of its impoverished gentry. Sir Charles Wood expressed the unanimous view of the British cabinet when he declared in May 1848: 'There is no real prospect of regeneration . . . for Ireland till substantial proprietors possessed of capital and will to improve their estates are introduced into that country.'[2] In short, the strong wind on which Lord John Russell had counted for the salvation of the revised Irish poor law system had largely failed to materialise.

When Irish landowners did not fill the employment gap, the deficiencies of the poor law system were glaringly exposed. Its defects were so serious that they gave plausibility to charges (then and later) that there was a genocidal intent at work. Before these charges can be fairly assessed, the policies that governed the revised system and the local practices that prevailed under it must first be considered. The main poor law statute of June 1847 provided that the destitute who were not able-bodied (the aged, the infirm, the sick, orphans, and widows with two or more legitimate dependent children – often called the impotent poor) were to be relieved either in or out of the workhouse, with the local boards of guardians having the right to decide between these two modes of assistance. In addition, the able-bodied, if without employment and destitute, were also declared entitled to relief. But this had to be administered in the workhouse (as a test of destitution) unless there was no room or unless the prevalence of infectious disease had rendered the workhouse unfit for their reception. Where accommodation was exhausted or disease rife, the poor law commissioners in Dublin could authorise the local guardians to furnish outdoor relief to the able-bodied for a maximum of two months, but only in the form of food and only to those willing to engage in the hard labour of stone-breaking (another test of destitution). Lastly, no one occupying more than a quarter of an acre of land could be relieved out of the poor rates.[3] This provision, the infamous quarter-acre clause, was appended to the law at the urging of William H. Gregory, Conservative MP for Dublin city (1842–7), future husband of Lady Gregory, and heir to a substantial Galway estate (he succeeded to it in 1847) which he largely dissipated by gambling debts on the turf in the late 1840s and early 1850s.[4]

The purpose of this clause was to arm landlords with a weapon that would enable them to clear their estates of pauperised smallholders who were paying little or no rent. Only by surrendering their holdings above one rood to the landlord could these tenants qualify themselves and their families for public assistance. Although not all the consequences of the quarter-acre clause were fully appreciated in advance, its enormous potential as an estate-clearing device was widely recognised in parliament.[5] Defending his proposal in the Commons, where it initially stirred some controversy, Gregory used language that was dismissive and even contemptuous of the capacity of his amendment to inflict grievous injury. Many MPs, he declared, had 'insisted that the operation of a clause of this kind would destroy all the small farmers. If it could have such an effect [he said], he did not see of what use such small farmers could possibly be.'[6] Gregory's amendment was carried by a vote of 119 to 9, and only a few Irish MPs were among the tiny band of dissentients.[7] Throughout the rest of the famine years the Gregory clause, or 'Gregoryism', became a byword for the worst miseries of the disaster – eviction, exile, disease, and death.[8]

Workhouse Conditions

Even before the quarter-acre clause made the situation worse, conditions within the workhouses had underlined the woeful defects of the poor law system as the main instrument for confronting the effects of famine. The 130 union workhouses of Ireland in 1847 had been planned and built for relieving the abnormal distress of a poor country in normal times, not to contend with the mass starvation and disease of a catastrophic famine. In March 1847 fewer than 115,000 inmates could strictly be accommodated at one time, and the facilities available for separating the diseased from the healthy were initially not merely inadequate but often disastrously so. At the beginning of March, for example, the Fermoy workhouse in County Cork, with proper accommodation for only 800 persons, was inundated with more than 1,800 paupers. In the absence of a fever hospital at Fermoy the sick and the healthy were all mixed up together, and the consequent mortality was appalling: out of 2,294 persons admitted since 1 January 1847 and not discharged, as many as 543, or nearly 24 per cent, had perished within two months.[9]

The sufferers depicted in this contemporary lithograph were presumably victims of so-called 'famine fever'. In fact, there were two distinct kinds of fever that wreaked havoc during the famine – typhus and relapsing fever. The real causes of their generation and spread were then unknown, though it was common to list food deprivation along with poverty and its attributes as principal or subsidiary reasons. Both of these fevers actually shared the same vector: the human body louse. By prompting migration on a vast scale and by bringing crowds together at relief works, poorhouses, and food depots, the famine created ideal conditions for the transmission of lice and the twin scourges they carried. (National Library of Ireland)

Many other workhouses in the south and west were in a state similar to that of Fermoy. The average *weekly* rate of mortality per thousand inmates rose from 4 at the end of October 1846 to 13 at the end of January 1847, and then almost doubled to 25 in the middle of April – the highest rate of workhouse mortality recorded during the famine years.[10] Already there was a marked tendency for the seriously or fatally ill to delay their entry into the workhouse until they were so debilitated by disease that medical attention was virtually useless. Resigned to death, many entered merely to assure themselves of a coffin and burial at public expense. This pattern was to persist throughout the famine years and was largely responsible for making the workhouses places of notoriously high mortality and refuges of the very last resort – a mutually reinforcing process.

The workhouse horrors of the early months of 1847 compelled the relief authorities to institute a series of changes: the construction of separate fever hospitals and additional dispensaries, the expansion of workhouse accommodation (both permanent and temporary), and the granting of outdoor relief even to the able-bodied poor. The building of the fever hospitals, making possible medical differentiation among paupers, was an unmixed blessing. It kept workhouse mortality from again reaching the fearsome peaks of early 1847. Even so, the sanitary condition of the workhouses at the beginning of 1848 was anything but reassuring to potential applicants for admission, to say nothing of actual inmates. The average weekly mortality rate stood as high as 11 or 12 per thousand inmates during the months of January and February. Much lower rates generally prevailed thereafter, mainly because of the institution of outdoor relief on a greatly extended scale. The outbreak of cholera early in 1849, however, again pushed workhouse death rates up to the high levels prevailing at the start of 1848. The average weekly mortality rate per thousand inmates increased from 7.7 in mid-January 1849 to 9.4 at the beginning of March and 12.4 by early May, before falling to 6.3 at the end of June.[11]

Together with this relative improvement in sanitary conditions in 1848 and 1849, there occurred a gradual expansion of workhouse accommodation. Between September 1847 and September 1848 the original accommodation was increased by about one-third, thus creating space for a maximum of over 150,000 inmates at any one time. This enlargement of facilities continued over the next twelve months, so that by September 1849 the total number of places available in the workhouses, auxiliary buildings, and fever hospitals had reached about 250,000. Even with this steady expansion, however, some workhouses in the south and west continued to suffer from severe overcrowding at the periods of maximum seasonal pressure in the winter and spring. An extreme example was the Skibbereen workhouse, which was originally designed to accommodate only 800 persons, but contained nearly 2,800 inmates early in December 1848, even though the local guardians had provided only three small timber sheds as additional room.[12]

The persistence of overcrowding was usually attributable to the determined efforts of local boards of guardians to avoid giving outdoor relief to the able-

The fever hospitals of Ireland before the famine, such as this one at Lismore in 1842, were generally far too small to address major epidemics. The authorities had to scramble madly to narrow this enormous gap when epidemic diseases – typhus, relapsing fever, dysentery, and scurvy – began to rage in late 1846 and early 1847. The general answer was found in the 'temporary fever hospitals', often no more than sheds, which treated some 580,000 patients between July 1847 and August 1850. Most fever victims, it is thought, never entered a hospital during the great famine. (National Library of Ireland)

bodied poor or to restrict such assistance as narrowly as possible. In those districts of Munster and Connacht where labourers and cottiers dominated the social structure, the guardians dreaded that the abandonment of the workhouse test of destitution would bring incalculable hordes of poverty-stricken people on to the outdoor relief lists. This common view was forcefully expressed in late March 1848 by Captain Arthur Kennedy, the poor law inspector in Kilrush union in west Clare, where appointed vice-guardians had recently replaced an incompetent and probably corrupt group of elected guardians:

> A formal closing of the house under any circumstances would swamp the union and the vice-guardians together. The great danger of giving outdoor relief in this union to any but the impotent classes arises from the wretched wages given. Any number of men can be procured for 5d. per day without their food; so that [the outdoor relief] ration on the lowest scale would be, in nine cases out of ten, worth more than their wages. Six days' wages at 5d. would be but 2s. 6d., not an equivalent to two and a half stones of meal, which a small family on outdoor relief would be entitled to.[13]

In order to have workhouse places available to test the destitution of able-bodied applicants for assistance, the guardians of Kilrush and other unions repeatedly shunted the qualified impotent poor who were not seriously ill to the outdoor relief rolls. In addition, the poor law commissioners authorised the granting of outdoor relief to certain classes of persons who technically were not entitled to such assistance: widows with only one dependent child, childless widows over sixty years of age, women deserted by their husbands before June 1847, and orphans whose relatives or friends were prepared to shelter them.[14] But above all, it was essential in the eyes of relief officials to increase workhouse accommodation so as to restrain the otherwise irresistible pressure for outdoor relief. It was notorious among relief officials that the poor loathed the harsh discipline of the workhouse and dreaded contracting a fatal disease there. As Captain Kennedy informed the poor law commissioners in February 1848, 'The repugnance to enter the workhouse is beyond credence, and I am satisfied the outdoor relief list might be reduced one-third by testing them.' He rejected the idea of actually doing this as 'neither politic nor humane', given the undoubted destitution of those on the list and 'the utter absence of any employment or mode of earning'.[15] Yet like relief officials generally, he was extremely anxious to acquire additional workhouse accommodation as a defence against a great and very costly increase in outdoor assistance. Reasons of economy and not of humanity basically controlled the near-tripling of workhouse places from slightly more than 114,000 in March 1847 to almost 309,000 by March 1851.

Once the workhouses of the south and the west were filled to capacity in February and March 1848, however, the poor law commissioners were compelled to sanction outdoor relief for the destitute able-bodied poor as well as for certain categories of women and children technically not eligible for such assistance. The extension of outdoor relief, under the second section of 10 & 11 Vict., c. 31, to others besides the impotent poor had begun in the last few months of 1847, and already by the first week of February 1848 over 445,000 persons were receiving this kind of assistance. Of this number, almost one-quarter consisted of the able-bodied and others qualified under the second section of the law. By the end of June the outdoor relief rolls had swollen to nearly 834,000, and now the proportion qualified under the second section had increased to slightly more than two-fifths of the total. The pressure of destitution was so great in 1848 that in as many as 71 out of the 131 unions the poor law commissioners authorised outdoor relief in the form of food under the second section of the act. Only in 23 of these 71 unions, however, was such assistance sanctioned 'without distinction of class'. In 35 other unions outdoor relief was restricted to the impotent poor under the first section of the law, and in the remaining 25 unions no assistance was granted outside the workhouse, apart from occasional urgent cases. The same pattern was repeated in the following year. The outdoor relief rolls expanded from 423,000 persons at the beginning of January 1849 to 784,000 in the first week of July, and the portion represented by the able-bodied and others qualified under the second section rose over the same period from 18 to 37 per cent.[16]

In 1850, on the other hand, assistance outside the workhouse was confined almost exclusively to the impotent poor, with the number of such persons in receipt of outdoor relief fluctuating between 100,000 and 150,000 at any one time between January and June. The great increase in workhouse accommodation over the previous three years allowed the local guardians to apply the workhouse test rigidly to the able-bodied, and the total number of inmates rose to 264,000 in the third week of June – the highest level so far attained. In 1851 even the impotent poor were invariably required to submit to workhouse discipline, since in that year outdoor relief was virtually eliminated altogether. The workhouses themselves, however, were still nearly full in the first half of 1851, at least in Munster and Connacht, with over 263,000 inmates early in June of that year.[17]

Keeping Costs Down

Throughout the famine years cost was a primary consideration in nearly all administrative decisions about the character and quantity of relief. On a per capita basis outdoor relief was actually far cheaper than the expense of maintenance in the workhouse. Thus in the week ending on 1 July 1848 the total cost of providing outdoor relief to almost 834,000 persons amounted to £21,800, or slightly more than 6d. per head. By contrast, the average weekly expense of maintaining a pauper in the workhouse was as much as 2s. 4d. throughout 1847, 1s. 9d. in 1848, and 1s. 7d. in 1849.[18] The relative cheapness of outdoor relief on a per capita basis was not the result of the handsomeness of the workhouse diet but rather of lower overhead costs in outdoor assistance and the avoidance of expense for such items as clothing, bedding, firing, and medicine.

But for the economy-minded authorities, the much lower per capita cost of outdoor relief was completely cancelled by the almost universal preference of the poor for this form of assistance and their eagerness to avail themselves of it wherever it was offered. Unless this eagerness could be cooled, the resources of local ratepayers would be overwhelmed. The enormous difficulty that the guardians experienced in collecting the rates throughout most of Munster and Connacht was a constant reminder of the financial fragility of the poor law system. Another motive for fiscal restraint was the common assumption of officials that the Irish poor were thoroughly unscrupulous in claiming public assistance, and capable of almost limitless imposition and duplicity. (It rarely occurred to the authorities that the niggardliness of the poor law system itself greatly encouraged cheating and lying.) Erecting defences against the profligate abuse of outdoor relief by those who craved it therefore became an unending official preoccupation.

One such defence was the insistence of the poor law commissioners that only cooked food be issued by the local guardians to those qualified for outdoor relief, and that these paupers come each day to receive it. When food rations were distributed once a week instead of every day (Sundays excepted), observed the commissioners, the thriftless paupers too often consumed their weekly supply in three or four days.[19] This problem might have suggested to the commissioners and to the local guardians as well that the cause of the premature exhaustion of a weekly supply was less the paupers' improvidence and more the scantiness of the rations. These usually contained 1 lb of Indian meal for adults and ½ lb for children under twelve years of age. A dietary scale very similar to this had been sanctioned by the central Board of Health early in 1847 as sufficient to prevent malnutrition. In some unions, however, the guardians distributed less than the recommended quantity or its equivalent in soup. And yet even the approved scale was eventually recognised as seriously inadequate. Early in May 1848, after having again sought the opinion of the Board of Health but this time with a different result, the commissioners informed boards of guardians that 'the daily allowance to an able-bodied man [who is] required to work for eight or ten hours each day should be not less than 1¾ lb of raw meal or 2½ lb of baked bread – a scale which . . . may be considered applicable to the daily ration of oatmeal, Indian cornmeal, or wheaten meal'.[20] The numerous reports of deaths among paupers in supposedly regular receipt of outdoor relief probably prompted this belated reassessment by the central authorities, but it does not appear that local boards of guardians generally increased the rations.[21]

This is hardly surprising. The insistence of the commissioners on the daily issuance of cooked rations was prompted at least as much by their desire to cut costs as by their concern to ensure adequate nutrition. As they told the vice-guardians of Clifden union in west Galway in March 1848, 'The great point to be borne in mind is the due relief of destitution in the manner which is at the same time the most effectual and the most economical.'[22] It was obvious (or it should have been) that such factors as sickness, infirmity, inclement weather, and the necessity for long walks to the depots all served to reduce the number of claimants when rations had to be collected as often as once a day. (Some boards of guardians, however, did grant weekly allowances in food or money to the impotent poor relieved outside the workhouse.) It was also commonly observed by relief officials, as pointed out earlier, that the substitution of cooked food for raw meal also had the effect of lessening the number of claimants for assistance, and largely for this reason the commissioners strongly urged local boards of guardians early in 1848 to set up again the soup boilers that had been used so effectively and so economically in 1847.

But it proved extremely difficult to resurrect the elaborate local administrative machinery that had sustained the soup kitchens. Boards of guardians found it much easier to delegate the task of food distribution to meal contractors or shopkeepers. As a result, many fewer soup kitchens were set up or re-established, thus often leaving the destitute with longer journeys to make for their cooked rations. By placing their boilers four miles apart, the Clifden vice-guardians hoped in March 1848 to limit the travels of the poor in that union to

Hard physical labour was a major feature of workhouse discipline for the able-bodied. In some workhouses male inmates were made to do the tiring work of turning a capstan mill for grinding corn (pictured here). Strenuous as this was, it may well have been preferable to stone-breaking, an even more widespread form of workhouse labour. Forcing inmates to turn capstans, break stones, and do other forms of taxing and disagreeable work were ways of testing their destitution and discouraging people in general from seeking admission. (National Archives of Ireland)

a maximum of two miles coming for soup and two miles returning home. But in numerous unions this level of density was not achieved. Unless the length of the journey could be kept within reasonable bounds, the cooked food carried by able-bodied labourers to their dependants was apt to spoil by the time they arrived home, and in addition the impotent poor were liable to suffer extreme hardship. In the great majority of unions the guardians were therefore unable to comply with the commissioners' instructions. In May 1849 all food rations were distributed raw in as many as twenty-three of the thirty-one unions which then employed labourers outside the workhouse. In six other unions some of the food was issued cooked and some in a raw state; only in the remaining two unions was cooked food alone distributed.[23]

The labour test of destitution was a great deal more effective as a defence against what the authorities considered the inveterate propensity of the poor to abuse outdoor relief. The work usually assigned – stone-breaking – was itself hated. The popular attitude towards such work was epitomised by some applicants for outdoor assistance in Newcastle union (County Limerick), who declared in February 1848 that 'they would rather die than break stones'.[24] Many ratepayers objected to this type of unproductive labour as well, believing that their precious money might have been put to better use. But the poor law commissioners patiently explained that such barren work was the best calculated to hold down the rates, or rather to keep them from rising even higher. Just as the nature of the labour itself discouraged applicants, so too did the long hours of toil. At first, as many as ten hours were prescribed by the commissioners, although later eight hours of stone-breaking were required in most unions. The overseers initially employed to enforce this harsh regime often showed too much laxity and were replaced by tougher taskmasters. The overseers were generally obliged to call the roll of all the labourers in each working party at two or three stated intervals every day, and those not in attendance (a substantial portion frequently were not) could be and often were removed from the outdoor relief lists.

THE OPERATION OF THE GREGORY CLAUSE

The last major test of destitution – the Gregory clause barring from public relief anyone holding more than a quarter-acre of land – was by far the worst in its consequences. Before this draconian provision was inserted in the Irish poor law in June 1847, the central relief authorities had regularly urged local boards of guardians to extend assistance to smallholders and their families on the sensible grounds that a refusal to do so would only increase the likelihood that their current destitution would become a permanent condition. Once the law was altered drastically in this respect, the central relief authorities believed that they had no choice but to enforce the new provision. At first, the general inclination of the poor law commissioners and inspectors was to regard the change as beneficial. They saw the Gregory clause as another effective instrument for a more economical administration of public relief, another valuable bulwark against the deceptions and impositions practised by the poor.

But it soon became all too apparent that the drawbacks of the clause were quite serious even from the administrative viewpoint, and that they were no less than murderous from a humanitarian perspective. On the one hand, the poor law commissioners received a stream of reports in 1848 and 1849 that landlords in the south and west were using – and abusing – the quarter-acre clause to turn bankrupt smallholders out of possession *en masse*. This was a matter of deep concern at least partly because the mass evictions reduced the effectiveness of the various tests of destitution, raised the costs of relief substantially, and further weakened the already precarious financial structure of the poor law system. In response to early reports of clearances the commissioners lamely asked their local officers to furnish written statements, given under oath, about the evictions. This time-wasting bureaucratic punctilio eventually gave way to a more sensible insistence that local relieving officers be given sufficient prior notice of impending evictions – itself a recognition that in the face of the law or even abuses of the law, there was little or nothing that the commissioners or their local agents could do to stem the rage for clearances.

On the other hand, it also became obvious that the quarter-acre clause was indirectly a death-dealing instrument. A second stream of reports from Munster and Connacht conveyed to the commissioners the news that destitute smallholders were starving themselves and their families to death by refusing to surrender all but a quarter-acre of their land, thus disqualifying them from assistance out of the poor rates. Hardened relief officials could of course say, as they often did, that they were powerless to help those who would not help themselves by doing what the law required. But when specific cases of 'voluntary' starvation were investigated closely, it was repeatedly found that the victims had substantial reasons for their refusals, particularly the entirely justifiable fear of the demolition of their houses or the loss of an opportunity for landlord-assisted emigration. As the vice-guardians of Scariff union in west Clare explained to the commissioners in February 1848,

> There is the greatest reluctance to surrender to the landlord, even in cases where many years' arrears of rent are due; in most cases the land would be given up if the cabin could be retained, but the consequence of surrendering the cabin with the land is that the cabin is immediately demolished, and the recent tenant becomes a permanent pauper, without a home.[25]

Cottiers who retained only their cabins and then secured assistance in the workhouse often found that landlords took advantage of their absence to unroof their houses. Other tenants were cajoled into giving up possession of their land with false assurances that they would be granted outdoor relief. Still others engaged in bogus surrenders, but these were usually detected by their landlords or the guardians (often the same people). Under these circumstances a great number of smallholders simply clung to their ground against the odds of survival. The case of Michael Bradley, who 'died from want' early in 1848, was typical of thousands of others. Bradley 'held two or three acres of land [near Louisburgh in Mayo] and therefore never applied to the relieving officer for assistance, but left his home for the purpose of begging and died on the side of the road, within two miles of the town of Westport'. Bradley's neighbours were also 'now actually starving but still are unwilling to abandon their little farms'. In concluding his report on the Bradley case to the poor law commissioners, the inspecting officer of Westport union remarked: 'I may add that such cases are not peculiar to Louisburgh but are to be found in almost every district in the union.'[26] Indeed, his observation was applicable all over the south and west of Ireland.

Although the poor law commissioners steadfastly adhered to the strict letter of the law against relieving the actual occupiers of more than a quarter-acre, the Gregory clause was eventually relaxed for their wives and children. For almost a year after the enactment of this provision in June 1847, the commissioners had opposed giving assistance to such dependants, even when assured that they were starving. But in late May 1848, after taking legal advice on this question, the commissioners sent a circular letter to all boards of guardians informing them that the destitute dependants of 'obstinate' smallholders were now eligible to be relieved in the workhouse or even outdoors if the workhouse was full.[27] The guardians were needlessly cautioned, however, against granting assistance 'systematically and indiscriminately to the wives and children of persons occupying more than a quarter of an acre of land when the legislature has expressly declared that such occupiers are not to be deemed destitute'. Rather ludicrously, the guardians were also instructed that they could prosecute such occupiers under the vagrancy laws if through wilful neglect they allowed their wives or children to become destitute and chargeable to the rates. (That wilful neglect would be hard to prove in the midst of famine seems to have been grudgingly admitted.) The commissioners concluded by congratulating themselves for giving to the local guardians the legal means 'for the better securing [of] an object which must be regarded as the principal aim of every poor law, viz., the preservation of human life'.[28] How hollow this expression of sentiment rings in the modern ear!

Once again, however, the perceived problem of imposition and deception resurrected itself. Already, the local guardians were contending with innumerable applications for relief from women who asserted that they had been deserted by their husbands, and from children whose parents had allegedly died or abandoned them. Most such applications were bona fide, but a substantial number were bogus in the sense that the husbands or fathers (and sometimes mothers) were unwilling to submit themselves to workhouse discipline or to stone-breaking out of doors. After the dependants of destitute smallholders were declared eligible for assistance in May 1848, the difficulties of sorting out bogus claimants from legitimate ones were compounded. Almost all boards of guardians felt duty-bound to make the effort, but many experienced frustration and anger as they went about the task. The guardians of Mallow union in County Cork complained to the poor law commissioners in June 1849 that '30 individuals having 23 children have this day applied for admission to the workhouse, stating that they had been deserted by their wives or husbands respectively, an increasing evil for the prevention of which the legal remedies are not found efficacious'.[29] In some unions the guardians adopted a restrictive interpretation of the policy on dependants enunciated by the commissioners. Thus in Bandon union the guardians instructed the master of the workhouse in September 1848 to discharge all paupers whose husbands, fathers, or mothers were outside the house, although he was cautioned to 'use a discretion in [the] case of children who were too young & not strong enough to be sent away'.[30]

Seizing and Destroying Cabins

Even more consequential was the issue of whether, in order to be eligible for poor relief, a tenant was required to surrender his house as well as his holding to his landlord. Strictly speaking, the law mandated that only the land in excess of the one rood be yielded up, but often when tenants took this approach, the landlord or his agent refused to accept the partial surrender or declined to

Landlords or agents who evicted tenants were likely to say that the dispossessed went to the poorhouse, but most did not – at least not initially. If they could find shelter with other families or in makeshift dwellings by the roadside, they attempted to avoid entering the local workhouse, which they generally regarded with extreme distaste. For food, they begged, stole, or sought outdoor relief. Here are two illustrations of 1848 and 1849 showing former tenants living in huts after their evictions. In the first a disconsolate father stands at the entrance to his lean-to while one of his children seemingly points towards their old home; in the second an evicted tenant stands in front of his 'scalpeen' (from the Irish word *scailp*, for shelter), a hut built within the ruins of his unroofed house near Kilrush, Co. Clare. Fatal disease, assisted by malnutrition and exposure, soon swept many of the dispossessed into the grave. (*Illustrated London News*)

supply the certification of compliance with the law until both the house and all the land had been given up. Eventually, the poor law commissioners informed local guardians that the refusal of a landlord to accept a partial surrender could not be held to disqualify an otherwise eligible tenant from public assistance.[31] Yet in the all-important matter of the disposition of the surrendering tenant's house, landlords and agents almost always held the whip hand. Tenants frequently unroofed their own cabins as part of a voluntary surrender in which they were graciously allowed to take away the timber and thatch of their former dwellings. But in many thousands of cases estate-clearing landlords and agents used physical force or heavy-handed pressure to bring about the destruction of cabins which they sought. Many pauper families had their houses burned, often quite illegally, while they were away in the workhouse. Many others were reportedly told when they sought admission that the law, or at least the guardians, required that their cabins be unroofed or levelled before they would be allowed entry, and so they went back and did the job themselves. Where tenants were formally evicted, it was usually the practice for the landlord's bailiffs – his specially hired 'crowbar brigade' – to level or burn the affected dwellings there and then, as soon as the tenants' effects had been removed, in the presence of a large party of soldiers or police who were likely to quell any thought of serious resistance.[32]

The gross illegality of some evictions, and the extreme hardship inherent in all clearances, prompted the raising of questions in parliament, not only about especially egregious cases of inhumanity but also about whether the government would intervene to restrict evictions and the wholesale destruction of houses on so many estates. Protesting MPs drew attention on several occasions to the large-scale evictions and house levellings occurring in late 1847 and early 1848 on the Blake estate in County Galway, particularly to certain ejectments in the depth of winter which led to the death of several dispossessed tenants from exposure. There were even demands that the government institute criminal proceedings for manslaughter in this case.[33] But the home secretary, Sir George Grey, saw no grounds for such action. Responding lamely to critics in March 1848, Grey admitted that 'it was impossible to read without feelings of considerable pain of the destruction of a great number of houses in the county of Galway'. He pointed out unhelpfully that a tenant unjustly treated by his landlord 'would have a right of civil action' against him, but he rejected the notion that house-destroying landlords 'were open to any criminal proceedings on the part of the government'.[34] When the matter was pressed again at a subsequent session, the attorney-general, as a critic bitingly noted, in effect 'declared on legal authority that the law did not reach outrages of this kind'.[35] The government's posture elicited a scathing public letter from Archbishop John MacHale of Tuam to prime minister Russell. Instead of hearing loud 'denunciations of oppression' or the announcement of 'any prospective measures which would check the repetition of such cruelties', declared MacHale,

> the people received only the chilling assurance that in those deaths, however numerous, there was nothing illegal or unconstitutional! It is, then, it seems, no matter what may be the amount of the people's sufferings, or what may be the number of those who fall victims to the famine, provided that nothing illegal or unconstitutional is done in vindicating the rights of property.[36]

What is surprising is that Russell actually agreed with MacHale on the urgent need to curb ejectments and privately used language about evicting Irish landlords which sounded like that of a Whiteboy or a Rockite. As he told his cabinet colleague Lord Clarendon in March 1848, 'Of course, Irish proprietors would dislike such measures [i.e., curbs on evictions] very much; but the murders of poor cottier tenants are too horrible to bear, and if we put down assassins, we ought to put down the lynch law of the landlord.'[37] Russell had to contend, however, with two great Irish proprietors in his own cabinet – Lord Palmerston, the foreign secretary, and Lord Clanricarde, the postmaster-general – with hard-line views on the economic necessity of clearances. Palmerston told the cabinet in a memorandum of 31 March that 'it was useless to disguise the truth that any great improvement in the social system of Ireland must be founded upon an extensive change in the present state of agrarian occupation, and that this change necessarily implies a long continued and systematic ejectment of smallholders and of squatting cottiers'.[38] The cabinet was said to have exhibited a 'general shudder' when Lord Clanricarde made pronouncements as ruthless as Palmerston's.[39]

Emblematic of the evictions in the Kilrush district of Clare were these unroofed houses in Tullig village. Evicting landlords and agents in this area specially dedicated themselves to the wholesale demolition of houses. This prevented the former tenants from returning, saved the costs of an expensive new ejectment proceeding, reduced food stealing from the remaining tenants, and allowed the property to be rearranged and newly let to 'better' and solvent tenants. The greatest of the house destroyers was Marcus Keane, who exercised control as agent over 'about 60,000 acres' in Kilrush union, equal to almost 40 per cent of its territorial extent. He alone reportedly levelled some 500 houses with the help of the proverbial 'crowbar brigade'. (*Illustrated London News*)

Opposed not only by these two Irish landlords but also by the 'moderates' in his cabinet, Russell was forced to water down his original proposals 'in favour of a bill which aimed merely to slow down ejectments and make them more expensive to the proprietor'.[40] Even so, early in April Sir George Grey promised the Commons a bill which would not only prohibit evictions without proper notice to the local poor law guardians but also 'prevent the pulling down of huts and homes of tenants, although a legal right to do so might exist'.[41] This sounded too good to be true, and in the end it was. Although Russell's bill quickly passed the Commons early in May, it came under fierce assault in the Lords, especially from Irish peers like Lord Monteagle, whose wrecking amendments further blunted the prime minister's measure.[42] The legislation that finally emerged reduced the advance notice required to be given to local relief officials in cases of eviction to as little as forty-eight hours, and its provisions relating to the destruction of houses had been shorn of nearly all their protective features. The new law made it a misdemeanour to unroof, pull down, or otherwise demolish the dwelling house of a person whose tenancy had expired only if the tenant or members of his family were actually within the house at the time that the demolition took place. (In a concession of stunning magnanimity this law also prohibited evictions on Christmas Day and Good Friday as well as before sunrise or after sunset.)[43] This outcome was all too typical of the general Irish record of Russell's ministry, as Peter Gray has shown in his recent and excellent book. Instead of being the master of his cabinet, Russell presided weakly and sometimes powerlessly over a badly divided set of colleagues, and between cabinet divisions and parliamentary opposition the constructive side of Russell's legislative agenda, such as it was, frequently was neutered.[44]

RICKETY FINANCIAL STRUCTURE

What made the rigid enforcement of the quarter-acre clause as well as the workhouse and labour tests of destitution seem so essential to central and local relief officials was the inability of the financial structure of the poor law system to sustain a greatly increased burden. On this vital point British policy was terribly misguided. The dictum that Irish property should carry the full weight of relieving Irish poverty may have been a reasonable proposition for ordinary times and circumstances, but in the face of a catastrophic famine it was a prescription for both horribly inadequate resources and the ruination of much Irish property. Though the famine years witnessed intense conflict between landlords and tenants, they were both agreed on at least one point: the British government and parliament had scandalously abdicated their responsibility for meeting a major share of the costs of famine relief after September 1847. Irish landlords were not happy to pay rates. Indeed, the active or passive opposition of ordinary ratepayers to the collection of taxes was often attributed to the instigation or bad example of their disgruntled betters among the landed élite. Landlord hostility to the poor law system during the famine was thoroughly understandable. First of all, landlords were responsible for paying half the poor rates of all holdings valued at more than £4 and for discharging the entire rates of every holding valued at £4 or less. This latter liability served as a major inducement to the mass eviction of bankrupt smallholders so that the landlords would not have to endure both heavy rates and unpaid rents at once. Second, each poor law union was supposed to be self-financing, and proprietors whose estates were located in the impoverished unions of the south and west felt deeply aggrieved that the burden of providing for an extraordinary calamity like the great famine should fall so disproportionately on their shoulders. They saw no reason why they should be held financially accountable for the peculiar geographical incidence of an event for which the responsibility should have been national and ultimately imperial.

Above all, it was the towering burden of the rates in unions where mass destitution prevailed which condemned the poor law system in the eyes of its taxpaying critics. In the province of Munster, with thirty-six unions, there were as many as eleven where rates of between 5s. and 10s. in the pound on the valuation would have been necessary to meet the expenses incurred under the poor law during the year ending 29 September 1848. In two additional Munster unions – Kenmare in Kerry and Scariff in Clare – average poor rates of 10s. 3d. and 12s. 6d. on the valuation would have been required respectively. The position in the province of Connacht was even worse. In more than half of the unions there (ten out of eighteen), a sum equal to *at least* 25 per cent of the valuation (5s. in the pound) would have been necessary in rates to satisfy poor law expenditures in the year 1847–8. In four Connacht unions – Ballina, Ballinrobe, Clifden, and Westport – rates exceeding 50 per cent of the valuation would have been required. In Clifden union, the worst placed in this respect in all of Ireland, not even a sum equivalent to the whole valuation would have sufficed, for an average rate of 24s. 4d. in the pound would have been necessary to discharge expenditures.[45] As if this were not bad enough, the year 1848–9 brought even heavier financial pressures.

Not surprisingly, where the poor rates actually levied surpassed 25 per cent of the valuation, resistance to their collection was widespread. Indeed, opposition was common even in some unions where the assessments did not reach that level. Little of the resistance involved violence. Ratepayers hid their livestock from the collectors and engaged in generally non-violent rescues when cattle, sheep, or pigs were seized. But the guardians and their collectors were relentless in pursuing defaulters, and the massive arrears of 1847 were greatly reduced in 1848 and 1849. Apart perhaps from scrutinising applications for relief, the business of supervising the collection of the rates occupied more of the time of the guardians and inspecting officers than any other issue.

In the most distressed unions of the south and the west, however, the guardians were unable to collect enough money to meet their liabilities, and they often hesitated to strike additional rates in the knowledge that to do so would be largely futile or even counterproductive for the collection of rates which had been struck earlier. As arrears accumulated in these unions and bills fell due, the government had to issue loans from its own coffers or to call upon the funds of the philanthropic British Association. The need was actually greater in the financial year 1848–9, when expenditures under the poor law reached nearly £2.2 million, as compared with £1.7 million in the previous twelve months.[46]

By mid-1849 twenty-two unions in the west and the south-west, with a combined population of almost 1.5 million, were more or less bankrupt; some of them in fact had been in that condition for many months. Characteristically, the government was unwilling to continue subsidising them with loans. It therefore instituted in June 1849 what was called a rate-in-aid. This device entailed the levying of a special rate of 6d. in the pound, or 2.5 per cent of the valuation of all electoral divisions throughout the country, and was designed to raise nearly £323,000. A second rate-in-aid of 2d. in the pound was imposed in December 1850 and netted about £99,000.[47] Outside the unions which benefited from them, the rates-in-aid were highly unpopular. There were loud complaints that if the act of union of 1800 meant anything tangible, these special rates should have been levied not on Irish unions alone but on those of England, Scotland, and Wales as well. Harried ratepayers in Connacht and Munster could now say that the government had in effect conceded their point about the unfairness of the fiscal structure of the Irish poor law system, but the step had been taken so belatedly and its overall impact was so restricted that even in the west and the south the government reaped little credit from its decision.

British Relief Expenditures

It will be convenient here to summarise the contributions of the British government towards the costs of famine relief in Ireland. The treasury calculated in 1850 that its total outlay since 1845 amounted to £8.1 million. Of this sum, less than half consisted of grants from imperial resources. The most important grant came in 1848 when the government remitted half of the total cost (£4.8 million had been spent altogether) of the public works carried out between October 1846 and June 1847. This remission, together with the grants extended under the relief schemes of 1845–6 and the soup kitchen act of 1847, amounted to less than £3.6 million. The rest of the treasury outlays – a sum of slightly more than £4.5 million – consisted of loans that were supposed to be repaid out of Irish taxes. But only a small portion of these liabilities (less than £600,000) had been discharged by 1850, when most of the outstanding debts (about £3.7 million) were consolidated and refinanced, with repayment to come in annuities extending over forty years and bearing interest at an annual rate of 3.5 per cent. The burden of liquidating these debts fell most heavily on the western and south-western unions, which continued to be distressed after 1850 and therefore had great difficulty in paying their annuities. Finally, Lord Aberdeen's coalition government decided in 1853 to cancel all remaining debts completely, although it destroyed any possibility of Irish gratitude for this concession by imposing duties on Irish spirits and by extending the income tax to Ireland at the same time.[48] Thus in the end, taking into account treasury grants since 1845 and the annuities remitted in 1853, British governments – Peel's, Russell's, and Aberdeen's – contributed about £7 million to the costs of famine relief.

While it has frequently been said that this was not nearly enough, it has less often been pointed out that the British government contribution was considerably less than what was raised in Ireland itself. By far the most important Irish contribution to the costs of famine relief came through the collection of poor rates. Altogether, expenditures under the poor laws from 30 September 1846 to 29 September 1851 amounted to almost £7.3 million. To this figure should be added about £300,000 incurred for poor law expenses in the first nine months of 1846 (the sum of £435,000 was spent during that year as a whole).[49] Although a small portion of poor law outlays was covered by advances (unrepaid) from the treasury, the great bulk of the money was actually extracted from Irish ratepayers. The other main Irish source of famine relief was the exceptional employment furnished by landowners. In part, this was financed out of private income, and we can only guess at its magnitude. But most of the money was borrowed from the government under the land improvement acts, and nearly all of these loans were eventually repaid. Between mid-1847 and the end of 1851 proprietors borrowed a total of £1.2 million for land improvement projects, the great majority of which were designed to alleviate distress associated with the famine.[50] Even if private subscriptions for relieving destitution that were raised within the country are left out of the account (perhaps they amounted to £1 or £2 million in addition), it is clear that Ireland itself contributed more to the costs of famine relief than did the well-endowed but miserly British treasury.

But the British treasury, or rather the political élite that controlled its disbursements, was not always miserly, and that is just the point. In assessing the woeful inadequacy of government outlays for famine relief, Joel Mokyr has drawn attention to the fact that Britain spent no less than £69.3 million on 'an utterly futile adventure in the Crimea' during the mid-1850s, and as Mokyr plausibly maintains, 'half that sum spent in Ireland in the critical years 1846–9 would have saved hundreds of thousands of lives'.[51] Another way of putting British government expenditure on famine relief into perspective is to note that British outlays for national defence since 1815 had averaged over £16 million a year, and that the annual average tax revenue of the United Kingdom in the late 1840s was about £53 million.[52] Had the political will existed to do more for the starving masses in Ireland, what happened there could have been far less tragic.

After this extended consideration of the application of British relief policies in Ireland during the famine, it is appropriate to ask if there is any justification for the charge of genocide levelled by (among others) the revolutionary Irish nationalist John Mitchel (1815–75) and the respected British historian A.J.P.

THE ENGLISH LABOURER'S BURDEN;
OR, THE IRISH OLD MAN OF THE MOUNTAIN.

'Famine fatigue' had become deeply entrenched in Britain by February 1849, when *Punch* published 'The English labourer's burden', a cartoon suggesting that the crafty and conniving Paddy had succeeded in extracting major tax benefits from Britain at the expense of the poor English labourer. Though an economic recession in Britain in 1847–8 played some role in lessening British sympathy for Irish suffering, a far greater influence was British revulsion over the abortive Irish rebellion of 1848, which seemed in Britain to betoken monstrous Irish ingratitude. The 'racialisation' of Paddy in *Punch* also became more pronounced, as in this cartoon. (*Punch* Archive)

Taylor. In his extraordinary book, *The last conquest of Ireland (perhaps)*, first published in 1860, Mitchel passionately maintained that Britain possessed the power and wealth needed to save Ireland from the famine disaster and that the withholding of the means of salvation could only be ascribed to malignant motives. In spite of his evident distortions of fact and his suppression of evidence that did not fit his thesis, Mitchel's scathing book has great rhetorical force, a power that it gains from its savage irony. As Thomas Flanagan has well said, 'Surely, the reader of Mitchel's account finds himself thinking against his will, surely this intricate machinery of ineffective relief, these proliferating committees and commissions which produce nothing save lists of the dead and the starving, could not have issued from a wholehearted desire to keep the Irish people alive, however great the expense to British trade and the British treasury?'[53]

Without attributing malevolent intentions to the responsible British ministers and officials, A.J.P. Taylor has also characterised their policies as genocidal. In reviewing Cecil Woodham-Smith's *The great hunger* (1962) in the *New Statesman* shortly after its publication, Taylor compared famine-stricken Ireland to Bergen-Belsen ('all Ireland was a Belsen' – a gross exaggeration) and declared: 'The English governing class ran true to form. They had killed two million Irish people.'[54] But unlike Mitchel, Taylor does not argue that the English rulers of Ireland deliberately chose to pursue a campaign of extermination. As he points out, 'Russell, Wood, and Trevelyan were highly conscientious men, and their consciences never reproached them.' Instead, they were led hopelessly astray by their economic convictions: 'They were gripped by the most horrible, and perhaps the most universal, of human maladies: the belief that principles and doctrines are more important than lives. They imagined that rules, invented by economists, were as "natural" as the potato blight.'[55]

If the charge of genocide could be sustained simply by showing that blind adherence to the doctrines of *laissez-faire* led to countless thousands of deaths (though certainly not two million) in Ireland during the late 1840s, then it may be taken as proved. But if, as most scholars would hold, there must also be a demonstration that English statesmen and their agents in Ireland were knowing and willing collaborators in a deliberate campaign of extermination, then the allegation of genocide is not only unproven but not even worth making. Still, that the charge has been levelled at all is one gauge of how radically mistaken were the actions and inactions of the politicians and administrators responsible for relief measures during the great famine. It is true that at times, especially during the operation of the soup kitchen scheme, accepted economic principles were reluctantly thrown to the wind. Yet what made by far the greater impression was not how many people were kept alive by soup in the late spring and summer of 1847, but rather how many people were allowed to die at other times because they were not fed when they could have been. Many aspects of British relief policy deserve censure, but the severest condemnation should be aimed at the paltry level of financial aid rendered by the British government after September 1847. In this sense A.J.P. Taylor is essentially correct in saying of Peel's successors that 'when crisis arose, they ran away from it'.[56]

BRITISH PUBLIC OPINION

But British ministers were not the only ones to walk away from the famine crisis in Ireland. Much of the British middle-class and upper-class public eventually set aside their initially strong sympathies with Irish suffering and adopted attitudes displaying tightfistedness and hardheartedness. Recognition of the tragic consequences of the amended poor law of June 1847 was slow to emerge among the British public and press. But an awareness of its devastating impact gradually took hold. The *Illustrated London News* conceded early in March 1848 that 'its immediate revision' was 'absolutely necessary to prevent a large and aggravated augmentation of the social evils which afflict the unhappy sister country'. The paper condemned as an 'absurd resolve' the Whig government's refusal to accede to a request from Irish MPs for a committee of inquiry into the operation of the poor law in Ireland.[57] And by November 1848 the *Illustrated London News* seemed ready to recant altogether its earlier faith in the amended poor law and to grant the Irish landlords' case against it. 'All argument' originally supported its introduction, but

> alas! such is the wide extent of the misery and destitution of that country that the poor law, so just in theory, so fair-sounding, so applicable elsewhere, has broken down. . . . Small farmers and great landed proprietors are equally pinched or crushed beneath the operation of the law. Without the poor law the people would have died of famine; with a poor law the people are not elevated above habitual and constant pauperism, and the property of the landlords is all but confiscated.[58]

In fact, however, neither the *Illustrated London News* nor *The Times* was ready to jettison the poor law, even if occasionally the language of their editorials suggested otherwise. As late as January 1849 *The Times* still pronounced itself in favour of 'giving effect to the provisions of the poor law. We urge its adoption now, in this season of gloom, despondence, and dismay, because we recognise this to be the only sure protection against the recurrence of other seasons as gloomy and as dismal as the present.'[59] Almost forgetting its past severe criticisms of the poor law, the *Illustrated London News* had insisted a month earlier: 'The people of this country must listen to no representations or remonstrances intended to shake their faith in the efficacy of that enactment.'[60] What these quotations suggest is the existence in Britain of a widespread public ambivalence about the real and perceived practical consequences of strictly administering the poor law, an ambivalence that surely contributed heavily to a paralysis of the moral and political will to take effective countermeasures. And the abortive Irish rebellion of July 1848, even though it ended quickly and ignominiously, did nothing to induce sympathy for Irish suffering in Britain. On the contrary, there was a tendency to regard the rebellion as a monstrous act of ingratitude for prior British benevolence.[61]

British Reactions to Mass Eviction

What was true of British attitudes towards the amended poor law was also true of British responses to the clearances. Indeed, these two matters were intimately related to each other. On the one hand, prior to the widespread availability of outdoor relief, British commentators invariably condemned the clearances and their perpetrators out of hand for driving the unrelieved rural poor into the country towns and port cities of Ireland. These 'sinks and cesspools of destitution', declared *The Times* in May 1847, 'are a creation of landlordism – the work of a class without social humanity, without legal obligation, without natural shame'.[62] To some extent, moral outrage of this kind persisted in the midst of outdoor relief as clearances mushroomed under the spurs of the Gregory clause and heavy poor rates. Mass evictions, such as the especially cruel ejectments on the Blake estate in County Galway, prompted the *Illustrated London News* in April 1848 to declare sternly:

> In November [1847] a coercion act was most properly passed through parliament to defend the Irish landlords from the murderous revenge of their exasperated tenants. Justice demands that with equal celerity a bill should now be passed to protect defenceless tenants from the equally murderous clearances of tyrannical landlords.[63]

The British response to the clearances, however, was by no means unambiguously disapproving. How could it be? One of the principal aims of the new poor law adopted in mid-1847 was, in the words of *The Times*, 'to compass indirectly the destruction of very small holdings and to convert the cottier, who is nicknamed a farmer and who starves on a *cow's grass*, into a labourer subsisting on competent wages'. If this aim could only be accomplished, *The Times* dared to hope, 'we shall also cease to witness the insane competition for land . . . , degrading men to the appetite and food of beasts and peopling the land with a race savage, reckless, and irreconcilable'.[64] As pointed out earlier, part of the theory of the amended poor law was that Irish landlords would spend a great deal of money giving large-scale employment to their former tenants as labourers in the improvement of their estates. And if they did not employ them, they would at least have to support them in or out of the workhouse. Thus the mere passage of the amended poor law had the potential to shift British attitudes about the clearances, and this is partly what happened. Before its passage, asserted the *Illustrated London News* in December 1848, clearances were 'cruel and unjust in the extreme', but now, with outdoor relief widely available, 'we have no right, how great soever the apparent or real hardship may be, to find fault with the landlord'. Indeed, claimed this editorial writer with a breathtaking leap into unreality, ejectment in Ireland, 'which was horrible before the poor law came into operation, *has now become harmless* [my italics]'.[65]

Repeatedly after 1847 attitudes that were much less critical of clearances, or even mildly approving, found a definite place in the British press. Alongside reports from Irish newspapers that condemned evictions and their perpetrators in the harshest terms were other reports or editorials that palliated, excused, or justified landlord actions. A resigned tone of inevitability suffused an account in the *Illustrated London News* in April 1849 about the impending clearance of 731 persons from Toomyvara in north Tipperary ('nearly the entire village'), which was part of the Massy-Dawson estate. The landlords, remarked the *Illustrated*

This illustration highlights the difficulties of harrowing land on a mountain farm in Mayo in 1880. Its message was even more relevant to the Ireland of forty years earlier, when the proportion of the population eking out an existence in unrewarding places was far higher. In Mayo on the eve of the famine three-quarters of all agricultural holdings were valued at £4 or less for the purposes of poor law taxation. Though the case of Mayo was extreme, other western counties contained high proportions of very small holdings, many of which were scattered here and there in odd-shaped patches under the custom known as 'rundale'. Reform-minded landlords and agents regarded this situation as an intolerable abomination. (*Illustrated London News*)

London News indulgently, 'are abused in the popular journals, but it is not suggested what {else} they should do. The more stringent the poor law, the more surely will the clearance system continue.'[66] When Massy-Dawson later carried out the mass eviction of at least 500 persons and levelled the whole village, it was said in exculpation that he 'got no rent lately' from Toomyvara, and that 'the village was a receptacle for all the evicted tenantry of the neighbouring estates'.[67] And in an editorial devoted exclusively to the subject of clearances in October 1849, the *Illustrated London News* offered the classic defence of the political economists:

> The truth is that these evictions . . . are not merely a legal but a natural process; and however much we may deplore the misery from which they spring, and which they so dreadfully aggravate, we cannot compel the Irish proprietors to continue in their miserable holdings the wretched swarms of

> people who pay no rent, and who prevent the improvement of property as long as they remain upon it.[68]

Lastly, there was a growing readiness in Britain to accept that, given their financial condition, which was assumed to be highly precarious, many Irish proprietors simply could not afford the kind of costly estate improvements, such as thorough drainage, that might have enabled them to transform cottiers into labourers. Earlier, this point had been conceded only grudgingly, as in the sneering remark of *The Times* in May 1847 that 'human drainage' was 'the only drainage an Irish landlord will ever think of doing at his own expense'.[69] But later, at the end of 1848, the *Illustrated London News* portrayed clearances and the consolidation of evicted holdings as 'the easiest mode of improvement, and therefore', it said excusingly, 'poor landlords are compelled to resort' to them.[70] Even so humane an English politician and friend of the Irish poor as George Poulett Scrope, who had roundly denounced the Gregory clause before its adoption, was prepared to place the blame for the clearances elsewhere than on the landlords, whom he saw as generally acting under compulsion and out of an instinct for self-preservation:

> It sounds very well to English ears to preach forbearance and generosity to the landowners. But it should be remembered that few of them have it in their power to be merciful or generous to their poorer tenantry. . . . They are themselves engaged in a life and death struggle with their creditors. Moreover, the greater number of the depopulators are mere agents for absent landlords or for the law-receivers under the courts acting for creditors. . . . Those landlords who have yet some voice in the management of their estates . . . think themselves justified – most of them, indeed, are compelled by the overwhelming pressure of their own difficulties – to follow the example [of the often evicting receivers of estates under Court of Chancery jurisdiction].[71]

Whereas Scrope considered it 'absurd' to blame 'a few, reckless, bankrupt, wretched landlords', he did not hesitate to accuse the Russell government of the 'crime' of refusing to mitigate the 'ferocity' of the amended poor law. In strident language of which even the revolutionary nationalist John Mitchel would have approved, Scrope thundered that the government would 'be held responsible for it by history, by posterity – aye, and perhaps before long, by the retributive justice of God and the vengeance of a people infuriated by a barbarous oppression, and brought at last to bay by their destroyers'.[72] A similar verdict was rendered by a special correspondent of the *Illustrated London News* whose articles in late 1849 and early 1850 sought to publicise the heartless severities of the amended poor law, especially in relation to the clearances. With the Gregory clause particularly in mind, this correspondent declared bluntly:

> The poor law, said to be for the relief of the people and the means of their salvation, was the instrument of their destruction. Calmly and quietly . . .

> from Westminster itself, which is the centre of civilisation, did the decree go forth which has made the temporary but terrible visitation of a potato rot the means of exterminating, through the slow process of disease and houseless starvation, nearly half of the Irish [people].[73]

Or, as this same correspondent put it succinctly and with brutal clarity in a later article, 'The system intended to relieve the poor, by making the landlords responsible for their welfare, has at once made it the interest and therefore the duty of the landlords to get rid of them.'[74]

Thus for this writer and for many others in Britain, the Irish landlord, though to some extent the half-willing agent of irresistible forces and pressures, remained devoid of any redeeming features. At the end of his remarkable series of articles the *Illustrated London News* correspondent characterised Irish landlords, 'speaking of them as a body and admitting many exceptions', as 'extremely selfish, ignorant, negligent, profligate, and reckless. To the serf-like people they have always been more oppressors than protectors, and have thought of them only as sponges out of which they were to squeeze the utmost possible amount of rent, to squander on their own pleasures.'[75] That quintessential voice of the English middle classes, the Lancashire cotton manufacturer and Quaker John Bright, was equally disparaging of Irish landlords. Speaking at the Corn Exchange in Manchester in January 1850 on the need to remedy Irish popular grievances, he declared that Irish landed proprietors, with 'some brilliant exceptions', were 'for the most part . . . beggared', 'almost universally despised, and to a large extent detested' – calculated remarks which, no doubt as he had expected, elicited loud cheers from his audience. The landlords, insisted Bright in phrases that by now were almost formulaic, 'very grossly neglected all the duties of their office and of their position'. Bright's severe strictures on landlords, of course, were not limited to those of Ireland, for in closing this address, he roundly asserted that 'the aristocracy of the United Kingdom has heaped evils unnumbered upon Ireland'.[76] Appreciating the sensitivities of the urban middle classes, British radicals made a practice of abusing the aristocracy and landed gentry in the early and mid-nineteenth century. Indeed, Bright's denunciation of the British and Irish 'aristocracy' at Manchester was part of a wider movement for 'free trade in land' – an ineffective campaign aimed at the middle classes and seeking to eliminate certain legal privileges (especially primogeniture) currently enjoyed by the landed élite of both countries.[77]

EARLY DONOR FATIGUE

But did not the English middle classes have any complicity in the imposition of an amended poor law on Ireland in mid-1847? Surely they did. This had been reflected above all in middle-class determination to shift the financial burden of relieving Irish destitution on to the shoulders of Irish landed proprietors. The terms in which Irish landlords were discussed in parliament and in the British press clearly display the telltale features of scapegoating, and perhaps it is not fanciful to see in all this the displacement of British middle-class guilt. The shifting of the financial burden was accomplished under the poor law amendment act in the face of many protests and much evidence that Irish property could not bear this huge burden without pushing many landlords towards bankruptcy and causing the collapse or near-collapse of the poor law system in some areas. Even after the dire consequences of the amended poor law became plain in Britain, there was no widespread disposition to reassume any substantial share of the costs of relieving the mass destitution associated with the famine. In March 1849, some eighteen months after any significant expenditure by the British government had ended, the *Illustrated London News* proclaimed, 'Great Britain cannot continue to throw her hard-won millions into the bottomless pit of Celtic pauperism.'[78] This may safely be taken as the authentic or at least the dominant voice of the British middle classes. What has been called 'donor fatigue' manifested itself in Britain at an early stage of the great famine.

Admittedly, this was very far from the way in which the educated British public assessed the overall British contribution to the relief of an Ireland prostrated by famine. The common British view, well expressed by the *Illustrated London News* in November 1848, was that 'in a time of commercial pressure and distress we have consented to enormous pecuniary sacrifices for the sake of Ireland and are ready to do so again if we can be assured that our bounty will not do harm rather than good to its recipients'. Coupling a grossly inflated claim with a threadbare excuse, the paper declared:

> If Ireland has offered to the world the spectacle of a gigantic misery, England has also offered to the world the spectacle of an unparalleled effort to relieve and to remove it. If the splendour of our benevolence has not kept pace with the hideousness of her misery, it has not been from any want of inclination on the part of the living race of Englishmen, but from the sheer impossibility of remedying in one year the accumulated evils of ages, and of elevating the character of a people too poor and sorrow-stricken to attempt to elevate themselves.[79]

'A NATION OF BEGGARS'

Here, in the slighting reference to 'the character' of the Irish people, we have a highly significant pointer as to why donor fatigue displayed itself in Britain at such an early stage of the famine. If Britons were well along the way towards spending a claimed £10 million (an exaggerated figure) to relieve Irish starvation by the spring of 1847, without being able to see any signs of permanent improvement, the question arose as to whether the root of the problem was financial or – as seemed much more likely to most educated Britons – moral and 'racial' or cultural.[80] What Britons confronted in Ireland,

HEIGHT OF IMPUDENCE.

Irishman to John Bull.—"SPARE A THRIFLE, YER HONOUR, FOR A POOR IRISH LAD TO BUY A BIT OF —— A BLUNDERBUSS WITH."

Months before threats of revolution became a feature of radical Irish nationalism in late 1847 and early 1848, some segments of public opinion in Britain showed signs of believing that neither the suffering Irish poor nor the middle-class Young Irelanders could be trusted to remain peaceful or loyal. These two *Punch* cartoons of late 1846 point to growing British suspicions of lurking Irish rebellion. In the first, entitled 'Height of impudence', the cartoonist suggests that the ape-like Irishman begging money from John Bull is really a rebel ready for violence. In the second, entitled 'Young Ireland in business for himself', the cartoonist puts a Young Irelander wearing a Milesian cap behind the counter of a weapons store, from where he encourages Paddy to load up with arms and ammunition. The racial stereotyping in these *Punch* cartoons was already quite blatant. (*Punch* Archive)

YOUNG IRELAND IN BUSINESS FOR HIMSELF.

proclaimed *The Times* in March 1847, was 'a nation of beggars', and thus the challenge was enormous: 'We have to change the very nature of a people born and bred, from time immemorial, in inveterate indolence, improvidence, disorder, and consequent destitution.'[81] England, claimed the paper, had been trying for years to eradicate or correct the worst features of the Celtic character – 'its inertness, its dependence on others, its repulsion of whatever is clean, comfortable, and civilised'.[82] Irish Catholic priests, representatives of a religion despised by *The Times*, were roundly chastised as a body because allegedly they never preached against 'that which is notoriously the crying evil of Ireland – its universal sloth'.[83] It was not exactly all their fault that the Irish people were in this lamentable condition. If Englishmen had been 'goaded by oppression and stupefied by neglect', declared *The Times*,

> they would sit, like the Irish, with folded arms on the edge of subterranean or untried wealth, or in the face of anticipated but unrepelled famine; they would lounge, like the Irish, on the shore of a sea whose produce they never sought, and cumber the surface of a soil whose fertility they never cared to augment.[84]

In this situation, what was England's duty, its mission? 'We must educate and elevate Ireland', insisted *The Times*, 'by teaching her people to educate and elevate themselves.'[85] The paper pointed in self-satisfied fashion to all that the English people and government had already done for famine-stricken Ireland – as much as 'the most exacting foe or the most jealous rival could have imposed on our submission or our conscience'. Even greater feats could be achieved by English charity 'were it absolutely needful that England should take the work upon herself'. But such extreme generosity was neither necessary nor advisable while Ireland and the Irish, though not deficient in resources, displayed only 'a crafty, a calculating, a covetous idleness' and 'a thorough repudiation of all self-exertion'.[86] In the face of such deep-seated Irish moral incapacity, what could large additional amounts of British money really accomplish? This was the thrust of one of the most callous lines ever to appear in the pages of *The Times* in all the famine years: 'But what art, what policy, what wealth is cunning enough, wise enough, rich enough to assuage the moral evils and stay the moral disease of a vast population steeped in the congenial mire of voluntary indigence and speculating on the gains of a perpetual famine.'[87] Even though this 'voluntary indigence' was considered extremely difficult to eradicate, *The Times* had urged the adoption of an amended poor law partly in the belief that it would 'give to the peasant a right and a title which may at once insure his industry and his independence'.[88] Since the diagnosis was horribly wrong, it is scarcely surprising that the prescribed course of treatment failed to yield the desired cure.

But if the amended Irish poor law disappointed British expectations in several critical respects, on balance its consequences probably satisfied most educated Britons. In April 1849 *The Times* distilled its results in a quite positive manner:

> The rigorous administration of the poor law is destroying small holdings, reducing needy proprietors to utter insolvency, compelling them to surrender their estates into better hands, instigating an emigration far beyond any which a government could undertake, and so leaving the soil of Ireland open to industrial enterprise and the introduction of new capital.

Like many other Britons, this editorial writer was not at all blind to the huge accompanying social dislocation, but what mattered in the end was that the ground had apparently been cleared for a new agrarian era: 'We see Ireland depopulated, her villages razed to the the ground, her landlords bankrupt – in a word, we see the hideous chasm prepared for the foundation of a future prosperity. . . .'[89] For numerous people in Britain a 'hideous chasm' was, however regrettably, the price which had to be paid for 'a future prosperity'.

CHAPTER 6

Landlords and Tenants

It was possible for Irish landowners who looked back upon the great famine from the vantage point of the mid-1850s to regard that cataclysmic event as advantageous on balance to their interests. A Kerry proprietor who dined with the visiting Sir John Benn-Walsh in October 1852 crudely went 'the whole length of saying that the destruction of the potato is a blessing to Ireland'.[1] But it was much more difficult for landowners to adopt such a view during the famine itself. Over much of the country the difficulties created by the famine seemed decidedly to outweigh the opportunities which it opened up. The two most serious problems facing landlords, especially in the west and the south, were those of collecting rents and finding the means, out of their diminished incomes, to discharge heavy poor rates and to provide additional employment. Though no landowner is known to have starved during the famine, a substantial number wound up in the special bankruptcy court established for insolvent Irish proprietors in 1849.

Because there were enormous variations, even within the same region, it is dangerous to generalise about the degree to which the rental incomes of landowners were reduced during the famine years. It is essential, however, to distinguish between the fortunes of the larger proprietors and the losses of small landlords, especially those who held only or mostly intermediate interests and were not owners in fee. Two highly important determinants of the rate of collection or default were of course the location of the property in relation to the varied geography of destitution and the distribution of holdings by size on the estate. Whereas many owners of overcrowded estates in the west and the south-west were threatened with ruin because of unpaid rents, their counterparts in the north-east, the east midlands, and the south-east often escaped with modest or light losses. In addition, a great deal depended on whether the proprietor generally let his land directly to the occupiers or to intermediate landlords, commonly called middlemen, who sublet their holdings to smaller tenants and cottiers. For a variety of reasons but especially because it entailed a loss of income and of control over tenant access to land, the middleman system had been under attack from proprietors and their agents since the late eighteenth century. But its eradication was a highly protracted process, lasting much longer on some estates than on others, and not completed in many districts until the famine or even later. A survey of the estates of Trinity College, Dublin, carried

Powerscourt at Enniskerry in Wicklow is perhaps the most famous Irish country house. Until gutted by fire in 1974, it was long the imposing Palladian seat of the Viscounts Powerscourt of the third creation, a noble family that gave every appearance of prosperity right through the great famine. With almost 41,000 acres in Wicklow and another 12,000 acres in the counties of Wexford and Dublin (in 1876), the Viscounts Powerscourt ranked among the great landowners of the country, and their estates were generally free of the deep destitution that burdened so many properties in the south and the west. Though numerous landlords in some parts of Ireland battled insolvency in the late 1840s, many others came through the famine more or less unscathed. (National Photographic Archive/National Library of Ireland)

The gardens at Powerscourt (seen here from an elevation, with Sugarloaf Mountain in the background) are one of the man-made splendours of Ireland. They were created immediately before and during the famine. According to the leading authority Mark Bence Jones, 'From 1842 onwards, [the] 6th viscount employed Daniel Robertson of Kilkenny to transform [Richard] Castle's unadorned terraces into an Italian garden in the grand manner, with balustrades and statues, broad flights of steps and inlaid paving.' It is sobering, to say the least, to recall that this monument to human vanity (for such it was in part) was created essentially alongside the horrendous human suffering of the famine. (National Photographic Archive/National Library of Ireland)

out in 1843, showed that there were 12,529 tenants on the 195,000 acres owned by the college in sixteen different counties, mostly in Kerry and Donegal. But less than 1 per cent of these 12,500-odd tenants 'held directly from the college, while 45 per cent held from a college lessee, and 52 per cent held from still another middleman who was a tenant to a college lessee'.[2]

GETTING RID OF MIDDLEMEN

For perhaps a majority of the middlemen who had escaped eradication earlier, the famine and the agricultural depression of 1849–52 spelled the extinction of their position as intermediate landlords. They were ground into dust between the upper and nether millstones. Head landlords, having long wanted to oust them and to appropriate their profit rents, generally refused to grant them abatements. 'I have never made an allowance to middlemen or tenants having beneficial interest [i.e., the benefit of a long lease]', declared the agent of the Cork estates of Viscount Midleton in February 1852,[3] and few agents or their employers departed from this rule: it was either pay up or leave. But to pay up was a tall order. In the typical case the minor gentleman or large farmer who assumed the role of middleman had as his tenants a horde of small farmers, cottiers, and sometimes labourers – the very classes which were reduced to destitution or worse by the famine. When his tenants defaulted in their payments, sometimes in spite of large abatements, the middleman's profit rent sharply contracted or disappeared altogether, and he himself often fell into serious arrears in discharging the head rent owed to the proprietor. Some intermediate landlords whose profit rents were greatly reduced still managed to meet their obligations to the head landlord, but when they did not, proprietors were usually quick to oust them.

The liquidation of middlemen had been the consistent policy of Sir John Benn-Walsh ever since he succeeded to extensive estates of over 10,000 acres in Cork and Kerry in 1825, and the impact of the famine allowed him to bring the process almost to completion. At Grange near Cork city, as he noted in August 1850, the main middleman 'got greatly into arrear and I brought an ejectment for £800', a sum that represented more than twice the annual head rent.[4] On Benn-Walsh's much larger Kerry property three townlands near Listowel were in the hands of a middleman named Leake, whose doubtful legal title and financial embarrassment made him a tempting target for attack. By 1850 Leake 'was getting into arrear, and in consequence of the distressed state of the country we understood that he had little or no profit out of the farm', observed Benn-Walsh. 'We accordingly brought an ejectment, to which Mr Leake took no defence, and entered into possession last July [1851].'[5] Among the other middlemen remaining on his Kerry estate at the start of the famine, one was evicted in 1846, the lease of a second expired in 1849 and was not renewed, and a third, noted Benn-Walsh in 1850, 'has fallen a victim to the times'.[6]

But while the impact of the famine enabled Benn-Walsh to oust nearly all the surviving middlemen on his estates, it also greatly reduced the income

The severe effects of the famine prompted many landlords to grant at least some reduction of the usual rent, but tenants were often compelled to plead or threaten in order to extract substantial concessions. It was hardly unknown for struggling tenants to literally beg for special consideration, either verbally or (among the literate) in writing. It *was* unusual for tenants to do so in a body, as in this illustration of tenants pleading for a rent reduction on their knees. The incident depicted here reportedly occurred on the large Shirley estate in County Monaghan in 1843, soon after the appointment of William Steuart Trench as the new agent, and after the rejection of a written petition from the tenants seeking an abatement because of the low prices of grain and cattle. (By permission of the British Library)

which he derived from his Irish properties. Because he had been methodically removing middlemen long before the famine, when that crisis arrived, he had to contend directly with a mass of defaulting smallholders. This problem was especially acute on his Kerry estate, which was entirely concentrated in the poor law union of Listowel. Destitution in Listowel union was not nearly as bad as in Kenmare or several of the unions in Connacht, but it was still severe. As Benn-Walsh recorded with alarm and dismay in mid-August 1849, 'since last year the debts [under the poor law] have increased eightfold and the union owes about £40,000. There are now 22,000 paupers on outdoor relief out of a population by the last census of 78,000, now probably 10,000 less.'[7] Even though destitution on Benn-Walsh's own property was probably substantially less than in the rest of Listowel union, he could hardly expect well-paid rents. The combined annual rental of his Cork and Kerry estates in 1847 was £5,317, but, as Benn-Walsh later pointed out, during the famine years his rents were 'merely nominal'.[8] The surviving documentation does not permit any precise estimate of his losses, but to judge from a telling remark made in October 1852, they must have been enormous. The collection of the half-year's rent then payable had netted only £1,200, and yet Benn-Walsh observed with some glee, 'this is the best haul I have had since the famine'.[9] Allowances to his tenants for agricultural improvements certainly contributed to his losses, and so too did the heavy burden of poor rates, both directly and indirectly. 'The vice-guardians', he fumed in mid-August 1849, 'have already collected all the produce of the butter in rates, and they are prepared to strike another in September to secure the produce of the harvest. The fact is that the landed proprietors are now the mere nominal possessors of the soil. All the surplus produce is levied by the poor law commissioners.'[10] The bitter experience of Sir John Benn-Walsh, whose rental income may have fallen by more than half between 1846 or 1847 and 1852, can probably be taken as representative of the fortunes of landowners with a multitude of small direct tenants in regions of acute destitution.

A strikingly more favourable situation existed for another and greater Kerry proprietor, the earl of Kenmare. His huge property in that county was concentrated in the poor law union of Killarney, where the degree of destitution was almost as severe as that in Listowel, and yet Lord Kenmare managed to collect as much as £69,500 out of £81,100, or 86 per cent of the rents due between 1846 and 1850. In his case the explanation is simple: of the twenty-three townlands on his estate in Killarney union, no fewer than nineteen were still in the hands of middlemen as late as 1850, and these middlemen neither defaulted heavily (a rare happening in this region during the famine) nor received any abatement from Lord Kenmare. On all of his property in Kerry in 1850, the earl had only 300 direct tenants – a tiny fraction of the total number of occupiers – and they paid an average rent of almost £56.[11]

Other proprietors did almost as well as Lord Kenmare and occasionally better, even when they were not so heavily shielded by rent-paying middlemen. On the duke of Devonshire's great estates in the counties of Cork and Waterford, his agents were able to collect 84 per cent of the total of £359,200 due from the tenants between 1846 and 1853. But his properties, besides having been carefully managed for decades, were favourably situated – around Lismore in Waterford and Bandon in Cork – with respect to the geography of destitution. Even at their worst in 1850 his payments for poor rates and other taxes represented only about 9 per cent of his annual rental.[12] A much smaller landowner, Sir Charles Denham Jephson-Norreys, whose estate was centred in and around the town of Mallow in Cork, received as much as 90 per cent of the rents owed by his tenants between 1846 and 1853. Well might his agent tell him in August 1850: 'Taking everything into account, you have come off well with your tenants. Indeed, you are the only man I know who gets anything like his income.'[13] Partly, the reason was that a relatively high proportion of the receipts came from town tenants and the holdings of the rural ones were apparently much larger than average in size. Moreover, the estate was again favourably situated. As measured by poor law expenditures in the year 1847–8 in relation to the property valuation, Mallow had less pauperism than any other union in the county.

But even proprietors in districts with comparatively low levels of destitution could not expect to be as fortunate as Jephson-Norreys if their tenants were not large farmers. The experience of Robert Cole Bowen is instructive in this regard. From his tenants in the counties of Cork and Tipperary, Bowen managed to collect 81 per cent of the rents actually due from 1848 to 1853. But his income was not preserved even as well as this figure might suggest. Over the same period his yearly rental declined by about 14 per cent as tenants failed or were evicted without the prompt reletting of their farms. That numerous tenants disappeared from the rent roll is not at all surprising. On neither his Tipperary nor his Cork estate were the holdings large. On the Tipperary property the average yearly rent payable by the 144 tenants of 1848 was £19, and by the 111 tenants of 1853 it was £23. On the Cork estate the corresponding figure for the 37 tenants of 1848 was £27, and for the 28 tenants of 1853 it was £23.[14] To have numerous small or middling tenants spelled substantial losses for proprietors even when, as in this case, their estates lay outside zones of heavy pauperism.

If many landowners in relatively advantaged regions lost between 15 and 25 per cent of their rents during the late 1840s and early 1850s, it is easy to appreciate how badly the proprietors of Mayo, west Galway, and much of Clare must have fared. There the appalling degree of destitution and the extremely small size of holdings combined in a doubly destructive assault on landlord incomes. This combination was at its worst in County Mayo. According to a parliamentary return of 1846, no fewer than 75 per cent of the agricultural holdings in that county were valued at £4 or less for poor law taxation.[15] This meant, on the one hand, that the vast majority of tenants there quickly became unable to pay rent, and it also meant, on the other hand, that proprietors and other landlords were responsible for bearing nearly the whole burden of the poor rates. The marquis of Sligo, whose property was concentrated in Westport union, informed Lord Monteagle in October 1848 that for three years he had received no rent from his tenants. Though Lord Sligo undoubtedly obtained at least some money, it must have been only a small fraction of his nominal rental of about £7,200 a year, for in Westport union as many as 85 per cent of the occupiers had holdings valued at £4 or less. As early as March 1848 Lord Sligo owed almost £1,650 to the Westport board of guardians, a body that he served as chairman. This debt he was able to discharge only by borrowing £1,500, thus adding to his already heavy incumbrances, which reportedly cost him £6,000 annually. As he told Lord Monteagle, his dire financial condition placed him 'under the necessity of ejecting or being ejected'.[16]

In an effort to collect arrears of rent from tenants unable – or sometimes unwilling – to pay, landlords and agents had long been accustomed to seize tenants' livestock and to 'drive' the beasts to the local pound, where they were held until either redeemed by payment of the arrears or sold in satisfaction of the debt. The proper legal term for this procedure was distraint. This illustration shows the 'driving' or distraining of cattle and sheep for unpaid rent in County Galway in 1849. As the overall level of arrears increased enormously during the famine, so too did the practice of 'driving'. But many tenants took care to sell their livestock or grain before it could be seized. The money thus raised often helped 'runaway' tenants to emigrate. (*Illustrated London News*)

THE CLEARANCES

Evict their debtors or be dispossessed by their creditors – this perceived choice provided a general rationalisation among landlords for the great clearances of defaulting or insolvent tenants that were carried out during the famine and its immediate aftermath. 'The landlords are *prevented* from aiding or tolerating poor tenants', declared the large Galway proprietor Lord Clanricarde at the end of 1848. 'They are compelled to hunt out all such, to save their property from the £4 clause.'[17] Time diminished only slightly the force and currency of this exculpation. In 1866 Jephson-Norreys, the owner of Mallow, was still insisting that the £4 rating clause had 'almost forced the landlords to get rid of their poorer tenantry'.[18] From his experience as a poor law inspector in Kilrush union, Captain Arthur Kennedy (later Sir Arthur) carried away a different perspective. Many years later, he bitterly recalled: 'I can tell you . . . that there were days in that western county when I came back from some scene of eviction so maddened

Both before and during the famine Irish agrarian conflict was a complicated phenomenon. Rent disputes not only pitted tenants of varying means against landowners but also brought large or even middling farmers into conflict with labourers or cottiers holding ground from them. The famine had the general effect of heightening tensions at all levels of the land system. Threatened eviction of any kind could prompt resistance in individual cases, as in this illustration of January 1847 involving a farming family and perhaps some assisting relatives or neighbours. But organised, sustained, and violent resistance to eviction during the famine was quite uncommon. (*Pictorial Times*/By permission of the British Library)

by the sights of hunger and misery I had seen in the day's work that I felt disposed to take the gun from behind my door and shoot the first landlord I met.'[19]

There was remarkably little resistance and still less shooting. Some large clearances occurred in 1846, but the great campaigns of what were soon branded 'extermination' got under way in 1847 as the quarter-acre clause, starvation, and disease loosened the grip of smallholders on their land, and as the mounting tide of poor rates and arrears of rent propelled landlords into frenzied destruction of cabins. The number of evictions for the years 1846–8 can only be estimated very roughly from the records of ejectments, but beginning in 1849 the constabulary kept count of the evictions that came to the knowledge of the local police. In the earliest years of this effort, when estates were being cleared wholesale as well as piecemeal, it is likely that the police figures considerably understated the real total of dispossessions. From the two sets of statistics it is clear that evictions

Table 4
Evictions recorded by the constabulary, 1849–54

Year	Evicted		Readmitted		Not Readmitted	
	Families	Persons	Families	Persons	Families	Persons
1849	16,686	90,440	3,302	18,375	13,384	72,065
1850	19,949	104,163	5,403	30,292	14,546	73,871
1851	13,197	68,023	4,382	24,574	8,815	43,449
1852	8,591	43,494	2,041	11,334	6,550	32,160
1853	4,833	24,589	1,213	6,721	3,620	17,868
1854	2,156	10,794	331	1,805	1,825	8,989
Total	65,412	341,503	16,672	93,101	48,740	248,402

soared in 1847 and increased every year until 1850, when they reached a peak; they remained high in 1851 and 1852 before tailing off to a much lower level by 1854. Altogether, as Table 4 shows, the police recorded the eviction of 65,412 families from 1849 to 1854, but of this number 16,672 families were readmitted to their holdings either as legal tenants (after paying rent) or as caretakers (without payment). Thus a minimum of 48,740 families were permanently dispossessed between 1849 and 1854. The average evicted family included about five members, and the total number of persons dispossessed amounted to almost a quarter of a million.[20]

This figure, however, does not take account of the 'voluntary' surrenders of possession by tenants headed for the workhouse or the emigrant ship, or simply reduced to begging along the roads and especially in the towns. Although such surrenders usually were not reckoned officially as evictions, they often amounted to virtually the same thing, and they were legion. The Kerry and Cork estates of Sir John Benn-Walsh, for example, were 'very much weeded both of paupers and bad tenants during the famine'. This had been decorously managed by his agent, noted Benn-Walsh in September 1851, 'without evictions, bringing in the sheriff, or any harsh measures. In fact, the paupers and little cottiers cannot keep their holdings without the potato, and for small sums of £1, £2, and £3 have given me peaceable possession in a great many cases, when the cabin is immediately levelled.'[21]

LANDLORD-ASSISTED EMIGRATION

Some of the clearances were associated with landlord-assisted emigration. One of the largest such schemes was carried out by Francis Spaight, a famine-enriched partner in the 'great firm of merchants & corn dealers at Limerick', after he bought the Derry Castle estate around Killaloe on the Clare–Tipperary border in 1844. Spaight told an obviously impressed Sir John Benn-Walsh in 1849 that he 'had emigrated 1,400 persons, that this estate was now to be formed . . . into an electoral division to itself, and that he then anticipated that the poor rates would be within his controul [*sic*] and that the property would be a valuable and improving one'.[22] Spaight reported elsewhere that he had spent £3 10s. per emigrant,[23] so that the whole operation, which extended over several years, probably cost just under £5,000. An even more far-reaching scheme was undertaken for the marquis of Lansdowne by William Steuart Trench after he became the agent for Lansdowne's congested estate in bankrupt Kenmare union in south Kerry during the winter of 1849/50. As Trench analysed the daunting situation, some 3,000 of the 10,000 paupers then receiving poor law relief in that union were chargeable to Lansdowne's property. For the landlord to give employment to so many people, Trench rejected as thoroughly impractical after a short and partial experiment. To maintain them in the workhouse would, he claimed, cost a minimum of £5 per head a year, thus leaving Lansdowne with an annual bill for poor rates of £15,000 when the entire valuation of his property there barely reached £10,000 a year. He explained to Lansdowne that 'it would be cheaper to him, and *better for them* [i.e., his pauper tenants], to pay for their emigration at once than to continue to support them at home'.[24] Lansdowne concurred, and over the course of three or four years in the early 1850s, slightly more than 4,600 persons were shipped off to the United States or Canada. The total expense exceeded £17,000, and the average cost per emigrant (£3 14s.) was a few shillings more than that incurred by Francis Spaight.[25]

Perhaps the most notorious episode of a clearance associated with landlord-assisted emigration occurred on the Roscommon estate of Major Denis Mahon and led to his murder in November 1847.[26] It was later stated that Mahon, the only large landlord to suffer such a fate in all the famine years, had ejected over 3,000 persons (605 families) before he was slain.[27] To a substantial portion of his tenants (more than a thousand), however, Mahon and his agent offered the opportunity of emigration to Canada. They aimed their scheme at 'those [tenants] of the poorest and worst description, who would be a charge on us for the poor house or for outdoor relief', and whose departure 'would relieve the industrious tenant'.[28] Ineffective efforts were made to screen out anyone with disease, and a sum of about £4,000 was expended on the passages and provisioning of his emigrants. But unfortunately for his reputation, as many as a quarter of his emigrants perished during the Atlantic crossing, and 'the medical officer at Quebec reported that the survivors were the most wretched and diseased he had ever seen'.[29] Thus the distressing tale of Major Mahon's clearance became a conspicuous part of the much larger and more dreadful story of the 'coffin ships' and the horrors of Grosse Île, or as one contemporary called it, 'the great charnel house of victimised humanity'.[30]

By an extraordinary turn of events this clearance and landlord murder became the focus of an extensive journalistic controversy that polarised political and cultural attitudes on both sides of the Irish Sea. In a public letter addressed to Archbishop John MacHale of Tuam and given wide publicity in the English and

In response to evictions and other grievances, agrarian violence flared in late 1847 and 1848. Among a series of agrarian murders during this period was the assassination in November 1847 of Major Denis Mahon, who had presided over the clearance of more than 3,000 persons from his Roscommon estate. Another flare-up occurred in the early 1850s and was associated with 'Ribbonism' – an organised form of agrarian and sometimes sectarian violence – in north Leinster and south Ulster. The first illustration here depicts two 'Ribbonmen' crouching behind a stone fence, waiting to shoot the Monaghan land agent William Steuart Trench in 1852. The second illustration shows a tenant lying dead on the ground after being killed with an axe for having taken an evicted farm. But compared with the decades before the famine, concerted agrarian violence was remarkably less frequent and less widespread in the late 1840s and early 1850s. (By permission of the British Library)

Irish press, the earl of Shrewsbury, a prominent English Catholic, accused Father Michael McDermott, the parish priest of Strokestown, of having denounced Major Mahon from the altar on the Sunday before he was shot. Shrewsbury demanded that the offending priest be disciplined for contributing to the landlord's murder. Adding insult to injury, Shrewsbury also observed in his letter that English public opinion held the Irish Catholic church to be 'a conniver at injustice, an accessory to crime, [and] a pestilent sore in the commonwealth'.[31] Fr McDermott produced credible evidence that he had never publicly denounced Major Mahon at any time, but the furore soon broadened to embrace rival English and Irish religious and political stereotypes and clashing images of the Catholic clergy in general. The *Nation* newspaper in Ireland insisted early in January 1848 that 'every line that has been written in the English papers for the last two months' proved that 'the English charge the whole priesthood with instigations to murder'. 'Hang a priest or two and all will be right' was claimed to be 'the prevalent sentiment in England'.[32] In response to Shrewsbury's public letter MacHale produced one of his own, heaping bitter scorn on the calumniators of the Irish Catholic clergy, vehemently defending priests for their protests against mass evictions, and blasting the Whig government for doing nothing to check the clearances. Indeed, in his much-quoted response MacHale displayed his adherence to the genocidal view of the famine. 'How ungrateful of the Catholics of Ireland', he acidly remarked to Shrewsbury, 'not to pour forth canticles of gratitude to the [Whig] ministers, who promised that none of them should perish and then suffered a million to starve.'[33] From the dismal catalogue of tragedies, accusations, and wounds that surrounded the Mahon clearance, relations between the British government and the Irish Catholic church suffered a severe blow, as did landlord-assisted emigration.

Most proprietors who undertook such schemes did so, like Mahon and Spaight, in the years 1846–8, when landlord-assisted emigration was at its height. In contrast to Lansdowne, very few landowners engaged in the practice extensively after 1850. The schemes of these three men, however, were highly atypical in their scale. Oliver MacDonagh has concluded that landlord-assisted emigration from all of Ireland in the years 1846–52 'can scarcely have exceeded 50,000 in extent'.[34] Since all of Spaight's 1,400 tenants as well as about 3,500 of Lansdowne's had departed before 1853, this would mean that these two proprietors alone were responsible for nearly 10 per cent of the estimated total. But like the usually much smaller emigration enterprises of other landlords, those of Spaight and Lansdowne were portrayed as entirely voluntary. Spaight insisted that his tenants left willingly and without rancour,[35] and, according to Trench, Lansdowne's paupers greeted the offer of free passage to any North American port as almost 'too good news to be true' and rushed to seize the unexpected opportunity.[36] Everyone who accepted, Trench asserted, did so 'without any ejectments having been brought against them to enforce it, or the slightest pressure put upon them to go'.[37] Yet by no means all of those whom landowners assisted to leave were given a choice between staying and going. For a great many, the choice, sometimes implicit and at other times made quite explicit, lay between emigrating with modest assistance and being evicted. Moreover, as MacDonagh has argued, it was a pretence to say that a pauperised tenant without the ability to pay rent or to keep his family nourished had a 'free' choice in the matter.

Mass Evictions in Kilrush Union

Yet even if the choice was highly constrained, it was far less inhumane than the total absence of an alternative, which is what the vast majority of estate-clearing landlords offered. West Clare in particular presented in the years 1847–50 the appalling spectacle of landlords cruelly turning out thousands of tenants on to the roadside. This heartless practice first became intense in the winter of 1847/8 and the following spring, as one landlord after another joined the campaign. Furnishing a list of the many cabins unroofed or tumbled on six different properties in just two of the electoral divisions of Kilrush union, Captain Arthur Kennedy informed the poor law commissioners early in April 1848, 'I calculate that 1,000 houses have been levelled since November and expect 500 more before July.' Those dispossessed, he declared, 'are all absolute and hopeless paupers; on the average six to each house! Enough to swamp any union or poor law machinery when simultaneously thrown upon it.'[38] Deceit and small sums of money were used to bring about acquiescence: 'The wretched and half-witted occupiers are too often deluded by the specious promises of under-agents and bailiffs, and induced to throw down their own cabins for a few shillings and an assurance of outdoor relief.'[39] Many of the evicted

> betake themselves to the ditches or the shelter of some bank, and there exist like animals till starvation or the inclemency of the weather drives them to the workhouse. There were three cartloads of these creatures, who could not walk, brought for admission yesterday, some in fever, some suffering from dysentery, and all from want of food.[40]

Other dispossessed families crowded into cabins left standing in neighbouring townlands 'till disease is generated, and they are then thrown out, without consideration or mercy'.[41] The larger farmers in the vicinity of these clearances took advantage of them by getting 'their labour done in exchange for food alone to the member of the family [whom the farmer] employs, till absolute starvation brings the mother and helpless children to the workhouse; this is the history of hundreds'.[42] (It is little wonder that Kennedy wanted to take his gun and shoot the first landlord he met.)

Such was the scale and intensity of the clearances of 1847–50 within its bounds that Kilrush union eventually acquired a gruesome notoriety throughout Ireland and Britain that was similar to that held earlier by the

This sketch of 1849 shows the young daughter of the poor law official Captain Arthur Kennedy in 'her daily occupation' of distributing clothing to wretched children in the town of Kilrush. Kennedy became poor law inspector for Kilrush union in November 1847 and remained the chief administrative officer there until 1850. Unusually for such an official, he became an increasingly forceful and vocal opponent of the mass evictions carried out by local landlords. The biggest depopulator was Colonel Crofton M. Vandeleur, who evicted over 1,000 persons from his estate. Vandeleur was chairman of the Kilrush board of guardians for most of the late 1840s. He and other local landlords deeply resented and publicly rejected Kennedy's fusillade of criticism. The controversy attracted much publicity to the Kilrush clearances. (*Illustrated London News*)

charnel-house district of Skibbereen. Kennedy's relentless drumbeat of criticism thoroughly antagonised the local landed gentry and their agents. Some of them vigorously contested the statements and eviction statistics presented in Kennedy's reports to the poor law commissioners in Dublin, especially after portions of this information began appearing in newspapers and became the basis for highly critical parliamentary speeches. Kennedy fought back with a tenacity, resourcefulness, and effectiveness which local landlords and agents found galling. The bitter controversy led to the publication (in the British parliamentary papers) of a large sheaf of Kennedy's reports and eviction lists, and it culminated in the appointment in 1850 of a select committee of the House of Commons under the spirited chairmanship of the independent Radical MP George Poulett Scrope, a rare and zealous champion of the Irish poor throughout the famine years.[43]

From this controversy a firm picture emerged of the enormity of the destruction wrought by the landlords and agents of Kilrush union. Relying on the notices served on relieving officers and their statements to him, Kennedy told Scrope's select committee in July 1850 that the total number of evicted persons in Kilrush union since late 1847 amounted – 'as accurately as I can ascertain it' – to 'between 16,000 and 19,000'.[44] These figures were contested by Colonel Crofton M. Vandeleur, one of the two largest landowners in the union and for most of the late 1840s the chairman of the Kilrush board of guardians. In his testimony before Scrope's committee Vandeleur declared that Kennedy's figure of over 16,000 evicted persons should be reduced by as much as half.[45] Also quarrelling with Kennedy's statistics was Marcus Keane, a man whose enthusiasm for evictions prompted one unfriendly newspaper to say of him that he was 'unhappy when not exterminating'.[46] Though a modest landowner himself, Keane's great importance derived from his extensive activities as land agent for some of the biggest proprietors in Kilrush union, including the Marquis Conyngham and Nicholas Westby. Altogether, by 1850 Keane exercised sway as agent over 'about 60,000 acres', equivalent to nearly 40 per cent of the land area of the union.[47] Kennedy had claimed that in nine cases out of ten, when tenants were evicted, their houses were levelled. Yet Keane insisted that on the estates he managed in the union, 'I have pulled down very few houses.'[48] Neither Keane nor Vandeleur was telling the truth.

Their testimony was thoroughly shredded by the painstaking investigations of Francis Coffee, who presented his results to Scrope's committee in mid-July 1850. Coffee had special and impressive credentials for the inquiry that he conducted. A land agent, civil engineer, and professional surveyor, he was exceptionally well acquainted with the whole area of Kilrush union, having previously revised the poor law valuation for the Kilrush guardians.[49] But what made Coffee's findings so conclusive and so difficult to controvert were his methods of work. His basic source was a set of Ordnance Survey maps showing the exact location of all houses existing in the union in 1841, supplemented by markings indicating all new houses built since that year. Proceeding townland by townland and taking information from relieving officers, land agents, bailiffs, and others, Coffee carefully checked the evidence of his maps against what he could see – or now could not see – on the ground.[50] From his exhaustive work he was able to reproduce for the edification of the select committee a detailed Ordnance map, suitably coloured and marked, showing with 'black spots' the precise location of the 2,700 instances of eviction identified in Kilrush union. In addition, Coffee's data distinguished three different degrees of eviction: first, cases in which the affected families had had their houses levelled; second, cases in which families were 'unhoused' from a dwelling that was left standing; and third, cases in which families were restored as caretakers. Accompanying this map was a comprehensive list of seventy-six proprietors and middlemen who had engaged in evictions in Kilrush union from November 1847 to 1 July 1850, along with details about the number of families and persons evicted by each, divided into the three aforementioned categories.[51]

EXPULSION OF 12,000 PEOPLE

Coffee's cold statistics framed a local story of human distress that stood out boldly even in the endless sea of misery that was the great famine. He found that the houses of 1,951 families had been levelled and that a further 408 families had been displaced (or 'unhoused') from their dwellings. Calculating that there had been five people in each of the combined total of 2,359 dispossessed families, Coffee noted with appropriate emphasis that the expulsions amounted to some 12,000 people.[52] In addition, another 341 families in a third category, though evicted, had been restored to their houses (if not to their lands) as caretakers. Coffee rightly regarded the caretakers' position as highly precarious, for they held their houses merely 'at the will of the proprietor or until their respective tenements were relet to other tenants'.[53] Coffee's data also clearly established the dimensions of the depopulation carried out by Vandeleur and Keane. Vandeleur had dispossessed from his estate as many as 180 families, including just over 1,000 persons – a greater number than any of his landlord peers in Kilrush union.[54] Moreover, on the properties which Keane administered as agent, some 500 houses had been levelled. Another 50 families on Keane's properties had been unhoused, while a third group of 67 families, though evicted, had been allowed to reoccupy their dwellings as caretakers. This was certainly a dramatic and appalling record of depopulation for a single agent. A total of about 2,800 persons had their houses levelled or were displaced from their dwellings on estates in Kilrush union where Keane was in charge.[55] Yet in another self-deluded statement before Scrope's committee in June 1850, Keane could declare, 'I say that there was more consideration [shown] for the feelings and wants of the poor people who were removed than there was for an increase of [landlord] income.'[56]

One measure of the intensity of the clearances in Kilrush union is that 17 per cent of its 1841 population suffered some form of eviction between November 1847 and the end of June 1850.[57] Clearance and depopulation were greatest in the extensive and once densely settled coastal areas of the union. Speaking of the small coastal holdings stretching from Miltown Malbay down to Kilkee, a distance of 14 miles, Francis Coffee remarked, 'About three-fourths [of the population] along the coast have been evicted and unhoused.'[58] Similar, if perhaps somewhat less savage, events took place in other coastal areas of the union, as on both sides of the peninsula running out to Loop Head.[59] Indeed, the worst was over in Kilrush union by mid-1850 precisely because the clearances there had already been carried to such grotesque lengths. Francis Coffee told Scrope's committee in mid-July of that year that the rate of eviction was likely to slow to less than half of its earlier pace because landlords were now finding that they had carried the clearances too far for their own good. Rates and taxes on evicted lands in the owners' hands, as well as lost rents therefrom, would, he maintained, 'reduce their gross income by a very considerable amount'.[60]

Among the thousands evicted in Kilrush union were Bridget O'Donnell and her children. Her destitution was mirrored in that of the union as a whole. The vast majority of its population were cottiers or landless labourers. Most of the smallholders so densely settled in the long coastal districts of Kilrush union had doubled as fishermen, but the impact of the famine quickly and thoroughly disrupted this customary resource. Fishermen almost universally pawned their nets and parted with their tackle in order to buy food. Unable to pay their rents and standing in the way of 'agricultural improvement', they were removed *en masse* from their little holdings of a few acres. (*Illustrated London News*)

PRESSURES AND MOTIVES

Who were these Kilrush landowners who executed such enormous clearances, and what were their economic circumstances and motives? It appears that the intensity of mass eviction in this region of Clare was a function, first of all, of the pervasiveness of the mania for clearances among its landlords, from the magnates down to the small fry. Admittedly, the mammoth clearances were the work of a very restricted group. A mere eight Kilrush landlords each dispossessed more than 400 people and were collectively responsible for almost half of the total of 12,000 unhoused persons recorded by Francis Coffee. Five of these eight actually ousted more than 700 people apiece. Another small group of five landlords each evicted between 300 and 400 persons and collectively accounted for 15 per cent of those dispossessed. The rest of the evicted army (almost 4,600 persons) were the responsibility of the remaining sixty-three proprietors or middlemen on Coffee's list of seventy-six evictors.[61] In this general landlord mania for large-scale evictions in Kilrush union, imitation almost certainly played a significant role, in the sense that the evident ubiquity of evictions there allowed initially hesitant landlords to cast aside their inhibitions and join the common onslaught against small holdings and 'cottierisation'. Colonel Vandeleur excused the mass evictions locally on the false plea in 1850 that 'the clearances in our union have been nothing to what I have understood have been the clearances in other unions' in the west of Ireland.[62] Just as Vandeleur invoked the sanction of allegedly greater depopulators elsewhere, so too lesser Kilrush landowners could point to his example as a ready excuse for their own evictions.

The relative poverty of Kilrush landowners was also an important factor in their heavy penchant for clearances. Along with the generality of Clare proprietors, those of Kilrush union must have belonged to the poorer section of the Irish landed élite at the time of the great famine. Admittedly, little of the land of Clare – surprisingly little – was sold during the 1850s in the Incumbered Estates Court, a fact which strongly suggests that crushing indebtedness was not the common condition of the generality of Clare's proprietors before or during the famine.[63] But the structure of landownership in Clare, as revealed by the well-known return of Irish landowners in 1876, giving the acreage and valuations of their estates, is suggestive of quite modest wealth at best. Only four proprietors then had estates in that county larger than 20,000 acres, and even the largest of them, Lord Leconfield's estate of 39,000 acres, had a valuation of less than £16,600. Edmund Westby's property of some 27,300 acres, perhaps the largest in Kilrush union, was valued at under £7,900, and in the hands of Nicholas Westby, its owner during the famine years, this estate had an annual rental of about £6,000. Even those Clare landowners with sizeable properties had unimpressive valuations.[64] Among the telltale signs of the pinched circumstances of proprietors in Kilrush union during the famine was the extreme dearth of landlord-provided employment. Among the seventy-six landowners and middlemen named in his comprehensive list of Kilrush evictors, there were, remarked Francis Coffee in July 1850, only three 'who afford what I would consider employment', and a fourth who furnished some work, but not as much 'as should be expected from his property'.[65] Also conspicuous by its absence was landlord-assisted emigration. Coffee had a short and depressingly stark answer when asked before Scrope's committee whether many of the 12,000 dispossessed persons in Kilrush union had emigrated: 'I should say not one per cent.'[66]

Having in general only modest means to start with, and having in their view little or nothing to spare for such costly projects as employment schemes or assisted emigration, the landed proprietors of Clare and Kilrush union were deprived of much of their rents by the shattering impact of the famine on their tenants, the vast majority of whom were land-poor, with fewer than 15 acres.[67] Where there were no middlemen in place to absorb some of the default below them, the losses could be dramatically large. Marcus Keane, whose land agency business covered as much as two-fifths of Kilrush union, told Scrope's committee in June 1850 that of all the rents due from tenants, 'I suppose the sum actually received by my employers was about half'. And he said the same thing about the usual experience of the owners of other estates in Kilrush union and Clare generally: 'About one-half of the amount of the rental was received by the landlords.'[68] If Keane was right, part of the reason may well have been that Kilrush proprietors had relatively few middlemen to buffer them against the insolvency and destitution of so many occupying tenants. Keane was adamant that the clearances there did not usually stem from the actions of middlemen or the non-payment of rents to them. On the contrary, he estimated that as many as five out of every six evictions noted in Captain Kennedy's reports and returns concerned the direct tenants of head landlords, not middlemen.[69]

Among these direct tenants were swarms of smallholders, as befitted a county whose population had grown at double the national rate and more rapidly than that of any other Irish county between 1821 and 1841. It has been suggested that 'on the eve of the famine landless or near-landless households accounted for two-thirds of the population of Clare'.[70] Kilrush union was an exaggerated version of the county in this respect, as its devastating famine experience demonstrated. Cottier tenants holding fewer than 3 or 5 acres in the coastal district between Kilkee and Miltown Malbay were 'immediately swept away' by the successive potato failures of 1846 and 1847.[71] Most of the smallholders so densely settled in the long coastal areas of Kilrush union doubled as fishermen, but the impact of the famine rapidly and almost completely sapped the foundations of this traditional resource. 'Generally', declared Coffee, 'five-sixths of those who previously lived as fishermen were obliged to pawn their nets or part with their fishing tackle for their means of subsistence in 1847 and 1848.'[72] From the masses of such tenants, landlords and agents could extract very little rental income, if indeed they got anything at all.

On the side of expenditure poor rates were a heavy charge. Admittedly, the rates struck and collected in Kilrush union between 1847 and 1850 were far less than those of many other distressed western unions. A general rate of almost 5s. in the pound (25 per cent of the valuation) was struck in August 1847, but the rates imposed in the following three years were all lower, and that of 1848 was only 3s. in the pound – certainly modest in relation to the extraordinary scale of destitution.[73] But for landlords already squeezed by lost rents, the rate burden pinched hard enough, and it seems to have weighed even more heavily on their minds. Marcus Keane asserted that on Nicholas Westby's estate, with a rental of about £6,000 a year, the rates paid in 1849 had amounted to between £1,800 and £1,900, or almost a third of rents due. Speaking more generally of Kilrush proprietors, Keane observed in June 1850, 'Their incomes have been greatly reduced, and their charges are so heavy, and the rates so much, that it is with difficulty the proprietors can get money enough to live on.'[74] Colonel Vandeleur echoed this gloomy assessment in the following month: 'I may say that in many instances the landlords have only barely lived.'[75]

The £4 rating clause of the Irish poor law, which made landowners liable for paying all the rates for holdings on their estates valued at £4 or less, was a source of intense concern, and as elsewhere it impelled Kilrush landlords into mass evictions. The pressure created by the clause, said Colonel Vandeleur in July 1850, 'has been particularly severe, especially in towns' – and, he might have added, in the densely crowded rundale villages so common in Kilrush union and rural Clare generally. He cited the case of a street of boatmen, fishermen, and labourers in the town of Kilrush, which he owned. Their forty-nine houses owed a collective rent of £11 14s. a year, but the rates on those houses – all of which he apparently had to pay – amounted to £22 12s. Almost in the same breath Vandeleur pronounced the £4 rating clause 'a great inducement to get rid of small tenants' – a conviction which he practised with little restraint.[76] In this instance his antagonist Captain Kennedy could not have agreed more with Vandeleur. The £4 rating clause, Kennedy insisted in June 1850, after the avalanche of local clearances had finally begun to abate, 'induces excessive evictions. The landlord must do it as a measure of self-defence. . . . I think in both cases, whether the rent be paid or not, there is a great inclination to get rid of that class of occupiers.'[77]

Whatever the real rate burden, fears of being swamped by pauperism probably pushed the landlords and agents of Kilrush union towards clearances. A considerable number of them may have been panicked into starting mass evictions by the gigantic scale of relief in the spring of 1847: as many as 47,000 persons were then assisted under the soup kitchen scheme.[78] This was much more than half the total population of the union. And as Captain Kennedy told the poor law commissioners in late February 1848, after the clearances had commenced locally, 'All who received relief last year . . . naturally expected its continuance and still continue to importune and besiege the relieving officers.'[79] Outdoor relief in Kilrush union under the poor law in 1848 and 1849 never attained the level of public assistance granted in 1847; it reached its peak of almost 31,000 people in the summer of 1849 before decreasing to about 9,000 or 10,000 during the winter of 1849/50.[80] But in the initiation of clearances Kilrush proprietors were probably moved to such drastic action by the enormous wave of destitution that seemed ready to overwhelm their property in late 1847 and early 1848.

LAW: THE EVICTING LANDLORD'S FRIEND

To expel tenants and level houses on the massive and perhaps unprecedented scale of the Kilrush clearances required landlords and agents to bring to bear a whole complex battery of legal, administrative, physical, and psychological resources before they could accomplish the immense task to which they had committed themselves. Simplifying their task was the fact that clearances could usually be executed with little cost or legal trouble. Where the landowner or his agent aimed to evict any large number of tenants, the cheapest and easiest legal course was to sue for an ejectment on the title in one of the superior courts and to avoid as much as possible the facilities offered by the lower courts – the assistant barrister's court or the quarter sessions court. The reason was quite simple. In these lower courts each tenant had to be sued separately and at considerable cost – £5 or £6 for the solicitor acting on behalf of the landlord and lessor, according to Marcus Keane, whose vast experience made him an expert in such matters.[81] In the superior courts, on the other hand, a landlord could take aim with one ejectment against the tenants of an entire townland, a whole district, or even (in theory) all his property in a given county. As the matter was expressed by Colonel Vandeleur, the biggest of the Kilrush evictors, 'by civil bill ejectment [in the lower courts] only one party could be included, but by the superior court ejectment you may include as many different parties as you please'.[82] Marcus Keane made the same point even more succinctly: 'You must sue each [tenant] separately in the sessions court, whereas you may sue a whole county in the superior court.' Every tenant served with a copy of a superior court ejectment who did not resist the proceeding by taking formal defence was 'liable to be turned out on the issuing of the *habere*' [i.e., a decree for possession]. Indeed, as long as the *habere* was in force, every occupier on the lands could be removed at an hour's notice.[83] This was Keane's standard procedure, and apparently that of Colonel Vandeleur and most of the other Kilrush evictors as well. 'I have not resorted', said Keane in June 1850, 'to the quarter sessions court in any case [of ejectment], except on one property; I always proceed in the superior court.'[84]

Among the advantages of the superior court ejectment was the way in which it allowed landowners and agents to weed out those considered bad tenants and to rearrange the farms among the remaining occupiers. 'What I generally did', explained Marcus Keane, was to bring the ejectment against all the tenants of a given townland, 'then take the land from the bad and enlarge the holdings of the good. I had, besides turning out the bad tenants, to remodel the farms and allot to the good tenant the portion it was desirable he should have.'[85] What made this practice so attractive to Keane and others like him in Kilrush union was the great prevalence there of the rundale system, with its inefficient scattering of small bits of land belonging to the same tenant in different locations.[86] It should be noted that the widespread use of the superior court ejectment as a tool of estate management during the famine years makes it highly problematic to take such ejectments as a measure of evictions, as historians have sometimes done for the years 1846–8, prior to the start of the constabulary returns in 1849.[87] Marcus Keane offered a hypothetical example in 1850 in which he said that, using a superior court ejectment, he might evict ten tenants from lands once in the hands of thirty, and then rearrange the holdings among the remaining twenty. In this case what would appear in the records as thirty tenants ejected should really have been only ten.[88]

Unroofing and Levelling Houses

The wholesale demolition of houses was obviously a special preoccupation of the evicting landlords and perhaps the supreme defining feature of the Kilrush clearances. Marcus Keane, who might be called the greatest of the house levellers, was not bashful about explaining why he and others pursued the practice with such enthusiasm. Partly, it was a device to obviate an immediate

The mass evictions in the poor law union of Kilrush in County Clare were probably unprecedented in their scale and intensity. Belatedly, they were brought to the notice of the British reading public. Just as Skibbereen became horribly familiar through a series of never-to-be-forgotten sketches early in 1847 in the *Illustrated London News*, so too the Kilrush region commanded similar attention in 1849–50 when the same periodical published numerous haunting images relating to the clearances and their lethal effects there. A careful investigation disclosed in mid-1850 that since November 1847 alone, over 14,000 persons (from 2,700 families) had been evicted from their holdings in Kilrush union. Whole villages were cleared, including that of Moveen, depicted in this illustration. (*Illustrated London News*)

risk and its serious financial ramifications. If cabins were not levelled, he told Scrope's committee in June 1850, 'you would have the family return again in six hours after they were put out'. And if they did return, 'you would be obliged to resort to a new ejectment, and in the most expensive court, for you must go into the superior court to prove title in order to expel a pauper who returns and locates himself upon the property'. Such a suit, he claimed, might cost as much as 150 guineas, and he grimly recalled that the large Clare landowner Colonel George Wyndham had been put to the outrageous expense of £200 'to get that pauper out of a shed in which he had located himself'.[89] But there were other important considerations behind the mania for levelling, tumbling, and knocking down houses. The bigger, solvent tenants – of the kind associated with the much-desired restructuring of the whole agrarian order in Clare and elsewhere in Ireland – were constantly subject to the depredations of the acutely distressed and starving people around them. As Captain Kennedy told the poor law commissioners in February 1848, 'The farmers complain loudly of the universal pilfering and theft by widows and their children, of which class there is an immense proportion along the coast. A haggard [stack-yard] or garden cannot be left without a night guard.'[90] The attitudes of the bigger farmers and their perceived needs heavily influenced the way in which land agents like Marcus Keane approached the conduct of clearances. He made the farmers' viewpoint his own. 'Every respectable farmer in the country', he declared in June 1850, 'is obliged to keep watch over his effects at night; that is the case throughout the whole of the county Clare.'[91] Unless such farmers were protected from these constant depredations, they would abandon their lands and leave the country. To guard against that calamity, the houses of a great many paupers simply had to be levelled. Though he claimed to have avoided knocking down houses wherever he could, 'there are districts where, if the houses were not levelled, the produce of the whole farm would go to the paupers. When people become poor, they very often become dishonest, to supply the very calls of nature; and when they are scattered about upon the townlands, they have more opportunities of exercising their propensities.'[92] Keane asserted that he worked in accordance with certain rules or principles in deciding whether or not to level paupers' houses. If the continued presence of the paupers would have prevented the land from being 'occupied by anyone else . . . , as a matter of course, I removed the paupers [and their houses]; but where I thought the presence of the poorer people would not prevent the profitable use of the land by others, or prevent others from taking it, I left them in their houses'.[93] To judge from the total of some 500 houses reportedly levelled on estates which he managed, as against fewer than eighty evicted tenants restored as caretakers, Keane's application of these rules can only be described as draconian.

Those evicted tenants who did not seek or gain the shelter of the workhouse lived precariously. Many reportedly crowded into inhabited dwellings on the same property from which they had been dispossessed. But landlords and agents usually took stern measures to discourage the provision of long-term shelter by occupying tenants. Marcus Keane was said to have given orders that any occupier on the Marquis Conyngham's estate who gave shelter to an evicted tenant and his family should at once be distrained for the 'hanging gale', that is, the half-year's rent that was commonly allowed to stand in arrears. Moreover, Captain Kennedy asserted that it was 'usual throughout the union [of Kilrush] to do that'.[94] And it is highly probable that in this regard Colonel Vandeleur's attitudes and conduct were also typical of Kilrush landlords and agents. In a printed notice sent in April 1850 to the ratepayers of Kilrush electoral division, Vandeleur warned 'all persons holding small tenements under me' to harbour no vagrants or pauper families in their houses under pain of the penalties specified in their agreements. He observed in the notice that every pauper allowed to settle in Kilrush electoral division might add £4 a year 'to your rates'.[95]

Chased in this way from their old estates, perhaps most evicted tenants erected makeshift accommodation for themselves and their families by the roadside, in the bogs, or on pieces of waste ground where they hoped to be left unmolested – a vain hope in numerous instances. Scrope summarised the position well in the draft report of his select committee. Evicted families, he observed, 'perhaps linger about the spot and frame some temporary shelter out of the materials of their old homes against a broken wall, or behind a ditch or fence, or in a boghole (scalps as they are called), places totally unfit for human habitations . . . '.[96] Against severe cold or heavy rains scalps and similar ramshackle dwellings obviously provided little protection, and such inclement weather, often combined with disease and the denial of outdoor relief, would eventually drive the dispossessed (if they had not died first) to the workhouse as a last resort, in spite of their detestation of the place.[97] But squatters in such temporary dwellings might also simply become the targets of a new round of burnings, tumblings, or levellings engineered by remorseless landlords or agents. Under all these circumstances eviction in Kilrush union was very often a death-dealing instrument. Captain Kennedy gave the only truthful answer when he was asked in July 1850 if house levellings had been 'greatly destructive to life' during the past three winters. His firm answer: 'It greatly induced disease and death. I think that cannot be doubted.'[98]

But dedicated evictors like Marcus Keane and Colonel Vandeleur could not bring themselves to see or speak the truth. Vandeleur was asked in July 1850, 'Was there much sickness and mortality amongst the class of persons who were ejected?' Deflecting responsibility, he responded: 'Not that I am aware of.'[99] Questioned as to the fate of evicted tenants, Vandeleur gave a less than truthful reply to Scrope's committee. 'They have', he averred, 'generally obtained relief from the board of guardians.'[100] Marcus Keane also shielded himself from the excruciating reality. When pressed by Scrope to say what became of evicted tenants, he answered: 'I do not know of any great change having taken place in them since their eviction.' Destitute before being ousted, they were destitute still, he declared.[101] What presumably made it much easier for Keane and Vandeleur to hold such views about the almost 'benign' human consequences of mass evictions was their deep conviction that the clearances were absolutely essential to both the economic improvement of the country and their own financial well-being. 'It would have been utterly impossible', insisted Vandeleur in July 1850, 'that the country could have progressed, or that improvements could have been carried out, or that either rates or rent could have been paid in the union if ejectments had not taken place.'[102] Keane put this economistic doctrine even more succinctly: 'In fact, I think the evictions, and driving paupers off [the] land, were absolutely necessary to the welfare of the country.'[103] This was exactly the kind of justification, self-evident to its exponents, that allowed most of the depopulators of Ireland to conceal from themselves the enormity of their crimes.

The eviction mania so evident in Kilrush union from 1847 to 1850 was prevalent throughout most of Clare during and immediately after the famine, even if not on quite the same scale. A greater number of permanent evictions occurred in Clare in the period 1849–54, relative to the size of its population in 1851, than in any other county in Ireland. For that period as a whole its eviction rate was 97.1 persons per thousand. Altogether, nearly 21,000 people were permanently dispossessed in Clare from 1849 to 1854, according to the constabulary returns. Thus a county that comprised only 3.2 per cent of the population of Ireland in 1851 experienced 8.3 per cent of the total number of officially recorded evictions between 1849 and 1854. The eviction rate for Clare was even much higher than that for nearly all the other western counties. The corresponding rates for Kerry and Galway were 58.4 and 65.3 per thousand respectively, although for west Galway alone the rate of dispossession was much closer to that for Clare.[104]

CLEARANCES IN MAYO

Only in Mayo were evictions almost as numerous, relative to population, as those in Clare. From 1849 to 1854 over 26,000 Mayo tenants were permanently dispossessed, a figure which represented a rate of 94.8 persons per thousand of the 1851 population. With only 4.2 per cent of the inhabitants of the country, Mayo was the scene of no less than 10.5 per cent of all evictions in Ireland during the years 1849–54. But the temporal pattern of the clearances in Mayo was strikingly different from that in Clare, the rest of Connacht, or indeed the rest of Ireland. Whereas the total number of evictions in Ireland declined sharply after 1850, the toll in Mayo remained remarkably high during the early 1850s. Permanent dispossessions were more numerous there throughout the years 1851–3 than in 1849 and dropped below the level of 1849 only in 1854.[105] Part of the reason for this difference between Mayo and the rest of Ireland, it has been argued, is that Mayo landlords had less cause to engage in clearances before 1850 because a much higher proportion of the tenants there, 75 per cent of whom occupied holdings valued at £4 or less, surrendered their tiny plots to the landlords in order to qualify themselves for poor law assistance.[106] In addition, Mayo provided a much higher than average share of

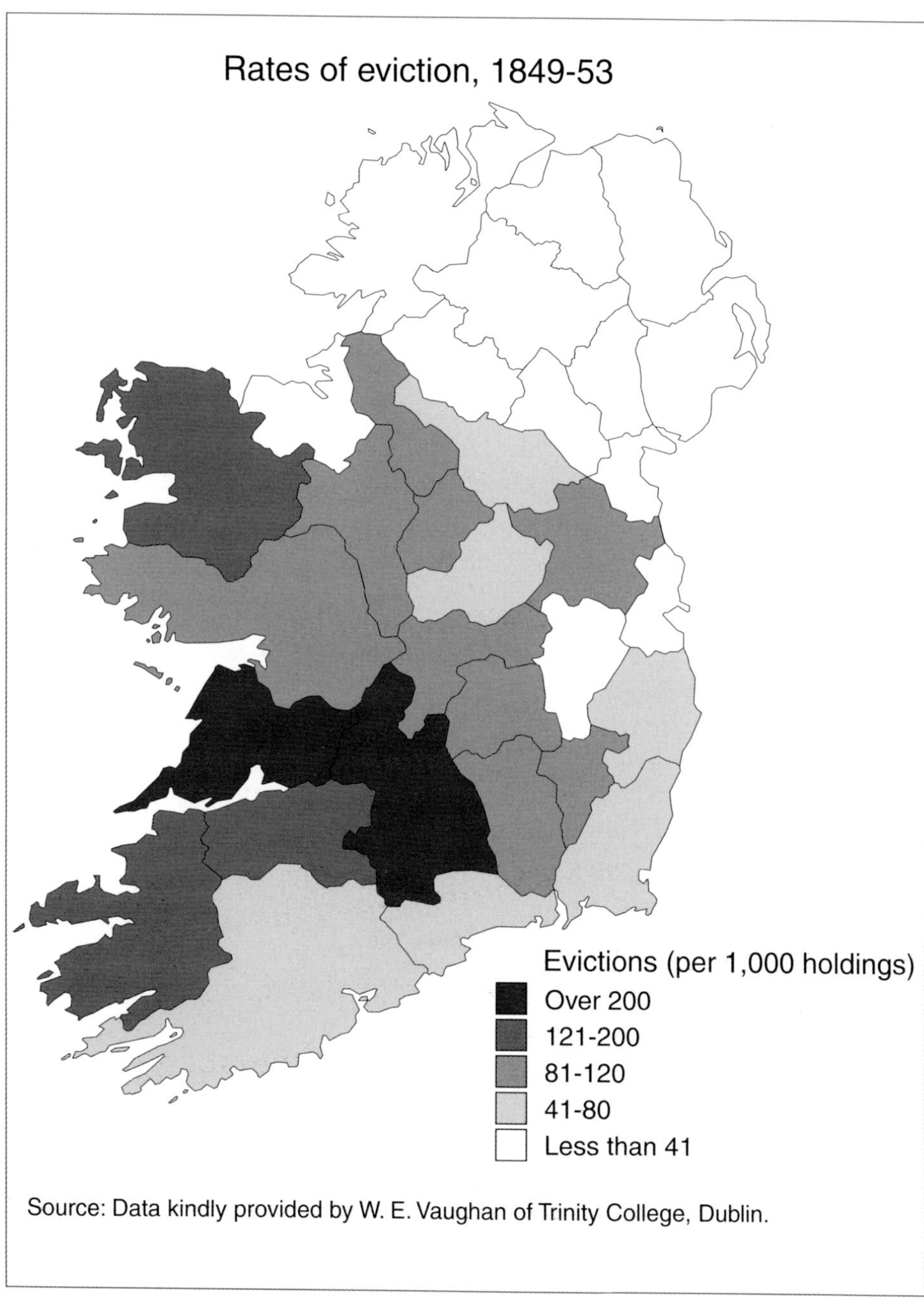

Having long wanted to reduce the 'overpopulation' of their estates, many landlords and agents were given strong motives and large opportunities to do so by the great famine. The result was the 'clearances' of the late 1840s and early 1850s. Evictions could be either formal and legal or informal and without the strong arm of the law. About 250,000 persons were formally and permanently evicted from their holdings between 1849 and 1854, but this number may represent only half of all those dispossessed formally and informally from 1846 to 1854. As this map shows, the clearances were highly skewed geographically. Counties in the south-west, the far west, and the middle of the country (as far south as Tipperary) recorded the heaviest toll, whereas mass eviction was almost unknown in the northern counties. (Joan Murphy Donnelly)

insolvent proprietors to the Incumbered Estates Court, and there is an abundance of evidence that the new purchasers of these properties actively engaged in extensive evictions during the early 1850s.[107]

But even by long-established proprietors, and before 1850, there were some enormous clearances in Mayo, with entire villages of smallholders being erased from the map. Among the greatest of these depopulating landlords was the earl of Lucan, who owned over 60,000 acres. Having once said that he 'would not breed paupers to pay priests', Lord Lucan was as good as his word. In the parish of Ballinrobe, most of which was highly suitable for grazing sheep and cattle, he demolished over 300 cabins and evicted some 2,000 people between 1846 and 1849. Some of those dispossessed here may have been included among the almost 430 families (perhaps 2,200 persons) who, as Lucan's surviving but incomplete rent ledgers show, were 'removed' between 1848 and 1851. In this campaign whole townlands were cleared of their occupiers. The depopulated holdings, after being consolidated, were sometimes retained and stocked by Lord Lucan himself as grazing farms, and in other cases were leased as ranches to wealthy graziers.[108]

Also belonging to the 'old stock' of Mayo proprietors who cleared away many tenants was the marquis of Sligo. His policy, he claimed in 1852, was rigorously selective. Though 'large evictions were carried out', only 'the really idle and dishonest' were dispossessed, while 'honest' tenants were 'freed from all [arrears] and given [land] at a new, fairly valued rent'. Once he had finished implementing this policy, he thought that perhaps one-quarter of his tenants would be forced to leave. Despite his earlier assertion that his was a case of 'eject or be ejected', Lord Sligo had a troubled conscience about his evictions. He despised more indulgent landowners, such as Sir Samuel O'Malley and his own cousin G.H. Moore. He professed to be convinced that by refusing to evict for non-payment of rent, they were pursuing a course that would ultimately make necessary clearances far greater in scope than his own. To prove his point, he cited the fact that the indulgent O'Malley was eventually forced to evict on a large scale: on O'Malley's property in the parish of Kilmeena near Westport 'the houses are being levelled till at least half [the tenants] are evicted and legally removed'. He severely upbraided Moore, saying that he would become 'a second Sir Samuel'. In concluding his shrill, self-exculpatory letter to Moore, Lord Sligo declared, 'In my heart's belief you and Sir Samuel do more [to] ruin and injure and persecute and exterminate your tenants than any [other] man in Mayo.'[109]

But while the old stock of Mayo proprietors did a fair share of the 'extermination' for which landlords were assailed in the national and local press, they received a strong helping hand in the early 1850s from the numerous new purchasers under the incumbered estates act. Quite a few of the new owners had in fact invested their money in the west of Ireland on the explicit understanding that the property which they were buying had already been or was in the process of being cleared of superfluous tenants. As the prospectus for the sale of the Martin estate in the Ballinahinch district of Galway delicately put the matter,

> The number of tenants on each townland and the amount of their rents have been taken from a survey and ascertained rental in the year 1847; but it is believed many changes advantageous to a purchaser have since taken place, and that the same tenants by name and in number will not be found on the land.[110]

When new owners discovered that the contrary was true, they secured special court injunctions for the removal of such tenants, or they simply proceeded to oust the unwanted occupiers themselves, sometimes avoiding formal evictions by persuading the tenants to accept small sums as inducements to depart. Among the numerous new Mayo purchasers who behaved in one or another of these ways were Edward Baxter at Knockalassa near Cong, Captain Harvey de Montmorency at Cloongowla near Ballinrobe, Joseph Blake on the Abbey Knockmoy estate, and Lord Erne at Barna near Ballinrobe. Similar scenes – the succession of new landlords followed by the eviction of the old tenants and the consolidation of their holdings into much larger units – were occurring during the early 1850s in west Galway and parts of adjacent counties, where among the clearance-minded new owners were John Gerrard at Kilcoosh near Mount Bellew, Francis Twinings at Cleggan near Clifden, and James Thorngate on the Castlefrench estate.[111] 'In the revolution of property changes', observed the *Roscommon Journal* in July 1854, 'the new purchaser accelerates the departure of the aborigines of the country, by which he seems to imagine he has not only rid himself of their burden but enhanced the value of his property.'[112]

These clearances in Mayo and west Galway set the stage for a considerable expansion of the grazing or ranch system there during the 1850s. Both the old proprietors who escaped the Incumbered Estates Court and the new owners avidly promoted the grazing system. Many of them retained at least part of the depopulated holdings in their own hands and, like Lord Lucan, stocked the land with cattle and sheep. But they also leased recently cleared tracts to new settlers, a substantial number of whom were of Scottish or English origin and set themselves up as graziers on a large scale. The land agent Thomas Miller estimated in 1858 that as many as 800 English and Scottish farmers had secured leases of large holdings in Mayo and Galway, which were almost exclusively devoted to the raising of livestock. Miller indicated that there were particularly heavy concentrations of new settlers in the districts of Hollymount, Newport, and Westport in Mayo as well as around Ballinasloe and Tuam in Galway.[113] In a few cases the new settlers were the victims of agrarian violence, but the vast majority escaped any immediate retribution, as did the proprietors who facilitated their entry into the western countryside. Yet the local resentment against these intruders from England and Scotland remained strong for decades and would eventually erupt into violence during the various phases of the land war in the late nineteenth and early twentieth centuries. Like the clearances themselves, their beneficiaries were remembered with a poisonous, ineradicable hatred.

The extreme destitution of the west became a much-discussed political topic in Britain early in 1849, when there were calls for a 'new plantation of Connaught', championed especially by the Conservative leader Peel. Radical structural change under government auspices, with new landlords and tenant farmers from England and Scotland introducing large-scale capitalist agriculture on the British model, was seen by some as the only, or the best, permanent answer. Not everyone agreed, as suggested by this *Punch* cartoon of 17 March 1849 entitled 'The new St. Patrick; or, Sir Robert [Peel] turning the reptiles out of Ireland', which ridiculed the notion of a 'new plantation'. Whigs objected not to the desired outcome but rather to the implied costs and scale of such government-led social engineering. (*Punch* Archive)

Consolidation of Holdings

Through the great clearances of the late 1840s and early 1850s, as well as through mass emigration and mass death, Irish landowners were able to achieve their long-desired objective of the consolidation of holdings on a large scale. The painstaking work of P.M.A. Bourke convincingly demonstrated that the statistics on farm size appearing in the 1841 census cannot be used to gauge the degree of consolidation that took place between 1841 and 1851. The two most serious flaws of those statistics for comparative purposes are that in 1841 farm size was overwhelmingly expressed in terms of the larger, Irish acre (the equivalent of 1.62 statute acres), and that in the computation of farm size waste land was excluded in 1841. 'Together', declared Bourke, 'the two factors led to *a reduction of about one-half* in the apparent farm size', in contrast to the real picture that would have emerged if, as in 1847 and later, the statute acre had been taken as the invariable unit of measurement and waste land had been included along with pasture and arable.[114] Though it is possible to reconstruct the 1841 figures by applying some rough corrections to those data, Bourke found it preferable to use in a modified form the returns on farm size compiled in 1844 or 1845 by the poor law commissioners. These returns are not fully comparable in all respects with the figures which appear in the annual series of agricultural statistics beginning in 1847, but the discrepancies are relatively minor. The results of Bourke's reworking of the poor law returns, together with the official statistics for 1847 and 1851, are presented in Table 5.[115]

The discarding of the 1841 census data on farm size results in making the change effected by the events of the famine 'less sensational' but nevertheless quite striking. The number of holdings in the two smallest categories of size declined between 1845 and 1851 by almost three-quarters and by slightly over one-half respectively, and even holdings of 5 to 15 acres fell in number by nearly two-fifths. Farms above 15 acres increased modestly in number between 1845 and 1851, and rather dramatically in proportional terms – from less than a third of all holdings in 1845 to almost a half by 1851. There was never again so sudden and drastic a change in the structure of landholding in Ireland as that

Table 5
Changes in the distribution of holdings by size in Ireland, 1845–51

Year	1 acre or less		1–5 acres		5–15 acres		Over 15 acres	
	(no.)	(%)	(no.)	(%)	(no.)	(%)	(no.)	(%)
1845	135,314	14.9	181,950	20.1	311,133	34.4	276,618	30.6
1847	73,016	9.1	139,041	17.3	269,534	33.6	321,434	40.0
1851	37,728	6.2	88,083	14.5	191,854	31.5	290,404	47.8
% change, 1845–51		–72.1		–51.6		–38.3		+5.0

which occurred during and immediately after the famine. Though consolidation continued in the post-famine generations, it was usually a very gradual and piecemeal process. Furthermore, for the 50 per cent of Irish tenants whose holdings did not exceed 15 acres, there were severe limits to the gains that could be conferred even by a long period of agricultural prosperity like that of 1853–76, and such tenants of course remained highly vulnerable to the effects of economic downturns on their precarious condition.

INDEBTED LANDLORDS AND THE LAND MARKET

In undertaking clearances of pauper tenants, landlords proved to be pitiless creditors, but they too had creditors who became equally remorseless in pressing their claims during the famine. A lavish style of living assumed before 1815 and not easily supportable under the conditions of depressed markets and lagging rents in peacetime, together with defective laws which permitted the accumulation of debts far beyond the value of the security, meant that even before the famine a substantial section of the Irish landed élite was in a precarious financial condition. In fact, a significant number of heavily indebted landowners were past rescue. In 1844 receivers appointed by the Court of Chancery were administering as many as 874 Irish estates with a combined annual rental of almost £750,000.[116] The owners of some of these properties were simply minors or mentally incompetent, but most of them were bankrupts. Under different circumstances these insolvent proprietors might have satisfied their creditors by selling all or part of their estates. But because of further defects in the law, especially the great difficulty and cost of tracing the incumbrances in separate registers in different courts and in the Registry Office of Deeds, prospective purchasers were extremely wary of buying Irish property. Many estates of bankrupts continued under chancery administration for years (some for decades), and thus the backlog of insolvent landowners was very slow to be cleared. From such proprietors tenants obviously received little or no assistance during the famine.

The great famine had the short-term effect of exacerbating the extreme sluggishness of the land market. On the one hand, it added substantially to the number of bankrupt and acutely embarrassed proprietors. Lost rents, heavy poor rates, and (in some cases) significant expenditures for employment erased what was for many a narrow margin of safety between income and outgoings even before 1845. Foreclosure notices and execution warrants soon began to rain down upon the heads of landowners unable to discharge the claims of mortgagees, bond holders, annuitants, and other creditors. As early as December 1846 one newspaper reported that 'within the last two months twelve hundred notices have been lodged in the Four Courts to foreclose mortgages on Irish estates'.[117] Certain proprietors known to be embarrassed were hounded from pillar to post. Against Earl Mountcashell 'execution upon execution was issued . . . until in December 1849 there were in the sheriff's hands executions to the

Whereas

I, JAMES HUNT,

of Danesfort, in the County of Cork, Esquire, by virtue of a Conveyance from the Commissioners for the Sale of Incumbered Estates in Ireland, duly executed on the 16th day of August, 1851, am now the Owner in Fee of the Lands of DYSURE and LISNACUDDY, situate in the Barony of West Muskerry and County of Cork, and entitled to the Rents and Profits thereof:

NOW TAKE NOTICE,

That I require you, and each of you, from henceforward to pay to me all Rents to grow due, and payable by you and each of you out of your respective holdings in said Lands.

Dated this 6th day of September, 1851.

To the several and respective occupying Tenants of the said Lands of Dysure and Lisnacuddy, and all others concerned.

James Hunt
Danesfort,
Mallow.

R. Lindsey, Printer, Main-street, Mallow.

The famine deflated Irish land values, and the passage of the incumbered estates act in 1849 made the decline even steeper, creating an unprecedented buyers' market. Like most new buyers, James Hunt already belonged to the Irish landed gentry. By paying only 11 years' purchase (i.e., 11 times the annual rental), he got a great bargain when he bought these 530 acres in the Mallow district of Cork. He issued this notice in September 1851 so that his new tenants would be in no doubt about where to pay their rents. The avalanche of land sales in the early 1850s was concentrated in the west and the south, generally matching the incidence of distress, but sales were relatively rare in Kerry, Clare, and Leitrim, all of which acutely felt the impact of the famine. (Author's collection) amount of £15,000', and others in 1850 soon brought the total to about £20,000.[118] The earl derived some temporary relief from the fact that his son Lord Kilworth was then the high sheriff of County Cork, and the agent of his estates there was the sub-sheriff, but other landowners in similar straits were not even that lucky.

On the other hand, the famine and the agricultural depression of 1849–52 had the result of greatly lowering the value of Irish land. According to one reliable report, the average rate of sale had fallen from 25 years' purchase of the annual rental before 1845 to only 15 years' purchase by the spring of 1849.[119] Even though financially embarrassed proprietors needed to sell at least some property to stay afloat, they were generally unwilling to let it go at so great a sacrifice, and therefore they themselves were not about to initiate such ruinous transactions. Even creditors might not wish to force sales in cases where there was reason to fear that the proceeds would not be sufficient to discharge their claims in full because of a low sale price. Yet unless prices were low, and unless secure titles could be obtained, it was difficult to imagine that purchasers would be forthcoming, since the immediate prospects for reasonable returns on their investments were anything but attractive.

The Incumbered Estates Court

After an abortive effort to resolve the problem in 1848 by using the cumbersome machinery of the Court of Chancery, the Whig government finally broke the impasse in July 1849 by carrying into law the incumbered estates act, which established a new tribunal with drastic powers.[120] The three commissioners or judges of the court received authority to order sales upon the application of a single incumbrancer as long as the annual charges and interest payments exceeded half the net yearly income of the land or leasehold. The creditors' interests were taken into account in the provision that allowed all incumbrancers to bid for the property or lease to be sold, with the single exception of the incumbrancer upon whose application the sale had been ordered, and even he could become the purchaser with the consent of the commissioners. The judges were also authorised to arrange exchanges and divisions, even of lands not subject to be sold under the act, if such steps would facilitate the sale of the incumbered property. And they were empowered to sell lands included in different applications in the same sale. Finally, the court received the authority to grant to purchasers of property sold under its aegis an indefeasible parliamentary title, secure against the claims of all previous creditors. The passage of the act signalled that the long-standing log-jam in the land market was about to be broken, and the release of so much property to the auction block at once could only drive land values still lower. Even proprietors who had no reason to expect forced sales themselves were disheartened. 'I am deeply affected by this most heavy stroke', moaned Sir John Benn-Walsh in August 1849, 'by which my Irish property is rendered as valueless as a Jamaica estate.'[121]

The early operations of the court confirmed the worst fears of heavily indebted proprietors. In one of the largest sales some 62,000 acres in Cork and Antrim belonging to Lord Mountcashell, with a combined yearly rental of £18,500, were bought for £240,000, or 13 years' purchase. During the proceedings a distraught Mountcashell 'was heard to exclaim that it was bad enough to have his estates confiscated, but to be sold up by a dwarf in a garret was more than he could endure!' – a reference to Commissioner Charles Hargreave, a very short man whose office was located in the bedroom storey of a house in Henrietta Street in Dublin.[122] An even greater loser was Viscount Gort, whose case aroused widespread popular sympathy because he had opposed clearances and had reputedly evicted no one from his property around Lough Cutra in south Galway. Moreover, though his unsettled estates were charged with debts of about £60,000, they had been valued at £150,000 as recently as 1842. When a mortgagee who had not received his due during the famine forced the sale of these estates in the court, the various purchasers acquired great bargains. Thirteen years' purchase was apparently 'the highest [price] given at this sale' and 'many lots were sold at five'.[123] Lord Gort was even forced to part with his mansion, Lough Cutra Castle, which was also sold for much less than its value.

The many victims of this drastic process of course protested bitterly, but the commissioners stoutly defended the prevailing prices. In May 1851 they asserted that to calculate the rates of purchase from the printed rentals was a 'fallacious' exercise for several reasons: first, because the rents specified there were often excessive even before 1846; second, because arrears amounting to several years' rent were usually owed to the previous owners; and third, because the generally dilapidated condition of the property 'would necessarily require a heavy outlay by the incoming purchaser'.[124] Their case, however, is not very persuasive, nor was it then. The cheapness of most of the property sold before 1854 was repeatedly demonstrated by the far higher rates of purchase given for the same lands when they were resold through the court only a few years later. In fact, there was considerable speculation in the underpriced estates of bankrupt landowners during the early 1850s. The London *Morning Herald* reported in November 1853 that two English land companies were pooling small capitals to buy Irish property with the intention of selling it again at a substantial profit.[125] Solvent Irish proprietors were hardly above playing the same game of speculation, and the rewards could be handsome. The west Cork landowner John Becher was said to have bought a portion of the Holybrook estate in 1853 for £1,950 and to have resold it six years later for £4,050.[126] The Castle Hyde estate, purchased in December 1851 for £14,425 by Vincent Scully (MP for County Cork, 1852–7, 1859–65), was sold again in court in 1860 for nearly £45,000.[127] The superior of the Sisters of Mercy had paid £17,000 for Lord Gort's castle on Lough Cutra, intending to convert it into a noviciate for her order, but this plan was dropped and the castle was soon resold at a tidy profit of £7,000 above the original purchase price.[128]

Prices were at their lowest (generally from 10 to 15 years' purchase) during the early 1850s, when in fact the bulk of the most heavily incumbered estates were sold. Of the almost 4,300 petitions for sale presented to the court between January 1850 and March 1858, over three-quarters were lodged before 1855.[129] By the late 1850s Irish land had not only recovered but had probably surpassed the levels of the late 1830s and early 1840s. By that time a large portion of the petitions for sale were actually being lodged by necessitous landowners themselves rather than by their creditors. Only 6 of the first 100 petitions to the court in 1849 had come from the owners, but as many as 53 out of the last 100 before September 1857 emanated from them.[130] There was little reason to hang back now that the land market was so buoyant. When the marquis of Thomond sold almost all of his property in Clare and Cork in 1857, the 48,000 acres involved, with a combined yearly rental of about £13,500, realised nearly £360,000, representing a rate of over 26 years' purchase. His 39,000-acre Clare estate alone, situated in the Ennis district, reaped more than 32 years' purchase. The buyers of his property were almost exclusively Irish; in the case of his Clare estate they were all said to be 'connected with that county and resident in it'.[131]

This was not what the Whig ministers who framed the incumbered estates act had anticipated. They had fervently hoped that wealthy English capitalists would invest their money in Irish property in large numbers and begin to manage their new possessions on the most advanced English lines. To some educated Britons, it seemed that no part of Ireland stood in greater need of British investment or was more likely to receive it than the impoverished west. 'In a few years more', *The Times* of London had declared hopefully at the start of this experiment, 'a Celtic Irishman will be as rare in Connemara as is the Red Indian on the shores of Manhattan.'[132] In fact, however, although most of Connemara did fall into the hands of the English Law Life Assurance Society, British capitalists formed only a small proportion of the purchasers throughout Ireland. Out of a total of 7,489 buyers up to the end of August 1857, just 309, or 4 per cent, were of English, Scottish, or foreign background; all the rest were Irish. Admittedly, the non-Irish purchasers often bought large estates, but of the gross proceeds of all sales conducted between October 1849 and August 1857 (about £20.5 million was realised), they provided only £2.8 million, or less than 14 per cent.[133]

A.M. Sullivan, editor of the *Nation* from 1855 to 1876, is mainly responsible for the legend that the overwhelmingly Irish purchasers were drawn predominantly from a commercial background. In his popular work *New Ireland*, first published in 1877, Sullivan claimed that the new owners were 'chiefly mercantile men who have saved money in trade and invest it for a safe percentage. They import what the country people depreciatingly call "the ledger and day-book principle" into the management of their purchases, which contrasts unfavourably in their minds with the more elastic system of the old owners.'[134] The appearance of a significant number of individuals, though not even close to a majority, from outside the ranks of the traditional landowning

GOG AND MAGOG GIVING PADDY A LIFT OUT OF THE MIRE.

"A Special Court of Common Council was held on Thursday to consider the propriety of purchasing estates in Ireland, with a view to cultivate and improve the same. * * * That London can and will do this work, her own history affords the most abundant guarantees."

British economic success encouraged many in Britain around mid-century to believe that its businessmen could fix Irish agrarian problems in a hurry. This *Punch* cartoon of July 1849 – 'Gog and Magog giving Paddy a lift out of the mire' – was inspired by a meeting of the London Common Council concerned with the question of buying and improving the estates of insolvent Irish landowners. The theory was that rich Londoners and other wealthy Britons would boost the depressed Irish economy by investing some of their abundant capital in cheap Irish land. Talk raced far ahead of action: the eventual British investment was small. (*Punch* Archive) class naturally attracted contemporary attention, and the fact that some of them aroused intense popular hostility by raising rents, pressing for arrears, or carrying out evictions gave rise to a prevalent view that the new owners in general were a breed different from and worse than the old masters of the soil whom they replaced. But a systematic analysis of the social backgrounds of the purchasers under the incumbered estates act in County Cork indicates that most of the new owners there came from the established landed and professional élites, with the sons of the gentry and nobility as well as landed gentlemen and aristocrats themselves constituting the most numerous group of buyers.[135]

Moreover, for every indulgent Lord Gort or Lord Kingston who crashed in the Incumbered Estates Court, there was a Lord Lucan or a Lord Sligo who was anything but lax or elastic. The new owners in Mayo and Galway may have intensified the clearances there during the early 1850s, but whether the eviction rate in those counties would have been substantially lower without their coming is doubtful. Given what the old landlords were doing in Clare before 1850, tenants in that county would presumably have applauded a thoroughgoing change. There is, in short, no need to invent an invasion of the ranks of landowners by commercial men after 1850 to account for the tighter administration of Irish estates. What Sullivan termed 'the ledger and day-book principle' (this was not a country expression) was as evident among the continuing owners as among the new purchasers. The transformation of estate management and of landholding among tenants was the product of historical forces larger than mere changes of personnel.

CHAPTER 7

Excess Mortality and Emigration

L.M. Cullen has argued that the great famine 'was less a national disaster than a social and regional one'.[1] This provocative statement has the merit of drawing attention to the wide social and regional variations in the incidence of famine-related destitution, mortality, and emigration. But to hold that the famine had the character of a national calamity is a defensible position, especially if one considers the combined effects of both excess deaths and emigration on the population levels of individual counties. Only six of the thirty-two counties lost less than 15 per cent of their population between 1841 and 1851. In another six counties the population in 1851 was from 15 to 20 per cent lower than it had been a decade earlier. Of the remaining twenty counties, nine lost from 20 to 25 per cent of their population, while eleven lost over 25 per cent between 1841 and 1851.[2]

Since the intensity of excess mortality and levels of emigration often differed in individual counties, it will be best to consider these two matters separately. With respect to mortality, both the overall magnitude and the regional variations are now known with some statistical precision. The geographer S.H. Cousens did the pioneering work on this subject. Cousens based his calculations mainly on the deaths that were either recorded on census forms in 1851 or reported by institutions, though he had of course to derive estimates of 'normal' death rates before and during the famine. His calculations for each of the thirty-two counties yielded a country-wide total of excess mortality amounting to 800,645 persons for the years 1846–50. Cousens also suggested that the inclusion of the excess deaths that occurred in the first quarter of 1851 (census night was 31 March) would raise the total to approximately 860,000.[3] For more than two decades historians were content to regard Cousens's estimates as generally reliable.

More recently, however, Cousens's dependence on the 1851 census data has been sharply and effectively criticised by the economic historian Joel Mokyr. His chief objection is to the serious undercounting of deaths in the census, a deficiency arising from the fact that when whole families were obliterated by mortality or emigration, there was no one to report the deaths in such families to the census takers. Cousens was in fact aware of this problem, but his attempt to offset it must now be regarded as insufficient. Adopting a different approach, Mokyr calculates excess death rates as a residual for each county (and for the

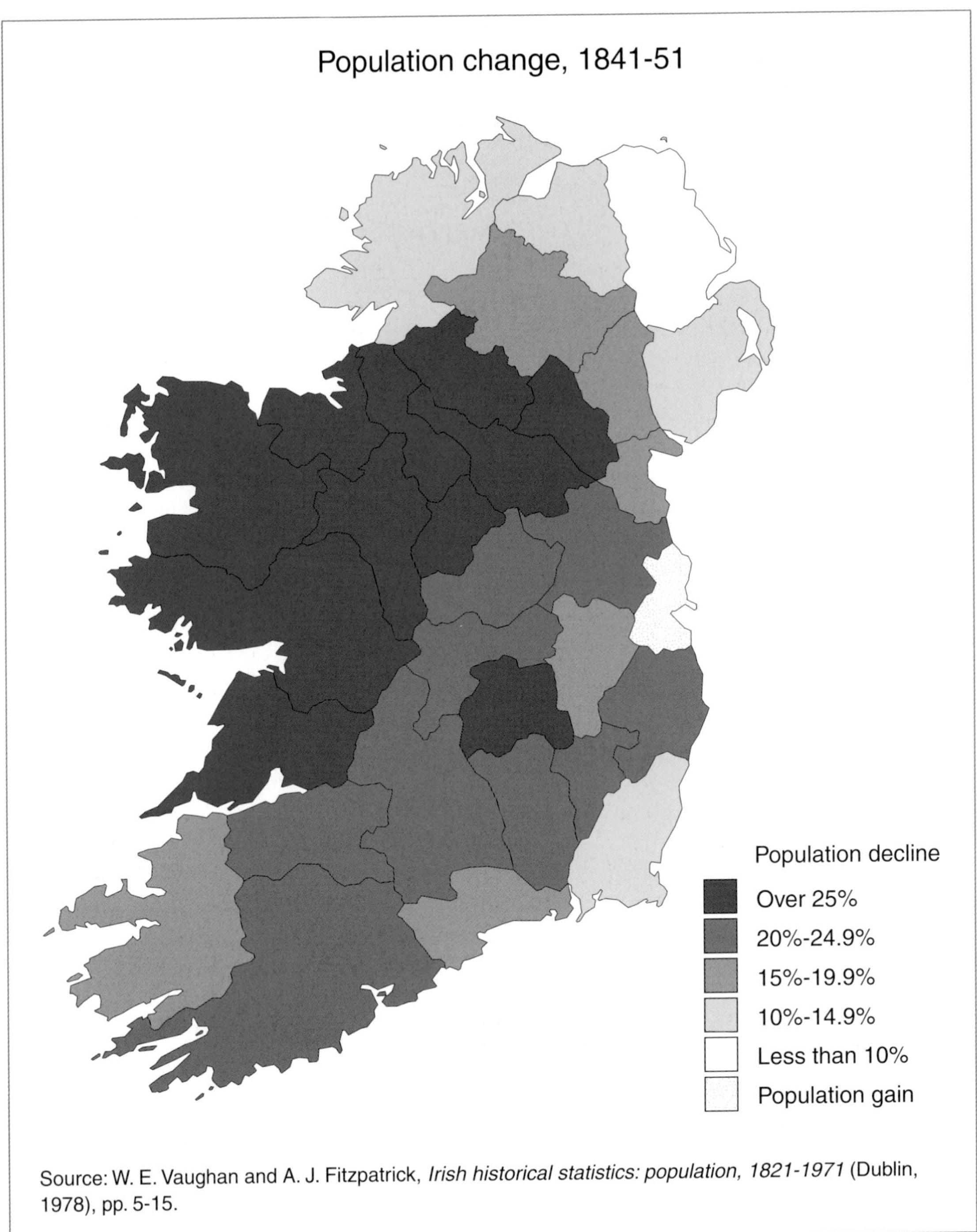

Mass death and mass emigration during the famine reduced the total population of Ireland from almost 8.2 million in 1841 to fewer than 6.6 million in 1851. There were marked regional variations in the severity of both excess mortality and emigration, but their combined effect, when viewed nationally, produced extremely widespread population losses, as this map demonstrates. The famine initiated a long period of demographic contraction. By the end of the century the Irish population had fallen below 4.5 million. (Joan Murphy Donnelly)

country as a whole) by comparing the estimated population of 1846 with the officially reported population of 1851 after first accounting for births, emigration, and internal migration. As he frankly admits, the results of these elaborate calculations are not free from ambiguities and possible sources of error. The chief uncertainty is how steeply the birth rate fell during the famine years and whether or not to count averted births as a part of the excess mortality. This problem is sensibly resolved by the presentation of lower-bound and upper-bound estimates of excess deaths between 1846 and 1851. (Actually, Mokyr offers two slightly different versions of these sets of estimates and the discussion here relates to the second version in which the national totals are insignificantly higher.) According to these figures, overall excess mortality in the years 1846–51 amounted to 1,082,000 persons if averted births are not counted, and to 1,498,000 if they are. To count averted births among the casualties of the great famine is a thoroughly defensible procedure, though some might not wish to go so far.[4]

Epidemics of Disease

Of the more than one million who died, by far the greater number perished from disease rather than from sheer starvation. This was not so much because starvation was not rampant as because one or another of the many famine-related diseases killed them before prolonged nutrition deficiency did. In the absence of sufficient replacement foods, starvation on a massive scale became inevitable when the loss of the potato deprived the people of Ireland of the prolific root which before 1845 had provided an estimated 60 per cent of the national food supply.[5] Even though food imports belatedly swelled beginning in the spring and summer of 1847, there remained a significant gap between food needs and available resources throughout the famine years, and besides the overall gap there were serious problems in ensuring that the food in the country reached those deprived of it. Recent research by Peter Solar has highlighted both the enormous food shortfall created by repeated epidemics of potato blight and the relative narrowness of the overall gap owing mostly to the major contribution to supply made eventually by food imports. According to Solar's elaborate and painstaking calculations, total food consumption in the years 1846–50 was only about 12 per cent less than in the period 1840–5.[6] This fact only reinforces the points made earlier about the catastrophically uneven distribution of the overall supply and the far greater importance of epidemic disease in producing unprecedented mass mortality.

The initially enormous food gap in the autumn of 1846 and the following winter (when the government refused to stop grain exports) gave epidemic diseases the opportunity to commence their ravages. It was during 1847 that the scourges of 'famine fever' and dysentery and diarrhoea wreaked their greatest havoc, as indicated by official statistics – part of three volumes of data on disease and death collected in conjunction with the 1851 census. These scourges

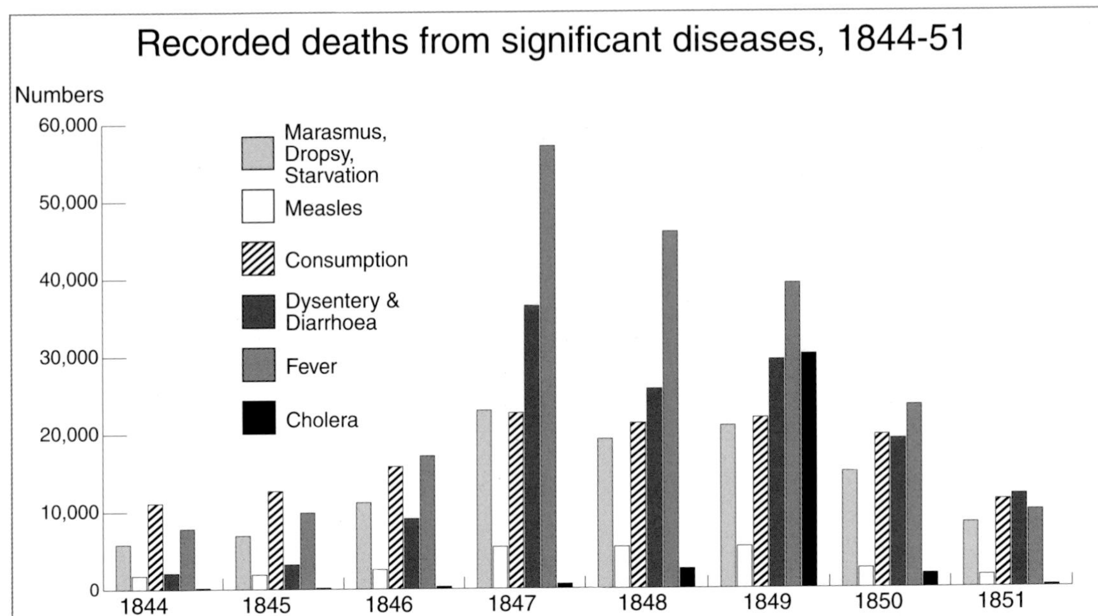

The limitations of medical knowledge and administrative inadequacies meant that many famine-related deaths were improperly diagnosed or not recorded at all. Thus the official figures of deaths from significant diseases in the years 1844–51, depicted in this graph, suffer from numerous imperfections, but the graph demonstrates dramatically the ravages of 'fever' and of dysentery and diarrhoea in the years 1847–50. Also distinctly elevated by the effects of the famine were deaths from 'consumption', most of which were undoubtedly attributable to tuberculosis. At the end of the decade, in 1849 and early 1850, Asiatic cholera suddenly became a great killer. Radical nutrition deficiencies could and did lead to death directly (witness the category of 'marasmus, dropsy, and starvation'), but such deficiencies also contributed to the incidence of fatal epidemic diseases. (Joan Murphy Donnelly)

persisted at extremely high levels through 1850. Only in 1851 did their incidence fall to about the rates of 1846.[7] Moreover, the great killing diseases were joined in the late 1840s by a series of lesser ones which collectively took a tremendous additional toll. Piled on top of the multitude of infectious and nutrition-deficiency diseases of the famine years was a ferocious epidemic of 'Asiatic cholera' in 1849. 'To the beleaguered Irish', as the medical historian Laurence Geary has aptly said, 'it must have seemed as if the hand of providence were raised against them.'[8]

As in every famine, the quest for food or the means to buy it uprooted large segments of the population and sent them streaming to places where they hoped to find what they so critically lacked. Vagrancy and mendicancy, already prominent features of Irish life before the famine, soared to record heights, and large crowds from the countryside congregated in cities and towns, where they besieged the sellers of provisions, the houses of the well-to-do, the gates of the workhouses, and the doors of food depots and soup kitchens. Similar crowds thronged the public works in the last quarter of 1846 and the first quarter of 1847. These were exactly the disrupted social conditions which promoted the spread of 'famine fever'. There were actually two distinct types of fever that acted as grim reapers during the late 1840s – typhus and relapsing fever. Among the elements that these different epidemic diseases had in common was the same vector: the human body louse. The micro-organisms which are at the root of typhus fever, and which lice transmit, invade the body through skin lesions, at the eyes, and by inhalation. Relapsing fever usually gains entry by a similar process through scratches on the skin.[9] Lice 'feasted on the unwashed and susceptible skin of the hungry, multiplied in their filthy and tattered clothing, and went forth, carried the length and breadth of the country by a population who had taken to the roads, vagrants and beggars, as well as the evicted and those who had abandoned their homes voluntarily' in the search for relief from their afflictions.[10] Typhus fever was an age-old scourge among the poor in Ireland, especially in times of food scarcity, and as a result there was some natural immunity among them against this disease. The mortality rate from typhus was therefore greater among the better-off segments of the population, whereas relapsing fever made by far its heaviest inroads among the destitute.[11]

Next to typhus and relapsing fever, the worst killers during the great famine were dysentery and diarrhoea, infectious diseases which were the most widespread and lethal complications of their even more murderous cousins. Attacks of fever had the effects of increasing susceptibility to other infections, including bacillary dysentery, and of raising the risks of mortality when one of these other infections took hold after the body's resistance had been lowered by the ravages of fever. Again, the radical disruption of normal social life by the famine, and especially the insanitary and crowded conditions found in or around workhouses, fever hospitals, gaols, relief centres, and emigrant ports, facilitated the dissemination of these diseases. The bacillus responsible for dysentery is spread by direct contact with an infected sufferer, through water polluted with the faeces of other victims, and by flies carrying the bacillus.[12] The acute dietary deficiencies associated with the famine also inflated the death toll from dysentery and diarrhoea. Starving people will eat almost anything in their urge to assuage the sharp pangs of hunger. The green-smeared mouths of some of the famine dead indicated that they had been reduced to eating grass in their extremity. The famished eagerly sought 'many curious substitutes for the potato' – the leaves and barks of certain trees, the roots of fern and dandelion, the leaves of the dock and the sorrel, the berries of the mountains and the bogs, the nettles found in particular luxuriance in graveyards, the pickings of the seashore.[13] Though some nourishment was often found in these acts of desperation, in many cases the strange, inedible, or uncooked nature of what was ingested left victims with agonising bowel complaints or fatally aggravated pre-existing dysentery and diarrhoea. In a special category of this kind was 'Peel's brimstone' – the

Before the famine death was surrounded by certain ritual observances designed to ease the path of the deceased into the next world, console the bereaved, and reaffirm life. These rituals found expression in 'the wake' at the house of the deceased, with its classic mixture of sorrowful remembrance and raucous merriment. The emotional range is captured in this illustration of 1841, which shows women around the corpse keening the deceased while other people nearby (mostly men) enjoy the pleasures of the glass, the pipe, and lively conversation. Even the poor laid aside money to ensure themselves 'a fine wake' and 'a decent funeral'. (By permission of the British Library)

Indian corn so widely used as a substitute for the failed potato, and so much of which at first was poorly ground, poorly cooked (sometimes not cooked at all), or even unmerchantable altogether.[14] Discharges of infected faeces, of course, frequently led to the intensification of dysentery and diarrhoea epidemics.

Among the lesser killing infections of the famine were measles, scarlatina, consumption, and smallpox. Mortality from measles increased nearly threefold between 1845 and 1849, while scarlatina deaths were more than twice as high by 1850 than in 1845. Claiming even more lives than either of these diseases in the late 1840s was consumption, the most common form of which was tuberculosis of the lung. Deaths from consumption more than doubled between 1846 and 1847 and remained extremely high in 1848 and 1849. For the three years 1847–9 mortality from consumption and measles closely paralleled one another, with each accounting for about 20,000 officially recorded deaths annually. Measles and scarlatina, as childhood diseases, carried off the very

How different were most famine funerals! In the workhouses deaths were so numerous that the authorities resorted to coffins with hinged bottoms so that they could be reused after the bodies had been dumped in mass graves or pits. This sketch of January 1847 depicts a funeral near Skibbereen, Co. Cork, a district just then becoming notorious throughout the United Kingdom for its unspeakable horrors. To be buried in this way, without the presence of family, friends, or neighbours, and without the traditional wake and funeral, was perceived as one of the grossest indignities of the famine. (*Illustrated London News*)

young in great numbers; measles could be especially devastating and was known in some cases 'to wipe out the children of entire villages within days'. Consumption, on the other hand, was worst among adolescents and young adults. More than a third of all consumption deaths in the decade 1841–51 consisted of people between the ages of ten and twenty-five. As with fever, so too with measles, scarlatina, and consumption: attacks of these infections opened their victims to other diseases and raised the likelihood that they would be fatal.[15]

Most often lethal were two other diseases less closely linked to famine conditions but very much part of this dismal catalogue of destructive epidemics. The first was smallpox, an acute viral disease which seemed largely oblivious of class distinctions, affecting the wealthy as well as the destitute. The mortality rate from smallpox had tripled by 1849 in comparison with the immediate pre-famine years, and the disease was especially virulent in the western coastal counties from Cork to Mayo as well as in Dublin and its rural environs. Those who survived smallpox were invariably disfigured with pock marks on their faces for life, but they were fortunate to be alive at all, as this disease usually killed its victims quickly. Dreaded even more for the same reason was 'Asiatic' cholera, the last of the scourges of the famine era. Its appearance in Ireland (first in Belfast) at the end of 1848 was essentially unrelated to food scarcity or the prevailing syndrome of other infectious diseases. But cholera cut a wide swathe of death across much of the country, terrifying all segments of Irish society by the quickness with which it extinguished life (three or four days was usual, and sometimes death occurred within hours) and by its tendency to bypass class boundaries. Before cholera finally subsided in the summer of 1850, after about twenty months of carnage, the authorities had officially recorded nearly 46,000 cases of the disease, and 42 per cent of them – probably an underestimate – were listed as fatal.[16]

The Geography of Excess Mortality

How were the excess deaths distributed geographically? Excluding averted births, the provincial breakdown is as follows: Connacht accounted for 40.4 per cent of the total, Munster for 30.3 per cent, Ulster for 20.7 per cent, and Leinster for 8.6 per cent. With even relatively prosperous Leinster and Ulster recording 93,000 and 224,000 excess deaths respectively, it could be argued that although its geographical incidence was heavily skewed towards Connacht and Munster, the famine still had the dimensions of a national disaster. It is useful and instructive to disaggregate the provincial statistics since these mask significant intraprovincial variations. Mokyr's lower-bound estimates of excess mortality by county are set out in Table 6.[17]

Table 6
Average annual rates of excess mortality by county, 1846–51 (per thousand)

County	Rate	County	Rate
Mayo	58.4	King's	18.0
Sligo	52.1	Meath	15.8
Roscommon	49.5	Armagh	15.3
Galway	46.1	Tyrone	15.2
Leitrim	42.9	Antrim	15.0
Cavan	42.7	Kilkenny	12.5
Cork	32.0	Wicklow	10.8
Clare	31.5	Donegal	10.7
Fermanagh	29.2	Limerick	10.0
Monaghan	28.6	Louth	8.2
Tipperary	23.8	Kildare	7.3
Kerry	22.4	Down	6.7
Queen's	21.6	Londonderry	5.7
Waterford	20.8	Carlow	2.7
Longford	20.2	Wexford	1.7
Westmeath	20.0	Dublin	–2.1

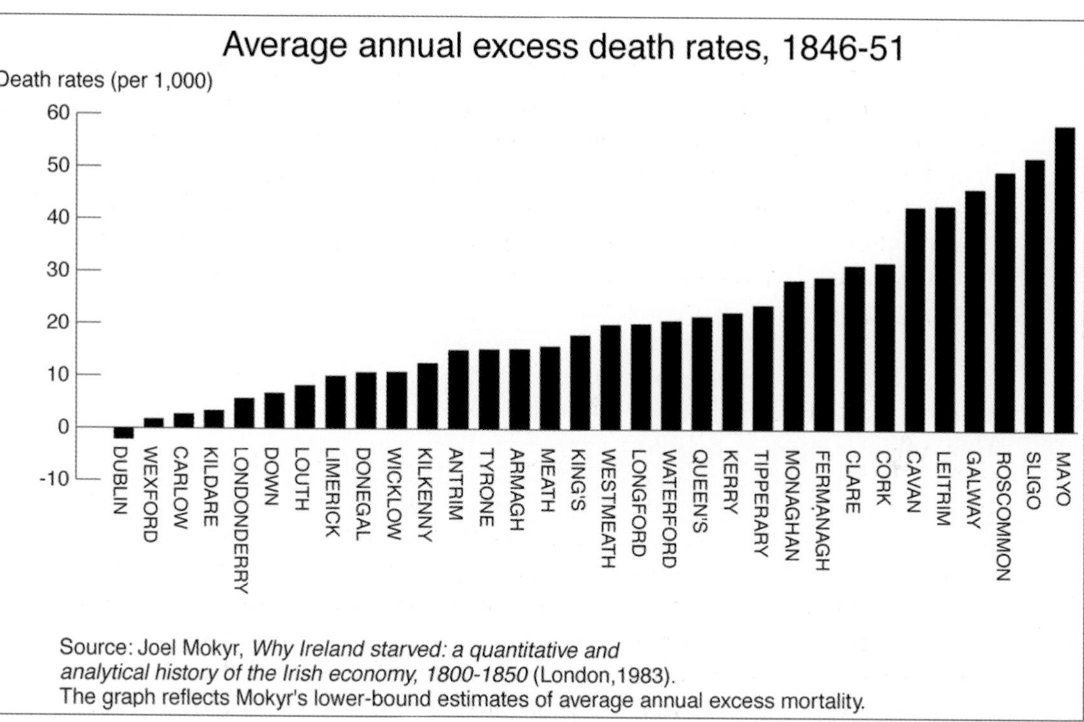

Source: Joel Mokyr, *Why Ireland starved: a quantitative and analytical history of the Irish economy, 1800-1850* (London,1983).
The graph reflects Mokyr's lower-bound estimates of average annual excess mortality.

The geographical distribution of famine-related mortality exhibited distinct regional patterns, as shown by the graph of annual average excess deaths in the years 1846–51. Led by Mayo and Sligo, the five counties in the western province of Connacht recorded the highest toll of excess deaths, followed closely by three counties in south Ulster (Cavan, Fermanagh, and Monaghan) and four counties in Munster (Cork, Clare, Tipperary, and Kerry). What had made these regions so vulnerable was their acute poverty on the eve of the famine, a predicament linked to their disproportionately large numbers of potato-dependent smallholders and labourers as well as to the decay of rural industry in south Ulster and parts of Connacht. Why the counties of Donegal in the north-west and Limerick in the south-west did not suffer much greater mortality is a question not yet sufficiently understood by historians. Clearly, however, the higher levels of material welfare in east Ulster, and in the eastern coastal counties generally, shielded their inhabitants from the calamities that overtook other regions. (Joan Murphy Donnelly)

Even within Connacht the difference between Mayo and Leitrim was substantial, though the most noteworthy fact is that all five counties in that province registered higher rates of excess deaths than any county elsewhere in Ireland. In a second group of counties covering most of Munster and the southern portion of Ulster, excess mortality was also fearfully high. On the other hand, the rate of excess deaths was comparatively moderate in mid-Ulster (Tyrone and Armagh) and in west Leinster, while a low rate was characteristic of east Leinster and the northern portion of Ulster. Given what is known of their social structures, it is somewhat surprising that Limerick in the south-west and Donegal in the north-west escaped the brutal rates of excess mortality suffered by the rest of the west of Ireland.

In seeking to explain these wide geographical variations, Mokyr used regression analysis to test the potency of an assortment of independent variables. The results of the regressions indicate that neither the pre-famine acreage of potatoes nor rent per capita was related to the differing geographical incidence of the famine. The factors that correlate most strongly with excess mortality are income per capita and the literacy rate. The counties with the lowest incomes per capita and the highest rates of illiteracy were also the counties with the greatest excess mortality, and vice versa. In addition, the proportion of farms above and below 20 acres correlates positively with excess death rates. As the proportion below 20 acres increases, the excess mortality becomes progressively worse, and as the proportion above 20 acres rises, the excess deaths progressively fall. The grim reality was that poverty, whether measured by dependence on wage labour or by reliance on inadequate landholdings, greatly increased vulnerability to the mortality of the famine. This was true even in regions of the country usually regarded as relatively prosperous. Sheer location offered little protection to labourers and smallholders cursed with inadequate personal resources. Ultimately, the successive failures of the potato claimed as many victims as it did in Ireland because so high a proportion of the population had come to live in a degree of poverty that exposed them fully to a horrendous accident of nature from which it was difficult to escape.[18]

EMIGRATION MEASURED AND DISSECTED

Emigration, of course, did offer the chance of escape, and that chance was seized by no fewer than 2.1 million Irish adults and children between 1845 and 1855. Of this horde, 'almost 1.5 million sailed to the United States; another 340,000 embarked for British North America; 200,000–300,000 settled permanently in Great Britain; and several thousand more went to Australia and elsewhere'. As Kerby Miller has observed in his monumental study of 1985, 'more people left Ireland in just eleven years than during the preceding two and one-half centuries'.[19] A significant portion of those who departed in these eleven years would undoubtedly have left even if there had been no famine, for the emigrant stream had been swelling in the decade immediately before 1845. As many as 351,000 had sailed from Ireland to North America alone between 1838 and 1844 – an average of slightly more than 50,000 a year, as compared with an annual average of about 40,000 from 1828 to 1837. If the rate of increase recorded between these two periods had simply been maintained in the years 1845–51, then 437,500 people would probably have journeyed to North America anyway. But the actual number of Irish emigrants who went overseas in those years amounted to more than a million. Departures during the immediate aftermath of the famine were almost as enormous as during the famine years themselves. Of the total of 2.1 million who left between 1845 and 1855, 1.2 million fled before 1851 but as many as 900,000 departed over the next five years.[20]

THE 'COFFIN SHIPS'

The mass emigration of the famine era has been associated ever since in the popular mind with the horrors of the 'coffin ships' and Grosse Île. And no serious account of the enormous exodus of those years can overlook these tragic events, their causes, and the deep imprint that they have left on the public memory of the famine. It should be stressed, however, that this disastrous episode was confined to 1847. The panic quality of so much of the emigration in that year meant, among other things, that many of the emigrants were already sick or infected with disease when they embarked, that both the cross-channel steamers and the transatlantic ships were more than usually overcrowded, and that passengers had often made too little preparation for the long journey of six or even seven weeks. Those who arrived in Liverpool in a healthy condition frequently went down with disease when they had to seek temporary shelter in the overcrowded, insanitary, and foul-smelling lodging-

By the spring of 1851, when this sketch of emigrants on the quay at Cork first appeared, the enormous wave of famine emigration was cresting. In that year alone, almost 250,000 persons departed the country. Altogether, between 1845 and 1855 some 2.1 million people – an astounding number – left Ireland, with 1.5 million sailing to the United States. In the earliest years of the famine a high proportion of all Irish emigrants (45 per cent in 1847) went to Canada, and many did so under appalling conditions at sea and upon landing at Grosse Île. But the horrors of the 'coffin ships' of 1847 did not persist, and emigration to Canada slackened to only 10 or 15 per cent of the total after 1848. Like their counterparts elsewhere, these Cork emigrants of 1851 faced a long journey – the Atlantic crossing then lasted about six weeks. (*Illustrated London News*)

houses and cellars of that city while awaiting passage to the new world. Liverpool was so overwhelmed by the Irish inundation of 1847, and so ravaged by epidemics of disease, that thousands of would-be emigrants either perished there or were deprived of the financial means to go overseas.[21] The panic quality of the exodus of 1847 also swept up a disproportionate number of the poorer members of Irish society (with a greater susceptibility to disease), and Canada was therefore the destination of an unusually high proportion of the emigrants of that year (about 45 per cent), for the simple reason that steerage fares to British North America might be as little as half of those on the now heavily trafficked routes to United States ports. But there was a steep price to be paid for cheapness. At this stage the passage to Canada was very loosely regulated, with the greatest overcrowding and the least adequate provision for food, water, sanitation, and medical facilities. The traffic also took place characteristically in the 'timber ships' whose normal load on the journey over to Europe consisted of the products of the great Canadian forests. Not only were such ships unsuitable in various ways for heavy passenger traffic on the return journey, but many of them were also in poor seafaring condition.[22]

The suffering associated with the 'coffin ships' need not only be imagined, for the Limerick landlord, philanthropist, and social reformer Stephen de Vere penned a vivid account after travelling as a steerage passenger to Canada in the late spring of 1847:

> Before the emigrant is a week at sea, he is an altered man. . . . How can it be otherwise? Hundreds of poor people, men, women, and children, of all ages, from the drivelling idiot of ninety to the babe just born; huddled together without light, without air, wallowing in filth and breathing a fetid atmosphere, sick in body, dispirited in heart . . . ; the fevered patients lying between the sound in sleeping places so narrow as almost to deny them the power of indulging, by a change of position, the natural restlessness of the diseased; by their agonised ravings disturbing those around them and predisposing them, through the effects of the imagination, to imbibe the contagion; living without food or medicine except as administered by the hand of casual charity; dying without the voice of spiritual consolation, and buried in the deep without the rites of the church.[23]

De Vere assured civil servants at the Colonial Office in London that the conditions on this particular ship, though wretched enough, were actually 'more comfortable than many'.[24] In retrospect, the multiple elements that contributed to the catastrophe at Grosse Île and further afield can be clearly delineated.

Already by the end of May 1847 there were forty vessels in the vicinity of Grosse Île, with as many as 13,000 emigrants under quarantine, stretching in an unbroken line two miles down the St Lawrence. Another report only a week later put the number of refugees on the island at 21,000.[25] The situation remained beyond control for months. Even in early September, with the shipping season drawing to an end, no fewer than 14,000 emigrants were still aboard ships in the river and being held in quarantine.[26] The death toll at sea had been extremely high on many of these ships, and disease of course continued its ravages as the surviving passengers were prevented from coming ashore for long periods. The dead lay among the living – or the barely alive – for days without removal or burial, and it was only with difficulty that bodies could be cleared from the holds. The quarantine authorities at Grosse Île were limited in what they could do to speed the release of such a horde of refugees, even when they recognised that keeping them on the ships was a death sentence from contagion. Frenzied efforts were made to expand the hospital and other medical facilities on the island, but as late as August accommodation still fell far short of needs. At that point the hospital sheds and tents could cater for about 2,000 sick and 300 convalescents, along with another 3,500 regarded as healthy but not yet qualified for release.[27]

Under these appalling conditions the death toll was extraordinary. Shortly after the arrival of the first ship, deaths numbered 50 a day, and as many as 150 people were buried on 5 June. The monument that was eventually erected over the mass grave at Grosse Île – located at the western end of the island and covering six acres – proclaims that 5,424 persons lie entombed there. This huge burial-ground is the largest of the mass graves of the great famine, in or out of Ireland. But the more than 5,000 dead lying there are only a fraction of those thought to have died on the coffin ships at Grosse Île, on the island itself, or elsewhere in Canada soon after their arrival. One careful recent scholar has estimated that a minimum of 20,000 persons perished on the island or on the ships around it, and he has emphasised that 'this number does not include the thousands of others who, having survived Grosse Île, reached Quebec city, Montreal, Kingston, Toronto, and Hamilton, only to die there in fever hospitals and emigrant sheds'.[28] Another expert, Kerby Miller, has calculated that the death toll among the almost 100,000 emigrants to British North America in 1847 reached at least 30 per cent of the total. To this minimum of 30,000 deaths on the Canadian route or in Canada itself are to be added another 10,500 people who perished on their way to the United States or shortly after arriving there in the same year (about 9 per cent of the total of more than 117,000).[29] In short, the combined mortality associated with the phenomenon of the 'coffin ships' was not far short of 50,000 persons.

But the tragic story of the 'coffin ships' and the appalling scenes at Grosse Île in 1847 must not be allowed to obscure the larger reality that the vast majority of the two million Irish emigrants of the period 1845–55 survived their arduous journey and began to carve out new lives for themselves in the United States, Canada, and Australia. From what social groups were the emigrants of these years drawn? We are better informed about the emigrants of the early 1850s than about those of the late 1840s. It would appear that in the years 1851–5 between 80 and 90 per cent of all Irish emigrants consisted of common or farm labourers and servants. Skilled workers never constituted more than 11 per cent of the total in the early 1850s (the unweighted average was about 9 per cent), and farmers never accounted for more than 8 per cent (the unweighted average in their case was less than 5 per cent). In the late 1840s the lower-class composition of emigrants was less pronounced but not markedly so. According to manifests of vessels sailing to New York City in 1846, three-quarters of the Irish passengers were either labourers or servants; artisans made up 12 per cent and farmers only 9.5 per cent of the remainder.[30] Admittedly, it was notorious that Irish emigrants disembarking at United States ports were much superior in condition to those arriving in British North America. But the exodus to Canada, though favoured by the poorest because of the lower fares, was also much smaller in scale and could not have changed the picture greatly. The conclusion is inescapable that in both the late 1840s and early 1850s the overwhelming majority of emigrants were drawn from the lowest classes of Irish society. Compared with pre-famine emigrants, they were less likely to be skilled or to have been farmers. And as Kerby Miller has emphasised, they were more likely to be Catholic, Irish-speaking, and illiterate.[31]

From which parts of Ireland was the exodus heaviest? Three areas stand out as having experienced high or very high rates of emigration: south Ulster, north Connacht, and much of the Leinster midlands. The same areas had been notable for a heavy stream of departures in the years 1815–45, and thus the famine period saw the continuation of the pre-famine trends in this respect. As Cousens showed, the prominence of these regions in the pre-famine exodus was mostly the result of the contraction and virtual collapse of the domestic textile industry, especially the home spinning and weaving of linens, under the withering impact of the industrial revolution in Britain and the north-eastern corner of Ireland. Although the decline of cottage industry was already far advanced by the late 1830s, with hand spinning having become altogether obsolete, the ruin of the handloom weavers was delayed until the 1840s, when many of them joined the famine exodus.[32]

But high rates of emigration during the famine years were usually the result of a combination of factors. According to Cousens, the extensive movement from Leitrim and Roscommon as well as from Longford and Queen's County was mainly owing to the coincidence of a heavy preponderance of small holdings with high rates of eviction. In addition, the pressure of heavy poor rates was a factor of considerable importance in promoting emigration from Cavan, Monaghan, Leitrim, and Longford, where not only were the rates high but a relatively large proportion of the ratepayers also occupied holdings valued at £4 to £5, or just above the threshold of liability to rates.

On the other hand, relatively low emigration was characteristic of most of Ulster, the south-west, and the south-east. Flight was reduced in most of the northern counties by the moderate level of destitution, the correspondingly low poor rates, the scarcity of evictions, landlord paternalism, and the availability of internal migration and factory employment as alternatives to emigration. By contrast, the high levels of destitution that prevailed throughout most of the

These two sketches of July 1850 show emigrants departing from Liverpool for America. Many intending Irish emigrants never got beyond Liverpool. In the first surge of departures in 1847, many of the fleeing were already infected with fever and died or suffered long agonies in Liverpool, which was overwhelmed by the Irish inundation in that year. Even if they arrived at Liverpool in sound health, Irish emigrants initially ran a high risk of contracting disease in the noisome lodging-houses and stinking cellars of the city. Long delays in departure owing to disease could strip would-be emigrants of their passage money. But by the early 1850s the Liverpool authorities had brought the health crisis well under control. (*Illustrated London News*)

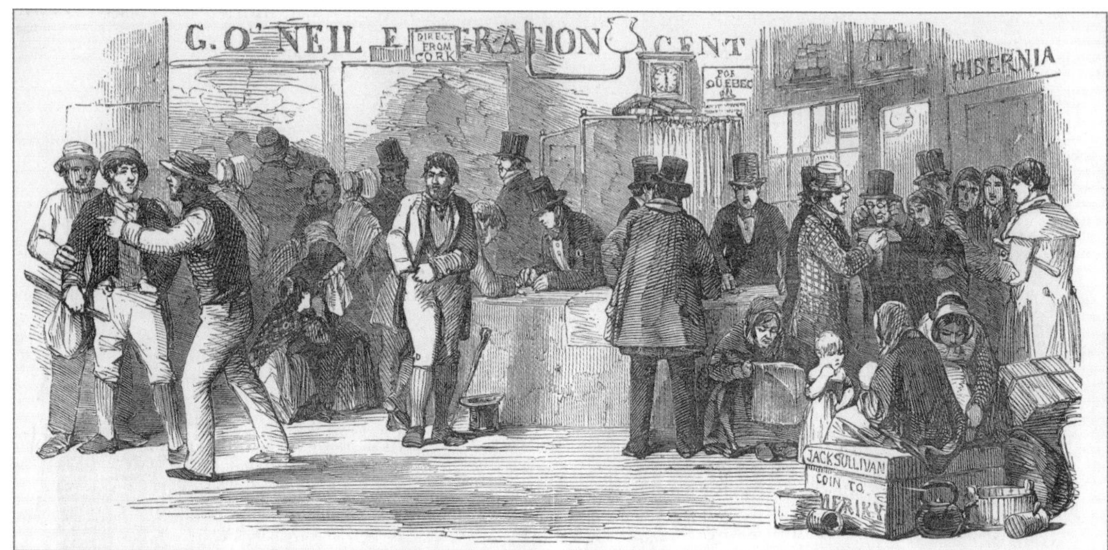

Departing emigrants usually arranged the details of their sea journeys at the office of an emigration agent, as depicted in this sketch of 1851. Fares were probably somewhat higher by the early 1850s than before 1845. Even the cheapest steerage passage to New York at the end of the famine period was usually at least 75s., or not far short of £20 for a family of five. Perhaps only about 5 per cent of all emigration during the famine was assisted, since neither the landlords nor the government gave much aid. Many emigrating farmers paid for their passage from sales of their crops and livestock, but an increasing proportion of emigrants in the early 1850s benefited from the flood of remittances sent home by relatives who had left earlier. (*Illustrated London News*)

south and in the far west operated to restrict departures among smallholders, agricultural labourers, and farm servants. Even though labourers and farm servants constituted the most numerous category of emigrants during the famine, they were also the groups who least possessed the resources needed to depart. This difficulty seems to have been most acute in the Munster counties, four of which (Clare, Cork, Kerry, and Tipperary) actually experienced an increase in the ratio of farm workers to farmers between 1841 and 1851. In Waterford there was a substantial decline, but the ratio there was still higher in 1851 than in any other Irish county (Dublin excepted), and not surprisingly, Waterford's rate of emigration was one of the lowest in the country.[33]

Destitution, however, did not always act as a sharp brake on emigration. In fact, four of the five counties with the highest rates of excess mortality during the famine years (Leitrim, Mayo, Roscommon, and Sligo) also ranked among the counties with the heaviest rates of emigration. Perhaps the likeliest explanation for this apparent anomaly is that north Connacht, as noted earlier, had been a centre of emigration before 1845, and that remittances from previous emigrants relieved their relatives and friends who now followed them from having to depend exclusively or largely on their own resources. In south Ulster as well, emigration was not checked by destitution. The exodus from Cavan, Monaghan, and Fermanagh was extraordinarily heavy, even though in all three counties the rate of excess mortality was considerably above the average. This region too had been remarkable as a centre of emigration in the pre-famine years, and presumably remittances again allowed many of its poor to escape abroad.

Apart from south Ulster and north Connacht, however, the relationship between emigration and excess mortality was usually inverse, as Kerby Miller has observed. This pattern was perhaps clearest in the mid-west and the south-west. In Galway, Clare, and west Cork, where excess deaths were high, emigration was relatively low. Conversely, in Donegal and Limerick, where excess mortality was quite low, emigration was either very heavy (Donegal) or moderately high (Limerick). An inverse relationship similar to that prevailing in Limerick and Donegal was also strikingly evident among certain of the Leinster counties. Carlow, for example, ranked very low in the scale of excess deaths but very high in the scale of emigration, and the same was true of Kildare, Kilkenny, and especially Louth. To be sure, the inverse relationship was often less pronounced, but it was rare for a low level of excess mortality to be associated with anything less than a moderate level of emigration. Even Wexford and Dublin, which ranked lowest in the excess mortality scale, experienced moderate rates of emigration.[34]

Even though emigration was already a normal occurrence in certain regions of the country before 1845, its acceptability increased enormously throughout most of Ireland in the late 1840s and early 1850s. The exodus of the late 1840s, and especially that of 1847, was characterised by an often panic-driven desperation to escape that swept aside the prudential considerations and customary restraints of former years. Neither reports of adverse conditions abroad, nor lack of adequate sea stores and landing money, nor the absence of safe vessels could check the lemming-like march to the ports. Most of those who left embraced emigration as their best – or their only – means of survival, even if it entailed, as it did for thousands, the perilous crossing of the North Atlantic in the middle of winter.[35] Inevitably, departures under such conditions produced disasters at sea or upon landing, as on the 'coffin ships' and at Grosse Île in 1847. Fortunately, the vast majority of emigrants escaped such depths of suffering. In 1848 the death rate among passengers to Canada fell to barely more than one per cent, and voyages to the United States throughout the famine years were much less dangerous to the health and safety of Irish emigrants, largely because of stricter regulation of passenger ships.[36]

At first, the mass exodus aroused little hostile comment in Ireland. Landlords who encouraged departures were not initially condemned, provided that they gave some modest assistance towards the emigration of their tenants; instead, such landlords were frequently praised for their generosity. For a time after 1845 Catholic priests generally accepted and often even promoted emigration, and nationalist newspapers and politicians usually acquiesced in it. But by late 1847 and early 1848 the whole tone of public discussion on the subject had changed drastically. Priests, editors of popular newspapers, and nationalist politicians of all factions were joining in a loud chorus of denunciation, stigmatising

The practice of calling the roll on the quarter-deck of an emigrant ship, depicted in this illustration of July 1850, may be taken to signify some tightening in the regulation and management of ships carrying transatlantic passengers after the horrors of 1847. But throughout the late 1840s and early 1850s there was considerable variability in the quality of the ships involved in the trade, and conditions below decks were far from satisfactory. American ships were much preferred to British because they were generally less crowded and had the advantage in design, accommodation, and speed. But whether the ships were American or British, emigrants invariably suffered from overcrowding in steerage, fetid quarters, poor food and sanitation, and a seemingly endless journey. (*Illustrated London News*)

emigration as forced exile. This radical shift in opinion coincided with, and was largely prompted by, the bitter realisation that the British government had laid aside any conception of the famine as an imperial responsibility and had terminated all major schemes of direct relief funded by the treasury. The hypercriticism of emigration evident among clerics and nationalists by 1848 did nothing to stem departures. But along with other factors, it helped to undermine earlier popular conceptions of the famine as divine punishment for sin or as the will of an inscrutable providence.[37] Increasingly after 1847, blame for emigration and indeed for the famine itself was laid at Britain's door, and political events, to be discussed in the next chapter, had much to do with this fundamental and long-lasting development.

CHAPTER 8

A Famine in Irish Politics

In Irish politics the famine years coincided with the splintering and decline of the once powerful popular movement for the repeal of the act of union.[1] Already before the famine the unity of the repeal movement had been badly shaken by the consequences of the failure of its basic strategy. The great 'monster meetings' of 1843 were intended to intimidate the British government into granting legislative independence to Ireland, just as an enormous popular agitation under Daniel O'Connell's masterful leadership in the 1820s had coerced the Wellington-Peel administration into conceding Catholic

O'Connell's repeal campaign – the greatest extra-parliamentary agitation yet – was designed to compel the British government and parliament to repeal the act of union by the sheer force of overwhelming public opinion in Ireland. Central to this strategy in 1843 was the holding of some forty 'monster meetings' at places of historic significance, such as this vast gathering in August at Tara Hill, the seat of the Irish high kings. Sympathetic reporters estimated the attendance there – much too generously – at from 750,000 to 1.5 million people. At the heart of the monster meetings were enormous processions, heavily laden with symbolism, which brought Irish political mobilisation to a new peak. (*Illustrated London News*)

emancipation in 1829. But in the early 1840s the use of essentially the same strategy and tactics as in the 1820s failed to produce a similar political breakthrough. This was not because the implied threat of possible revolution appeared less credible in British eyes than it had earlier, but rather because British politicians feared the consequences of Catholic emancipation far less than they did those of repeal. However much O'Connell might stress Irish Catholic loyalty to the crown and to Queen Victoria personally, the British political élite persisted in regarding the repeal agitation as a crypto-revolutionary movement whose goal, if achieved, would lead ultimately to the disintegration of the British empire. Given this dominant attitude towards repeal in British political circles, and given O'Connell's deeply rooted aversion to violence, the result of the so-called showdown at Clontarf in October 1843 was entirely predictable. When the Tory government of Sir Robert Peel banned this planned monster meeting and dispatched troops to prevent it from taking place, O'Connell called it off rather than risk serious bloodshed.

Alienation of Young Ireland

This decision was not repudiated by the Young Ireland allies of O'Connell who had done so much to boost his movement and to trumpet in the weekly *Nation* their own special cause of Irish cultural nationalism. But privately the Young Irelanders harboured misgivings, and these were intensified when O'Connell showed in the aftermath of Clontarf that he was willing to negotiate with both the Whigs and the federalists. O'Connell did not embrace federalism, and there was as yet no question of a formal alliance with the opposition Whigs. But his apparent readiness to enter into discussions with these groups was profoundly disturbing to the Young Irelanders, who were especially haunted by the not unreasonable fear of a repetition of the O'Connellite-Whig alliance of 1835–41. That earlier episode had in effect required O'Connell to shelve his demand for repeal in return for distinctly inferior concessions that were not widely applauded or appreciated in Ireland. For most of the Young Irelanders, repeal was a non-negotiable minimum demand, and its eventual achievement was inseparably linked in their eyes with maintaining the political independence of the O'Connellite party at Westminster.

The fissures that opened up in 1844 between the idealistic Young Irelanders and the opportunistic O'Connellites were considerably widened in 1845 by their sharp clash of views over the colleges bill.[2] This was one of three measures devised by Peel's government with the general aim of undercutting Catholic support for repeal by detaching moderates, especially Catholic churchmen, from the O'Connellite political machine. During the debates over the bill in the Repeal Association in Dublin, it became evident that despite the strictures of most Catholic bishops against the proposed colleges, many of the leading Young Irelanders took a favourable view of the measure. Strongly associated as they were with a non-sectarian cultural nationalism, and including numerous middle-

The government's banning of the scheduled 'monster meeting' at Clontarf early in October 1843 was the prelude to O'Connell's arrest, trial, and conviction on a charge of seditious conspiracy. His short spell in Richmond prison in Dublin came to an end in September 1844 when the House of Lords narrowly overturned his conviction on appeal. With masterful skill O'Connell converted his release from Richmond gaol into an immense popular political triumph, as depicted in this illustration. The chief spectacle of the celebratory procession was the liberated O'Connell himself riding atop a huge and magnificently decorated triumphal car drawn by six horses. The enormous procession took over two hours to pass each of its stages. (*Illustrated London News*)

class Protestants within their ranks, the Young Irelanders were not bothered by the refusal of Peel's government to entrust control of the colleges to the Catholic hierarchy or to provide public money for the teaching of Catholic theology. On the contrary, from their perspective these omissions actually enhanced the attractiveness of the colleges. The projected establishment of non-denominational institutions of higher education in Belfast, Cork, and Galway was fully consistent with the non-sectarian cultural nationalism that Thomas Davis, John Blake Dillon, and Charles Gavan Duffy had been propagating in the *Nation*. According to Young Ireland ideology, even the Protestant landed gentry might be won over to repeal through the power of the nationalist ideal to blunt sectarian and class divisions. So deep was this faith that the impact of the famine itself was slow to dislodge it.

O'Connell, however, cast himself as the political guardian of the interests of the Catholic church on this issue, and in a lamentable display of rhetorical

For Peel's Tory government the partial failure of the potato crop in 1845 spelt increased pressure from numerous quarters – nationalists and agrarian rebels in Ireland as well as Tory protectionists and free-trade radicals in Britain. This *Pictorial Times* cartoon of November 1845 entitled 'The minister's dream' neatly illustrates how the onset of blight in Ireland brought together all of Peel's political nightmares – O'Connell, Irish agrarian unrest, the vexed issue of repeal of the corn laws, and the demands of British Radicals. Peel hoped that the Irish crisis would make repealing the corn laws less objectionable to protectionists, but they rebelled against him and helped to bring him down. (*Pictorial Times*/The Trustees of the National Library of Scotland)

excess he branded the proposed colleges as 'godless' or 'infidel'. In May 1845 there was an ugly row over the issue in the Repeal Association, with O'Connell in one of his most insensitive and belligerent moods. The fundamental differences of opinion were at once papered over by mutual expressions of personal regard, and the opportunity for further acrimony was reduced by another round of monster meetings as well as by the common grief over the premature death of the young Thomas Davis in September 1845. But the uniform nationalist reaction to this latter event could not conceal that the breach between the two groups was growing steadily wider and might soon produce an open rupture.

When it came, the rupture was linked in a roundabout way with the famine, and the famine helped to make it permanent, except for a brief interlude in 1848. At the end of 1845 and in the early months of 1846 the energies of Peel's government were directed towards repealing the corn laws, largely as a means of alleviating the food crisis created in Ireland by the partial failure of the 1845 potato crop. The measure was regarded as base treachery by a large majority of Tories, whose anxiety to maintain agricultural protection in Britain led them at this stage to minimise Irish suffering. The votes of Peelite, Whig, and O'Connellite MPs were more than sufficient to ensure the repeal of the corn laws in June 1846. But the protectionist Tories were so enraged by their defeat that, oblivious to their own past political behaviour, they joined with the Whigs and the O'Connellites in voting against an Irish coercion bill sponsored by Peel's government. Thus the protectionist Tories and the O'Connellites provided the ladder by which the Whigs climbed back into office early in July under the leadership of Lord John Russell.

FORCING A SHOWDOWN

O'Connell's desire to oust Peel and to give general political support to the Whigs, provided that the Whigs reciprocated with what he called 'sweeping measures' for Ireland,[3] was a primary consideration in the decision to force a showdown with the fractious Young Irelanders in the Repeal Association. Six months earlier, in December 1845, when it seemed that the Whigs might be able to form a government because of a split in Peel's cabinet over the corn laws, O'Connell soothingly told the future Young Ireland leader William Smith O'Brien exactly what he wanted to hear: 'We ought to observe a strict neutrality between the two great English factions, supporting good measures as they may be proposed by either, and creating for ourselves an Irish national party entirely independent of both.' O'Connell assured Smith O'Brien that he could never be a party to 'placing the Irish nation under the feet of the English Whigs'.[4]

By late June 1846 O'Connell had conveniently forgotten these fine words. No longer was he stressing either parliamentary independence or the urgency of repealing the act of union. Instead, he was insisting that 'something must be done by the [Whig] government for the benefit of the Irish people during the present session' of parliament.[5] Accordingly, O'Connell asked the Repeal Association to endorse a list of eleven measures that he hoped to persuade the Whigs to adopt. The list contained few items that were new. Included were proposed reforms of the franchise, municipal government, the grand jury system, and landlord–tenant relations, coupled with a tax on the rents of absentee proprietors and the provision of denominational university education.[6] Except for the last item, which resurrected the contentious issue of the 'godless colleges', the Young Irelanders were not hostile to these measures in themselves. But the whole package implied much greater O'Connellite fraternisation with the Whigs than the Young Irelanders could stomach. Moreover, O'Connell apparently considered it essential to demonstrate to the Whigs that he was in complete control of the repeal movement, and that it was free of even the slightest taint of unconstitutionality or illegality. Such a demonstration would presumably make it easier for the Whigs to adopt, and for parliament to accept, the O'Connellite package of reforms.

The device chosen by O'Connell to dramatise his control came to be known as the 'peace resolutions'. At this juncture only a tiny minority of the Young Irelanders could even be suspected of harbouring thoughts of armed revolution. Nevertheless, O'Connell demanded that every member of the Repeal Association agree to an all-embracing renunciation of the use of physical force to achieve repeal or any other political objective, whether in Ireland or elsewhere. As the key resolution put it, 'We emphatically announce our conviction that all political amelioration . . . ought to be sought for . . . only by peaceful, legal, and constitutional means, to the utter exclusion of any other. . . .' Despite serious objections to such a sweeping repudiation of physical force under virtually all circumstances (only defence against unjust aggression was to be allowed), the Young Irelanders at first sought to avoid a break. With only one dissentient (Thomas Francis Meagher), the statement of which this resolution formed part was adopted by acclamation by the Repeal Association on 13 July 1846. But further debate about its meaning and interpretation led to the secession of the principal Young Irelanders before the end of that month.[7]

The showdown that O'Connell had deliberately provoked had ended much as he had expected. Immediately, his own leadership position was strengthened. The seceders were relatively few in number, and as individuals they had no considerable following in the country. But otherwise, O'Connell's political calculations missed their mark. Once again, and this time disastrously, he had overestimated the willingness and capacity of the Whigs to 'do something' for Ireland, and his successful assertion of control failed to pay political dividends in the parliamentary arena.

Though the social and economic condition of Ireland had almost nothing to do directly with the split of July 1846 within the Repeal Association, it had a great deal to do with the course of Irish politics after the total failure of the potato crop in the autumn of 1846. The beginning of mass death in the winter of 1846/7 and the tragic shortcomings of the Whigs' relief measures

THE REAL POTATO BLIGHT OF IRELAND.
(FROM A SKETCH TAKEN IN CONCILIATION HALL.)

A hero in Ireland, Daniel O'Connell was a much-hated figure among the Protestant upper and middle classes of Britain, especially those of the Tory persuasion. As the leader of a resurgent and overwhelmingly Catholic nationalism, he was particularly obnoxious to the growing and highly influential evangelical wing of British Protestantism. Shortly after the blight had made its first appearance in Ireland in late 1845, *Punch* published 'The real potato blight of Ireland', a cartoon savagely depicting O'Connell as a corpulent potato. Since O'Connell's vanity in matters of physical appearance was well known, this characterisation was designed to deliver maximum personal injury. (*Punch* Archive) underscored for most nationalists the folly of disunity between O'Connellites and Young Irelanders. If the Whigs were to be persuaded to alter their policies, it seemed highly desirable to achieve a reunion among nationalists and, if possible, to broaden the basis of political cooperation even more by including non-repealers. O'Connell's denunciation of Whig relief measures in December 1846 narrowed the gap separating him from the Young Irelanders, and the growing disenchantment of Irish landlords with Whig policies appeared to create an opportunity for repealers and non-repealers to join hands in an effort to push the Whigs into adopting a different course.

To heal nationalist divisions, however, proved an impossible task. The conference on reunion held in December 1846 ended in failure when neither side displayed sufficient readiness to compromise. O'Connell refused to jettison the notorious peace resolutions; at most, he was willing to limit their application to Anglo-Irish relations alone. He also declined to discuss certain other issues, such as cooperation with the Whigs and the acceptance of government jobs by repealers, until the Young Irelanders rejoined the Repeal Association. There was too little in these proposals to tempt the Young Irelanders to terminate their secession.[8]

THE IRISH CONFEDERATION AND IRISH LANDLORDS

Instead, the Young Irelanders decided to launch in January 1847 their own organisation, which they christened the Irish Confederation. The confederation was eventually to acquire a solid base of support among the artisans of the towns, but it began its life with, and long retained, completely unrealistic hopes about the power of nationality to resolve sectarian and class divisions within Irish society. There was a naive belief among Confederate leaders such as Gavan Duffy and Smith O'Brien, a Protestant landlord, that if they eschewed 'the ultra-democratic and ultra-Catholic tendencies' that they ascribed to the Repeal Association, they would be able to attract substantial support from Protestants and landlords as well as from moderate Catholics and tenant farmers.[9] Special emphasis was placed on the landed gentry, whose conversion to repeal in significant numbers was thought possible. They were by now intensely dissatisfied with Whig relief measures, which neglected reproductive works and laid heavy fiscal burdens on landlord shoulders. Though he was soon to repent his faith in the landlords, at this point even John Mitchel firmly believed that they had an important role to perform in the nationalist movement.

Overtures to the landed gentry were hardly confined to the Young Irelanders of the Irish Confederation. For several months O'Connell had been sounding the same note just as insistently, and in December 1846 he called publicly for a great national conference that would include the landlords and address the calamity facing the country. Though not really a national conference, the meeting held in Dublin on 14 January 1847 could reasonably claim to speak for the Irish upper and middle classes, Protestant and Catholic alike. In attendance were several peers, twenty-six Irish MPs, and many landowners and professional men. Broad agreement was reached on four points: (1) private enterprise alone could not be expected to satisfy the food needs of a starving population; (2) the imperial exchequer should bear all the costs of emergency employment schemes because the famine was an 'imperial calamity'; (3) insofar as possible, relief monies ought to be spent on reproductive works, such as thorough drainage, waste land reclamation, and harbour construction; and (4) legislation should be passed that would provide evicted or departing tenants with reasonable compensation for their agricultural improvements. This gathering was the prelude to a new political departure. In its immediate aftermath as many as eighty-three Irish peers and MPs, including the O'Connellites, agreed to act in unison as an Irish parliamentary party, with the object of pressing on the government the proposals adopted at the Dublin meeting. This was the high-water mark of Irish political unity during the famine years, but it was an unnatural alliance fated to endure for only a few months.[10]

Divisions within the party began to appear as early as February 1847 over the proposal of the Tory protectionist leader Lord George Bentinck to have the British treasury advance as much as £16 million for Irish railway projects. Once the minimisers of Irish suffering, the Tory protectionists now came forward as the saviours of the famishing population. Here was a grand scheme of reproductive works bound to appeal to almost all political factions in Ireland. But the measure actually split the Irish MPs after Russell threatened to resign if Bentinck's bill were given a second reading. Thus weakened, the Irish parliamentary party collapsed altogether when faced with its next big test. What caused the collapse was the varied reaction of Irish MPs to the Whigs' Irish poor relief bill. Irish Tory MPs strongly opposed the bill for two main reasons. First, it made the relief of the destitute in effect a wholly local responsibility, with no prospect that other relief schemes such as public works or soup kitchens would ease the enormous pressure on the poor law system. Second, under certain circumstances the bill authorised outdoor relief not only for the impotent poor but also for the able-bodied, a provision whose anticipated costs frightened the landlords even more.

If the repeal MPs had been faithful to the terms by which the Irish parliamentary party came into existence, they would have voted against this bill because it was at the opposite pole from making relief of the famine an imperial responsibility. But the O'Connellites fixed their attention on the limited authorisation of outdoor relief. Though dissatisfied with other provisions of the bill, they found in the issue of outdoor relief sufficient reason to support the measure, albeit reluctantly. O'Connell's last parliamentary speech came during the debates over this bill, and he pathetically told the Commons that he was willing to accept anything likely to help the poor. Had O'Connell known how the bill would be administered after it became law, he would perhaps have been less ready to see his cooperation with the non-repeal Irish MPs terminated, as it soon was, over this measure.[11] It is a sad comment on the last phase of

O'Connell's career that he gave even grudging approval to the measure that, above all others, signalled the disengagement of British ministers from bearing fiscal responsibility for the famine.

O'CONNELL'S DEATH

By the time the poor law amendment act reached the statute book in June 1847, Daniel O'Connell was among the shades. Partly on the advice of his doctor that a warmer climate might improve his health, which had been deteriorating sharply for several months, and partly because O'Connell himself recognised that his end was near, he decided to make a pilgrimage to Rome. On his way there in May, at Genoa, he died. In accordance with his last wishes, his heart was removed and taken to the eternal city, while his remains were returned to Ireland for burial. No other leader of the modern era dominated Irish politics for as long as O'Connell, with the exception of de Valera, and no other leader, again excepting de Valera, was held in greater popular esteem by his Catholic contemporaries.

But whereas de Valera made a career of setting British governments at defiance, O'Connell in two notable phases of his public life shaped his policies in such a way as to persuade Whig ministers to 'do something' for Ireland. Each time the results were disappointing, and during the famine profoundly so. Admittedly, O'Connell had to work within a political system that made the task of a constitutional nationalist leader exceedingly difficult. The Irish parliamentary franchise was still so restricted, and the limited electorate was so variable in its socio-economic composition, that O'Connell's following at Westminster bore little relation to the real strength of his grassroots support in Ireland.[12] As a result, he was unable to acquire the kind of tactical political leverage that Parnell exploited later in the century.

But a comparison with Parnell also suggests that O'Connell's overwhelming aversion to violence and his strong faith in the rights of private property severely restricted his willingness to use agrarian unrest for worthwhile political ends. Parnell also knew how to harness the energies of Fenians in the cause of Irish nationalism, whereas O'Connell forced the Young Irelanders out of the Repeal Association almost against their will. Parnell could justify his alliance with the Gladstonian liberals in the years 1886–90 on the grounds that the Liberal party was firmly committed to Irish home rule and strongly anti-landlord in temper, but O'Connell could make no similar defence of the Whigs. His last years as the pre-eminent Irish political leader were surely not his best, and his final year was almost unrelieved agony. He saw the abyss into which the country was falling and called for heroic measures to avert catastrophe. When these were not forthcoming, he denounced Whig policies as hopelessly inadequate. But he could not bring himself or the movement he led to the point of resolute, thoroughgoing opposition because he regarded the Tories as a far worse alternative. Whether the Conservatives, Peelite or protectionist, would have

Emigration was rising substantially in the three decades before the famine, when altogether the exodus carried off nearly a million people to North America. Many thousands more left for Britain. The Catholic proportion of the emigrant stream was growing, with Catholics outnumbering Protestants by the early 1840s. Emigrant ranks also contained increasing numbers from the poorer segments of Irish society and from the three southern provinces after 1815. By the early 1840s the Liverpool–New York route had become commonplace, and passage rates to the States were now only modestly higher than those to Canada. But the journey itself – first (usually) to Liverpool and then across the Atlantic – was filled with suffering. This anonymous painting – *Emigrants at Cork* – of *c.* 1840 depicts emigrants of the farming class, as yet untroubled, on the quay at Cork, with a cross-channel steamer behind them going down the River Lee. (Courtesy of the Department of Irish Folklore, University College Dublin)

Some emigrant ships sailed directly to America from Irish ports, as reflected in these two paintings of 1852 and 1853 – James Glen Wilson's *Emigrant ship leaving Belfast* and Edwin Hayes's *An emigrant ship, Dublin Bay, sunset.* But the great bulk of famine emigrants had first to face the adversities of the crossing to Liverpool. These were at their worst in 1847–8, during the widespread panic to leave the country, when 'there were frequently from 600 to 800 deck passengers on board of one steamer at a time, arriving [at Liverpool] from the ports of Dublin, Drogheda, Dundalk, and Sligo, crowded together on deck, mixed among the cattle and besmeared with their dung, clothed in rags, and saturated with wet'. (Photograph reproduced with the kind permission of the Trustees of the National Museums & Galleries of Northern Ireland/National Gallery of Ireland)

Stories of economic success were a staple of the emigration phenomenon, retailed in promotional literature, many emigrant letters, and folklore. The reality, of course, was much more complex. Upward social mobility was particularly difficult for the famine emigrants in the United States, though many of them no doubt lived on a higher material plane than if they had remained at home. The contrast was underlined by Erskine Nicol in his two companion lithographs of *c.* 1850 – *Outward bound* and *Homeward bound*. The 'returned Yanks' of the post-famine years had usually done well in America, and even better according to the folklore about them in Ireland, but there were very few of them. Only a minute fraction returned to stay, and even the number of those who came back for a visit before 1900 was nearly as small, though lack of means was certainly not the reason. (National Library of Ireland)

The famine emigrants arriving in the United States concentrated themselves in the cities of the north-eastern seaboard. For at least a generation their lot was usually a hard one. In New York around mid-century the Irish accounted for only about 10 per cent of the foreign-born workers in the building trades and the clothing industry, but for almost 90 per cent of foreign-born unskilled labourers. Housing conditions for these new Irish immigrants in New York were also typically bleak. Many wound up in the 'Bloody Old Sixth' Ward, with its notorious Irish slum known as the Five Points. The Irish in this painting of *c.* 1855 by Samuel Waugh – *Immigrants disembarking at the Battery, Castle Garden, New York* – have an air of wellbeing that sits oddly with what we know about general living and working conditions for Irish New Yorkers of this time. (Museum of the City of New York)

The floodgates of emigration that opened with the famine never really shut before 1900. Though the rate of departures slowed down considerably after 1854, the numbers going overseas in later decades were still impressively large – a total of nearly 2.6 million from 1861 to 1900. Emigration thus figured prominently in the thoughts and plans of most of those who survived the famine and of their children, as a reality either for themselves or for their close relatives. In thought or action emigration prompted conflicted feelings, as the advantages of going – real and imagined – were weighed against the sacrifices which leaving entailed. As departures loomed, the sense of loss induced by the inevitable separations was usually dominant, even if it did not exclude other emotions. Erskine Nicol depicted various degrees of sadness on the faces of the figures in his painting of 1864 – *Irish emigrants waiting for the train.* (Sheffield Galleries & Museums Trust, UK/Bridgeman Art Library)

News from the wider world had long been penetrating Irish rural areas by the time of the famine. Illiteracy was still the norm before 1845, but this did not necessarily mean that the poor were cut off from politics or from information about the outside world. In rural areas it had long been the practice for certain literate people to 'read the news' aloud to the unlettered. In this painting of *c.* 1850 by Henry McManus (*c.* 1810–78) entitled *Reading the 'Nation'*, a well-dressed gentleman with the newspaper in his hand and the people around him look middle-class, but numerous sources confirm that the *Nation* and other papers were often read to illiterate country people. After 1850 rural illiteracy steadily declined, and the number of provincial newspapers soared. (National Gallery of Ireland)

An important source of news at the popular level throughout much of the nineteenth century were emigrant letters, many more of which have survived the ravages of time than was once thought. The arrival of a letter from America or Australia was an event of the first magnitude in almost every Irish rural (and indeed urban) household, not least because the letters often contained – or were thought to contain – remittances of money or prepaid passages. The remittances were the foundation of what scholars frequently call 'chain-link emigration', with established emigrants in the new world sending back the means to take out new ones in a seemingly endless flow. When such letters arrived, the fortunate family commonly gathered round to listen to an oral reading, as depicted in *Letter from America*, a painting of 1875 by James Brenan, 1825–89. (Crawford Municipal Art Gallery, Cork)

Irish emigrants stopping temporarily at Liverpool had to contend with a host of tricksters and con-artists who were determined to relieve them of their money and possessions. This was true before, during, and long after the famine. One famine emigrant declared that even if humans possessed seven senses, it 'would take 500 senses largely developed to counteract the sharpers of Liverpool'. The hapless victim at the centre of this painting of 1871 – *Irish emigrant arriving at Liverpool* – by Erskine Nicol would no doubt have agreed wholeheartedly. (National Galleries of Scotland, Edinburgh)

With much of Ireland prostrated by starvation and epidemic disease in May 1847, the death of O'Connell at Genoa while on his way to Rome was felt as an especially cruel blow in Ireland. Even the *Illustrated London News*, not a periodical sympathetic to O'Connellite nationalism, was capable of capturing the significance of this funereal conjuncture. It published this allegorical representation of the death of the Liberator, with a grieving Ireland at the foot of his statue, and with heavy black clouds hanging over the land, presumably to signify the catastrophe of famine as well as the loss of his leadership. (*Illustrated London News*)

The identification of Irish nationalism with Catholicism in the nineteenth and twentieth centuries owes a great deal to the political career of Daniel O'Connell. His personal attachment to the Catholic faith was also intense. His practice of fingering his rosary beads while sitting in the House of Commons at Westminster attracted comment, and even more so did his pious plan to make a pilgrimage to the eternal city at the close of his life. Entirely appropriate, then, were the solemn and elaborate obsequies for O'Connell early in August 1847 at the Catholic church in Marlborough Street in Dublin, shown here. The funeral procession drew immense crowds of mourners. (*Illustrated London News*)

performed much better during the famine than the Whigs can be debated, but what is certain is that the Whigs never came close to proving the worth that O'Connell saw in them.

Although O'Connell's death was not an event of great political significance, his passing made it even less likely that repealers of either faction would be able to breathe new life into the Irish body politic. Upon the Liberator's death the mantle of leadership within the Repeal Association fell to his son, John O'Connell, who lacked his father's charisma and the capacity that his father had once shown for political decisiveness. Besides these defects, John O'Connell possessed neither the policies nor the funds needed to revive his largely moribund organisation. The Young Irelanders were in no better shape. As the general election of mid-1847 demonstrated, they were widely held responsible for having hastened the death of the revered Liberator. Moreover, their chief leaders Gavan Duffy and Smith O'Brien still clung tenaciously to the forlorn hope of converting the landed gentry to repeal and ensured that the Irish Confederation adhered strictly to a constitutionalist and conservative nationalism in which agrarian agitation, much less social revolution, had no place. The overall result was that neither group was capable of accomplishing anything.

Various attempts were made in 1847 both to achieve a nationalist reunion and to resuscitate the spirit that had propped up the Irish parliamentary party. With the Whig alliance so thoroughly discredited, the ground separating John O'Connell from the Young Ireland leaders was much narrower than it once had been. And in negotiations with the Confederate chieftains John O'Connell was more conciliatory than his father on such points as the interpretation to be placed on the peace resolutions and the barring of place-hunting by repealers. But he rejected the Young Irelanders' insistence that an entirely new repeal organisation should take the place of both the confederation and the Repeal Association.[13] And just as these efforts at reunion failed, so too did the attempts of both groups to win any significant number of landlord recruits to a strategy of broad-based opposition to government policy. That many landlords were deeply discontented with the Whig ministry was obvious, but nationalist leaders were extremely reluctant to admit that the unionism of the landed gentry was much stronger than their current alienation from the Whig government. Many landlords also had reason to doubt the soundness of repealers on the land question.

AGRARIAN ISSUES

The land question, and more specifically tenant right, became the focus of much political discussion as the clearances gathered momentum in late 1847 and as the destitute multitudes faced another winter of starvation and pestilence.[14] Among Irish politicians who advocated tenant right as a solution to the problem of insecurity of tenure, there was no agreement as to its precise meaning or as to how it might be given legislative embodiment. For William Sharman Crawford, the best known Irish advocate of tenant right and its foremost parliamentary champion, the phrase had no radical implications. A claim to tenant right, he held, arose only in those cases where the tenant had made substantial permanent improvements to his holding; in such instances the tenant deserved reasonable compensation if his landlord evicted him or if he wished to surrender his farm. Under this interpretation the achievement of tenant right would have been of limited practical significance during the famine years. Only a small proportion of the tenants then facing eviction or planning to emigrate could legitimately have claimed to be responsible for really substantial improvements. In contrast to Sharman Crawford, John O'Connell apparently took a more advanced position and viewed the tenant 'as having, in effect, a property right in the land itself, once he had paid his rent'.[15] But as much as O'Connell was interested in somehow linking the demand for tenant right to the cause of repeal, he showed no disposition to subordinate the latter to the former (not even temporarily) or to lead a popular agitation with tenant right as one of its primary goals.

Such views, however, were forcefully advocated by James Fintan Lalor in the pages of the *Nation*, and they were eventually taken up and pressed by John Mitchel and other radicals in the Irish Confederation.[16] Lalor was the crippled son of a prosperous farmer in the Abbeyleix district of Queen's County; his father Patrick Lalor had played a prominent part in the great anti-tithe agitation of the early 1830s and had briefly sat in parliament as an O'Connellite MP for Queen's County (1832–5). But Fintan Lalor had no time for the O'Connells or their policies. While regarding himself as a nationalist, he rejected repeal as 'an impracticable absurdity', not attainable by constitutional methods and much too abstract to have any real attractiveness in the famine-stricken Irish countryside.[17] Although he accepted private property as the basis of the social system, Lalor repudiated the notion of absolute ownership in land. He held instead that the land belonged ultimately to the whole community, and he insisted that the current occupiers of the soil possessed rights amounting to co-ownership with the proprietors. From this premise it followed that the tenants were entitled at least to fair rents and security of tenure. Perhaps more important than Lalor's radical philosophy was his advocacy of what he called 'moral insurrection', which meant in practice a national strike against the payment of rent until the British government and Irish landlords conceded a new agrarian order that would recognise the justice of the tenants' claims to economic security. Lalor was convinced that the traditional agrarian regime was collapsing under the destructive impact of the famine, so that replacing it should not be all that difficult. With the help of local activists he tried to start a militant tenant right movement in south Leinster and north Munster.

Lalor's strategy, however, failed to win acceptance either at the grassroots level or within the Irish Confederation. Strong farmers would not begin to show deep interest in a tenant right movement until 1849 or 1850, after an agricultural depression took hold. And even tenant right seemed remote from the elemental concerns of smallholders and agricultural labourers in the years 1847–8. There was truth in Gavan Duffy's biting criticism that Lalor's 'angry peasants, chafing like chained tigers, were creatures of the imagination – not the living people through whom we had to act'.[18] Lalor was no more successful within the confederation. By the end of 1847 John Mitchel had at last abandoned his earlier hopes that the landlords would concede tenant right without open warfare. Though he did not endorse all of Lalor's views, Mitchel now agreed that the confederation ought to give enthusiastic support to the kind of agrarian campaign that Lalor advocated. A few others in that body had also come to the same conclusion. But the moderate majority still accepted the judgement of Gavan Duffy and Smith O'Brien, who decried class conflict and insisted upon

PUNCH AND PADDY.

"PUT AWAY THAT NASTY THING, AND LET'S HAVE A MERRY CHRISTMAS."

Recalling the winter of 1847/8, John Mitchel remarked trenchantly: 'A kind of sacred wrath took possession of a few Irishmen at this period. They could endure the horrible scene no longer and resolved to cross the path of the British car of conquest, though it should crush them to atoms.' *Punch* appeared sensitive to the new mood among the most extreme nationalists. In this cartoon of December 1847 a festive Mr Punch urges a distracted Paddy with a blunderbuss under his arm to 'put away that nasty thing' so that they can all have a Merry Christmas. (*Punch* Archive) adhering to constitutional agitation alone. In disgust Mitchel and his friends began to sever their ties with the confederation. They concurred with the *Nation* writer who declared: 'It is indeed full time that we cease to whine and begin to act. . . . Good heavens, to think that we should go down without a struggle.'[19] There was no whining in Mitchel's new newspaper, the *United Irishman*, which began publication early in February 1848. It preached revolution more or less openly, but few were listening to its message. Futility and division seemed to have an iron grip on Irish politics as the year 1848 opened.

DRIFTING TOWARDS REBELLION

Everything appeared to change, however, when beginning in February the fever of revolution swept across Europe. Especially invigorating was the spectacle of the overthrow of Louis Philippe in France by an almost bloodless revolution in Paris. It encouraged Irish nationalists to believe that repeal could now be won without spilling much blood – without having to make a real revolution. To instil fear would be enough. If British ministers should lose their nerve, as others had, the goal could be attained. Fearful of attack by revolutionary France, fearful of social revolution by domestic Chartists, and fearful of nationalist revolution in Ireland, Britain would soon concede repeal.

It was quickly made plain, however, that the new revolutionary government in France, valuing good relations with Britain, would not commit itself to open support of Irish nationalism. An Irish nationalist delegation to Paris, headed by Smith O'Brien, came away empty-handed early in April. The Chartists in Britain were much more accommodating. In the north of England numerous combined Chartist and Confederate meetings were held in the spring of 1848, and Irish Confederates were much in evidence at the great Chartist demonstration on Kennington Common in London on 10 April, when Feargus O'Connor extolled the justice of Ireland's cry for repeal. But the main lesson to be drawn from the Kennington Common episode was that social revolution by the Chartists was simply not in the offing. Consequently, it was hardly necessary for Whig ministers to concede repeal to Irish nationalists so as to be able to concentrate on the Chartist menace at home. Thus nationalists in Ireland were gradually thrown back on their own resources, which were still divided and mostly rhetorical.[20]

Then the government unintentionally rescued the nationalists from their divisions, though not from their rhetoric. In March 1848 the authorities decided to prosecute three of the leading Young Irelanders on charges of sedition: Mitchel for articles appearing in the *United Irishman*, and Smith O'Brien and Thomas Francis Meagher for inflammatory speeches. The lord lieutenant feared that unless the agitators were muzzled, they would raise a storm throughout the country, and because the government had no new measures of relief to offer, their opportunities for making mischief or worse would be much enhanced. Those officials who advised against the prosecutions for fear of making martyrs were overruled, but they had the cold comfort of seeing their predictions confirmed when the trials took place in May. The prosecutions of both Smith O'Brien and Meagher ended in hung juries and the prisoners were discharged amid nationalist jubilation. After this stinging defeat the authorities went to great lengths to pack the jury in the case of Mitchel, who was tried ten days later under the recently passed treason-felony act, the earlier charges of sedition having been dropped. Mitchel was duly convicted and sentenced to fourteen years' transportation. The severity of the sentence, together with the flagrant packing of the jury, at once aroused a wave of sympathy for Mitchel among all nationalist factions. Not for the first or last time, it was difficult for Irish political moderates to gainsay the spell cast by a martyr, however unpalatable his extreme views.[21]

The character and outcome of Mitchel's trial increased the pressures for a nationalist reunion, especially within the Repeal Association, which was financially crippled and faltering badly under John O'Connell's less than masterful leadership. And on this occasion, though O'Connell fought a rearguard action against merger, the negotiations finally led in early July 1848 to the establishment of the short-lived Irish League, which replaced both the Repeal Association and the confederation. The terms of the merger were more favourable to the Young Irelanders than to O'Connell and his followers, since the Confederate clubs scattered around the country were not only allowed to remain in being but were also permitted, as the nucleus of a national guard, to arm themselves. Thus, even though the league was officially a constitutionalist organisation, its members were left free as individuals to champion the use of physical force.[22]

In practice, nationalist reunion signified little. Attention was focused not on building up the league but rather on extending the network of local Confederate clubs. In the dispiriting circumstances of the time this work was bound to proceed slowly. Even at their widest extent the clubs never numbered more than about seventy, each with a membership reportedly ranging from 200 to 500. If the average membership is generously assumed to have been about 300, the total may have slightly exceeded 20,000. Had club members been properly armed and well trained, they might have constituted a potentially troublesome, if not really formidable, force. But arms were in short supply and drilling was sporadic. Moreover, the clubs were very unevenly distributed geographically. Almost all of them were concentrated in the towns, with nearly half located in Dublin alone; organisation in the countryside, not surprisingly, was virtually non-existent.[23] Under such conditions the prospects for the success of a possible rebellion were scarcely encouraging, as the Young Irelanders themselves recognised in their sober-minded moments.

In the end, the principal Young Irelanders or Confederates became the prisoners of all their bold talk of action. By calling on the people to arm themselves so that they might be ready if the day for action ever came, the Confederate leaders instilled the belief that they meant business, sooner rather than later. They felt wounded when some of their fanatical adherents in effect accused them of being fine talkers rather than courageous men of action. As a result, they themselves drifted aimlessly towards action. They were helped along this path by the widespread notion that the preservation of self-respect, their own and that of a famishing people, required action. This attitude was strengthened in July, when the government suspended *habeas corpus*, instituted a series of arrests, and declared illegal the holding of arms in Dublin and certain other counties. It was only by a small majority that the council of the Irish League voted against an immediate rising in response to the government proclamation. Instead, the majority, still awaiting a better opportunity to strike, opted for a policy of defensive resistance against efforts to disarm the clubs. As the main proponent of immediate action bitterly declared, they were forever waiting – till aid came from France or America, 'till rifles are forged in heaven and angels draw the trigger'.[24]

THE 1848 RISING AND ITS LEGACY

It is unnecessary to rehearse here the confused events of late July which finally brought the Young Ireland leaders to their brief and inglorious encounter with the police in the Widow McCormack's cabbage garden near Ballingarry, County Tipperary. As Robert Kee has well said, the so-called rising of 1848 'was not in any practical sense a rising at all, nor until the very last minute was it ever intended to be one'.[25] Its reluctant, half-hearted leaders had made hardly any preparations. They had nothing that could be dignified with the name of a strategy. They discovered again what they already knew – that the peasantry in the south-east were incapable of being roused or were too intelligent to take the risk. And even in the towns where clubs existed, they found that most members were without firearms. It was a pure mercy that such a ridiculous escapade collapsed almost as soon as it started. Mitchel's acid comment when he received the news two months later was apposite: 'What is this I hear? A poor extemporised abortion of a rising in Tipperary, headed by Smith O'Brien'. Coming from the arch-revolutionary, this might be considered strange criticism, but Mitchel professed to know his business: 'In the present condition of the island, no rising must begin in the country. Dublin streets for that.' The revolt, he added, 'has been too long deferred', implying that if only the rebels had taken up arms earlier, and in Dublin, they would have given a much better account of themselves, though even Mitchel accepted that the ultimate military outcome would have been the same.[26] He seems to have wanted what would later be called a blood sacrifice, one that would redeem military defeat by the political success of its after-effects, and his disappointment over the pathetic farce of a revolution was acute.

But Mitchel's immediate reaction to the rising was unduly pessimistic, just as Sir Robert Peel was too optimistic when he claimed in late August 1848, 'Smith O'Brien has rendered more service than I thought he was capable of rendering

A rebellion without a military plan, or adequate supplies of arms and ammunition, or a committed rebel army was bound to end badly, even ludicrously. That was the misfortune of the 'Irish rebellion' of July 1848, which effectively concluded with the inglorious affray on 29 July in the Widow McCormack's cabbage garden on Boulagh Commons at Ballingarry, Co. Tipperary. In the encounter, depicted in this sketch, a hundred or so rebels (mainly local miners) temporarily cornered a body of police in the Widow McCormack's house. The police held them off, killing several of the rebels, until they were relieved by large numbers of troops and constabulary who poured into the neighbourhood. A *Times* writer sneered at 'the cabbage-garden revolution'. (*Illustrated London News*)

by making rebellion ridiculous.'[27] In spite of the pathetic character of the rising, its political effects were profound and literally far-reaching. Some of these were slow to mature while others manifested themselves more quickly. Many Young Ireland rebels evaded arrest and took ship to North America, where they later helped to give focus and a sharp edge to the anti-English hostility of the famine emigrants and their children. A few others escaped to Paris, where they continued to nurture their fierce resentment against British misrule. This small band included James Stephens and John O'Mahony, the co-founders in the late 1850s of the Fenian movement in Ireland and America. Indeed, in its leadership before 1865 and in its ideology, Fenianism was essentially the product of 1848.

Other Young Irelanders, however, paid the price for their involvement in the events of 1848 either by imprisonment in Ireland or by transportation to Van Diemen's Land. The judicial repression that followed the rising was by no means severe. Presented with the gift of a ridiculous rebellion, the government was not disposed to throw it away through an excess of repressive zeal. Not a single one of the captured rebels was executed. Four of them (Smith O'Brien, Meagher, Terence Bellew McManus, and Patrick O'Donoghue) were convicted of high treason and sentenced to death, but the authorities were strongly against letting

In the aftermath of the rebellion the government arranged a series of state trials of the principal leaders. Among the chief targets of this repression was Smith O'Brien. This illustration depicts the impressive opening of the special commission for his trial and those of three others at Clonmel on 28 September 1848. Their trials lasted for almost a month altogether, and their speeches from the dock, along with those of certain other 1848 prisoners, became staples of revolutionary and constitutional nationalist propaganda. (*Illustrated London News*)

the law take its course. And when the four state prisoners embarrassingly refused to ask for the pardons that would have allowed their death sentences to be commuted to transportation, the government resolved the difficulty by quickly carrying into law a measure that made transportation permissible in treason cases without pardon.[28] But for all its calculated restraint the government could not prevent the martyr's crown from descending on those convicted in its courts. By refusing to crave pardons, the four state prisoners elevated and ennobled their farcical rising. Their steady courage during and after their trials, together with their eventual dispatch to Van Diemen's Land, captured the Irish popular imagination at home and abroad. A hero's welcome greeted McManus, Meagher, and Mitchel when they arrived in California in 1853 after escaping from Van Diemen's Land.[29]

Though less idolised, the Young Irelanders imprisoned at home also benefited politically from their rebel past and penal confinement. The fact that they were soon released did not prevent them from claiming some share in the martyrology of Irish nationalism, even when, chastened by their recent experience, they again embraced constitutionalism and non-violence.[30] Most of them soon resumed their political careers, and quite a few drew important lessons from their political isolation in 1848. Gavan Duffy, among others, recanted one of the cardinal tenets of the moderate Young Irelanders before the rising, namely, their belief in the necessity of avoiding class conflict between landlord and tenant. Soon after emerging from gaol, he revived the *Nation* at the beginning of September 1849 and at once announced that in the short run the quest for independence must give way to efforts 'to bring back Ireland to health and strength by stopping the system of extermination'.[31] A week later, he declared it to be 'the first duty of a national association to assault' the current land system.[32] Though not in the same words, many others – churchmen and politicians, Catholics and Presbyterians – were now saying much the same thing. Capitalising on this increasing public sentiment in favour of agrarian reform in the south as well as in Ulster, Duffy was instrumental in organising a national conference in November 1849 that helped to lay the basis for the great tenant right agitation of the early 1850s.[33]

Collectively, what the Young Ireland rebels did was to politicise the events of the famine, especially its appalling mortality and its mammoth emigration.[34] The interpretation of famine deaths as a grotesque act of genocide perpetrated by the British government owed much to the Young Irelanders. Long before John Mitchel in 1860 gave systematic expression to this view in his book *The last conquest of Ireland (perhaps)*, even the moderate Gavan Duffy was calling the famine 'a fearful murder committed on the mass of the people' – in the *Nation* at the end of April 1848.[35] Similarly, the interpretation of famine emigration as forced exile or banishment found some of its most vociferous exponents among Young Irelanders who were themselves compelled to flee their native land. Not only did they dramatise in their own persons that emigration was forced exile, but they also propagated the same view relentlessly in their venomously anti-English writings and speeches in those countries to which they had been 'banished'. Of course, these interpretations of mortality and emigration were not the exclusive property of the politically sophisticated, middle-class Young Irelanders. Often, they arose spontaneously at the popular level out of bitter common experience. But the Young Irelanders certainly gave them a currency and respectability that they would not otherwise have had.

However acquired, such views gained wide popular acceptance in Ireland and among the famine Irish abroad largely because they served a deep psychological need to displace personal guilt. Apart altogether from 'extermination' by landlords and the deadly callousness of officials, the records of the great famine are replete with anti-social behaviour and acts of gross inhumanity – committed by wealthy farmers and shopkeepers against the poor, by the poor against others of their own class, by parents against their children, and by sons and daughters against their parents. By their very nature prolonged famine and epidemics of fatal disease lead to the large-scale erosion or collapse of traditional moral restraints and communal sanctions. For many of the survivors of the great famine of the late 1840s, the recollection of their anti-social conduct against neighbours and even close relatives was a heavy psychological burden crying out for release and displacement. What made the displacement of this guilt on to Albion's shoulders so compelling was not only that England represented the ancient oppressor but also that its Whig government during the famine had such a damning record in Ireland. Who today should be surprised that many of 'Erin's boys' wanted 'revenge for Skibbereen'?

CHAPTER 9

Constructing the Memory of the Famine, 1850–1900

In a well-known, slightly notorious, article published in 1989 in *Irish Historical Studies*, Brendan Bradshaw drew our attention to the large gap that had developed between the popular and nationalist understanding of the great famine and the interpretation which had become fashionable among the academic 'revisionists', as he and others called them.[1] It may be that in the matter of the famine at least, historians of Ireland, even the native-born ones, taking them as a group, were not as revisionist in their perspective as Bradshaw seemed to indicate. And in the years since 1989 the scholarly works published about the famine, and the films made about it involving professional historians and other academics, have on balance tended strongly in the direction of the traditional nationalist interpretation.[2] Even so, there are several important aspects of the nationalist version of the great famine, especially those that relate to the charge of genocide levelled at the British government of the time, which academic historians strenuously refuse to credit, even if they do not belong at all to the so-called revisionist camp.[3] And so strong are popular feelings on these matters in Ireland and especially in Irish-America that a scholar who seeks to rebut or heavily qualify the nationalist charge of genocide is often capable of stirring furious controversy and runs the risk of being labelled an apologist for the British government's horribly misguided policies during the famine. This situation, which at times I have found personally unpleasant, prompts me to examine what I call the nationalist construction of the memory – the public memory – of the famine in Ireland and the Irish diaspora from roughly 1850 to 1900. One major purpose of this last chapter is to contribute to a further narrowing of the gap which separates the populist and nationalist understanding of the famine catastrophe from what I think is now the dominant post-revisionist academic one.

Food Exports and Mass Starvation

In the public memory of the famine as constructed by nationalists, no idea came to be lodged more firmly than the notion that throughout the famine years enough food (more than enough, many said) was produced to feed all of

Ireland's people, and that if this food had only been retained in the country, it would have prevented mass mortality. But instead of being retained, most of this food had been exported to Britain in order to satisfy the inexorable demands of Irish landlords (nationalists often said and say 'English landlords') for their rents, in the collection of which they enjoyed, whenever necessary, the armed assistance of soldiers and police – the British garrison in Ireland. The tenant producers of this food had no choice but to sell it for export if they wished to avoid the disaster of eviction, and, if they were inclined to resist, their crops and livestock were legally seized by the landlord's bailiffs, fully backed by the forces of the state. As a direct result of the 'forced export' of all this food, a million people starved to death or died of disease. This was and is the heart of the nationalist charge that the British government committed genocide against the Irish people.

As the years passed, constitutional nationalists were almost as likely to share and advocate this view as revolutionary ones. In his formidable book *The Parnell movement*, first published in 1886 and hugely popular on both sides of the Atlantic, the journalist and Parnellite MP T.P. O'Connor reduced the argument about the export of 'these vast provisions' to an irrefutable syllogism: 'The Irish land system necessitated the export of food from a starving nation. The English parliament was the parent of this land system; the English parliament was, then, responsible for the starvation which this exportation involved.'[4] In the revolutionary nationalist tradition this view often took the form (and still does so today) of denying legitimacy to the use of the very word 'famine' in referring to the disaster. In his *Recollections* Jeremiah O'Donovan Rossa showed what had long been the usual republican intolerance for calling it a famine. 'We adopt the English expression', he complained, 'and call those years the "famine years"; but there was no famine in the land. . . . [Instead] the English took the food away to England and let the people starve.'[5] Thus for revolutionary nationalists the preferred terminology became 'the great starvation' or 'the great hunger' and its equivalent in Irish, '*an gorta mór*'.

It is beyond question that the notions connecting huge food exports with mass starvation and British genocide became deeply rooted in the folk memory of the nationalist Irish at home and abroad during the first half-century after the famine. The autobiographical memoir of the Irish scholar Canon Peter O'Leary, first published in 1915, furnishes some confirming evidence. Born in 1839 in an area of north-west Cork (Liscarrigane near Macroom) that was hit hard by the famine, O'Leary was educated at Fermoy and Maynooth before becoming active (locally) in the Land League and later (nationally) in the Gaelic League. Though highly educated (indeed, he was once called 'the greatest living master of Irish prose'), he was also close to the oral traditions of his native Cork. In that portion of his memoir dealing with the start of the great famine, O'Leary declared: 'There was sent out from Ireland that year [apparently, 1846 is meant] as much – no! twice as much – corn as would have nourished every person living in the country. The harbours of Ireland were full of ships and the ships full of Irish

This cartoon from the *Looking Glass* of July 1831 was inspired by famine conditions in the western counties of Galway and Mayo in the spring and summer of that year. It depicts the export of food – in this case potatoes – in the face of protests from starving people. In allowing the export of grain from Ireland during the great famine, and especially after the disastrous potato failure of 1846, the Whig government opened itself to the nationalist charge that it was guilty of genocide against the famishing Irish people. This charge, made repeatedly by nationalist writers and orators in the decades after 1850, became deeply lodged in the popular memory. (Reproduced by courtesy of the Knight of Glin)

corn; they were leaving the harbours while the people were dying with the hunger throughout the land.' As to why no law prohibiting grain exports had been passed, O'Leary offered an answer filled with anti-English venom: 'It was not at all for the protection of the people that the English made laws [at] that time. To crush the people down and to plunder them, to put them to death by famine and by every other kind of injustice – that's why the English made laws in those days.'[6] Another clerical scholar with essentially the same views was Monsignor Michael O'Riordan, rector of the Irish College in Rome, who in 1916 made these ideas a theme of his St Patrick's day sermon in St Patrick's church in that city: 'Seventy years ago began in Ireland what are known as the "famine years". There was indeed a famine, but it was a famine in the midst of plenty. . . . Men made it but they threw the blame on God; as much corn was grown in Ireland during those years as would more than maintain the population; but it was taken and shipped out of the country under the protection of the law and was turned to other uses than to the support of those who grew it.'[7]

The memories of ordinary people, less likely perhaps to have been shaped directly by nationalist writings, closely paralleled those of the scholars Canon O'Leary and Monsignor O'Riordan. One Mayo informant of the Irish Folklore Commission (Martin Manning, born in 1875) recounted the following story in 1945: 'In the year 1847 fourteen schooners of about 200 tons each left Westport quay laden with wheat and oats for to feed the English people while the Irish were starving. This happened one morning on one tide and was repeated several times during the famine.'[8] And a Clare informant, a farmer by occupation (Tomás Aichir, born in 1859), told the Irish Folklore Commission in 1945: 'A shipload of American corn coming would pass a shipload of Irish corn going out of Ireland to England – corn which they had to sell to pay the landlord's rent and escape losing their homes and their all.'[9]

Are such views echoes of the extended and bitter discussion of food exports to be found in John Mitchel's *The last conquest of Ireland (perhaps)*, the first Irish edition of which appeared in 1861? While this is possible, there were in nationalist literature other, earlier potential sources as well as numerous later ones. And it also needs to be emphasised that a firm foundation for these views had been laid in political conflict during the famine itself. As Charles Gavan Duffy recalled in his autobiography, it was the consistent line of the *Nation* under its Confederate editors that tenant farmers should 'hold the harvest', and that somehow the export of corn should be stopped.[10] 'The *Nation* insisted over and over again', declared Duffy, that 'if there was a famine, it would be a famine created by the landlords.'[11] In August 1847 the radical Confederate priest Father John Kenyon proclaimed a stark form of this gospel to the readers of the *Nation*: 'Year after year our plentiful harvests of golden grain, more than sufficient even since the potato blight to support, and to support well, our entire population, are seen to disappear off the face of the land.'[12] The deep Confederate conviction that the stoppage of grain exports constituted 'the only alternative to famine' even found expression in an angry poem by Confederate barrister John O'Hagan which the *Nation* happily published:

Were we, saints of heaven! – were we, how we burn to think it – FREE!
Not a grain should leave our shore, not for England's golden store;
They who hunger where it grew, they whom heaven hath sent it to,
They who reared with sweat of brow, they, or none, should have it now.[13]

Nationalists quarrelled bitterly among themselves over issues relating to the food supply during the famine. In his autobiography Duffy harshly criticised Daniel O'Connell's conduct after the partial potato failure of 1845 in demanding the opening of Irish ports to foreign grain and in saying that the prohibition of Irish grain exports should not extend to England. In repudiating O'Connell's positions, Duffy went so far as to claim that 'opening

Charles Gavan Duffy (1816–1903) played a central role in Irish nationalist politics from 1842, when he co-founded the *Nation* newspaper with Thomas Davis and John Blake Dillon, until 1856, when he emigrated to Australia after becoming disillusioned with the failure of the Independent Irish party. Along with other Young Irelanders, he broke with Daniel O'Connell and the Repeal Association in mid-1846. A leader of the Irish Confederation from its foundation in January 1847, he drifted halfheartedly into rebellion in July 1848. Though he was tried no fewer than four times for his involvement in the 1848 'rising', he was acquitted on each occasion. His political career in Australia culminated in his appointment as governor-general of Victoria. Late in his long life he published heavily on Irish politics before, during, and after the famine. His autobiography – *My life in two hemispheres* – appeared in 1898 when he was over eighty years old. (National Gallery of Ireland)

the ports was entirely unnecessary, as the country produced more food than it consumed, and the prohibition against exporting cereals would have been precaution enough', as long as no exception was made for England. Duffy ridiculed O'Connell's statement that on balance Ireland was perhaps a net importer of food from England. This, he declared, was 'a statement as marvellous as if he affirmed that Newcastle gets more coal from Ireland than she sends to it'.[14]

Disagreement over food supply issues intensified after the permanent split between the O'Connellites and the Young Irelanders in mid-1846. By the spring of 1847 the Young Irelanders, now organised in the Irish Confederation, were loudly proclaiming a 'hold the harvest' line. 'If Ireland yields produce enough to feed eight millions', shouted Mitchel at a confederation meeting in April of that year, 'what particular eight millions in the world have the first claim upon it?'[15] In justification of their position the Confederates were quick to invoke a famous speech about the famine given at this time by Bishop John Hughes of New York. In this speech, often quoted in later years as well, Hughes maintained that 'the rights of life are dearer and higher than those of property; and in a general famine like the present, there is no law of heaven, nor of nature, that forbids a starving man to seize on bread wherever he can find it, even though it should be the loaves of proposition on the altar of God's temple'.[16] Even before John Mitchel took the 'hold the harvest' line to the extreme point of calling for a universal strike against both rents and poor rates, the O'Connellites denounced the Irish Confederation and its leaders as political adventurers or worse. Duffy bitterly recalled in his autobiography that 'the young men [of the confederation] were impeded at every step by the base falsehood which represented them as agents of anarchy, and Conciliation Hall [the meeting place of the O'Connellite Loyal National Repeal Association] was ready on the first alarm to point them out as dabbling in the blood of the people'.[17] Thus already during the famine itself, as part of their opposition to O'Connellite nationalists, Irish landlords, and the British government, the Young Irelanders or Confederates had staked out what had become a doctrinaire position on the scale of Irish grain production and on the role of grain exports, as encouraged by British laws and policies, in bringing about 'the great starvation'.

SETTING THE RECORD STRAIGHT

This doctrinaire position was based on a whole series of erroneous assumptions or miscalculations. First, grain exports during the famine years were far below normal, as much more of the corn grown in Ireland was in fact consumed there. Thus in 'black '47', according to one careful estimate by P.M.A. Bourke, only 146,000 tons of grain were exported, in contrast to an average of 472,000 tons annually in the three years from 1843 to 1845. Second, the inflow of grain from abroad, especially Indian corn and meal from North America, greatly exceeded the outflow of grain from Ireland after 1846. Thus in the years 1847 and 1848 total imports (1,328,000 tons) exceeded total exports (460,000 tons) by a factor of almost three to one.[18] Third, and most important, when blight destroyed the potato in the late 1840s, it destroyed the crop which had provided, according to Bourke's estimate, approximately 60 per cent of the nation's food needs on the eve of the famine. To the remaining 40 per cent of national requirements, oats contributed only 16 per cent, wheat only 9 per cent, and other foods 15 per cent.[19] The food gap created by the loss of the potato in the late 1840s was so enormous that it could not have been filled even if all the grain exported in those years had been retained in the country.

The extent of this gap, as already pointed out, has been illuminated by the imaginative and laborious statistical calculations of Peter Solar, who has shown in tabular form 'where the Irish people got their calories in the early and late 1840s'. Excluded from his calculations are meat and dairy products, mainly because their calorific content 'is quite small, so that the major changes in the calories available will be determined by what happens to potatoes and cereals'. In calorific terms Irish production of grain and potatoes plunged by slightly more than 50 per cent in the years 1846–50 as compared with the early 1840s, with the destruction of the potato being exclusively responsible for this staggering loss of calories. Smaller exports of grain and pork (essentially a potato-based product) after 1845 helped modestly to narrow the gap, as only 1.9 thousand million calories per day were exported in these forms in the late 1840s, in contrast to 6.4 thousand million calories per day in the years 1840–5. The retention of these exports during the famine years would have raised Irish food supplies from 12.6 to 14.5 thousand million calories per day, or by 15 per cent. Imports of grain and Indian corn actually made a far greater contribution than the complete retention of these exports could have achieved, since the imports of the late 1840s added 5.5 thousand million calories per day to food stocks, whereas the exports depleted them only at the rate of 1.9 thousand million calories per day. In other words, in calorific terms grain imports were worth almost three times as much as grain exports during the late 1840s.[20]

Ideology over Facts

Such statistical considerations as these were not altogether beyond the ability of Irish nationalists to entertain. The gross figures for Irish grain imports and exports, for example, were readily accessible in official and unofficial sources, and if honestly confronted, would at least have raised serious doubts about the accuracy of the nationalist perspective. Instead, the half-century after the famine witnessed a never-ending stream of books and newspaper articles on both sides of the Atlantic which repeated or developed the nationalist doctrine propounded by Confederate leaders in the *Nation* in 1847. First in the field was the 1848 exile Thomas D'Arcy McGee, who in 1851 published in Boston his extremely popular *History of the Irish settlers in North America*, which had already gone into its sixth edition by 1855.[21] Before escaping to America in the aftermath of the

Thomas D'Arcy McGee (1825–68) had multiple careers – journalism, politics, and historical writing – and made his mark in three countries – Ireland, the United States, and Canada. While still a supporter of Daniel O'Connell before 1846, he was parliamentary correspondent of the *Freeman's Journal* and then the *Nation*. After splitting from O'Connell along with other Young Irelanders, he was secretary of the Irish Confederation and fruitlessly sought help in Scotland for the 1848 'rising'. Escaping to America with the help of Bishop Edward Maginn of Derry, he founded newspapers first in New York and then in Boston. He published his *History of the Irish settlers in North America* in 1852 while presiding over the *American Celt*, his Boston paper. His rejection of his earlier republicanism prompted some leading Irish-Americans to denounce him. Their denunciations eventually led McGee to start a new and highly successful career in Canadian politics in the late 1850s. He was assassinated in Ottawa in April 1868 after condemning Fenian raids on Canada. (Notman Photographic Archives, McCord Museum of Canadian History, Montreal)

rising of 1848, McGee had acted as the London correspondent of both the *Freeman's Journal* and the *Nation*, and had served in 1847 as secretary of the Irish Confederation. Like so many other 1848 exiles, McGee was closely associated with journalism in North America and launched several newspapers.[22] Though he later became a convert to constitutional nationalism, the views about the famine which he expressed in his book of 1851 would easily have passed muster with revolutionary nationalists. Invoking the authority of a report by Captain Thomas Larcom of the Board of Works, McGee asserted that in the wake of the total potato failure of 1846 'there were grain crops more than sufficient to support the whole population – a cereal harvest estimated at four hundred millions of dollars, as prices were. But to all remonstrances, petitions, and proposals, the imperial economists had but one answer, "They could not interfere with the ordinary currents of trade."' The result, declared McGee, was that 'ships laden to the gunwales sailed out of Irish ports while the charities of the world were coming in'.[23] Or as he put it in another passage with a much sharper political point, 'England's flag drooped above the spoil she was stealing away from the famishing [Irish], as the American frigates passed hers, inward bound, deep with charitable freights.'[24] He even gave a malicious political twist to Sir Robert Peel's successful advocacy of free trade in 1846. Instead of underlining its significance for the massive food imports that came to Ireland in the late 1840s, McGee contented himself with observing that Peel's legislation 'had let in Baltic wheat and American provisions of every kind to compete with and undersell the Irish rack-rented farmers'.[25]

If McGee set the tone for post-famine nationalist writing about food exports and genocide, his influence was greatly exceeded by that of John Mitchel. The Mitchelite case was propounded again and again, always trenchantly and with rhetorical flair: first in his *Jail journal*, which initially appeared in instalments from January to August 1854 in the *Citizen*, Mitchel's own newspaper in New York City;[26] then in *The last conquest of Ireland (perhaps)*, which originally appeared as a series of letters published in 1858 in the *Southern Citizen*, a newspaper which he conducted in Knoxville, Tennessee, and later in Washington, D.C., from 1857 to 1859;[27] next in *An apology for the British government in Ireland*, published in Dublin in 1860; and lastly in his *History of Ireland from the treaty of Limerick to the present time*, which first appeared in New York in 1868 and was described in 1888 by Mitchel's biographer William Dillon as 'now the standard work upon that period of Irish history which it covers'.[28] All four of these works were frequently reprinted, both in cheap, popular forms and in more expensive editions, especially *Jail journal*, *Last conquest*, and the *History of Ireland*.

In his introduction to *Jail journal*, first published in book form in 1854, Mitchel greatly exaggerated the scale and significance of domestic Irish food production, and what's more, he did so in such a way as to suggest to his readers that his assertion was beyond dispute. There was, he declared, no need to recount 'how in . . . '46, '47, and '48 Ireland was exporting to England food to the value of fifteen million pounds sterling and had on her own soil at each harvest good and ample provision for double her own population, notwithstanding the potato blight'.[29] In his *Apology* of 1860 Mitchel employed the same assertion about the scale of Irish food production to propel more forcefully the charge of genocide against Britain:

> When the Irish nation, then being nine millions, produced by their own industry on their own land good food enough to feed eighteen millions, one cannot well say that *Providence* sent them a famine; and when those nine millions dwindled in two or three years to six and a half millions, partly by mere hunger and partly by flight beyond sea to escape it; and when we find [in] all these same years the English people living well and feeding full upon that very food for want of which the Irish died, I suppose the term British famine will be admitted to be quite correct.[30]

With this passage specifically in mind Thomas Flanagan has aptly said of Mitchel, 'his pen could not touch paper upon this subject without striking fire'.[31]

This comment is especially true of what Mitchel had to say of food exports and the Irish trade balance in grain in *Last conquest*, published in book form in the United States in 1860 and in Dublin in the following year. Speaking of Irish agricultural exports after the partial potato failure of 1845, Mitchel insisted, 'The great point was to put the English Channel between the people and the food which providence had sent them, at the earliest possible moment. By New Year's Day [1846] it was almost all swept off.'[32] Speaking of 'black '47', Mitchel asserted that 'insane mothers began to eat their young children, who died of famine before them. And still fleets of ships were sailing with every tide, carrying Irish cattle and corn to England.'[33] Mitchel did not deny the fact of very considerable grain imports from England and abroad, but he belittled their significance in numerous ways. Referring to the imports secured by Peel and his colleagues early in 1846, Mitchel declared, 'The quantity imported by them was inadequate to supply the loss of the grain *exported* from any one county, and a government ship sailing into any [Irish] harbour with Indian corn was sure to meet half a dozen sailing out with Irish wheat and cattle.'[34] In another place Mitchel firmly planted the notion that relief shipments from America were nullified by Irish exports to England, to the point that it would be perfectly futile for the United States to send aid 'if Ireland should again starve'. In that 'most likely' event, asserted Mitchel, 'let America never, never send her a bushel of corn or a dollar of money. Neither bushel nor dollar will ever reach her.'[35] In a third place Mitchel alleged that much of the grain that came to Ireland from England 'had previously been exported *from* Ireland and came back – laden with merchants' profits and double freights and insurance – to the helpless people who had sowed and reaped it'. He even went so far as to claim that 'many a shipload was carried four times across the Irish Sea, as prices "invited" it . . .'.

'This', Mitchel declared, 'is what commerce and free trade did for Ireland in those days.' Lest his readers be left in any doubt as to how the Irish balance of trade stood, he instructed them to bear in mind two facts: '*First*, that the net result of all this importation, exportation, and reimportation . . . was that England finally received our harvests to the same amount as before; and *second*, that she gave Ireland – under free trade in corn – less for it than ever.'[36] This very same language, and most of the rest of *Last conquest*, Mitchel simply reproduced in his *History of Ireland*, which the Sadleirs published in New York in 1868 and which in subsequent editions enjoyed extremely large sales on both sides of the Atlantic.[37]

Although no other nationalist writer exercised as much influence on this subject as Mitchel, some who reached large audiences managed to outdo him in exaggeration. Falling into this category was Bishop J.L. Spalding of Peoria, Illinois, whose book *The religious mission of the Irish people and Catholic colonization* enjoyed a wide circulation after its publication in 1880. Spalding claimed that under 'favorable circumstances' Ireland was capable of supporting as many as fifteen million people, not just eight million, as on the eve of the famine. As to the balance of trade in the late 1840s, Spalding flatly declared: 'During the four years of famine Ireland exported four quarters of wheat for every quarter imported.' To judge from the context of this assertion, Spalding seems to have been suffering from the double misunderstanding that wheat was the main Irish grain export and that wheat, a high-priced food, would have been a suitable imported substitute for the potato.[38] Another nationalist writer guilty of gross exaggeration was O'Donovan Rossa. In his *Recollections* of the late 1890s he meretriciously claimed the impartiality of a historian: 'Ireland [in] those three years of '45, '46, and '47 produced as much food as was sufficient to support three times the population of Ireland', but English ships carried most of it away. 'What I say', insisted Rossa, 'is historical truth, recorded in the statistics of the times.'[39] One measure of the impact of such exaggerated claims on the public memory of this aspect of the famine was the belief encountered by a collector for the Irish Folklore Commission in 1945 in the Dromore district of Sligo. 'The Indian meal', he reported, 'may have come perhaps in 1849; the people here could not say exactly, but they are positive it did not come during the three years of the failure of the potato crop.'[40]

Alone among nationalist writers in the late nineteenth century in paying some attention to agricultural statistics and trade figures was the journalist and Parnellite MP T.P. O'Connor. The show of statistical interest and acumen in his widely read book of 1886, *The Parnell movement*, no doubt gave added authority to his arguments and conclusions. Unfortunately, like other nationalists, O'Connor was not at all concerned with imports, which he left entirely out of consideration. Instead, he was preoccupied exclusively with exports, although he hardly noted how much Irish grain exports had declined during the famine years as compared with the early 1840s. What deeply impressed him was the absolute volume of grain exports. His figures for non-animal food exports (grains

T.P. O'Connor (1848–1929) had a long political career as a leader of the immigrant Irish in Britain and as a popular journalist and writer there. After moving to Britain in 1870, he strongly supported Irish home rule, the Land League, and Charles Stewart Parnell. He played a key role in persuading Irish voters in Britain to cast their ballots against the Liberals in the 1885 election, and the outcome helped to push the Liberal leader William Gladstone into embracing Irish home rule. O'Connor's book *The Parnell movement* (lauding the Irish leader) appeared in 1886, but he took the anti-Parnellite side in the great split of 1890–1 in the Irish parliamentary party over the O'Shea divorce. Of the three British newspapers he founded, the most successful was *T. P.'s Weekly*, launched in 1902. For almost five decades (1880–1929) he represented the Scotland division of Liverpool in the Westminster parliament, and was called the 'father of the House of Commons' in his later years. (Hulton Getty)

overwhelmingly) in the four years 1846–9 amounted to an average of 1,546,000 quarters annually. He suggested that one quarter of wheat was approximately equal to the 'average annual [bread] consumption of an individual'. Then, rather cavalierly, he declared, 'It is a simple sum in multiplication to find how many daily rations of bread for starving peasants were exported in each of these years.'[41]

Perhaps more tellingly, but still without much statistical rigour, O'Connor pointed out that the cost of the very material relief provided under the soup kitchen act between March and September 1847 had amounted to not much more than £1.5 million, which was substantially less than the estimated value (almost £2 million) of the Irish livestock exported in 1847. Or as he put it, 'Thus there was exported in cattle, sheep, and swine alone in this year – to say nothing whatever of the 969,490 q[uarte]rs of cereals – nearly half a million more in money value than was required to feed three millions of starving people in the same year.'[42] In short, the only nationalist writer in the half-century after the famine to show any significant interest in economic data reached essentially the same conclusion as all the others. Landlord demands for rent led inexorably to enormous food exports. 'It was,' said O'Connor, 'as Mitchel calls it, an artificial famine – starvation in the midst of food.'[43]

Mass Evictions Remembered

Next to the 'forced exports' of grain and other food from Ireland during the famine years, the mass evictions or clearances provided nationalists with what they considered the best and most compelling evidence of the malevolent intentions of the British government and parliament. Admittedly, the immediate agents of the clearances were Irish landlords, and in the public memory of the famine fashioned by nationalist writers and orators the suffering and death inflicted by many members of the Irish landed élite essentially obliterated the recollection of whatever good had been done by some members of that class. A.M. Sullivan was almost alone among nationalist writers of the second half of the nineteenth century in his generally positive view of landlord conduct. 'Granting all that has to be entered on the dark debtor side', argued Sullivan in 1877, 'the overwhelming balance is the other way. The bulk of the resident Irish landlords manfully did their best in that dread hour.'[44] No doubt, as Sullivan maintained, there were landlords whose generous relief of distress local people remembered to their credit, but they were much more likely to remember, and to remember much longer, the landlords whose large-scale evictions branded them as 'exterminators' in popular estimation. A century after the famine the Galway landowner Lord Dunsandle was still known in parts of that county as 'Lord Leveller', a man who had been fond of saying about his tenants, 'They're never tired [of] breeding beggars.'[45] Similarly, an informant of the Irish Folklore Commission (Martin Manning, born in 1875) not only called attention in 1945 to the clearances carried out by two Mayo landlords (the

O'Donnells of Newport and the Brownes of Westport), but he also recited the names of nine whole townlands cleared by the former and twelve townlands cleared by the latter.[46] In other cases informants at the remove of a century could still recite the names of the actual families who had been evicted from particular estates during the famine.[47]

In striking contrast to A.M. Sullivan's defence of at least resident Irish landlords stood a long line of nationalist authors who condemned the landlord class for its behaviour during the famine in the harshest terms. In his *Jail journal* Mitchel spoke of 'the extermination, that is, the slaughter of their tenantry' by the landlords.[48] Having noted that in 1849 alone they had allegedly evicted as many as 50,000 families, or 200,000 persons, Bishop Spalding of Peoria declared sweepingly, 'Everything, in a word, tended to make the Irish landlords the worst aristocracy with which a nation was ever cursed; and by the most cruel of fates this worst of all aristocracies was made the sole arbiter of the destinies of the Irish people. . . .' This all-embracing denunciation appeared first in the *Catholic World* newspaper in 1876 and was republished in 1880 in Spalding's widely read and highly influential book, *The religious mission of the Irish people and Catholic colonization*.[49] Even stronger language was used by Michael Davitt in his *Fall of feudalism* about how Irish landlords had completely discredited themselves during the famine. 'Nothing more inhumanly selfish and base', Davitt loudly insisted, 'is found to the disgrace of any class in any crisis in the history of civilised society.' Davitt grudgingly acknowledged that there had been a few exceptions to this black picture, but in his view they 'only bring into greater contrast the vulture propensities of the mass of Irish landowners of the time'.[50] Davitt's uncompromising anti-landlordism was probably related directly to his lively recollection of the eviction of his entire family from their holding at Straide, County Mayo, in 1850:

> I was then but four and a half years old, yet I have a distinct remembrance (doubtless strengthened by the frequent narration of the event by my parents in after years) of that morning's scene: the remnant of our household furniture flung about the road; the roof of the house falling in and the thatch taking fire; my mother and father looking on with four young children, the youngest only two months old, adding their cries to the other pangs which must have agitated their souls at the sight of their burning homestead.[51]

Like Davitt, O'Donovan Rossa also had bitter personal experience of dispossession and vied with Davitt in the vehemence of his denunciation of Irish landlordism. In his *Recollections*, first appearing in a newspaper serialisation in New York in the years 1896–8, Rossa indicated that his anti-landlord attitudes had been acquired almost with his mother's milk: 'Before I was ever able to read a book . . . , I heard [my] father and mother and neighbors rejoicing – "buidhechas le Dia!" – whenever they heard of an English landlord being shot in Tipperary or any other part of Ireland.'[52] Of the impact of the famine itself in

Michael Davitt (1846–1906) played a role in the Irish 'land war' of 1879–82 that was second only to Parnell's. A Fenian whose family had been evicted from their holding in Mayo during the famine, Davitt sought to bring about the destruction of landlordism in Ireland through the aggressive campaign waged by the Land League. He was alienated from Parnell and his supporters, however, when they turned away from agrarian agitation and towards home rule in 1882. In addition, Davitt's attachment to the idea of land nationalisation, as opposed to turning tenants into owner-occupiers, distanced him after 1882 from the mainstream of Irish agrarian reform. His book *The fall of feudalism in Ireland*, published in 1904, highlighted the contributions of Fenians and ex-Fenians like himself to the creation and accomplishments of the Land League. It also contained a fierce indictment of Irish landlord actions and British government policy during the famine. (The Board of Trinity College, Dublin)

Jeremiah O'Donovan Rossa (1831–1915) appears second from the right in this photograph of five recently released Fenians taken upon their arrival in the port of New York on the SS *Cuba* in January 1871. Along with John Devoy (top left), Rossa stood out among Irish expatriates in America for the intensity of his anti-British animus. He earned a justifiable reputation as the very embodiment of the spirit of Fenianism. Indelibly marked by searing personal memories of the famine, Rossa was the founder of the Phoenix National and Literary Society of Skibbereen, a cover for a revolutionary organisation dedicated to establishing an Irish republic. An early leader of the Irish Republican Brotherhood, he was rounded up along with other Fenians in 1865 and sentenced to life imprisonment. Though he was released in 1871, his harsh penal treatment only intensified his anti-British hostility, expressed verbally in his 1874 book *Prison life* (later reprinted as *Irish rebels in English prisons*), and physically in his association with a dynamiting campaign in England in the early 1880s. Thereafter he lived mostly in New York, where he inveighed against British imperialism in his newspaper *United Irishman* and in his lectures to Irish audiences throughout America. (Photo: National Museum of Ireland)

and around his native Skibbereen, Rossa had a host of searing adolescent memories: the death of his father on the public works in March 1847; his own near-death from fever; the canting of all the household effects of his family in the street as the result of a creditor's execution of a court decree; the serving of an eviction notice on his mother in the summer of 1847; and the breaking up of his home and the scattering of his family at the end of 1848.[53] Before his own family was evicted, Rossa recalled that another family to whom they had given shelter had apparently killed and eaten a pet donkey while staying with the Rossas, prompting him to remember fifty years later the still troubling and embarrassing expression, 'Skibbereen! where they ate the donkeys.'[54] Rossa also recalled the great clearances on the marquis of Lansdowne's estate around Kenmare just across the county border from Skibbereen in south Kerry, a clearance that, as already noted, was linked to a vast assisted-emigration scheme under the notorious land agent William Steuart Trench. Rossa compared Trench to Oliver Cromwell, under whose rule thousands of the Irish had been shipped to Barbados. Trench 'brought his shipmasters from England', declared Rossa indignantly, 'and shipped the Kerry people to the Canadas – in ships that were so unfit for passenger service that half his victims found homes in the bottom of the sea'.[55] With such bitter recollections it was easy enough for Rossa to endorse Mitchel in his most sanguinary disposition. 'Didn't John Mitchel say', Rossa asked rhetorically, 'that the mistake of it was that more landlords were not shot . . . .'[56]

In the public memory which Mitchel and his fellow revolutionary nationalists sought to shape about the clearances, the rancour and hostility were not reserved exclusively for Irish landlords and their agents. The finger of blame was aimed directly at the British government. Characteristically, Mitchel adopted the most extreme language in bringing responsibility home to the Whig ministry. He noted that the famous Devon commission of 1843–5 had said that the consolidation of holdings of up to 8 acres would require the removal of more than 192,000 families. 'That is', insisted Mitchel rather wildly, 'the killing of a million of persons. Little did the commissioners hope then that in four years British policy, with the famine to aid, would succeed in killing fully two millions and forcing nearly another million to flee the country.'[57] For Mitchel as for others, the mass evictions of the famine years eventuated from the joint actions of government and landlords. Pre-famine ejectment legislation had considerably cheapened the cost of eviction, 'so that when the famine and the poor laws came', declared Mitchel, 'the expense of clearing a whole countryside was very trifling indeed'. What is more, the greatly expanded availability of poor relief both in and out of the workhouses was intended to render evictions less objectionable to both their victims and their perpetrators, a fact which Mitchel appreciated and exploited: 'To receive some of the exterminated [smallholders], poorhouses were erected all over the island, which had the effect of stifling compunction in the ejectors. The poorhouses were soon filled.'[58] Nor did Mitchel overlook the obvious way in which state power had been used to smash traditional settlements and scatter their inhabitants. 'There is no need to recount', said Mitchel while doing that very thing, 'how the assistant barristers and sheriffs, aided by the police, tore down the roof-trees and ploughed up the hearths of village after village, how the quarter-acre clause laid waste the parishes, how the farmers and their wives and little ones in wild dismay trooped along the highways. . . .'[59]

Many constitutional nationalists also found in the mass evictions of the famine years murderous collusion between Irish landlords and the British government and parliament. One of the most influential was T.P. O'Connor, whose book of 1886, *The Parnell movement* (with numerous later editions), included a long chapter of some sixty pages entitled 'The great clearances'. As previously noted, O'Connor, though a constitutionalist, basically agreed with the genocidal view of revolutionary nationalists that 'forced exports' of Irish grain had been responsible for the mass mortality.[60] On the question of the clearances O'Connor was only slightly less vituperative against both the landlords and the British government than Mitchel himself. And he provided far more in the way of damning evidence, particularly a long set of extracts from the reports of the poor law official Captain Arthur Kennedy, who had recounted in gruesome detail mammoth clearances in the Kilrush union of Clare.[61] Writing of the agrarian violence of 1847–8 and of the government's response by means of another coercion act, O'Connor employed Mitchelite sarcasm to justify the one and condemn the other:

> Many of the tenants were indecent enough to object to being robbed [through eviction] of their own improvements even with the sanction of an alien parliament, and went the length of revolting against their wives and children being massacred wholesale, after the fashion described in Captain Kennedy's reports. In short, the rent was in danger, and in favour of that sacred institution all the resources of British law and British force were promptly despatched.[62]

It can be argued that the clearances contributed more than any other set of events associated with the famine to the generation and spread of anti-British hostility in Ireland and especially the Irish diaspora. Writing in 1868 after his extensive tour of North America, John Francis Maguire, editor of the *Cork Examiner* and nationalist politician (MP for Cork city, 1865–72), gave this assessment of the political significance of the clearances among Irish Americans: 'I do not care to speculate as to the number of the class of evicted tenants scattered through the United States . . . ; but wherever they exist, they are to be found willing contributors to Fenian funds and enthusiastic supporters of anti-British organisations.'[63] T.P. O'Connor's evaluation in 1886 was quite similar to Maguire's:

> To this day the traveler in America will meet Irishmen who were evicted from Ireland in the great clearances of the famine time, and they speak even to this

John Francis Maguire (1815–72) was a moderate nationalist in the O'Connellite tradition. Though very active in both local and national politics (he was four times mayor of Cork city and sat in parliament from 1852 until his death), he made an equally weighty impression as a distinguished journalist and author. He founded the *Cork Examiner* in 1841 and was its proprietor throughout his life. His enthusiasm for Irish industrial development and for the cause of temperance led to two notable works – *The industrial movement in Ireland* (1852) and his biography of the 'apostle of temperance', Father Theobald Mathew (1863). But even more important was his 1868 book, *The Irish in America*, a pioneering survey of recent Irish immigration to the United States and Canada. Maguire emphasised the intensity of anti-British feeling among Irish-Americans and traced much of it to bitter memories of the famine. (*Irish Examiner*)

> hour with a bitterness as fresh as if the wrong were but of yesterday. It was these clearances and the sight of wholesale starvation and plague, far more than racial feelings, that produced the hatred of English government which strikes impartial Americans as something like frenzy.[64]

Among the interviews with Irish Americans reported by Maguire in 1868 were several highly revealing ones with tenants evicted from their farms in Ireland. One was now a prosperous 400-acre farmer in a western state who was still angry about his dispossession by the 'crowbar brigade'. According to Maguire, 'in his heart he cherished a feeling of hatred and vengeance, not so much against the individual by whom the wrong was perpetrated, as against the government by which it was sanctioned and under whose authority it was inflicted'. In spite of his success in America, his mind kept returning to the day when, as he put it, 'he and his were turned out like dogs – worse than dogs – on the roadside'. Nothing could efface the bitter memory. Declared this farmer, 'I'll never forgive that government [the British] the longest day I live.' His wife was inclined towards forgiveness, but his sons, Maguire reported, 'sympathised more with the vengeful feeling of their father than with the Christian spirit of their mother'.[65]

In a second case discussed at some length by Maguire (as reported to him by an 'eminent Irish ecclesiastic' in an eastern state), another well-to-do immigrant farmer who had been evicted in Ireland had long refused to go to confession or receive the eucharist. Having been pressed often by the priest to do so, he finally admitted the reason: he simply could not forgive those who had evicted him, causing his father's death and that of his wife immediately after childbirth. His rheumatic father 'died that night [of the eviction] in the gripe of the ditch', and his wife 'died in my arms the next day'. After their deaths he swore an oath vowing revenge, and, he declared, 'I'll never forgive the bloody English government that allowed a man to be treated worse than I'd treat a dog . . . ', adding for emphasis, 'and what's more, I teach my children to hate them too.' In his acrid recollection the presence of the state's agents on the day of the eviction was still quite vivid: 'There didn't come out of the heavens a bitterer morning [than] when the sheriff was at my door with the crowbar men, and a power of peelers and the army too, as if 'twas going to war they were, instead of coming to drive an honest man and his family from house and home.'[66]

What is perhaps especially interesting about these two cases is that the victims of the evictions had both given a precise political meaning to their harsh experiences, instead of viewing only a particular landlord as the exclusive source of the calamity which had befallen them. This type of reaction appears to have been quite general and helps us to understand the remarkable strength of Irish-American support for the destruction of landlordism in Ireland during the late 1870s and the 1880s. It was also an astute politician's consciousness of widespread memories and persistent common fears in Ireland itself which prompted Charles Stewart Parnell to proclaim at Westport in June 1879: 'You must show the landlords that you intend to keep a firm grip of your homesteads and lands. You must not allow yourselves to be dispossessed as you were dispossessed in 1847.'[67] Through this famous speech, as Davitt later said, Parnell 'gave to the [Land League] movement one of its subsequent watchwords, "Hold a firm grip of your homesteads"'.[68] These words were in fact inscribed on all the membership cards of the Irish National Land League.

Clearly, nationalist writers and orators used bitter memories of the clearances to sustain or heighten anti-British feelings in Ireland and the diaspora. To some extent, they may have succeeded in politicising the clearances, giving them a sharp political meaning which at least some of their victims might not have adopted if left to themselves. On the other hand, did evicted tenants really need to be taught what to think by nationalist politicians and ideologues before concluding that the British state had played a crucial role in their dispossession? In many cases, perhaps in most, this seems quite unlikely. Harsh experience must itself have been a potent and embittering teacher. Of the roughly 500,000 people evicted formally or informally during the famine years, many died. But many of them survived in Ireland or emigrated to North America and elsewhere. To relieve their bitterness, if for no other reason, these survivors of the clearances must often have spoken of their memories of dispossession among their families and friends, and sometimes among a much wider public. In so doing, they gave a particular shape to nationalist memories of the great famine.

PROLONGED AND BITTER RECRIMINATIONS

In constructing the public memory of the famine, Irish nationalist writers and orators often focused their own resentment and that of their audience on English expressions of rejoicing or satisfaction at famine-related events. Perhaps the most notorious of such expressions was the apparent relish of the London *Times* over the way in which evictions and emigration (along with the anticipated workings of the Incumbered Estates Court) were emptying out the western countryside. 'In a few years more', declared *The Times*, 'a Celtic Irishman will be as rare in Connemara as is the Red Indian on the shores of Manhattan.'[69] It was this grossly insensitive comment which Jeremiah O'Donovan Rossa had in mind when at the start of 1858, in his first recorded speech, he told the members of the Phoenix National and Literary Society of Skibbereen that England

> has stained almost every hearthstone in the land with the heart's blood of a victim; and the other day, in savage exultation at the idea of her work being accomplished, she cried out, 'The Irish are gone, and gone with a vengeance' (groans). But the mercenary thunderer [*The Times*] lies. I read it in your countenances. The Irish are not gone; but part of them are gone, and in whatever clime their pulses beat tonight, that 'vengeance' which banished them is inscribed on their hearts. . . .[70]

Forty years later, Rossa's bitter resentment on this score had, if anything, grown more intense. Writing now (in the late 1890s) what would become his *Recollections* in his New York newspaper the *United Irishman*, Rossa still believed that Irish depopulation at English hands merited violent retribution: 'Nine millions in 1845; four and a half millions in 1895. And those English savages rejoice over the manner in which they destroy us. They thank God we are gone, "gone with a vengeance," they say. What a pity we haven't the spirit to return the vengeance.'[71]

Irish revolutionary nationalists from John Mitchel to John Devoy exploited English insensitivity about Irish depopulation. Referring again explicitly to *The Times*'s 'rejoicing over the disaster' in its notorious Connemara-Manhattan comparison, Devoy acidly commented in his *Recollections* of 1929 that while over a million Irish people were starving or suffering from fever, 'the English press read them solemn lectures on political economy and printed columns of claptrap about getting rid of the "surplus population"'.[72] Much earlier, in his hugely popular *Jail journal*, Mitchel had satirised the omission of such famine-stricken spots as Skibbereen and Westport from Queen Victoria's itinerary on her brief and sanitised visit in 1849: 'After a few years, however, it is understood that her majesty will visit the west. The human inhabitants are expected by that time to have been sufficiently thinned, and the deer and other game to have proportionately multiplied. The prince Albert will then take a hunting lodge in Connemara.'[73]

Many constitutional nationalists were as deeply affronted by the enthusiastic English public embrace of the need for Irish depopulation as were republicans. A.M. Sullivan, the former editor of the *Nation* and a leading exponent of constitutional nationalism, put a humorous coating in his *New Ireland* of 1877 on what would otherwise have amounted to a recriminative outburst:

> If the bullock being led to the abattoir could understand and be consoled by remarks upon the excellent sirloin and juicy steak which he was sure to furnish, so ought the Irish landlords and tenants to have taken kindly the able speeches and learned leading articles which declared they were being slaughtered for the public good. But they had not a philosophy equal to this lofty view of things, and they called it hard names.[74]

Earlier and without any humorous sugar-coating, the three Sullivan brothers, who in 1868 gave to the Irish and Irish-American political worlds their classic *Speeches from the dock*, long a *vade mecum* of nationalists in Ireland and throughout the Irish diaspora, had castigated 'above all' the way in which, after the abortive rising of 1848 and the onset of mass emigration, England 'found it much pleasanter . . . to felicitate herself on the reduction which had taken place in the Irish population'. From the English perspective Irish depopulation, insisted the Sullivans in *Speeches from the dock*, 'was the glorious part of the whole affair. The Irish were "gone with a vengeance!" – not all of them but a goodly

Alexander Martin Sullivan (1830–84) was the foremost moderate nationalist journalist of his generation. He was the proprietor and editor of the *Nation* from 1858 until 1876, when he handed over the reins to his brother T.D. Sullivan. The Sullivans pioneered cheap weekly journalism with their *Weekly News*; their most successful foray in mass marketing was undoubtedly their *Speeches from the dock* of 1868, a phenomenal bestseller on both sides of the Atlantic. A.M. Sullivan's fierce opposition to Fenianism in the early 1860s prompted the IRB to pass a death sentence on him in 1865, but his eulogy of the 'Manchester martyrs' in the *Weekly News* briefly landed him in prison in 1868. His influential books *The story of Ireland* (1867) and *New Ireland* (1878) reached very large audiences. His career as a home rule MP beginning in 1874 was shortened by a heart attack in 1881, and he died prematurely three years later. (*United Ireland*/By permission of the British Library)

proportion, and others were going off every day. . . . There appeared to be in progress a regular breaking up of the Irish nation. This, to the English mind, was positively delightful.' In droves the Irish were going to America or to the bottom of the sea – 'nearly the same thing', said the Sullivans acidly, 'as far as England was concerned' – and would trouble England no more. Their places were to be assumed by English farmers, drovers, and labourers, 'who would take possession of the deserted island. . . . O magnificent consummation! O most brilliant prospect in the eyes of English statesmen!'[75]

Whether by dint of indoctrination by literate and educated nationalists or through the local workings of lived experience, these Irish perceptions of English or Anglo-Irish receptivity to mass death and mass emigration became deeply embedded in the post-famine oral folklore. One informant of the Irish Folklore Commission (Martin Donoghue, a native of Ballinasloe, County Galway) told in 1945 of a conversation heard by his father between his father's landlord and a local poor law guardian during the famine:

> 'Well,' said the landlord, 'are they dying fast?'
> 'Oh,' said the guardian, 'they are dying so fast we can scarcely bury them.'
> 'That's good. That's good', said the landlord.[76]

Similarly, Rossa retold in his *Recollections* the story given to him about the chairman of the Skibbereen board of guardians during most of the famine years, a small local landlord and magistrate named Lioney Fleming, by Neddie Hegarty, the porter at the main gate of Skibbereen workhouse. According to Hegarty, Fleming always asked him whenever the guardians met at the workhouse, '"Well, Hegarty, how many [dead] this week?" and if I told him the number this week was less than the number last week, his remark would be, "Too bad, too bad; last week was a better week than this."'[77] Another informant of the Irish Folklore Commission (Pádraig Pléimionn of Killarney, County Kerry) told the following story about famine deaths in and around the Killarney workhouse: '"Bring the carrion as soon as possible" was the order from the local magnate, Irish or Anglo-Saxon, to his hirelings, who were brutal enough to cart away [to the local paupers' graveyard] dying men and women in the hope that they "would be dead enough to bury" by the time the graveyard was reached.' Concluded this informant, 'But why say more? I used to get sick listening to such tales as a youngster.'[78] Two other informants from the Enniskeane district of County Cork delivered the following assessments of the attitudes of landlords and officials towards food exports during the famine. The first remarked, 'If the people starved, all the better [in the landlords' eyes].'[79] The second observed, 'The men in power were all Protestants. . . . They were in league with England, and it was their delight to see the population decreasing by the thousands, dying with hunger and what followed.'[80] This second informant also related a genocidal story about a copper boiler for making soup that was operated by 'the big Protestants of Manch', supposedly for the relief of the local poor. Even though for some reason the boiler was allegedly poisoning the people, one of the Manch Protestants was said to have knowingly told another, 'That's right, that's right. . . . Keep the copper boiler going.'[81]

Such beliefs about the intentions and feelings of the English government and of officials and landlords in Ireland were extremely widespread in America. Following his grand tour of the United States and Canada, John Francis Maguire, the editor of the *Cork Examiner*, drew attention in 1868 in his book *The Irish in America* to 'the profound belief which lies at the very root of this hostility [against Britain] and gives life to every anti-British organisation – that Ireland is oppressed and impoverished by England; [and] that England hates the Irish race and would exterminate them were it in her power . . .'.[82] Even a writer as hostile to the Irish and to Irish nationalism as the Englishman Philip Bagenal conceded in 1882, in his book *The American Irish and their influence on Irish politics*, that the treatment given to the mass famine exodus of 1847–54 'by the English press was indignantly resented by the emigrant Irish themselves and by their countrymen in America'. Bagenal singled out 'the tone of such journals as *The Times* and *Saturday Review*' as having been 'well calculated to excite the indignation of the principal actors in the heartrending exodus of those days'.[83]

NATIONALIST REJECTION OF PROVIDENTIALISM

Just as Irish nationalists were made furious by English rejoicing over Irish depopulation, so too they became indignant when they recalled, as they did often, the ease with which leading British politicians and wide sections of the British press had resorted to providentialist interpretations of the famine, as if God himself for his own good reasons was, in wiping out the Irish potato crop, rendering some divine judgement on Ireland and the Irish people. English invocations of providence irritated or enraged Irish nationalists primarily because they seemed so strongly to indicate divine rather than human causation and to relieve the British government and people of responsibility for mass death and emigration. Thus Mitchel applied the corrective in his famous dictum, 'The Almighty indeed sent the potato blight, but the English created the famine.'[84] Mitchel was certainly not the first nationalist to pour scorn on English providentialist interpretations of the famine. That distinction may well belong to Bishop John Hughes of New York, who in a long speech in March 1847 (published later that year), given under the auspices of the General Committee for the Relief of the Suffering Poor of Ireland, made the following ringing declaration: 'I may be told that the famine in Ireland is a mysterious visitation of God's providence, but I do not admit any such plea. I fear there is blasphemy in charging on the Almighty what is the result of man's own doings.'[85] Hughes's declaration in this lecture was noted approvingly soon afterwards in the *Nation*, and much later (in 1904) Michael Davitt referred to it specifically in his *Fall of feudalism*.[86]

Though its dimensions have often been exaggerated, some Protestant proselytism aimed at the Irish poor occurred during the famine, giving wide currency to the term 'souperism' for this use of soup and other benefits to persuade destitute Catholics to embrace Protestantism. The proselytising efforts of Protestant evangelicals had long been centred on western coastal areas. Much attention was focused on the Protestant missionary settlement on Achill Island in Mayo shown in this illustration, where the Anglican clergyman Edward Nangle boasted of huge increases in converts in 1848 and 1849. Nangle and other evangelicals saw the conversions as a sign of divine approval, just as they interpreted the famine itself as a divine judgement against Irish Catholicism and the existing structure of Irish agrarian society. This kind of providentialism was widespread among British Protestant evangelicals. (National Library of Ireland)

Indeed, numerous nationalist writers and orators in Ireland and the diaspora explicitly connected English providentialism with genocide against the Irish people. In his rousing speech to the Phoenix Society of Skibbereen early in 1858 the young O'Donovan Rossa declared that nationalists must strive to regenerate their country 'so as to prevent a recurrence of the national disasters of '46 and '47, when England allowed thousands of our people to starve and blasphemously charged God Almighty with the crime, while the routine of her misgovernment compelled the cereal produce of the country to be exported'.[87] In his *Recollections* Rossa linked providentialism with mass evictions and landlord depopulation. In the face of crop seizures and mass mortality, he insisted in words reminiscent of Mitchel, 'The English press and the English people rejoiced that the Irish were at last conquered; that God at last was fighting strongly at the side of the

English.'[88] Rejecting in another place the idea of the famine as a 'visitation of providence', he noted instead the innumerable seizures of grain crops for unpaid rent and branded this 'a visitation of English landlordism – as great a curse to Ireland as if it was the arch-fiend himself [that] had the government of the country'.[89] Davitt's condemnation of providentialism in his *Fall of feudalism* was even more blistering: 'Hundreds of thousands of women, children, and men were, on this hideous theory, murdered by starvation because of some inscrutable decree of the God of the poor. . . .' Concluded Davitt sweepingly: 'No more horrible creed of atheistic blasphemy was ever preached to a Christian people than this. . . .'[90]

Not all nationalists went as far as Mitchel, Rossa, and Davitt in connecting English providentialism with genocide, but they still believed that providentialism helped to explain the slowness and inadequacy of the British government's response. In his recollections of 1905 the famous nationalist newspaper editor and poet T.D. Sullivan put the point in this way: 'There was only too much reason to believe that the ministry regarded the situation as one that would eventuate in a mitigation of "the Irish difficulty", and which therefore they need not be in a great hurry to ameliorate. Some of the British newspapers spoke plainly out in that sense, intimating their belief that the whole thing was an intervention of an all-wise providence for England's benefit. . . .'[91] Other nationalists underscored the rabid anti-Catholicism of some strands of providentialist thought on the famine. Canon John O'Rourke contemptuously explored a small portion of this literature in his classic of 1874, *The history of the great Irish famine of 1847*. He quoted from an 1847 tract by the notorious anti-papist Philip Dixon Hardy, in which the author claimed that 'in the heartrending scenes around us do we witness punishment for national idolatry', and he also quoted from an issue of the *Achill Missionary Herald*, an evangelical Protestant proselytising journal, which claimed that the famine was God's punishment for the Maynooth act of 1845, a law 'to endow a college for training priests to defend and practise and perpetuate this corrupt and damnable worship in this realm'.[92] O'Rourke gave ammunition to later nationalists and helped to root this aspect of the famine, which he connected directly to 'souperism', in the public nationalist memory. T.D. Sullivan cited O'Rourke's work for his assertion in 1905 that in England 'the extreme Protestant organs and some of their pulpit orators confidently declared that the famine was a divine chastisement of the Irish people for their adherence to "popery"'.[93]

But it was undoubtedly the connection commonly drawn by nationalists between providentialism and genocide that did most to engender this kind of Irish and Irish-American hostility towards England. Philip Bagenal recalled in 1882 that in thanking heaven for the relief which England had felt over the mass famine exodus, the London *Times* had quoted the Virgilian motto '*Deus nobis haec otio fecit*' ('It is God that has made this peaceful life for us'). 'For an Englishman to quote the motto, comfortably seated at home', declared Bagenal, 'was no doubt translated by the Irish in America as a paean on the providence which slew millions of the pauper Irish and banished the rest.'[94] Obviously, very few, if any, of the Irish in America had ever heard of *The Times*'s quotation from Virgil, but great numbers of them had most certainly heard of the attitude and body of thought which it epitomised, and their translation was not at all far from that postulated by Bagenal.

REBELS: HEROICISED OR VILIFIED

The impact of English pronouncements on divine providence and on Irish depopulation was intensified by the treatment of the Irish rebellion of 1848 and its aftermath in the British press. Again, nationalist writers and orators seized on the offensive language and portrayals and hurled them back at their opponents before nationalist audiences on both sides of the Atlantic. In *The last conquest of Ireland (perhaps)* Mitchel assured his readers in Ireland and the diaspora that 'the whole British press, which never strikes so viciously at an enemy as when he is down and in chains, sent after me on my dark voyage [to Van Diemen's Land] one continuous shriek of execration and triumph that came to my ear even in my Bermuda prison'.[95] In nationalist memory Mitchel was scarcely the only target of English journalistic derision and scorn. In their enormously influential *Speeches from the dock* the Sullivan brothers made the broad and acerbic claim that after the abortive rising of 1848 England 'found it much pleasanter to chuckle over the discomfiture of the Irish patriots, to ridicule the failure of their peaceable agitation, to sneer at their poor effort in arms, [and] to nickname and misrepresent and libel the brave-hearted gentleman [William Smith O'Brien] who led that unlucky endeavour . . . '.[96]

But it was Mitchel's view that soon after the failed 1848 revolt a much more intensive and altogether nastier campaign of racial or ethnic vilification got under way in England. He associated it especially with the promulgation of Sir Robert Peel's scheme for a 'new plantation' of Ireland, with feckless Irish landlords and tenants in the west giving way to enterprising Anglo-Saxons and Scots. This proposal was enthusiastically endorsed by Thomas Carlyle, among many others. Mitchel quoted Carlyle's crude anti-Irish rant: 'Ireland is a starved rat that crosses the path of an elephant: what is the elephant to do? *Squelch* it, by heaven! Squelch it!' Mitchel saw Carlyle's outburst as marking a turning point:

> From this time commenced that most virulent vilification of the Celtic Irish in all the journals, books, and periodicals of the 'sister island', which has been so faithfully reproduced (like all other British cant) in America, and which gave such venom to the Know-Nothing agitation. Then, more than ever, English writers were diligent in pointing out and illustrating the difference of 'race' between Celt and Saxon, which proved to their own satisfaction that the former were born to be ruled by the latter.[97]

It is perhaps worth noting here that Mitchel's views about increasing British antagonism have been partly confirmed by recent research on the depiction of the famine in the pages of *Punch*. As Peter Gray remarks, 'in the wake of the abortive 1848 rising *Punch* returned repeatedly to the theme of inveterate Irish barbarity and ingratitude. Agrarian unrest and political rebellion were rolled together . . . , and images of famine-related suffering were ignored.'[98]

A reprise of this mutually embittering pattern of English vilification and Irish nationalist retort occurred in the days of Fenianism in the 1860s. Philip Bagenal provided a whole series of examples of vituperative remarks made in the London press that were bound to intensify Irish and Irish-American hostility to England. In one instance it was said that Ireland 'has no snakes or vermin except among its peasantry and clergy', and in another case that 'Ireland is boiling over, and the scum flows across the Atlantic'. With some reason Bagenal remarked that 'these are expressions which have rankled deeper than coercion acts and sentences of transportation'.[99] If nationalists in Ireland and the diaspora clasped the so-called 'Manchester martyrs' of 1867 to their bosoms, it was at least partly because nationalists were so offended by the reported behaviour of the English crowd attending the execution of Allen, Larkin, and O'Brien. It was said that this English crowd 'made the air resound with laughter at obscene jokes, shouts, cries, and repartees, and [beneath the very gallows] chorused in thousands . . . snatches of "comic" ballads and pot-house songs, varied by verses of "Rule Britannia" and "God save the queen," by way of exultation over the Irish'.[100] Greatly magnifying the impact of this report among nationalists was its appearance in that phenomenal bestseller *Speeches from the dock*, whose circulation almost certainly exceeded that of any other Irish nationalist work ever published. Whether the occasion was Irish depopulation during the famine, the failed 1848 rising, the threat of Fenianism, or the fate of the 'Manchester martyrs', English exultation over Irish reversals was repeatedly exploited by nationalists.

If the 'rising' of 1848 could be validated negatively by arousing nationalist anger over the satisfaction which Britons took in its abject failure, it could also be legitimised positively by valorising the patriotic motives of its self-sacrificing leaders. Though John Mitchel himself at times pilloried the failings of Smith O'Brien and Duffy, he gave in his *Jail journal* the classic revolutionary nationalist defence of this doomed project: 'Even as she [i.e., Ireland] was, depopulated, starved, cowed, and corrupted, it seemed better that she should attempt resistance, however heavy the odds against success, than lie prostrate and moaning as she was. Better that men should perish by the bayonets of the enemy than by their laws.'[101] Or as he declared in July 1849, after learning that Smith O'Brien, John Martin, and Thomas Francis Meagher were to be sent, like him, by convict ship to Van Diemen's Land, 'They would not be parties to the slaughter of their countrymen by [the] millions [so] that this foul pretence of [British] law might flourish for ages to come.'[102]

SPEECHES FROM THE DOCK,

OR

PROTESTS OF IRISH PATRIOTISM.

CONTAINING,

WITH INTRODUCTORY SKETCHES AND BIOGRAPHICAL NOTICES

BY T. D., A. M., AND D. B. SULLIVAN

SPEECHES DELIVERED IN THE DOCK

BY

THEOBALD WOLFE TONE
WILLIAM ORR
THE BROTHERS SHEARES
ROBERT EMMET
THOMAS RUSSELL
JOHN MITCHEL
JOHN MARTIN (1848)
WILLIAM SMITH O'BRIEN
THOMAS FRANCIS MEAGHER
TERENCE BELLEW M'MANUS
WILLIAM P. ALLEN
MICHAEL LARKIN
MICHAEL O'BRIEN
THOMAS C. LUBY

JOHN O'LEARY
CHARLES J. KICKHAM
J. O'DONOVAN ROSSA
COLONEL THOMAS F. BURKE
CAPTAIN JOHN M'AFFERTY
STEPHEN J. MEANY
EDWARD DUFFY
CAPTAIN JOHN M'CLURE
JOHN EDWARD KELLY
COLONEL JOHN WARREN
AUGUSTINE E. COSTELLOE
CAPTAIN MACKAY
A. M. SULLIVAN
JOHN MARTIN (1868)

THIRTY-NINTH EDITION.

DUBLIN:

T. D. SULLIVAN, ABBEY-STREET.

1887.

This portrayal of 1848 as a patriotic protest in arms against British genocide or brutal oppression was frequently reiterated by Irish nationalists in later years. John Savage, who escaped from Ireland to New York after writing for Mitchel's *United Irishman* and helping to found the *Irish Tribune*, was among the more prominent nationalists to do so in America. In 1882, in his popular book *'98 and '48: the modern revolutionary history and literature of Ireland*, he reprinted several documents which developed this theme. In one, an address by the executive council of the Irish Confederation to the citizens of Dublin (15 March 1848), the council proclaimed: 'Death has raged among us like an invading army – emigration has drained our land of wealth and strength; we are justified before God and man in refusing to endure our wrongs any longer.'[103] In another document reprinted by Savage, an address from the Irish Students' Club to O'Brien, Meagher, and Mitchel (6 May 1848), the students used searing language to urge resistance to the holocaust around them: 'Guiltless millions perish unavenged. . . . Law is the poniard with which England stabs her victims before she undisguisedly proceeds to noonday murder.'[104]

In their famous *Speeches from the dock* the Sullivan brothers powerfully contributed to enshrining this perspective on 1848 by recalling the words of the defeated rebels in the courtroom. Here could be found John Martin's speech declaring that he had entered politics to 'make an end of the horrible scenes that this country presents – the pauperism, starvation, and crime, and vice, and hatred of all classes against each other'.[105] And here too was the unvarnished speech of Kevin O'Doherty: 'I had but one object and purpose in view. I did feel deeply for the sufferings and privations endured by my fellow countrymen. I did wish by all means . . . to assist in putting an end to that suffering.'[106] What many Confederates had found unbearable was the chasm between their idea of what Ireland should be and what under British rule it had become in the midst of the famine. Savage recaptured their burning indignation. Meagher, he recalled, had spoken in the dock of how he had wanted 'to lift this island up – to make her a benefactor of humanity instead of being the meanest beggar in the world'.[107] And Thomas Devin Reilly, hoping to stir Irishmen to resistance, had declared that they were 'the most humiliated, the most pitiable, the most helpless, the most despised people with a white skin on the face of God's whole earth'.[108]

Opposite: *Speeches from the dock* emerged in 1868 from the hands of constitutional nationalists. It demonstrates how much shared ideological ground there was at this juncture between constitutional and revolutionary Irish nationalists, especially in their attitudes towards Britain and its role during the famine. The execution of the three 'Manchester martyrs' – William Allen, Michael Larkin, and Michael O'Brien – in Salford jail in November 1867 had inflamed Irish and Irish-American public opinion against Britain. British leniency in the aftermath of the risings of 1848 and 1867 only made matters worse. These were the first Irishmen executed for an alleged political crime since Robert Emmet in 1803. The condemned men had spoken emotionally from the dock themselves, and even constitutional nationalists embraced them and their sacrifice. (National Library of Ireland)

Apportioning Blame at Home

If the Irish people behaved like slaves rather than men during the famine, as Reilly and others claimed, much of the blame, according to revolutionary nationalists in later years, belonged to Daniel O'Connell and his successors in the leadership of constitutional nationalism. From the day in July 1846 that the Whigs took office, asserted Duffy in his autobiography of 1898, O'Connell's 'remedy for the famine was confidence in the government; it would do all that could be done if the people were peaceful and patient'.[109] Discussing prime minister Russell's refusal to use the Royal Navy to bring Indian corn to starving Ireland, Duffy charged: 'Our submission to this shameful wrong in silent indignation was a natural result of the Whig compact' made by O'Connell, whose policy 'was submission'.[110] In a similar vein Michael Davitt, father of the Land League, opened the chapter dealing with the famine in his famous book of 1904, *The fall of feudalism in Ireland*, with a striking story about how John O'Connell, the Liberator's eldest son, had read aloud in 1847 in Dublin's Conciliation Hall a letter from a Catholic bishop in west Cork. In this letter the bishop reportedly observed, 'The famine is spreading with fearful rapidity, and scores of persons are dying of starvation and fever, but the tenants are bravely paying their rents.' Having quoted the bishop's remark, John O'Connell exclaimed proudly (according to Davitt), 'I thank God I live among a people who would rather die of hunger than defraud their landlords of the rent!' Davitt promptly heaped scorn on this 'perverted morality', as he called it: 'It is not, unfortunately, on record that the author of this atrocious sentiment was forthwith kicked from the hall into the sink of the Liffey.'[111] The harshest indictment of O'Connellism and its role in mass mortality came from the acid pen of John Mitchel. 'Because the Irish have been taught peaceful agitation in their slavery', declared Mitchel in his *Jail journal*, 'therefore they have been swept by a plague of hunger worse than many years of bloody fighting. Because they would not fight, they have been made to rot off the face of the earth, that so they might learn at last how deadly a sin is patience and perseverance under a stranger's yoke.'[112] Having deluded the Irish people into believing that repeal could be obtained by peaceful means, O'Connell became, in Mitchel's words, 'the magician' who 'bewitched them to their destruction'.[113] Davitt too was firmly convinced that violent resistance would have been less destructive of human life than passive acceptance of doom; it would, he claimed extravagantly, 'have saved three-fourths of the slaves who subsequently died like sheep without leaving on record one single redeeming trait of courageous manhood to the credit of their memories'.[114] Thus, for revolutionary nationalists, though not for them alone, the public memory of the famine was one which had at its core a great absence – the failure to resist the slaughter which British government policies entailed, a failure for which O'Connellite constitutional nationalism had to answer.

In this failure to resist, the Catholic church and its clergy were held by revolutionary nationalists to have been deeply implicated. Part of their criticism centred on the role of certain priests in actively opposing the efforts of Confederate leaders to mobilise the peasantry in 1848. Thus in his book *'98 and '48* the former Confederate John Savage unfavourably compared the political behaviour of a half-dozen named priests in Tipperary and Waterford in 1848 with that of certain of their counterparts in 1798 – 'a sad contrast', noted Savage, 'to those [illustrious names] of the Kearns[es], Roches, and Murphys of fifty years previous'.[115] Constitutional nationalist writers agreed that the Catholic clergy possessed enormous influence and that in 1848 they had used it against political violence with devastating effect. In his *New Ireland* of 1877, A.M. Sullivan declared flatly that the clergy's antagonism to the 1848 rebellion 'was fatal to the movement'.[116]

But the heavy strictures of revolutionary nationalists against Catholic bishops and priests were not limited to their conduct in 1848 alone. Many of the same republican nationalists who roundly denounced O'Connell and his followers for their 'peace policy' or 'policy of submission' excoriated the clergy in almost the same breath. This practice started during the famine itself and continued long afterwards. Thus in March 1848, in the second of his *Letters to the small farmers of Ireland*, John Mitchel told his readers to 'be well assured of this – that the priest who bids you perish patiently amidst your own golden harvests preaches the gospel of England . . . , bears false witness against religion, and blasphemes the providence of God'.[117] In his *Jail journal*, contemplating early in 1850 the prostrate condition of the country even in the face of the continuing 'clearance devastations', Mitchel ticked off the leading internal culprits: 'The O'Connell-Duffys are preaching constitutional agitation; and the Orangemen are crying "To hell with the pope", and the Catholic bishops are testifying their loyalty; and murder and famine and idiocy are dancing an obscene Carmagnole among the corpses.'[118] Mitchel's thunderings against the clergy were echoed a half-century later by Michael Davitt. In his *Fall of feudalism* Davitt asserted that the passivity preached during the famine by the Catholic church had undermined popular resistance at a time when political developments had 'left the mass of the people . . . under the all but absolute leadership of the bishops and priests'. Responsibility for 'the holocaust of humanity', he insisted, 'must be shared between the political and spiritual governors of the Irish people'.[119] As one of the countless thousands of readers of Mitchel's *Last conquest*, Davitt remarked that in that famous book Mitchel had primarily blamed the priests 'for persuading the people not to fight'. This prompted Davitt to engage in one of his bitterest anti-clerical outbursts on record. Of the priests in famine times, he declared: 'Begging alms and making paupers of men they had already taught to be slaves was more in their line, and the taunt of Mitchel is only too well deserved. . . .'[120]

It is clear, however, that this republican nationalist indictment of the church's role did not really become a salient part of the public memory of the famine. On the contrary, the public memory of the church's role was much closer to the heroic image portrayed by such constitutional nationalist writers as A.M.

Sullivan, who stressed in 1877 the 'countless deeds of heroism and self-sacrifice' carried out by Catholic priests and dispensary doctors. Providing striking evidence of their courage was the 'lamentable' rate of mortality among both groups. They were, declared Sullivan, 'Christian heroes, martyrs for humanity'.[121] Never forgotten was the readiness of so many priests (and sometimes nuns) to attend to the sick and the dying, often under the most appalling conditions, not only in Ireland but in Liverpool, in Grosse Île, and elsewhere. Favourably remembered too was the way in which so many Catholic clerics at the local level had loudly raised their voices against the evictions and clearances of 'exterminating landlords'. Truly was it said in 1877 that the Catholic Irish fondly 'revere the memory of their own priests who suffered with and died for them in that fearful time'.[122]

Admittedly, these strongly favourable memories rarely extended to individual Catholic prelates or to the hierarchy as a collective entity. At this elevated level silence or reticence had been too much in evidence, especially in the earlier years of the famine. But there were some notable exceptions who attracted attention at the time and later. In this category were Dr John MacHale, the archbishop of Tuam, and Dr Edward Maginn, the coadjutor bishop of Derry. Maginn achieved notoriety partly through his stirring letters to the local press denouncing 'exterminating landlords' and embracing repeal, and partly by sheltering the fugitive Thomas D'Arcy McGee before his escape to America in 1848. McGee repaid the favour by publishing a highly complimentary biography of Maginn in 1857 in which he highlighted the bishop's career during the famine. MacHale too achieved fame through his journalistic efforts during the late 1840s, most notably for his ringing defence of the Catholic priesthood in the wake of scurrilous English assaults that followed the assassination of the Roscommon landlord Major Denis Mahon in November 1847.[123] From an early stage MacHale also savagely criticised the Whig government of Lord John Russell for its policy blunders. One of MacHale's public letters, addressed to Russell from Tuam on 15 December 1846, at the onset of mass starvation and epidemic disease, was such a brilliant indictment of English misgovernment and landlord greed that more than fifty years later (in 1902), it was given a prominent place in the second edition of the four-volume *Cabinet of Irish literature*, a hugely successful collection of Irish prose and poetry with a wide appeal to the rapidly growing Irish middle classes of Ireland and America.[124]

Even Paul Cullen, still in Rome in 'black '47', was hardly less anti-British at this stage than MacHale or even Mitchel. Writing to his nephew Hugh Cullen in late May 1847, the future archbishop of Armagh declared with great vehemence: 'Only our rulers are such Turks, or worse than Turks, they would not let so many thousands die of pure starvation. They will have a terrible responsibility.'[125] After Cullen became archbishop of Armagh in 1849, episcopal reticence about the catastrophic impact of the famine soon fell away. And in their address at the close of the famous national synod of Thurles in September 1850, the assembled archbishops and bishops protested that the Irish poor were

The appointment of Paul Cullen (1803–78) as archbishop of Armagh in 1849 soon led to the adoption of a much more forthright public stance by the Irish Catholic hierarchy concerning the social misery connected with the famine. This new assertiveness found clear expression at the famous synod of Thurles, held for three weeks at St Patrick's College in that Tipperary town in August and September 1850. The four archbishops and twenty bishops who attended, and whose procession to the college is depicted here, agreed to condemn Protestant proselytism and to endorse Catholic denominational education and the establishment of a Catholic university. They also denounced evictions and proclaimed that bishops would commit 'criminal neglect if they suffer the poor to be oppressed without raising their voice in their defence and vindication'. But priests at the local level had long been at the forefront of relief efforts and opposition to clearances and needed no episcopal prompting. (National Library of Ireland)

'the victims of the most ruthless oppression that ever disgraced the annals of humanity'. For the cruelties inflicted on them, cried these prelates, 'it would be difficult to find a parallel save in the atrocities of savage life'. Of course, there was again the formulaic warning, so loathed by revolutionary nationalists, that the poor 'should bear their trials with patience and avoid secret societies and illegal combinations which the church so severely condemns'.[126] But there is no persuasive evidence that such warnings did any permanent damage to the popular reputation of the church. There was such an abundance of anti-British and anti-landlord rhetoric in the public statements of some of its leaders and a great many of its foot-soldiers, the parish priests and curates, that its ritualistic exhortations to non-violence could easily be overlooked or forgiven – and also forgotten. What was much harder to forget were the many clergy-led campaigns against wholesale evictions and the courageous performance of religious duties, often to the point of total physical exhaustion and even death.

Conclusion

This chapter has traced the firm establishment of the nationalist interpretation of the great famine – the public memory of it as constructed by nationalists between 1850 and 1900. Despite its numerous fallacies and exaggerations, this interpretation faced little criticism in Catholic Ireland or in Irish America before Irish independence in the early 1920s, and even afterwards it long enjoyed impressive staying power. This remarkable situation obviously requires some explanation. Part of the explanation must be that while the horrific experiences of the great famine contributed in a major way to a powerful nationalist critique of British rule after 1850, nationalist constructions of the famine also fitted all too neatly within a critique of British misgovernment that already existed before then and that had already defined the main lines of conflict and responsibility. Thus, for example, Archbishop MacHale, writing in December 1846, attributed what he viewed as the persistent immiseration of rural Ireland since the act of union in 1800 to 'a systematic collusion between the Irish landlords and the English legislature'; he insisted that 'Ireland never would have been reduced' to this condition 'had she the protection of a native parliament'.[127] What is especially notable about MacHale's widely shared perspective, and what is equally notable about nationalist constructions of the public memory of the famine after 1850, is the absence of class conflict apart from that which pitted Irish landed proprietors against 'the Irish people', usually portrayed (quite falsely) as a great undifferentiated mass. Under these circumstances the boundaries of responsibility were most unlikely to extend beyond heartless Irish landlords and oppressive English colonial masters – a gallery of well-known rogues. And if ideological filters were already in place prior to 1845, the filters grew even thicker in the decades after 1850. Public reflection on the great famine in this later period was almost inevitably part of the highly politicised atmosphere that surrounded Fenianism, the home rule movement, and the land war, to say nothing of the new cultural nationalism arising towards the end of the nineteenth century and extending in its influence far into the twentieth.[128]

As a result of these enduring ideological filters, it was extremely difficult or even impossible for nationalists to find a place in their interpretation or memory of the famine for facts or circumstances that contradicted or conflicted with reigning nationalist orthodoxies. Heavy food imports beginning in 1847, and the positive contribution of British government policy to this major development, certainly contradicted nationalist ideology and therefore failed to penetrate the public memory of the famine. Instead, nationalist writers chose to exaggerate the role of food exports in mass death and even in many cases to insist that this was a central part of a deliberate policy of starvation and extermination. The Irish popular mind fastened, understandably enough, from the outset of the famine on a moral outrage – the immensely disturbing fact of large exports of food while the masses starved, and nationalist writers repeatedly returned to this ghastly image after 1850.

No doubt, as revisionist historians have shown, this image is seriously inadequate and badly distorts the real story of what happened to the food supply in Ireland during the famine years. But what has sustained the nationalist perspective on the famine in the face of more recent revisionist assaults is a lively appreciation of a truth more fundamental than the case for rewriting the meaning of food exports and imports during the late 1840s. What is that fundamental truth? As the great majority of professional historians of Ireland now recognise, it is that a million people should not have died in the backyard of what was then the world's richest nation, and that since a million did perish while two million more fled, this must have been because the political leaders of that nation and the organs of its public opinion had at bottom very ambivalent feelings about the social and economic consequences of mass eviction, mass death, and mass emigration. Too many Britons of the upper and middle classes came to think in the late 1840s and early 1850s that major long-term economic gains could not be achieved in Ireland without a massive amount of short-term suffering and sacrifice.[129] Irish and Irish-American nationalists were and long remained outraged at what such Britons were prepared to tolerate and at how they justified their tolerance. Historians do well to remember and to preserve that sense of moral outrage among nationalists as well as the record of what provoked it.

Notes

Introduction

1. P.M.A. Bourke, *'The visitation of God'?: the potato and the great Irish famine*, ed. Jacqueline Hill and Cormac Ó Gráda (Dublin, 1993), p. 52.
2. Ibid., pp. 42–3, 94, 99.
3. Ibid., pp. 99, 101–2, 104.
4. *Census Ire., 1841*, p. xiv; T.W. Freeman, *Pre-famine Ireland: a study in historical geography* (Manchester, 1957), pp. 148–52; Líam Kennedy, P.S. Ell, E.M. Crawford, and L.A. Clarkson, *Mapping the great Irish famine: a survey of the famine decades* (Dublin and Portland, Oregon, 1999), pp. 76–87.
5. Cormac Ó Gráda, *Ireland before and after the famine: explorations in economic history, 1800–1925* (Manchester and New York, 1988), p. 18.
6. Kennedy *et al.*, *Mapping*, pp. 94–101. See also Ó Gráda, *Ireland before and after the famine*, pp. 199–200; idem, *Ireland: a new economic history, 1780–1939* (Oxford and New York, 1994), pp. 81–2.
7. Bourke, *'Visitation of God'*, p. 100.
8. Kennedy *et al.*, *Mapping*, pp. 142–3.
9. Joel Mokyr, *Why Ireland starved: a quantitative and analytical history of the Irish economy, 1800–1850* (London and Boston, 1983), p. 26.
10. Kennedy *et al.*, *Mapping*, p. 143.
11. David Dickson, Cormac Ó Gráda, and Stuart Daultrey, 'Hearth tax, household size, and Irish population change, 1672–1821', *R.I.A. Proc.*, lxxxii, sec. C, no. 6 (Dec. 1982), p. 155; W.E. Vaughan and A.J. Fitzpatrick (eds), *Irish historical statistics: population, 1821–1971* (Dublin, 1978), p. 3.
12. Kennedy *et al.*, *Mapping*, p. 76.
13. S.H. Cousens, 'The regional variation in emigration from Ireland between 1821 and 1841', *Transactions and Papers of the Institute of British Geographers*, no. 37 (Dec. 1965), pp. 15–30.
14. This is one of the major arguments made in the pioneering work by K.H. Connell, *The population of Ireland, 1750–1845* (Oxford, 1959), pp. 47–85.
15. L.M. Cullen, 'Irish history without the potato', *Past & Present*, no. 40 (July 1968), pp. 72–83. But see also Joel Mokyr, 'Irish history with the potato', *Ir. Econ. & Soc. Hist.*, viii (1981), pp. 8–29.
16. Mokyr, *Why Ireland starved*, pp. 10, 26.
17. Dickson, Ó Gráda, and Daultrey, 'Irish population change, 1672–1821', pp. 169–71.
18. For the positive correlation between the development of proto-industrialisation and population growth, see E.L. Almquist, 'Mayo and beyond: land, domestic industry, and rural transformation in the Irish west' (PhD dissertation, Boston University, 1977).

19. Mokyr, *Why Ireland starved*, pp. 35, 43.
20. Ó Gráda, *Ireland before and after the famine*, pp. 6–8.
21. E.R.R. Green, *The Lagan valley: a local history of the industrial revolution, 1800–50* (London, 1949); W.A. Maguire, *Belfast* (Keele, Staffordshire, 1993), pp. 31–58.
22. Ó Gráda, *Ireland before and after the famine*, pp. 22–3.
23. Mokyr, *Why Ireland starved*, p. 267.
24. Ó Gráda, *New economic history*, pp. 117, 120.
25. J.S. Donnelly, Jr, *The land and the people of nineteenth-century Cork: the rural economy and the land question* (London and Boston, 1975), pp. 26–52.
26. An editorial writer for *The Times* of London correctly saw this notion as a central purpose of the poor law amendment act of June 1847 (*The Times*, 1 May 1847).
27. These data come from a return compiled by the poor law commissioners and were submitted in evidence to the Devon commission of 1843–5 (*Devon comm. digest*, i, 394).
28. Ó Gráda, *New economic history*, p. 118.
29. Ibid., pp. 117–18.
30. Ó Gráda, *Ireland before and after the famine*, p. 54.
31. Bourke, *'Visitation of God'*, p. 66.
32. Quoted ibid., p. 65.
33. Ó Gráda, *New economic history*, pp. 17–22, 83–4, 105–10.
34. Ibid., pp. 86–90.
35. Ibid., pp. 82–3.
36. Ó Gráda, *Ireland before and after the famine*, pp. 19–20. See also idem, *New economic history*, pp. 81–2.
37. Ó Gráda, *New economic history*, p. 118; Donnelly, *Cork*, pp. 16–26, 45–52.
38. Ó Gráda, *New economic history*, pp. 105–8.
39. Mokyr, *Why Ireland starved*, p. 12; Ó Gráda, *Ireland before and after the famine*, p. 22.
40. Ó Gráda, *Ireland before and after the famine*, p. 78.
41. *In Dublin*, 13 Dec. 1984.
42. Brendan Bradshaw, 'Nationalism and historical scholarship in modern Ireland', *I.H.S.*, xxvi, no. 104 (Nov. 1989), pp. 329–51.
43. Ibid., pp. 340–1.
44. See especially the essays by Hugh Kearney and Gearóid Ó Tuathaigh in Ciaran Brady (ed.), *Interpreting Irish history: the debate on historical revisionism, 1938–1994* (Dublin, 1994), pp. 246–52, 306–26. See also D.G. Boyce and Alan O'Day (eds), *The making of modern Irish history: revisionism and the revisionist controversy* (London and New York, 1996); Kevin Whelan, 'Come all your staunch revisionists – towards a post-revisionist agenda for Irish history', *Irish Reporter*, ii (Second Quarter, 1991), pp. 23–5; L.P. Curtis, Jr, 'The greening of Irish history', *Éire-Ireland*, xxix, no. 2 (Summer 1994), pp. 7–28.
45. Cormac Ó Gráda called attention to the negative reception given by Irish academic historians to Woodham-Smith's book in his pamphlet *The great Irish famine* (Basingstoke, Hampshire, 1989), pp. 10–11.
46. Lyons's review appeared in *I.H.S.*, xiv, no. 53 (Mar. 1964), pp. 7–9.
47. A.J.P. Taylor, *Essays in English history* (Harmondsworth, Middlesex, 1976), pp. 73, 75, 78.
48. Lyons's review, p. 77.
49. Ibid., pp. 78–9.
50. Ó Gráda, *Great Irish famine*, p. 11.
51. Idem, 'Making history in Ireland in the 1940s and 1950s: the saga of *The*

great Irish famine', *Irish Studies Review*, no. 12 (Spring/Summer 1992), pp. 87–107.
52. Ibid., pp. 87–8.
53. Ibid., pp. 96–7.
54. K.B. Nowlan, 'Foreword' in Edwards & Williams, *Great famine* (New York, 1957), p. xi.
55. Ibid., pp. xiii–xiv.
56. Ibid., pp. xiv–xv.
57. Quoted in Ó Gráda, 'Making history', p. 95.
58. Quoted ibid., p. 100.
59. References in this book to Mitchel's *The last conquest of Ireland (perhaps)* are to the so-called author's edition published in Glasgow without a date by Cameron, Ferguson, & Co. See Mitchel, *Last conquest*, p. 148.
60. 'To make an addition to the national debt', Mitchel declared, 'in order to preserve the lives of a million or two of Celts would have seemed in England a singular application of money. To kill so many Celts would have been well worth a war that would cost forty millions' (ibid., p. 94).
61. Ibid., p. 219. See also ibid., pp. 102, 126.
62. Ibid., pp. 112, 134. See also Chapter 9 of this book.
63. Mitchel, *Last conquest*, p. 152.
64. See, for example, ibid., pp. 140, 211–12.
65. For an unconvincing exculpation of Trevelyan's conduct, based on the wrong-headed notion that he was simply the servant of his changing political masters, see Bourke, *'Visitation of God'*, pp. 170–7.
66. C.E. Trevelyan, *The Irish crisis* (London, 1848), p. 201. It could be argued that in this passage and elsewhere in his book Trevelyan was taking comfort, crudely and insensitively, from the social by-products of the famine rather than positively exulting in its destructive power. I owe this point to Líam Kennedy.
67. Peter Gray, 'Potatoes and providence: British government's responses to the great famine', *Bullán: An Irish Studies Journal*, i (1994), pp. 75–90. See also idem, *Famine, land, and politics: British government and Irish society, 1843–1850* (Dublin and Portland, Oregon, 1999), passim; Boyd Hilton, *The age of atonement: the influence of evangelicalism on social and economic thought, 1785–1865* (Oxford and New York, 1988).
68. It could be argued, however, that Trevelyan's importance and influence were inflated by the divisions over famine policy that existed among members of the Whig government led by Lord John Russell. These divisions are a major theme of Peter Gray's *Famine, land, and politics*.
69. Peter Gray, *The Irish famine* (New York and London, 1995), p. 40.
70 *The Times*, 23 Mar. 1847. See also ibid., 6, 8 Apr. 1847.
71. Trevelyan, *Irish crisis*, p. 190.
72. See Chapter 5 of this book.
73. Trevelyan, *Irish crisis*, p. 185.
74. Gray, *Famine, land, and politics*, p. 191.
75. Two of the great Irish landlords who sat in Russell's cabinet held and advocated such a view (ibid., p. 192).
76. Trevelyan, *Irish crisis*, p. 164.
77. Ibid., pp. 195–6.
78. J.S. Donnelly, Jr (ed.), 'The journals of Sir John Benn-Walsh relating to the management of his Irish estates, 1823–64', *Cork Hist. Soc. Jn.*, lxxx, no. 230 (July–Dec. 1974), p. 119.

79. N.W. Senior, *Journals, conversations, and essays relating to Ireland* (2 vols, 2nd edn, London, 1868), ii, 3.
80. Ibid.
81. Ibid., pp. 40–1.
82. M.E. Daly, 'Historians and the famine: a beleaguered species?', *I.H.S.*, xxx, no. 120 (Nov. 1997), p. 591.
83. Christine Kinealy, *A death-dealing famine: the great hunger in Ireland* (London and Chicago, 1997), p. 1.
84. Idem, 'Food exports from Ireland, 1846–47', *History Ireland*, v, no. 1 (Spring 1997), pp. 32–6; idem, *Death-dealing famine*, pp. 79–80.
85. M.E. Daly, 'Revisionism and Irish history: the great famine' in Boyce and O'Day, *Making of modern Irish history*, p. 85.
86. Peter Solar, 'The great famine was no ordinary subsistence crisis' in E.M. Crawford (ed.), *Famine: the Irish experience, 900–1900: subsistence crises and famines in Ireland* (Edinburgh, 1989), p. 123.
87. Cormac Ó Gráda, *Black '47 and beyond: the great famine in history, economy, and memory* (Princeton, 1999), pp. 122–5. The life-saving potential of a temporary embargo on grain exports immediately after the almost total potato failure of 1846 was pointed out in the work of P.M.A. Bourke on the Irish grain trade in the 1840s. See Bourke, 'The Irish grain trade, 1839–48', *I.H.S.*, xx, no. 78 (Sept. 1976), pp. 164–6.
88. Christine Kinealy, *This great calamity: the Irish famine, 1845–52* (Dublin, 1994), p. 352. See also J.S. Donnelly, Jr, '"Irish property must pay for Irish poverty": British public opinion and the great famine' in Christopher Morash and Richard Hayes (eds), *'Fearful realities': new perspectives on the famine* (Dublin and Portland, Oregon, 1996), pp. 60–76.
89. Daly, 'Revisionism', pp. 81–2.
90. Kinealy, *Great calamity*, pp. 227–31, 245–50, 350–3.
91. Ibid., pp. 262–3.
92. Quoted in Gray, *Irish famine*, p. 87.
93. See their writings cited in the select bibliography of this book.
94. W.E. Vaughan, *Landlords and tenants in mid-Victorian Ireland* (Oxford and New York, 1994), pp. 24–6.
95. J.S. Donnelly, Jr, 'Mass eviction and the great famine' in Cathal Póirtéir (ed.), *The great Irish famine* (Cork and Dublin, 1995), pp. 164–71. For the quotation from the *Limerick and Clare Examiner*, see *Nation*, 3 June 1848.
96. Donal Kerr, *'A nation of beggars'?: priests, people, and politics in famine Ireland, 1846–1852* (Oxford and New York, 1994), p. 107. See also ibid., pp. 92–107.
97. Gray, *Famine, land, and politics*, p. 26, and passim.
98. Idem, 'Ideology and the famine' in Póirtéir, *Great Irish famine*, pp. 102–3; idem, *Famine, land, and politics*, passim.
99. Gray, *Famine, land, and politics*, pp. 201, 218, 243–4, 275–6, 285, 288.
100. Quoted ibid., p. 288.
101. Kinealy, *Great calamity*, p. 359.
102. Ibid., pp. 285, 305–6; Gray, *Irish famine*, pp. 64, 79. Ó Gráda and others, however, have questioned the seriousness of the monetary and commercial crisis of 1847–8 (Ó Gráda, *Black '47 and beyond*, pp. 78–81).
103. Gray, 'Ideology and famine', p. 103. See also idem, *Famine, land, and politics*, pp. 331–3, 337–8.
104. Besides having to contend with the objections of 'moralists', Russell and

his strongest ministerial ally Lord Clarendon were also seriously weakened politically by the unwillingness of Irish landlords to submit to additional taxation in order to help finance emigration schemes (idem, *Famine, land, and politics*, pp. 307–11).

105. Quoted ibid., p. 310.
106. Quoted in K.A. Miller, *Emigrants and exiles: Ireland and the Irish exodus to North America* (New York and Oxford, 1985), pp. 306–7.
107. Cormac Ó Gráda and K.H. O' Rourke, 'Migration as disaster relief: lessons from the great Irish famine', *European Review of Economic History*, i, pt 1 (Apr. 1997), pp. 3–26.
108. Gray, *Famine, land, and politics*, pp. 308–9.
109. Ibid., p. 307.
110. R.J. Scally, *The end of hidden Ireland: rebellion, famine, and emigration* (New York and Oxford, 1995), pp. 222–4. Scally also considers the possibility that some of 'the missing' practised deliberate deception and remained behind (ibid., pp. 224–5).
111. Ruth-Ann Harris, 'Ballykilcline and beyond', *Irish Studies Review*, no. 15 (Summer 1996), pp. 39–42; Ó Gráda, *Black '47 and beyond*, pp. 105–6; T.M. Devine, *The Highland famine: hunger, emigration, and the Scottish Highlands in the nineteenth century* (Edinburgh, 1988).
112. Michael Quigley, 'Grosse Île: Canada's famine memorial', *Éire-Ireland*, xxxii, no. 1 (Spring 1997), pp. 20–40; idem, 'Grosse Île: "the most important and evocative great famine site outside of Ireland"' in E.M. Crawford (ed.), *The hungry stream: essays on emigration and famine* (Belfast, 1997), pp. 25–40. See also the works on Grosse Île by Marianna O'Gallagher and R.M. Dompierre cited in the select bibliography of this book.
113. Scally, *End of hidden Ireland*, pp. 184–216; Frank Neal, 'Lancashire, the famine Irish, and the poor laws: a study in crisis management', *Ir. Econ. & Soc. Hist.*, xxii (1995), pp. 26–48; Frank Neal, *Black '47: Britain and the famine Irish* (New York and London, 1998).
114. Ó Gráda, *Black '47 and beyond*, p. 113. See the discussion of the 'coffin ships' in Chapter 7 below.
115. David Fitzpatrick, *Oceans of consolation: personal accounts of Irish migration to Australia* (Ithaca and London, 1994); idem, 'The failure: representations of the Irish famine in letters to Australia' in Crawford, *Hungry stream*, pp. 161–74.
116. See, for example, R.H. Bayor and T.J. Meagher (eds), *The New York Irish* (Baltimore and London, 1996), pp. 87–192.
117. Crawford, 'Introduction: Ireland's haemorrhage' in idem, *Hungry stream*, p. 3.
118. Ó Gráda, *Black '47 and beyond*, p. 121.
119. See also Cormac Ó Gráda, 'The great famine and today's famines' in Póirtéir, *Great Irish famine*, pp. 248–58; idem, 'The great famine and other famines' in Cormac Ó Gráda (ed.), *Famine 150: commemorative lecture series* (Dublin, 1997), pp. 129–57.
120. Idem, *Black '47 and beyond*, pp. 4–5; idem, 'Today's famines', p. 250; idem, 'Other famines', pp. 132–3.
121. Peter Gray, 'Famine relief policy in comparative perspective: Ireland, Scotland, and northwestern Europe, 1845–1849', *Éire-Ireland*, xxxii, no. 1 (Spring 1997), p. 86.

122. Ó Gráda, *Black '47 and beyond*, p. 5. In parts of the country the potato may be said to have failed four or five years in succession, thus placing Ireland off the European scale of experience after 1600.
123. Ibid., pp. 5–8.
124. Mitchel condemned providentialism and political economy almost in the same breath in his book *The last conquest*. His contempt for providentialism sparked his most famous declaration about the Irish famine: 'The English indeed call that famine a "dispensation of Providence" and ascribe it entirely to the blight of the potatoes. But potatoes failed in like manner all over Europe; yet there was no famine save in Ireland. The British account of the matter, then, is first a fraud – second a blasphemy. The Almighty indeed sent the potato blight, but the English created the famine' (*Last conquest*, p. 219).
125. J.D. Post, *Food shortage, climatic variability, and epidemic disease in preindustrial Europe: the mortality peak in the early 1740s* (Ithaca and London, 1985), p. 177. See also idem, *The last great subsistence crisis in the western world* (Baltimore and London, 1977), pp. 53–67.
126. Gray, 'Famine relief policy', p. 107. See also ibid., pp. 101–3.
127. Ó Gráda, *Black '47 and beyond*, p. 83.
128. Ibid., p. 82. See also Peter Solar, 'The potato famine in Europe' in Ó Gráda, *Famine 150*, pp. 113–27.
129. Ó Gráda, *Black '47 and beyond*, pp. 122–5.
130. Niall Ó Ciosáin, 'Was there silence about the famine?', *Irish Studies Review*, no. 13 (Winter 1995–6), pp. 7–10; Carmel Quinlan, '"A punishment from God": the famine in the centenary folklore questionnaire', *Irish Review*, no. 19 (Spring/Summer 1996), pp. 68–86; Ó Gráda, *Black '47 and beyond*, pp. 194–225. See also Patricia Lysaght, 'Perspectives on women during the great Irish famine from oral tradition', *Béaloideas*, nos 64–5 (1996–7), pp. 63–131; Cathal Póirtéir (ed.), *Famine echoes* (Dublin, 1995). This last work is an important collection of folklore material from the archives of the Department of Irish Folklore in University College, Dublin, the successor to the Irish Folklore Commission.
131. Quinlan, 'Punishment from God', p. 68.
132. Ó Gráda, *Black '47 and beyond*, p. 197.
133. Idem, 'Famine, trauma, and memory' (unpublished paper presented at 'Conference on cultural trauma and national identity', Dublin City University, 28–9 Apr. 2000), pp. 7–8. I wish to express my thanks to Cormac Ó Gráda for kindly allowing me to cite this paper.
134. Ó Ciosáin, 'Was there silence?', pp. 7–10.
135. This possibility is suggested by Ó Gráda's observation that 'memories of more protracted catastrophes such as war or famine may be weighted towards their early phases' (Ó Gráda, 'Famine, trauma, and memory', p. 6).
136. Ó Gráda notes that the folklore record is not only 'rich in its condemnations of local landlords' (along with local merchants and officials) 'for their cruelties', but also kind to many other landlords for their generosity and charity (*Black '47 and beyond*, pp. 196–7).

137. Roger McHugh, 'The famine in Irish oral tradition' in Edwards & Williams, *Great famine*, p. 420.
138. Ibid., p. 425.
139. K.T. Hoppen, *Elections, politics, and society in Ireland, 1832–1885* (Oxford and New York, 1984), pp. 16–17.
140. Georges-Denis Zimmermann, *Songs of Irish rebellion: political street ballads and rebel songs, 1780–1900* (Dublin, 1967), passim; Gary Owens, 'Nationalism without words: symbolism and ritual behaviour in the repeal "monster meetings" of 1843' in J.S. Donnelly, Jr, and K.A. Miller (eds), *Irish popular culture, 1650–1850* (Dublin and Portland, Oregon, 1998), pp. 242–69.
141. Ó Gráda, *Black '47 and beyond*, pp. 216–22.
142. Ó Ciosáin, 'Was there silence?', p. 8. Quinlan has usefully pointed out that part of the 'distancing' to be noted in famine folklore may well result from the disproportionate survival rates of middling and strong farmers, many of whom would have succeeded to the holdings of famine victims or have themselves evicted labourers or cottiers during the famine. She also observes that many of the respondents to the centenary questionnaire were themselves farmers, but that there is little information about the size of their holdings. The questionnaire itself nowhere directly raised questions of political responsibility (Quinlan, 'Punishment from God', pp. 79–81, 85).
143. Ibid., p. 8.
144. Ibid., p. 10.
145. P.S. O'Hegarty, *A history of Ireland under the union, 1801 to 1922* (Dublin, 1952), p. 291. See also Ó Ciosáin, 'Was there silence?', p. 10.

Chapter 1

1. P.M.A. Bourke, 'Emergence of potato blight, 1843–46', *Nature*, cciii (Aug. 1964), pp. 805–8. See also Bourke, *'Visitation of God'*, pp. 129–54.
2. *Freeman's Journal* (hereafter cited as *F.J.*), 1 Oct. 1845 (quoting *Northern Whig*).
3. *F.J.*, 20 Nov. 1845.
4. *F.J.*, 1 Dec. 1845.
5. *F.J.*, 29 Oct. 1845.
6. E.C. Large, *The advance of the fungi* (London, 1940), p. 27.
7. T.P. O'Neill, 'The scientific investigation of the failure of the potato crop in Ireland, 1845–6', *I.H.S.*, v, no. 18 (Sept. 1946), pp. 123–38.
8. *F.J.*, 10 Nov. 1845.
9. Ibid.
10. *F.J.*, 5 Nov. 1845.
11. *F.J.*, 19 Dec. 1845.
12. *F.J.*, 5 Nov. 1845.
13. O'Neill, 'Scientific investigation', p. 128.
14. *F.J.*, 10 Nov. 1845.
15. *Copy of report of Dr Playfair and Mr Lindley on the present state of the Irish potato crop and on the prospect of approaching scarcity (dated 15th November 1845)*, p. 1, H.C. 1846 (28), xxxvii, 33.
16. Bourke, 'Emergence of potato blight', p. 807.
17. *F.J.*, 14, 17 Nov. 1845.
18. *Correspondence explanatory of the measures adopted by her majesty's government for the relief of distress arising from the failure of the potato crop in Ireland*, p. 5 [735], H.C. 1846, xxxvii, 57.
19. *F.J.*, 3 Dec. 1845.
20. *F.J.*, 3 Nov. 1845.
21. *F.J.*, 13 Nov. 1845.
22. *A statement 'of the total expenditure for purposes of relief in Ireland since November*

1845 . . .', p. 1, H.C. 1846 (615), xxxvii, 477.
23. T.P. O'Neill, 'The organisation and administration of relief, 1845–52' in Edwards & Williams, *Great famine*, pp. 215–16.
24. *Statement 'of total expenditure'*, p. 1; O'Neill, 'Administration of relief', p. 216.
25. *Correspondence explanatory of measures adopted*, p. 90.
26. *Correspondence from July 1846 to January 1847 relating to the measures adopted for the relief of the distress in Ireland and Scotland (commissariat series)*, p. 2 [761], H.C. 1847, li, 24.
27. Routh to Trevelyan, 6 Mar. 1846, quoted in *Correspondence explanatory of measures adopted*, pp. 56–7.
28. Cecil Woodham-Smith, *The great hunger: Ireland, 1845–1849* (New York and London, 1962), pp. 64–5, 73, 134–5.
29. Edward Pine Coffin to Trevelyan, 30 Mar. 1846, quoted in *Correspondence explanatory of measures adopted*, p. 84.
30. Routh to Trevelyan, 2 Apr. 1846, quoted ibid., p. 88.
31. O'Neill, 'Administration of relief', p. 216.
32. Routh to Trevelyan, 15 Apr. 1846, quoted in *Correspondence explanatory of measures adopted*, p. 105.
33. Hewetson to Trevelyan, 7 June 1846, quoted ibid., p. 158.
34. E.M. Crawford, 'Indian meal and pellagra in nineteenth-century Ireland' in J.M. Goldstrom and L.A. Clarkson (eds), *Irish population, economy, and society: essays in honour of the late K.H. Connell* (Oxford, 1981), pp. 113–15.
35. O'Neill, 'Administration of relief', p. 222.
36. Bourke, 'Irish grain trade', p. 163.
37. Ibid., p. 167; *Statement 'of total expenditure'*, p. 1.
38. Hewetson to Trevelyan, 7 June 1846, quoted in *Correspondence explanatory of measures adopted*, p. 158.
39. *Statement 'of total expenditure'*, p. 1; O'Neill, 'Administration of relief', pp. 219–21.
40. Trevelyan's memorandum, 15 Apr. 1846, quoted in *Correspondence explanatory of measures adopted*, p. 304.
41. Commissioners of public works to lords of the treasury, 8 Aug. 1846, quoted ibid., p. 352.
42. Ibid., pp. 332, 351; O'Neill, 'Administration of relief', pp. 220–1.
43. Commissioners of public works to lords of the treasury, 8 Aug. 1846, quoted in *Correspondence explanatory of measures adopted*, p. 352.
44. Ibid., p. 351.
45. Ibid., p. 349.
46. Quoted in Major Simmonds to Trevelyan, 4 July 1846, ibid., pp. 191–2.
47. Coffin to Trevelyan, 24 June 1846, quoted ibid., p. 175.
48. Routh to Trevelyan, 17 June 1846, quoted ibid., p. 167.

Chapter 2

1. *Cork Examiner*, 15 July 1846.
2. Quoted in *Correspondence from July 1846 to January 1847 (commissariat series)*, p. 4.
3. Ibid., p. 7.
4. Ibid., p. 57.
5. P.M.A. Bourke, 'The extent of the potato crop in Ireland at the time of the famine', *Stat. Soc. Ire. Jn.*, xx, pt 3 (1959), p. 11.
6. Ibid.
7. See note 2 above.
8. Captain Giffard to Trevelyan, 27 Feb. 1847, quoted in *Correspondence from*

January to March 1847 relating to the measures adopted for the relief of the distress in Ireland (commissariat series), pt ii, p. 178 [796], H.C. 1847, lii, 524.
9. Bourke, 'Extent of potato crop', p. 11.
10. Quoted ibid., p. 12.
11. Ibid., p. 11.
12. *Returns of agricultural produce in Ireland in the year 1853*, p. xix [1865], H.C. 1854–5, xlvii, 19.
13. *Thom's Irish almanac and official directory* (Dublin, 1855), p. 402.
14. *Returns of agricultural produce in Ireland in the year 1847*, pt i: *Crops*, p. vi [923], H.C. 1847–8, lvii, 6; *Returns of agricultural produce . . . 1853*, pp. vii, xii; Thomas Barrington, 'A review of Irish agricultural prices', *Stat. Soc. Ire. Jn.*, xv, pt 101 (Oct. 1927), p. 251.
15. See sources cited in note 14 above.
16. 'Corn exported from Ireland to Great Britain' in Ledgers of imports, England, 1843–9 (special abstract on last pages of each ledger), nos 32–5, 37, 39, 41 (P.R.O., Customs 5).
17. P.M.A. Bourke, 'The use of the potato crop in pre-famine Ireland', *Stat. Soc. Ire. Jn.*, xxi, pt 6 (1968), pp. 83–7.
18. *Cork Constitution*, 21 Jan. 1847.
19. Account of the total annual quantity of butter in casks, firkins, and kegs passed through the weigh-house, 1770–1869 (Cork Public Museum, Cork Butter Market MSS, C. 38). Because of a computational error the figures given in Donnelly, *Cork*, p. 77, are incorrect.
20. T.J. Clanchy and Co., *Half-a-century's butter prices . . .* (Cork, 1892), 1 p.
21. Barrington, 'Irish agricultural prices', p. 251.
22. Donnelly, 'Benn-Walsh journals', p. 115.
23. P.M.A. Bourke, 'The agricultural statistics of the 1841 census of Ireland: a critical review', *Econ. Hist. Rev.*, ser. 2, xviii, no. 2 (Aug. 1965), pp. 381–2.
24. *Returns of agricultural produce in Ireland in the year 1847*, pt ii: *Stock*, p. iv [1000], H.C. 1847–8, lvii, 112; *Returns of agricultural produce . . . 1853*, p. xix.
25. *F.J.*, 5 Oct. 1849.
26. *F.J.*, 9 Oct. 1849.
27. Barrington, 'Irish agricultural prices', p. 251.

Chapter 3

1. Quoted in *Correspondence from July 1846 to January 1847 (commissariat series)*, p. 15.
2. *Correspondence from July 1846 to January 1847 relating to the measures adopted for the relief of the distress in Ireland, with maps, plans, and appendices (Board of Works series)*, pt i, p. 76 [764], H.C. 1847, 1, 96.
3. O'Neill, 'Administration of relief', pp. 223–4.
4. *Correspondence from July 1846 to January 1847 (commissariat series)*, p. 31.
5. Quoted ibid., p. 80.
6. Trevelyan to Routh, 22 Sept. 1846, quoted ibid., p. 83.
7. Ibid., p. 103.
8. Ibid., pp. 93–6, 265.
9. Ibid., pp. 318, 428.
10. Trevelyan to Routh, 28 Dec. 1846, quoted ibid., p. 425.
11. O'Neill, 'Administration of relief', p. 225.
12. *Correspondence explanatory of measures adopted*, p. 215.
13. *Correspondence from July 1846 to January 1847 (commissariat series)*, pp. 22, 506–7.

14. Routh to Trevelyan, 22 Sept. 1846, quoted ibid., p. 84.
15. Routh to Trevelyan, 29 Sept. 1846, quoted ibid., p. 97.
16. Routh to Trevelyan, 30 Sept. 1846, quoted ibid., p. 104.
17. Trevelyan to Routh, 1 Oct. 1846, quoted ibid., p. 106.
18. Bourke, 'Irish grain trade', p. 165.
19. *Correspondence from July 1846 to January 1847 (commissariat series)*, pp. 48, 128, 199, 304, 313, 326, 335, 366.
20. Hewetson to Trevelyan, 23 Oct. 1846, quoted ibid., p. 185.
21. Hewetson to Trevelyan, 20 Oct. 1846, quoted ibid., p. 181.
22. Hewetson to Trevelyan, 18 Nov. 1846, quoted ibid., p. 278.
23. Ibid., pp. 479–82, 506.
24. Trevelyan to Routh, 30 Sept. 1846, quoted ibid., p. 101.
25. This and the next two paragraphs draw heavily on O'Neill, 'Administration of relief', pp. 227–34.
26. *Correspondence from July 1846 to January 1847 (Board of Works series)*, pp. 195, 344, 486; O'Neill, 'Administration of relief', pp. 232, 234.
27. *Correspondence from July 1846 to January 1847 (Board of Works series)*, pt i, p. 140.
28. Ibid., pp. 68, 150–1.
29. Ibid., pp. 152, 230, 346.
30. O'Neill, 'Administration of relief', p. 228.
31. Jones to Trevelyan, 10 Dec. 1846, quoted in *Correspondence from July 1846 to January 1847 (Board of Works series)*, p. 334.
32. *Clare Journal*, 7 Jan. 1847, quoted in *Correspondence from January to March 1847 relative to the measures adopted for the relief of the distress in Ireland (Board of Works series)*, pt ii, p. 3 [797], H.C. 1847, lii, 13.
33. Jones to Trevelyan, 18 Jan. 1847, quoted ibid., p. 17.
34. Quoted in *Correspondence from July 1846 to January 1847 (Board of Works series)*, pt i, p. 442.
35. Commissioners of public works to viceroy, 17 Jan. 1847, quoted in *Correspondence from January to March 1847 (Board of Works series)*, pt ii, p. 14.
36. Quoted in *Correspondence from July 1846 to January 1847 (Board of Works series)*, pt i, p. 445.
37. Quoted ibid., p. 448.
38. Ibid., pp. 441, 444, 446.
39. Quoted ibid., p. 285.
40. Quoted in *Correspondence from January to March 1847 (Board of Works series)*, pt ii, p. 5.
41. O'Neill, 'Administration of relief', p. 229.
42. Jones to Trevelyan, 12 Sept. 1846, quoted in *Correspondence from July 1846 to January 1847 (Board of Works series)*, pt i, p. 89.
43. Trevelyan to Jones, 5 Dec. 1846, quoted ibid., p. 299.
44. Quoted ibid., p. 414.
45. Quoted ibid., p. 413.
46. *Correspondence from January to March 1847 (Board of Works series)*, pt ii, p. 189.
47. Jones to Trevelyan, 13 Jan. 1847, quoted ibid., p. 8.
48. Ibid., p. 7.
49. Commissioners of public works to viceroy, 17 Jan. 1847, quoted ibid., p. 14.
50. Jones to Trevelyan, 13 Jan. 1847, quoted ibid., pp. 7–8.
51. Jones to Trevelyan, 16 Jan. 1847, quoted ibid., p. 13.

52. Jones to Trevelyan, 19 Jan. 1847, quoted ibid., p. 18.
53. Commissioners to viceroy, 17 Jan. 1847, quoted ibid., p. 14.
54. Jones to Trevelyan, 19 Jan. 1847, quoted ibid., p. 18.

Chapter 4

1. 10 & 11 Vict., c. 7 (26 Feb. 1847).
2. *Treasury minute dated 10th March 1847 and first report of the relief commissioners . . .* , p. 8 [799], H.C. 1847, xvii, 26.
3. Ibid., pp. 12–15, 22–4.
4. *Second report of the relief commissioners . . .* , p. 3 [819], H.C. 1847, xvii, 77.
5. *Treasury minute dated 10th March 1847*, pp. 4–5.
6. *Second report of relief commissioners*, p. 7.
7. Woodham-Smith, *Great hunger*, p. 288.
8. *Second report of relief commissioners*, p. 26; *Third report . . .* , p. 29 [836], H.C. 1847, xvii, 131; *Fourth report . . .* , p. 5 [859], H.C. 1847, xvii, 147; *Fifth report . . .* , p. 6 [876], H.C. 1847–8, xxix, 34; *Sixth report . . .* , p. 7 [876], H.C. 1847–8, xxix, 59; *Seventh report . . .* , p. 7 [876], H.C. 1847–8, xxix, 79.
9. *Third report of relief commissioners*, pp. 23–4; *Supplementary appendix to the seventh and last report of the relief commissioners . . .* , pp. 5–6 [956], H.C. 1847–8, xxix, 125–6.
10. *Treasury minute dated 10th March 1847*, pp. 22–3; *Second report of relief commissioners*, p. 4.
11. *Second report of relief commissioners*, pp. 6, 17; *Supplementary appendix to seventh and last report of relief commissioners*, p. 6.
12. *Third report of relief commissioners*, p. 24.
13. Ibid.
14. Ibid.
15. Woodham-Smith, *Great hunger*, p. 295.
16. *Supplementary appendix to seventh and last report of relief commissioners*, p. 6.
17. Ibid., p. 7.
18. Ibid., p. 6.
19. *Treasury minute dated 10th March 1847*, p. 23.
20. *Second report of relief commissioners*, p. 4.
21. *Supplementary appendix to seventh and last report of relief commissioners*, p. 7.
22. Ibid., p. 6. See also Woodham-Smith, *Great hunger*, p. 178.
23. *Second report of relief commissioners*, p. 7; *Fourth report . . .* , pp. 17–19.
24. *Supplementary appendix to seventh and last report of relief commissioners*, pp. 16–17.
25. Sir George Nicholls, *A history of the Irish poor law in connexion with the condition of the people* (London, 1856), p. 326.
26. *Papers relating to proceedings for the relief of the distress and state of the unions and workhouses in Ireland; fourth series, 1847*, p. 258 [896], H.C. 1847–8, liv, 294.
27. *Supplementary appendix to seventh and last report of relief commissioners*, p. 12.
28. Ibid., p. 7.
29. *Seventh report of relief commissioners*, p. 3.
30. For discussions of the poor law amendment act of June 1847 and the Gregory, or quarter-acre, clause, see Kinealy, *Great calamity*, pp. 180–4, 216–27. See also the following articles by Peter Gray: 'Punch and the great famine', *History Ireland*, i, no. 2 (Summer 1993), pp. 26–33; 'The triumph of dogma: ideology and famine relief', ibid., iii, no. 2 (Summer 1995), pp. 26–34; 'Ideology and famine', pp. 86–103.
31. *Illustrated London News* (hereafter cited as *I.L.N.*), 20 Mar. 1847.
32. *I.L.N.*, 20 Feb. 1847.
33. *The Times*, 2 Apr. 1847.
34. *I.L.N.*, 23 Jan. 1847.
35. *Hansard*, 3rd ser., lxxxix, 955.
36. *I.L.N.*, 6 Feb. 1847.

37. *The Times*, 10 Mar. 1847.
38. Ibid., 5 Apr. 1847.
39. Ibid., 20 Apr. 1847.
40. Ibid., 16 Apr. 1847.
41. Ibid.
42. *Hansard*, 3rd ser., xc, 1249–50, 1414.
43. *The Times*, 15 Mar. 1847.
44. Ibid., 8 May 1847.
45. *Hansard*, 3rd ser., xc, 1276.
46. Ibid., 1283.
47. *The Times*, 29 Mar. 1847.
48. *I.L.N.*, 23 Jan. 1847.
49. *Hansard*, 3rd ser., xc, 1273.
50. Quoted ibid., 1301.
51. *I.L.N.*, 22 May 1847.
52. *I.L.N.*, 15 May 1847.
53. *The Times*, 30 Mar. 1847.
54. *Hansard*, 3rd ser., xc, 1408.
55. *The Times*, 20 Apr. 1847.
56. *I.L.N.*, 3 Apr. 1847.
57. Ibid.
58. Ibid.

Chapter 5

1. Russell to Wood, 26 Mar. 1847, quoted in G.P. Gooch (ed.), *The later correspondence of Lord John Russell, 1840–1878* (2 vols, London, 1925), i, 172.
2. Wood to Russell, 20 May 1848, quoted ibid., p. 228.
3. 10 & 11 Vict., c. 31 (8 June 1847), sect. 10.
4. See his entry in the *Dictionary of national biography*. See also Brian Jenkins, *Sir William Gregory of Coole: the biography of an Anglo-Irishman* (Gerrards Cross, Buckinghamshire, 1986), pp. 71–5.
5. Objecting strenuously to the Gregory clause in the House of Commons, the English MP George Poulett Scrope declared, 'Its consequence would be a complete clearance of the small farmers in Ireland – a change which would amount to a perfect social revolution in the state of things in that country. Such a change might be desirable if effected by degrees; but to introduce it at once would have the effect of turning great masses of pauperism adrift on the community – a catastrophe which would undoubtedly not be without its effects in this country.' See *Hansard*, 3rd ser., xci, 588–9.
6. Ibid., 590.
7. Ibid., 592–3.
8. When in 1874 Canon John O'Rourke, the parish priest of Maynooth, came to publish his *History of the great Irish famine of 1847*, he declared of the Gregory clause, 'A more complete engine for the slaughter and expatriation of a people was never designed.' In case anyone might be inclined to forgive or forget, O'Rourke insisted that 'Mr Gregory's words – the words of . . . a pretended friend of the people – and Mr Gregory's clause are things that should be forever remembered by the descendants of the slaughtered and expatriated small farmers of Ireland'. See John O'Rourke, *The history of the great Irish famine of 1847, with notices of earlier Irish famines* (3rd edn, Dublin, 1902) pp. 332–3.
9. Minute book, Fermoy board of guardians, 1847–8, 10 Mar. 1847, pp. 26–9 (Cork Archives Council).
10. Nicholls, *Poor law*, p. 318.
11. Ibid., pp. 351, 404.
12. Ibid., pp. 342–3, 351–2; *Cork Examiner*, 8 Dec. 1848.
13. Kennedy to poor law commissioners, 30 Mar. 1848, quoted in *Papers relating to proceedings for the relief of the distress and state of the unions and workhouses in*

Ireland; sixth series, 1848, p. 811 [955], H.C. 1847–8, lvi, 849.
14. Ibid., p. 810.
15. Kennedy to commissioners, 24 Feb. 1848, quoted ibid., p. 796.
16. Nicholls, *Poor law*, pp. 343, 404.
17. Ibid., p. 404.
18. Ibid., pp. 397, 404.
19. *Papers relating to proceedings for relief of distress; sixth series, 1848*, pp. 297–8.
20. W. Stanley (secretary) to clerks of unions, 5 May 1848, quoted in *Papers relating to proceedings for the relief of the distress and state of unions and workhouses in Ireland; seventh series, 1848*, p. 13 [999], H.C. 1847–8, liv, 333.
21. O'Neill, 'Administration of relief', p. 252.
22. Commissioners to Clifden vice-guardians, 2 Mar. 1848, quoted in *Papers relating to proceedings for relief of distress; sixth series, 1848*, p. 298.
23. O'Neill, 'Administration of relief', p. 252.
24. Captain Maxwell to commissioners, 12 Feb. 1848, quoted in *Papers relating to proceedings for relief of distress; sixth series, 1848*, p. 584.
25. Scariff vice-guardians to commissioners, 12 Feb. 1848, quoted ibid., p. 506.
26. Richard Lynch to commissioners, 9 May 1848, quoted in *Papers relating to proceedings for relief of distress; seventh series, 1848*, p. 9.
27. Ibid., pp. 10–11.
28. W. Stanley to clerks of unions, 8 June 1848, quoted ibid., p. 12.
29. Minute book, Mallow board of guardians, 1849–50, 15 June 1849, p. 100 (Cork Archives Council).
30. Minute book, Bandon board of guardians, 1848–9, 23 Sept. 1848, p. 288 (Cork Archives Council).
31. *Nation*, 4 Mar. 1848.
32. *Nation*, 29 Jan., 5 Feb., 4 Mar., 3 June, 1 July 1848.
33. For the destruction of tenants' houses on the Blake estate and the ensuing parliamentary controversy, see *Nation*, 26 Feb., 4, 25 Mar., 1 Apr. 1848.
34. *Nation*, 25 Mar. 1848.
35. *Nation*, 1 Apr. 1848.
36. *Nation*, 15 Apr. 1848.
37. Quoted in Gray, *Famine, land, and politics*, p. 191.
38. Quoted ibid., p. 192.
39. Ibid.
40. Ibid.
41. *Nation*, 8 Apr. 1848.
42. Gray, *Famine, land, and politics*, p. 193.
43. 11 & 12 Vict., c. 47.
44. Gray, *Famine, land, and politics*, pp. 209, 224–6, 302, 322, 326–7.
45. *Papers relating to proceedings for the relief of the distress and state of unions and workhouses in Ireland; eighth series, 1849*, pp. xxxviii, xl [1042], H.C. 1849, xlviii, 478, 480.
46. Nicholls, *Poor law*, p. 395.
47. Ibid., pp. 359, 375–6.
48. O'Neill, 'Administration of relief', pp. 255–6.
49. Nicholls, *Poor law*, pp. 323, 395.
50. *Fiftieth report from the commissioners of public works in Ireland, with appendices, 1881–82*, p. 16 [3261], H.C. 1882, xx, 302.
51. Mokyr, *Why Ireland starved*, p. 292.
52. G.R. Porter, *The progress of the nation . . .* (London, 1851 edn), p. 506; J.H. Clapham, *An economic history of modern Britain: free trade and steel, 1850–1886* (Cambridge, 1932), p. 397.
53. John Mitchel, *Jail journal*, intro. Thomas Flanagan (University Press of Ireland edn, 1982), p. xxxi.

54. Taylor, *Essays in English history*, pp. 73, 78.
55. Ibid., p. 74.
56. Ibid.
57. *I.L.N.*, 4 Mar. 1848.
58. *I.L.N.*, 25 Nov. 1848.
59. *The Times*, 13 Jan. 1849.
60. *I.L.N.*, 16 Dec. 1848.
61. Gray, *Famine, land, and politics*, pp. 305–6.
62. *The Times*, 1 May 1847.
63. *I.L.N.*, 1 Apr. 1848.
64. *The Times*, 1 May 1847.
65. *I.L.N.*, 16 Dec. 1848.
66. *I.L.N.*, 14 Apr. 1849.
67. *I.L.N.*, 2 June 1849.
68. *I.L.N.*, 20 Oct. 1849.
69. *The Times*, 8 May 1847.
70. *I.L.N.*, 16 Dec. 1848.
71. *I.L.N.*, 20 Oct. 1849.
72. Ibid.
73. *I.L.N.*, 15 Dec. 1849.
74. *I.L.N.*, 22 Dec. 1849.
75. *I.L.N.*, 19 Jan. 1850.
76. *I.L.N.*, 12 Jan. 1850.
77. This campaign to abolish primogeniture as the legal foundation for the inheritance of land failed to attract much support from the middle classes at whom it was directed by its Radical leaders. It has been described as one in a series of unsuccessful attempts to 'prolong the Anti-Corn Law League for other purposes'. See Norman Gash, *Aristocracy and people: Britain, 1815–1865* (Cambridge, Mass., 1979), p. 349.
78. *I.L.N.*, 10 Mar. 1849.
79. *I.L.N.*, 25 Nov. 1848.
80. This issue of perceived racial differences requires careful handling. In the pages of *Punch*, as Roy Foster has remarked, hostility to the British working classes or to the French could lead to the same kind of 'racialist' caricatures as hostility to Irish peasants and Irish nationalists. In addition, as Foster notes, 'Irish comic papers of a nationalist bent represented the English as grasping, prognathous, subhuman bogeymen'. See R.F. Foster, *Paddy and Mr Punch: connections in Irish and English history* (Harmondsworth, Middlesex, 1993), p. 192.
81. *The Times*, 23 Mar. 1847.
82. Ibid., 6 Apr. 1847.
83. Ibid., 8 Apr. 1847.
84. Ibid., 31 Mar. 1847.
85. Ibid., 14 Apr. 1847.
86. Ibid., 26 Mar. 1847.
87. Ibid.
88. Ibid., 2 Apr. 1847.
89. Ibid., 2 Apr. 1849.

Chapter 6

1. Donnelly, 'Benn-Walsh journals', p. 119.
2. Samuel Clark, *Social origins of the Irish land war* (Princeton and Guildford, Surrey, 1979), p. 35.
3. Thomas Foley to Joseph Tatham, 12 Feb. 1852 (Guildford Muniment Room, Surrey, Midleton papers).
4. Donnelly, 'Benn-Walsh journals', p. 111.
5. Ibid., p. 113.
6. Ibid., pp. 102, 105, 108.
7. Ibid., p. 106.
8. Ibid., pp. 89, 119.
9. Ibid., p. 120.
10. Ibid., p. 106.
11. Rental of the earl of Kenmare's estates, 1830–50 (P.R.O.N.I., Kenmare papers); *Cork Examiner*, 31 Dec. 1849.
12. Rent receipts and disbursements of the duke of Devonshire's estates, 1818–90 (N.L.I., Lismore papers, MS 6929).

13. Rental of the Jephson-Norreys estate, 1846–55; J.W. Braddell to Sir Charles Denham Jephson-Norreys, 9 Aug. 1850, in folder marked 'Mallow workhouse and poor law commissioners, 1847–50' (Jephson-Norreys papers, Mallow Castle, Mallow, Co. Cork).
14. Rental of Robert Cole Bowen's estates in the counties of Cork and Tipperary, 1847–53 (Tipperary County Library, Thurles, Bowen papers).
15. *A return from the poor law commissioners . . .*, pp. 34–5, H.C. 1846 (262), xxxvi, 502–3.
16. Marquis of Sligo to Lord Monteagle, 8 Oct. 1848, quoted in Woodham-Smith, *Great hunger*, p. 364. See also D.E. Jordan, Jr, *Land and politics in Ireland: County Mayo from the plantation to the land war* (Cambridge, 1994), p. 111.
17. Marquis of Clanricarde to earl of Clarendon, 31 Dec. 1848, quoted in Woodham-Smith, *Great hunger*, p. 364.
18. *Cork Constitution*, 2 June 1866.
19. Sir W.F. Butler, *Sir William Butler: an autobiography* (2nd edn, London, 1913), p. 12. It was Butler who recorded what Kennedy said to Lord Carnarvon. Some transference of guilt was involved, since Kennedy had worked to keep a substantial number of the destitute from obtaining poor law relief.
20. *Return . . . of cases of evictions . . . from 1849 to 1880 inclusive*, p. 3, H.C. 1881 (185), lxxvii, 727. See also *Returns . . . of the number of ejectments* [1846–9], H.C. 1849 (315), xlix, 235.
21. Donnelly, 'Benn-Walsh journals', p. 117.
22. Ibid., p. 107.
23. Oliver MacDonagh, 'Irish overseas emigration during the famine' in Edwards & Williams, *Great famine*, p. 474, n. 9.
24. W.S. Trench, *Realities of Irish life* (Boston, 1880, originally published 1868), pp. 102–3.
25. Ibid., pp. 109–10.
26. For an account of this notorious case, see S.J. Campbell, *The great Irish famine: words and images from the Famine Museum, Strokestown Park, County Roscommon* (Strokestown, 1994), pp. 39–50.
27. *Nation*, 6 May 1848.
28. Campbell, *Great Irish famine*, pp. 40–1.
29. MacDonagh, 'Irish overseas emigration', pp. 336–7.
30. *Nation*, 19 Feb. 1848.
31. For Shrewsbury's letter to MacHale, see *Morning Chronicle*, 4 Jan. 1848. See also the excellent discussion of this episode and its far-reaching ramifications in Kerr, *'A nation of beggars?'*, pp. 92–107. Shrewsbury accepted as proven the charge made early in December 1847 by Lord Farnham in the House of Lords, namely, that Fr McDermott had proclaimed at Sunday mass that 'Major Mahon is worse than Cromwell and yet he lives' (quoted ibid., p. 92).
32. *Nation*, 8 Jan. 1848.
33. Ibid., 29 Jan. 1848.
34. MacDonagh, 'Irish overseas emigration', p. 335.
35. Ibid., p. 474, n. 9.
36. Trench, *Realities*, p. 103.
37. Ibid., p. 104.
38. Captain Arthur Kennedy to poor law commissioners, 8 Apr. 1848, quoted in *Papers relating to proceedings for relief of distress; sixth series, 1848*, p. 821.
39. Kennedy to commissioners, 13 Apr. 1848, quoted ibid., p. 823.
40. Kennedy to commissioners, 16 Mar. 1848, quoted ibid., pp. 803–4.

41. Kennedy to commissioners, 13 Apr. 1848, quoted ibid., p. 823.
42. Kennedy to commissioners, 6 Apr. 1848, quoted ibid., p. 817.
43. Much of this controversy is well treated in Ignatius Murphy, *A people starved: life and death in west Clare* (Dublin and Portland, Oregon, 1996), pp. 53–80.
44. *Report from the select committee on Kilrush union, together with the proceedings of the committee, minutes of evidence, etc.*, p. 160, H.C. 1850 (613), xi, 529 (hereafter cited as *Kilrush union*).
45. Ibid., p. 147. See also ibid., pp. 125–6, 128, 146.
46. *Limerick Reporter*, 24 Nov. 1848, quoted in Murphy, *People starved*, p. 53. See also *Kilrush union*, pp. 97–8.
47 *Kilrush union*, p. 86. According to a newspaper report in 1848, Keane was said to control as agent 'half the superficial land area of Clare'. See Ciarán Ó Murchadha, 'One vast abbatoir: County Clare, 1848–1849', *The Other Clare*, xxi (1997), p. 60.
48. *Kilrush union*, p. 95. See also ibid., pp. 93–4; *Reports and returns relating to evictions in Kilrush union*, p. 48 [1089], H.C. 1849, xlix, 315 (hereafter cited as *Kilrush evictions*).
49. *Kilrush union*, p. 217.
50. Ibid., pp. 219–20, 223.
51. Ibid., pp. 231, 247–9.
52. Ibid., pp. 217, 247.
53. Ibid., p. 224.
54. Ibid., p. 220.
55. Ibid.
56. Ibid., p. 95.
57. *Census Ire., 1851*, pt i (Munster), p. 46.
58. *Kilrush union*, p. 221.
59. Ibid., pp. viii, 105, 108–9.
60. Ibid., p. 231.
61. Ibid., pp. 247–9.
62. Ibid., p. 236.
63. Andrés Eiríksson and Cormac Ó Gráda, *Estate records of the Irish famine: a second guide to the famine archives* (Dublin, 1995), p. 51.
64. Apart from Westby and Leconfield, another half-dozen Clare landowners in 1876 had sizeable estates of between 10,000 and 20,000 acres, but the average valuation of the six properties was barely more than £6,400. Among the twenty-five Clare proprietors with estates ranging from 5,000 to 10,000 acres, the valuations extended from £776 in the case of the lowest to just under £3,900 in the case of the highest. Obviously, the general financial picture was even grimmer for the fifty-seven Clare landowners with 2,000 to 5,000 acres and lower valuations to match. See *Copy of a return of the names of proprietors and the area and valuation of all properties in the several counties in Ireland . . .* , p. 51, H.C. 1876 (412), lxxx, 395. The Leconfield title was created in 1859 for the Wyndham family.
A corrected figure of about 37,300 acres for Lord Leconfield's total acreage in Clare appears in John Batemen, *The great landowners of Great Britain and Ireland*, intro. David Spring (new edn, Leicester and New York, 1971), p. 261.
65. *Kilrush union*, p. 226. Colonel George Wyndham was cited as an unusual exception to the generality of Kilrush landowners. He reportedly provided considerable employment and 'paid very liberally for the emigration of pauper tenants', though he too was thought to be pinched financially by 1850. Even Wyndham eventually engaged in a large clearance

(278 persons) from a portion of his property (ibid., pp. 100, 249). For Wyndham's activities during the famine, see Ciarán Ó Murchadha, *Sable wings over the land: Ennis, County Clare, and its wider community during the great famine* (Ennis, 1998), pp. 7, 26, 55, 218, 249, 288.

66. Ibid., p. 231.
67. According to the 1841 census, almost 90 per cent of the holdings of over one acre in Clare were not larger than 15 acres (*Census Ire., 1841*, p. 454). Even if one were to make the necessary correction for the expression of these data partly in terms of the larger Irish acre, the conclusion would remain that smallholders were extremely numerous in this county.
68. *Kilrush union*, p. 88.
69. Ibid., p. 102.
70. Ó Gráda, *Black '47 and beyond*, p. 59. See also idem, *New economic history*, p. 94.
71. *Kilrush union*, p. 224.
72. Ibid., p. 227.
73. Ibid., p. 239.
74. Ibid., p. 94.
75. Ibid., p. 155.
76. Ibid., p. 154. Marcus Keane told Scrope's committee in June 1850 that rundale prevailed generally 'throughout the whole union. I do not know of any part of the union in which it did not prevail up to the last few years.' He also noted that though now all proprietors were working to eliminate rundale, 'I believe I was the first who commenced it' (ibid., p. 100).
77. Ibid., p. 188. Almost 75 per cent of all tenements in Clare in the early 1840s were valued at less than £10, according to a parliamentary return of 1844. See *Returns of parliamentary electors; also, of tenements valued under the act 1 and 2 Vict., cap. 56, for relief of the poor in Ireland, 1842–3*, p. 5, H.C. 1844 (533), xliii, 323. According to a later return in 1850, nearly 45 per cent of Clare holdings were valued at £4 or less, and another third at from £4 to £8 (*Kilrush union*, p. 240).
78. *Kilrush union*, p. viii.
79. *Papers relating to proceedings for relief of distress; sixth series, 1848*, p. 796.
80. *Kilrush union*, pp. x, 2.
81. Ibid., p. 91.
82. Ibid., p. 151.
83. Ibid., pp. 91–2.
84. Ibid., p. 91.
85. Ibid.
86. Ibid., p. 100.
87. Mary Daly, citing the letters of Alexander Somerville and recent work by Timothy P. O'Neill on ejectments during the famine, suggests that clearances were taking place before the impact of the poor law amendment act of June 1847 was felt. But this conclusion rests on statistics of ejectments which simply will not bear the weight which she and O'Neill place on them. See Daly, 'Historians and famine', pp. 593–4. There were some cases of clearance before the great famine, but they should not be compared with the mass evictions of the famine years. The newspaper evidence is clear that while evictions increased in 1846, what happened beginning in mid-1847 was on an altogether different scale.
88. *Kilrush union*, p. 92.
89. Ibid., pp. 90–1.
90. *Papers relating to proceedings for relief of distress; sixth series, 1848*, p. 790.
91. *Kilrush evictions*, p. 89.
92. Ibid., p. 196.
93. Ibid., p. 89.

94. Ibid., p. 159. See also ibid., p. 193.
95. Ibid., p. 153.
96. Ibid., pp. ix–x.
97. *Kilrush evictions*, p. 32; *Galway Vindicator*, 1 July, 11, 18 Nov. 1848; S.G. Osborne, *Gleanings in the west of Ireland* (London, 1850), p. 31.
98. *Kilrush union*, p. 102. Speaking especially of the clearances in Clare in the late 1840s, an English visitor, Revd Sidney Godolphin Osborne, declared in his book *Gleanings in the west of Ireland*, 'I think the reader must already have nearly arrived at the same conclusion with myself, that eviction as carried on in this part of Ireland is very much the same as extermination. . . ' (p. 155). See also the similar verdict of Francis Coffee (*Kilrush union*, p. 222).
99. *Kilrush union*, p. 153.
100. Ibid., p. 152.
101. Ibid., p. 98.
102. Ibid., p. 151.
103. Ibid., p. 195.
104. *Return of cases of evictions from 1849 to 1880 inclusive*, pp. 8–10.
105. Ibid.
106. Jordan, *Land and popular politics*, pp. 110–11.
107. P.G. Lane, 'The general impact of the encumbered estates act of 1849 on counties Galway and Mayo', *Galway Arch. Soc. Jn.*, xxxiii (1972–3), pp. 45–51.
108. Jordan, *Land and popular politics*, pp. 112–13.
109. Marquis of Sligo to G.H. Moore, [?] 1852, quoted in Joseph Hone, *The Moores of Moore Hall* (London, 1939), pp. 158–60.
110. Lane, 'General impact', p. 48.
111. Ibid., pp. 48–9.
112. Quoted ibid., p. 50.
113. Thomas Miller, *The agricultural and social state of Ireland in 1858* (Dublin, 1858), pp. 7, 12.
114. Bourke, 'Agricultural statistics', pp. 378–9.
115. Ibid., p. 380.
116. *Return from the registrar's office of the Court of Chancery in Ireland* . . . , H.C. 1847–8 (226), lvii, 213.
117. *Cork Examiner*, 14 Dec. 1846.
118. *Cork Constitution*, 24 Nov. 1857.
119. *Cork Examiner*, 13 May 1849.
120. 12 & 13 Vict., c. 77 (28 July 1849).
121. Donnelly, 'Benn-Walsh journals', p. 106.
122. A.M. Sullivan, *New Ireland* (2 vols, 3rd edn, London, 1877), i, 197.
123. Ibid., p. 292. See also ibid., pp. 291, 293–4.
124. Report of commissioners to viceroy, 3 May 1851, quoted in *Dublin Evening Post*, 13 May 1851.
125. *Cork Examiner*, 28 Nov. 1853 (quoting *Morning Herald*).
126. *Report of her majesty's commissioners of inquiry into the working of the landlord and tenant (Ireland) act, 1870* . . . , vol. iii: *Minutes of evidence*, pt ii, p. 916 [C2779-II], H.C. 1881, xix, 166.
127. *Cork Examiner*, 11 Dec. 1860.
128. Sullivan, *New Ireland*, i, 292.
129. *Hansard*, 3rd ser., cl, 27.
130. Sullivan, *New Ireland*, i, 295.
131. *Cork Constitution*, 29 Dec. 1857.
132. Quoted in Sullivan, *New Ireland*, i, 286.
133. Ibid., p. 296.
134. Ibid., p. 298.
135. Donnelly, *Cork*, p. 131.

Chapter 7

1. L.M. Cullen, *An economic history of Ireland since 1660* (London, 1972), p. 132.
2. Vaughan and Fitzpatrick, *Irish historical statistics*, pp. 5–15.

3. S.H. Cousens, 'Regional death rates in Ireland during the great famine, from 1846 to 1851', *Population Studies*, xiv, no. 1 (July 1960), pp. 55–74.
4. Mokyr, *Why Ireland starved*, pp. 263–8.
5. Bourke, *'Visitation of God'*, p. 52.
6. Solar, 'No ordinary subsistence crisis', p. 123.
7. Kennedy *et al.*, *Mapping*, p. 105.
8. L.M. Geary, 'What people died of during the famine' in Ó Gráda, *Famine 150*, p. 101.
9. Ibid., p. 102.
10. Ibid., pp. 103–4.
11. L.M. Geary, ' Famine, fever, and the bloody flux' in Póirtéir, *Great Irish famine*, p. 83.
12. Geary, 'What people died of', p. 106.
13. McHugh, 'Famine in Irish oral tradition', pp. 399–400.
14. Geary, 'Famine', pp. 84–5; McHugh, 'Famine in Irish oral tradition', pp. 407–9.
15. Kennedy *et al.*, *Mapping*, pp. 112–16.
16. Geary, 'What people died of', pp. 107–8; Kennedy *et al.*, *Mapping*, pp. 121–4.
17. Mokyr, *Why Ireland starved*, p. 267.
18. Ibid., pp. 268–75.
19. Miller, *Emigrants and exiles*, p. 291.
20. Ibid., pp. 199, 569.
21. For the Irish inundation of Liverpool in 1847 and its effects, see Neal, 'Lancashire', pp. 26–48; idem, *Black '47*, passim. Pauper burials, mostly of Catholics, increased by almost 5,000 in Liverpool in 1847, and Ó Gráda concludes that 'some tens of thousands of famine refugees perished' in Britain as a whole during the late 1840s. See Ó Gráda, *Black '47 and beyond*, pp. 111–13.
22. Miller, *Emigrants and exiles*, p. 292; Quigley, 'Grosse Île', pp. 20–40.
23. Quoted in Brendan Ó Cathaoir, *Famine diary* (Dublin and Portland, Oregon, 1999), p. 120. See also Woodham-Smith, *Great hunger*, p. 226; Quigley, 'Grosse Île', pp. 25–6.
24. Quoted in Quigley, 'Grosse Île', p. 25.
25. Ó Cathaoir, *Famine diary*, pp. 120–1; Quigley, 'Grosse Île', pp. 24, 27.
26. Quigley, 'Grosse Île' in Crawford, *Hungry stream*, p. 32.
27. Ibid., p. 31.
28. Ibid., p. 36.
29. Miller, *Emigrants and exiles*, p. 292.
30. Ibid., pp. 295, 582. The low percentages of farmers among the emigrants of both the late 1840s and the early 1850s are undoubtedly a reflection of the youthfulness of a large proportion of those who went overseas. Many of those recorded as farm labourers and servants were the sons and daughters of farmers.
31. Ibid., pp. 293–8.
32. Cousens, 'Regional variation in emigration, 1821–41', pp. 15–30; Miller, *Emigrants and exiles*, p. 293.
33. David Fitzpatrick, 'The disappearance of the Irish agricultural labourer, 1841–1912', *Ir. Econ. & Soc. Hist.*, vii (1980), p. 88.
34. My discussion of variations in the rate of emigration at the county level is based on an elaborate set of statistical calculations made by Joel Mokyr and not published in his book *Why Ireland starved*. I am deeply grateful to him for placing these data at my disposal.
35. Miller, *Emigrants and exiles*, pp. 298–300.
36. Mokyr, *Why Ireland starved*, pp. 267–8.
37. Miller, *Emigrants and exiles*, pp. 301–7.

Chapter 8

1. Thorough treatment of the politics of this period will be found in Nowlan, *Politics of repeal*; Robert Kee, *The green flag: a history of Irish nationalism* (London, 1972); and Malcolm Brown, *The politics of Irish literature: from Thomas Davis to W.B. Yeats* (Seattle and London, 1972). In this chapter I have relied most heavily on Nowlan's excellent work.
2. For the controversy over the colleges, see D.A. Kerr, *Peel, priests, and politics: Sir Robert Peel's administration and the Roman Catholic church in Ireland, 1841–1846* (Oxford, 1982), pp. 290–351.
3. Daniel O'Connell to William Smith O'Brien, 30 June 1846, in *O'Connell corr.*, viii, 61.
4. O'Connell to Smith O'Brien, 18 Dec. 1845, ibid., vii, 349–51.
5. O'Connell to David R. Pigot, 12 July 1846, ibid., viii, 66–7.
6. *Nation*, 4, 11 July 1846.
7. See O'Connell to Smith O'Brien, 18 July 1846, and editorial note 2 in *O'Connell corr.*, viii, 70–1. For a different interpretation of this episode, see Maurice R. O'Connell, 'O'Connell reconsidered', *Studies*, lxiv, no. 254 (Summer 1975), pp. 112–14.
8. Nowlan, *Politics of repeal*, pp. 113–15.
9. Gavan Duffy to Smith O'Brien, 26 Dec. 1846, quoted ibid., p. 128.
10. Ibid., pp. 125–9.
11. Ibid., pp. 132–7.
12. For the complexities of the Irish parliamentary franchise and the variability in the social composition of the electorate during the period 1832–50, see Hoppen, *Elections, politics, and society*, pp. 1–73.
13. Nowlan, *Politics of repeal*, p. 140.
14. Ibid., pp. 145–58.
15. Ibid., p. 148.
16. For Lalor's political career, ideas, and influence, see L.M. Fogarty, *James Fintan Lalor, patriot and political essayist (1807–1849)* (Dublin, 1918); Tomás Ó Néill, *Fiontán Ó Leathlobhair* (Dublin, 1962); Nowlan, *Politics of repeal*, pp. 148–51, 153–6; Kee, *Green flag*, pp. 259–61.
17. *Nation*, 17 July 1847.
18. Sir Charles Gavan Duffy, *Four years of Irish history, 1845–1849: a sequel to 'Young Ireland'* (Dublin, 1883), pp. 476–7.
19. Quoted in Kee, *Green flag*, p. 261.
20. Nowlan, *Politics of repeal*, pp. 182–93.
21. Ibid., pp. 194–6, 202–5.
22. Ibid., pp. 206–10.
23. Kee, *Green flag*, p. 268.
24. Quoted ibid., p. 275.
25. Ibid., p. 270.
26. John Mitchel, *Jail journal* (reprint, with intro. by Thomas Flanagan, University Press of Ireland, 1982, of M.H. Gill and Son edn, Dublin, 1913), pp. 72–3.
27. Peel to Sir James Graham, 24 Aug. 1848, quoted in Nowlan, *Politics of repeal*, p. 215.
28. Kee, *Green flag*, pp. 286–9; Nowlan, *Politics of repeal*, pp. 216–17.
29. Mitchel, *Jail journal*, pp. 349–50.
30. Miller, *Emigrants and exiles*, p. 310.
31. *Nation*, 1 Sept. 1849.
32. Ibid., 8 Sept. 1849.
33. Nowlan, *Politics of repeal*, pp. 230–1. For the origins of the Tenant League, founded in Aug. 1850, see Whyte, *Indep. Ir. party*, pp. 1–13.
34. In this paragraph and the next I am heavily indebted to the analysis of Kerby Miller, *Emigrants and exiles*, pp. 310–12.
35. *Nation*, 29 Apr. 1848.

Chapter 9

1. Bradshaw, 'Nationalism and historical scholarship', pp. 340–1.
2. Among the books, see especially Kerr, *'A nation of beggars?'*; Kinealy, *Great calamity*; Ó Gráda, *New economic history*; Gray, *Irish famine*; Póirtéir, *Great Irish famine*; Morash and Hayes, *'Fearful realities'*. Among the films, see especially the four-part series entitled 'Famine', produced by Louis Marcus for Radio Telefís Éireann and broadcast in Nov. and Dec. 1995. See the select bibliography at the end of this book for additional works published after 1996.
3. Even historians who are not revisionists generally reject the exaggerated role traditionally attributed by nationalists to food exports during the famine. See, for example, Gray, *Irish famine*, pp. 46–7.
4. T.P. O'Connor, *The home rule movement, with a sketch of Irish parties from 1843 and an addition containing a full account of the great trial instigated by the London 'Times'* (New York, 1891), p. 32.
5. Jeremiah O'Donovan Rossa, *Rossa's Recollections, 1838–1898* (1898; reprint, Shannon, 1972), p. 111.
6. Peter O'Leary, *My Story*, trans. Cyril T. Ó Céirin (1915; reprint, Cork, 1970), p. 52.
7. Peadar MacSuibhne (ed.), *Paul Cullen and his contemporaries, with their letters from 1820–1902* (5 vols, Naas, Co. Kildare, 1965), iii, 353.
8. Cathal Póirtéir (ed.), *Famine echoes* (Dublin, 1995), p. 210.
9. Ibid.
10. Sir Charles Gavan Duffy, *My life in two hemispheres* (2 vols, London, 1903), i, 201.
11. Ibid., p. 197.
12. *Nation*, 28 Aug. 1847.
13. Duffy, *Life*, i, 197.
14. Ibid., pp. 196–7.
15. Ibid., p. 205.
16. Bishop John Hughes, 'A lecture on the antecedent causes of the Irish famine in 1847, delivered under the auspices of the General Committee for the Relief of the Suffering Poor of Ireland', reprinted in *New York Irish History*, ix (1995), p. 48.
17. Duffy, *Life*, i, 201.
18. Bourke, *'Visitation of God'*, p. 168.
19. Ibid., p. 52.
20. Solar, 'No ordinary subsistence crisis', pp. 123–6.
21. Thomas D'Arcy McGee, *A history of the Irish settlers in North America from the earliest period to the census of 1850* (1851; reprint, n.p., 1971). This work is a reprint of the sixth edition, published by Patrick Donahoe in Boston in 1855.
22. J.S. Crone, *A concise dictionary of Irish biography* (1937; reprint, Nendeln/Liechtenstein, 1970), p. 139.
23. McGee, *Irish settlers*, p. 136.
24. Ibid., p. 140.
25. Ibid., p. 135.
26. Mitchel, *Jail journal*, p. iv.
27. William Dillon, *Life of John Mitchel* (2 vols, London, 1888), ii, 101, 118.
28. Ibid., p. 253.
29. Mitchel, *Jail journal*, p. xlix.
30. Mitchel, *An apology for the British government in Ireland* (1860; reprint, Dublin, 1905), pp. 6–7.
31. Thomas Flanagan, critical introduction, in Mitchel, *Jail journal*, p. xviii.
32. Mitchel, *Last conquest*, p. 104.
33. Ibid., p. 121.
34. Ibid., p. 112.
35. Ibid., pp. 127, 134.

36. Ibid., p. 121.
37. John Mitchel, *The history of Ireland from the treaty of Limerick to the present time, being a continuation of the history of the Abbé MacGeoghegan* (2 vols, London, n.d.), ii, 208, 212, 214.
38. J.L. Spalding, *The religious mission of the Irish people and Catholic colonization* (1880; reprint, New York, 1978), pp. 300–1.
39. Rossa, *Recollections*, p. 111.
40. Póirtéir, *Famine echoes*, p. 149.
41. O'Connor, *Home rule movement*, pp. 118–22.
42. Ibid., p. 122.
43. Ibid., p. 123.
44. Sullivan, *New Ireland*, i, 133.
45. Póirtéir, *Famine echoes*, p. 234.
46. Ibid., p. 238.
47. Ibid., pp. 234–5.
48. Mitchel, *Jail journal*, p. xlviii.
49. Spalding, *Religious mission*, p. 314. See also p. 300.
50. Michael Davitt, *The fall of feudalism in Ireland, or the story of the Land League revolution* (London and New York, 1904), pp. 53–4.
51. T.W. Moody, *Davitt and Irish revolution, 1846–82* (Oxford and New York, 1981), pp. 8–9.
52. Rossa, *Recollections*, p. 115.
53. Ibid., pp. 118–19, 121–2, 127–8, 130, 141–2.
54. Ibid., p. 117.
55. Ibid., pp. 161–2.
56. Ibid., pp. 115–16.
57. Mitchel, *Jail journal*, pp. xlvii.
58. Ibid., p. xlvi.
59. Ibid., p. xlviii.
60. O'Connor, *Home rule movement*, p. 123.
61. Ibid., pp. 82–102.
62. Ibid., p. 113.
63. J.F. Maguire, *The Irish in America* (New York and Montreal, 1868), p. 607.
64. O'Connor, *Home rule movement*, p. 117.
65. Maguire, *Irish in America*, pp. 603–4.
66. Ibid., pp. 604–7.
67. Robert Kee, *The laurel and the ivy: the story of Charles Stewart Parnell and Irish nationalism* (London, 1993), p. 189.
68. Davitt, *Fall of feudalism*, p. 154.
69. Sullivan, *New Ireland*, i, 286.
70. Rossa, *Recollections*, p. 191.
71. Ibid., p. 104.
72. John Devoy, *Recollections of an Irish rebel* (1929; reprint, Shannon, 1969), p. 4.
73. Mitchel, *Jail journal*, p. 203.
74. Sullivan, *New Ireland*, i, 286–7.
75. T.D., A.M., and D.B. Sullivan (eds), *Speeches from the dock, or protests of Irish patriotism, with introductory sketches and biographical notices* (42nd edn, Dublin, 1888), pp. 158–9.
76. Póirtéir, *Famine echoes*, pp. 201–2.
77. Rossa, *Recollections*, p. 166.
78. Póirtéir, *Famine echoes*, pp. 120–1.
79. Ibid., pp. 210–11.
80. Ibid., p. 211.
81. Ibid., pp. 145–6.
82. Maguire, *Irish in America*, p. 622.
83. Philip Bagenal, *The American Irish and their influence on Irish politics* (London, 1882), p. 128.
84. Mitchel, *Last conquest*, p. 219.
85. Hughes, 'Lecture on antecedent causes', p. 47.
86. Davitt, *Fall of feudalism*, p. 51.
87. Rossa, *Recollections*, p. 196.
88. Ibid., pp. 110–11.
89. Ibid., p. 110.
90. Davitt, *Fall of feudalism*, p. 50.
91. T.D. Sullivan, *Recollections of troubled times in Irish politics* (Dublin, 1905), pp. 3–4.
92. Canon John O'Rourke, *The great Irish famine* (1874; reprint, Dublin, 1989), pp. 264–5. See also pp. 266–7, 292.

93. Sullivan, *Recollections*, p. 4 and n.
94. Bagenal, *American Irish*, pp. 128–9.
95. Mitchel, *Last conquest*, p. 192.
96. Sullivan, *Speeches from the dock*, p. 158.
97. Mitchel, *Last conquest*, p. 207.
98. Gray, '*Punch* and great famine', p. 29.
99. Bagenal, *American Irish*, p. 129.
100. Sullivan, *Speeches from the dock*, p. 288.
101. Mitchel, *Jail journal*, pp. xlix–l.
102. Ibid., p. 156.
103. John Savage, *'98 and '48: the modern revolutionary history and literature of Ireland* (New York, 1882), p. 391.
104. Ibid., p. 398.
105. Sullivan, *Speeches from the dock*, p. 105.
106. Ibid., p. 152.
107. Savage, *'98 and '48*, p. 342.
108. Ibid., p. 371.
109. Duffy, *Life*, i, 198.
110. Ibid., p. 199.
111. Davitt, *Fall of feudalism*, p. 47.
112. Mitchel, *Jail journal*, p. 88.
113. Ibid., p. xlvi.
114. Davitt, *Fall of feudalism*, p. 53.
115. Savage, *'98 and '48*, pp. 328–9.
116. Sullivan, *New Ireland*, i, 183.
117. Savage, *'98 and '48*, p. 312.
118. Mitchel, *Jail journal*, pp. 219–20.
119. Davitt, *Fall of feudalism*, pp. 49–50.
120. Ibid., p. 64.
121. Sullivan, *New Ireland*, i, 137–8.
122. Ibid., p. 141.
123. Donnelly, 'Mass eviction', pp. 169–70.
124. K.T. Hinkson (ed.), *The cabinet of Irish literature: selections from the works of the chief poets, orators, and prose writers of Ireland, with biographical sketches and literary notices by Charles A. Read, F.R.H.S.* (new edn, 4 vols, London, 1902), iii, 92–4.
125. MacSuibhne, *Paul Cullen*, i, 301.
126. Ibid., ii, 56–8.
127. Hinkson, *Cabinet of Irish literature*, iii, 92–4.
128. I am indebted to Líam Kennedy of the Queen's University of Belfast for the thrust of the argument in this and the preceding paragraph. Kennedy also observes that constructions of the famine in nationalist polemical writings 'were costless and hence enormously attractive in hammering out denunciations of England'. See his essay entitled 'Out of history: Ireland, that "most distressful country"' in Líam Kennedy, *Colonialism, religion, and nationalism in Ireland* (Belfast, 1996), pp. 182–223.
129. Donnelly, 'Irish property must pay for Irish poverty', pp. 60–75.

Select Bibliography

This select bibliography heavily emphasises books and articles on the great famine that have appeared since about 1990. During the last decade or so there has been an explosion of research, writing, and publication about the famine, especially in connection with the official sesquicentenary of 1995–7. Also included in the bibliography are some other printed works of an earlier vintage which are considered important contemporary sources or significant scholarly contributions to the subject.

Aalen, F.H.A., Kevin Whelan, and Matthew Stout (eds), *Atlas of the Irish rural landscape.* Cork, 1997.

Akenson, D.H., *Small differences: Irish Catholics and Irish Protestants, 1815–1922: an international perspective.* Kingston and Montreal, 1988.

Akenson, D.H., *The Irish diaspora: a primer.* Toronto and Belfast, 1993.

Arnold, David, *Famine: social crisis and historical change.* Oxford and New York, 1988.

Aykroyd, W.R., *The conquest of famine.* London, 1974.

Bayor, R.H., and T.J. Meagher (eds), *The New York Irish.* Baltimore and London, 1996.

Bowen, Desmond, *Souperism: myth or reality: a study in souperism.* Cork, 1970.

Bourke, P.M.A., *'The visitation of God'?: the potato and the great Irish famine.* Ed. Jacqueline Hill and Cormac Ó Gráda. Dublin, 1993.

Bradshaw, Brendan, 'Nationalism and historical scholarship in modern Ireland', *Irish Historical Studies*, xxvi, no. 104 (Nov. 1989), pp. 329–51.

Brady, Ciaran (ed.), *Interpreting Irish history: the debate on historical revisionism, 1938–1994.* Dublin and Portland, Oregon, 1994.

Brown, Malcolm, *The politics of Irish literature: from Thomas Davis to W.B. Yeats.* Seattle and London, 1972.

Campbell, S.J., *The great Irish famine: words and images from the Famine Museum, Strokestown Park, County Roscommon.* Strokestown, 1994.

Central Relief Committee, *Transactions of the Central Relief Committee of the Society of Friends during the famine in Ireland in 1846 and 1847.* Dublin, 1852.

Clark, Samuel, *Social origins of the Irish land war.* Princeton and Guildford, Surrey, 1979.

Connell, K.H., *The population of Ireland, 1750–1845.* Oxford, 1950.

Connolly, S.J., 'Revisions revised?: new work on the Irish famine', *Victorian Studies* (Winter 1996), pp. 205–16.

Cosgrave, Marianne, 'Sources in the National Archives for researching the great famine: the relief commission papers', *Irish Archives*, ii, no. 2 (Autumn 1995), pp. 3–12.

Cousens, S.H., 'Regional death rates in Ireland during the great famine, from 1846 to 1851', *Population Studies*, xiv, no. 1 (July 1960), pp. 55–74.

Cousens, S.H., 'The regional pattern of emigration during the great famine, 1846–1851', *Transactions and Papers of the Institute of British Geographers*, no. 28 (1960), pp. 119–34.

Cousens, S.H., 'Emigration and demographic change in Ireland, 1851–1861', *Economic History Review*, ser. 2, xiv, no. 2 (Dec. 1961), pp. 275–88.

Cowman, Des, and Donald Brady (eds), *The famine in Waterford, 1845–1850: teacht na bprátaí dubha.* Dublin, 1995.

Crawford, E.M. (ed.), *Famine: the Irish experience, 900–1900: subsistence crises and famines in Ireland.* Edinburgh, 1989.

Crawford, E.M., 'The great Irish famine, 1845–9: image versus reality' in Raymond Gillespie and B.P. Kennedy (eds), *Ireland: art into history* (Dublin and Niwot, Colorado, 1994), pp. 75–88.

Crawford, E.M. (ed.), *The hungry stream: essays on emigration and famine.* Belfast, 1997.

Crotty, R.D., *Irish agricultural production: its volume and structure.* Cork, 1966.

Cullen, L.M., *The emergence of modern Ireland, 1600–1900.* London, 1981.

Curtin, Nancy, and Vera Kreilkamp (eds), *Éire-Ireland*, xxxii, no. 1 (Spring 1997), special issue devoted to the great famine.

Daly, M.E., *The famine in Ireland.* Dundalk, 1986.

Daly, M.E., 'Revisionism and Irish history: the great famine' in D.G. Boyce and Alan O'Day (eds), *The making of modern Irish history: revisionism and the revisionist controversy* (London and New York, 1996), pp. 71–89.

Daly, M.E., 'Historians and the famine: a beleaguered species?', *Irish Historical Studies*, xxx, no. 120 (Nov. 1997), pp. 591–601.

Davis, Richard, *The Young Ireland movement.* Dublin and Totowa, New Jersey, 1987.

Devine, T.M., and David Dickson (eds), *Ireland and Scotland, 1600–1850: parallels and contrasts in economic and social development.* Edinburgh, 1983.

Devine, T.M., *The great Highland famine: hunger, emigration, and the Scottish Highlands in the nineteenth century.* Edinburgh, 1988.

Dickson, David, Cormac Ó Gráda, and Stuart Daultrey, 'Hearth tax, household size, and Irish population change, 1672–1821', *Proceedings of the Royal Irish Academy*, lxxxii, sec. C, no. 6 (Dec. 1982), pp. 125–81.

Diner, H.R., *Erin's daughters in America: Irish immigrant women in the nineteenth century.* Baltimore and London, 1983.

Donnelly, J.S., Jr, *Landlord and tenant in nineteenth-century Ireland.* Dublin, 1973.

Donnelly, J.S., Jr, *The land and the people of nineteenth-century Cork: the rural economy and the land question.* London and Boston, 1975.

Donnelly, J.S., Jr, 'The journals of Sir John Benn-Walsh relating to the management of his Irish estates, 1823–64', *Journal of the Cork Historical and Archaeological Society*, lxxx, no. 230 (July–Dec. 1974), pp. 86–123; lxxxi, no. 231 (Jan.–June 1975), pp. 15–42.

Donnelly, J.S., Jr, 'The Kenmare estates during the nineteenth century: part 1', *Journal of the Kerry Archaeological and Historical Society*, no. 21 (1988), pp. 5–41.

Donnelly, J.S., Jr, 'Famine and government response, 1845–6'; 'Production, prices, and exports, 1846–51'; 'The administration of relief, 1846–7'; 'The soup kitchens'; 'The administration of relief, 1847–51'; 'Landlords and tenants'; 'Excess mortality and emigration'; 'A famine in Irish politics' in Vaughan, *A new history of Ireland*, v, pt 1, pp. 272–371.

Donnelly, J.S., Jr, 'Mass eviction and the great famine: the clearances revisited' in Póirtéir, *Great Irish famine*, pp. 155–73.

Donnelly, J.S., Jr, '"Irish property must pay for Irish poverty": British public opinion and the great Irish famine' in Morash and Hayes, *'Fearful realities'*, pp. 60–76.

Donnelly, J.S., Jr, 'The construction of the memory of the famine in Ireland and the Irish diaspora, 1850–1900', *Éire-Ireland*, xxxi, nos 1–2 (Summer 1996), pp. 26–61.

Donnelly, J.S., Jr, 'The great famine and its interpreters, old and new' in Hayden, *Irish hunger*, pp. 117–33.

Dooher, Johnny (ed.), *The great famine and Ulster (regional and local perspectives)*, special issue of *Ulster Local Studies*, xvii, no. 2 (Winter 1995).

Dooley, T.A.M., *Sources for the history of landed estates in Ireland.* Dublin and Portland, Oregon, 2000.

Edwards, R.D., and T.D. Williams (eds), *The great famine: studies in Irish history, 1845–52.* New York, 1957.

Eiríksson, Andrés, and Cormac Ó Gráda, *Estate records of the Irish famine: a second guide to famine archives, 1840–1855.* Dublin, 1995.

Elliott, B.S., *Irish migrants in the Canadas: a new approach.* Kingston and Belfast, 1988.

Ellis, Eilish, *Emigrants from Ireland, 1847–1852: state-aided emigration schemes from crown estates in Ireland.* Baltimore, 1983.

Fitzpatrick, David, *Irish emigration, 1801–1921.* Dundalk, 1984.

Fitzpatrick, David, *Oceans of consolation: personal accounts of Irish migration to Australia.* Ithaca and London, 1994.

Fitzpatrick, David, 'Famine, entitlements, and seduction: Captain Edmond Wynne in Ireland, 1846–51', *English Historical Review*, cx, no. 147 (1995), pp. 596–619.

Fitzpatrick, David, 'Women and the great famine' in Kelleher and Murphy, *Gender perspectives*, pp. 50–69.

Foster, R.F., *Paddy and Mr Punch: connections in Irish and English history.* London and New York, 1993.

Gallagher, Thomas, *Paddy's lament: Ireland, 1846–1847: prelude to hatred.* New York and London, 1982.

Garner, Edward, *To die by inches: an account of the Fermoy poor law union during the great famine, 1845–1850.* Fermoy, Co. Cork, 1986.

Geary, L.M., 'Famine, fever, and the bloody flux' in Póirtéir, *The great Irish famine*, pp. 74–85.

Geary, L.M., 'The great famine and Fethard temporary fever hospital', *Tipperary Historical Journal*, ix (1997), pp. 151–65.

Geary, L.M., 'What people died of during the famine' in Ó Gráda, *Famine 150*, pp. 95–111.

Goodbody, Rob, *A suitable channel: Quaker relief in the great famine.* Bray, Co. Wicklow, 1995.

Grant, James, 'The great famine and the poor law in the province of Ulster: the rate-in-aid issue of 1849', *Irish Historical Studies*, xxvii, no. 105 (May 1990), pp. 30–47.

Grant, James, 'Local relief committees in Ulster, 1845–7' in Crawford, *The hungry stream*, pp. 185–98.

Grant, James, 'The great famine in County Down' in Lindsay Proudfoot (ed.), *Down: history and society* (Dublin, 1997), pp. 353–82.

Gray, Peter, '*Punch* and the great famine', *History Ireland*, i, no. 2 (Summer 1993), pp. 26–33.

Gray, Peter, 'Potatoes and providence: British government's responses to the great famine', *Bullán: An Irish Studies Journal*, i (1994), pp. 75–90.

Gray, Peter, 'The triumph of dogma: ideology and famine relief', *History Ireland*, iii, no. 2 (Summer 1995), pp. 26–34.

Gray, Peter, *The Irish famine.* New York and London, 1995.

Gray, Peter, 'Famine relief policy in comparative perspective: Ireland, Scotland, and northwestern Europe, 1845–1849', *Éire-Ireland*, xxxii, no. 1 (Spring 1997), pp. 86–108.

Gray, Peter, *Famine, land, and politics: British government and Irish society, 1843–1850.* Dublin and Portland, Oregon, 1999.

Gribben, Arthur (ed.), *The great famine and the Irish diaspora in America.* Amherst, Mass., 1999.

Guinnane, Timothy, *The vanishing Irish: households, migration, and the rural economy in Ireland, 1850–1914.* Princeton and London, 1997.

Harris, Ruth-Ann, 'Ballykilcline and beyond', *Irish Studies Review*, no. 15 (Summer 1996), pp. 39–42.

Hayden, Tom (ed.), *Irish hunger: personal reflections on the legacy of the famine.* Boulder, Colorado, and Dublin, 1997.

Hickey, Patrick, 'Famine, mortality, and emigration: a profile of six parishes in the poor law union of Skibbereen, 1846–7' in Patrick O'Flanagan and C.G. Buttimer (eds), *Cork: history and society* (Dublin, 1993), pp. 873–918.

Hilton, Boyd, *The age of atonement: the influence of evangelicalism on social and economic thought, 1785–1865.* Oxford and New York, 1988.

Hood, Susan, 'The famine in the Strokestown Park House archive', *Irish Review*, nos 17–18 (Winter 1995), pp. 109–17.

Hoppen, K.T., *Elections, politics, and society in Ireland, 1832–1885.* Oxford and New York, 1984.

Houston, C.J., and W.J. Smyth, *Irish emigration and Canadian settlement: patterns, links, and letters.* Toronto and Belfast, 1990.

Jordan, D.E., Jr, *Land and popular politics in Ireland: County Mayo from the plantation to the land war.* Cambridge, 1994.

Kee, Robert, *The green flag: the turbulent history of the Irish national movement.* London, 1972.

Kelleher, Margaret, and J.H. Murphy (eds), *Gender perspectives in 19th century Ireland: public and private spheres.* Dublin, 1997.

Kelleher, Margaret, *The feminization of famine: expressions of the inexpressible?* Durham, North Carolina, and Cork, 1997.

Kennedy, Líam, *Colonialism, religion, and nationalism in Ireland.* Belfast, 1996.

Kennedy, Líam, and P.S. Ell, E.M. Crawford, and L.A. Clarkson, *Mapping the great Irish famine: a survey of the famine decades.* Dublin and Portland, Oregon, 1999.

Kennedy, Líam, 'Bastardy and the great famine: Ireland, 1845–1850', *Continuity and Change*, xiv, no. 3 (1999), pp. 429–52.

Kerr, D.A., *Peel, priests, and politics: Sir Robert Peel's administration and the Roman Catholic church in Ireland, 1841–1846.* Oxford and New York, 1982.

Kerr, D.A., *'A nation of beggars'?: priests, people, and politics in famine Ireland, 1846–1852.* Oxford and New York, 1994.

Kerr, D.A., *The Catholic church and the famine.* Dublin, 1996.

Kierse, Seán, *The famine years in the parish of Killaloe, 1845–1851.* Killaloe, Co. Clare, 1984.

Killen, John, *The famine decade: contemporary accounts, 1841–1851.* Belfast, 1995.

Kinealy, Christine, *This great calamity: the Irish famine, 1845–52.* Dublin, 1994.

Kinealy, Christine, *A death-dealing famine: the great hunger in Ireland.* London and Chicago, 1997.

Kinealy, Christine, and Trevor Parkhill (eds), *The famine in Ulster.* Belfast, 1997.

King, S.H., '" Pictures drawn from memory": William Carleton's experience of famine', *Irish Review*, nos 17–18 (Winter 1995), pp. 80–9.

Kinsella, Anna, *County Wexford in the famine years, 1845–1849.* Enniscorthy, Co. Wexford, 1995.

Kissane, Noel, *The Irish famine: a documentary history.* Dublin, 1995.

Knobel, D.T., *Paddy and the republic: ethnicity and nationality in antebellum America.* Middletown, Connecticut, 1986.

Lane, P.G., 'The general impact of the encumbered estates act of 1849 on counties Galway and Mayo', *Journal of the Galway Archaeological and Historical Society*, xxxiii (1972–3), pp. 44–73.

Lanigan, Anne, 'Tipperary workhouse children and the famine', *Tipperary Historical Journal*, viii (1995), pp. 54–80.

Lee, Joseph, *The modernisation of Irish society, 1848–1918.* Dublin, 1973.

Lindsay, Deirdre, and David Fitzpatrick, *Records of the Irish famine: a guide to local archives, 1840–1855.* Dublin, 1993.

Litton, Helen, *The Irish famine: an illustrated history.* Dublin, 1994.

Lyne, G.J., 'William Steuart Trench and post-famine emigration from Kenmare to America, 1850–55', *Journal of the Kerry Archaeological and Historical Society*, no. 25 (1992), pp. 51–137.

Lysaght, Patricia, 'Perspectives on women during the great Irish famine from oral tradition', *Béaloideas*, nos 64–5 (1996–7), pp. 63–131.

MacAtasney, Gerard, *'This dreadful visitation': the famine in Lurgan/Portadown.* Belfast, 1997.

MacAtasney, Gerard, *Leitrim and the great hunger, 1845–50: '. . . a temporary inconvenience . . .'?* Carrick-on-Shannon, Co. Leitrim, 1997.

McCorry, F.X., 'The famine in the Montiaghs' in F.X. McCorry, Art Hughes, and Roger Weatherup (eds), *Armagh: history and society* (forthcoming).

MacDonagh, Oliver, *The hereditary bondsman: Daniel O'Connell, 1775–1829.* London, 1988.

MacDonagh, Oliver, *The emancipist: Daniel O'Connell, 1830–47.* London, 1989.

McHugh, R.J., 'The famine in Irish oral tradition' in Edwards and Williams, *The great famine*, pp. 389–436.

Macintyre, Angus, *The Liberator: Daniel O'Connell and the Irish party, 1830–1847.* London, 1965.

MacKay, Donald, *Flight from famine: the coming of the Irish to Canada.* Toronto and London, 1990.

Mac Lochlainn, Antain, 'The famine in Gaelic tradition', *Irish Review*, nos 17–18 (Winter 1995), pp. 90–108.

Marnane, D.G., 'South Tipperary on the eve of the great famine', *Tipperary Historical Journal*, viii (1995), pp. 1–53.

Marnane, D.G., 'The famine in south Tipperary – part one', *Tipperary Historical Journal*, ix (1996), pp. 1–42.

Marnane, D.G., 'The famine in south Tipperary – part two', *Tipperary Historical Journal*, x (1997), pp. 131–50.

Miller, K.A., *Emigrants and exiles: Ireland and the Irish exodus to North America.* New York and Oxford, 1985.

Miller, K.A., and Paul Wagner, *Out of Ireland: the story of Irish emigration to America.* Washington, D.C., 1994.

Mitchel, John, *Jail journal.* Intro. by Thomas Flanagan. New edn. Dublin, 1982.

Mitchel, John, *An apology for the British government in Ireland.* Dublin, 1905. First published in Dublin, 1860.

Mitchel, John, *The last conquest of Ireland (perhaps).* Glasgow, n.d. Published in Dublin, 1861.

Mokyr, Joel, *Why Ireland starved: a quantitative and analytical history of the Irish economy, 1800–1850.* London and Boston, 1983.

Morash, Christopher, *Writing the Irish famine.* Oxford and New York, 1995.

Morash, Christopher, 'Spectres of the famine', *Irish Review*, nos 17–18 (Winter 1995), pp. 74–9.

Morash, Christopher, and Richard Hayes (eds), *'Fearful realities': new perspectives on the famine.* Dublin and Portland, Oregon, 1996.

Murphy, Ignatius, *Before the famine struck: life in west Clare, 1834–1845.* Dublin and Portland, Oregon, 1996.

Murphy, Ignatius, *A starving people: life and death in west Clare, 1845–1851.* Dublin and Portland, Oregon, 1996.

Neal, Frank, 'Lancashire, the famine Irish, and the poor laws: a study in crisis management', *Irish Economic and Social History*, xxii (1995), pp. 26–48.

Neal, Frank, *Black '47: Britain and the famine Irish.* New York and London, 1998.

Nicholls, Sir George, *A history of the Irish poor law in connexion with the condition of the people.* London, 1856.

Nicholson, Asenath, *Annals of the famine in Ireland.* Ed. Maureen Murphy. Dublin, 1998.

Nowlan, K.B., *The politics of repeal: a study in the relations between Great Britain and Ireland, 1841–50.* London and Toronto, 1965.

O'Brien, John, and Pauric Travers (eds), *The Irish emigrant experience in Australia.* Dublin, 1991.

O'Brien, W.P., *The great famine in Ireland and a retrospect of the fifty years 1845–95, with a sketch of the present condition and future prospects of the congested districts.* London, 1896.

Ó Cathaoir, Brendan, *Famine diary.* Dublin and Portland, Oregon, 1999.

Ó Ciosáin, Niall, 'Was there "silence" about the famine?', *Irish Studies Review*, no. 13 (Winter 1995–6), pp. 7–10.

O'Driscoll, Robert, and Lorna Reynolds (eds), *The untold story: the Irish in Canada.* 2 vols. Toronto, 1988.

O'Gallagher, Marianna, *Grosse Île: gateway to Canada, 1832–1937.* Quebec, 1984.

O'Gallagher, Marianna, and R.M. Dompierre (eds), *Eyewitness: Grosse Île, 1847.* Quebec, 1995.

Ó Gráda, Cormac, *Éire roimh an ngorta: an saol eacnamaíoch.* Dublin, 1985.

Ó Gráda, Cormac, *The great Irish famine.* London, 1989.

Ó Gráda, Cormac, '"Making history" in Ireland in the 1940s and 1950s: the saga of *The great famine*', *Irish Review*, no. 12 (Spring/Summer 1992), pp. 87–107.

Ó Gráda, Cormac, *Ireland before and after the famine: explorations in economic history, 1800–1925.* 2nd edn. Manchester, 1993.

Ó Gráda, Cormac, *Ireland: a new economic history, 1780–1939.* Oxford and New York, 1994.

Ó Gráda, Cormac, *An drochshaol: béaloideas agus amhráin.* Dublin, 1994.

Ó Gráda, Cormac, 'Making Irish famine history in 1995', *History Workshop Journal*, xlii (1996), pp. 87–104.

Ó Gráda, Cormac (ed.), *Famine 150: commemorative lecture series.* Dublin, 1997.

Ó Gráda, Cormac, and K.H. O'Rourke, 'Migration as disaster relief: lessons from the great Irish famine', *European Review of Economic History*, i, pt 1 (Apr. 1997), pp. 3–26.

Ó Gráda, Cormac, 'New perspectives on the Irish famine', *Bullán: An Irish Studies Journal*, iii, no. 2 (Winter 1997/Spring 1998), pp. 103–15.

Ó Gráda, Cormac, *Black '47 and beyond: the great Irish famine in history, economy, and memory.* Princeton, 1999.

O'Neill, T.P., 'The organisation and administration of relief, 1845–1852' in Edwards and Williams, *The great famine*, pp. 207–59.

O'Neill, Timothy P., 'Poverty in Ireland, 1815–45', *Folk Life: A Journal of Ethnological Studies*, xi (1973), pp. 22–33.

O'Neill, Timothy P., 'Fever and public health in pre-famine Ireland', *Journal of the Royal Society of Antiquaries of Ireland*, ciii, pt 1 (1973), pp. 1–34.

O'Neill, Timothy P., 'Clare and Irish poverty, 1815–1851', *Studia Hibernica*, no. 14 (1974), pp. 7–27.

O'Neill, Timothy P., 'The persistence of famine in Ireland' in Póirtéir, *The great Irish famine*, pp. 204–18.

O'Neill, Timothy P., 'Minor famines and relief in Galway, 1815–1925' in Gerard Moran and Raymond Gillespie (eds), *Galway: history and society* (Dublin, 1996), pp. 445–87.

Ó Murchadha, Ciarán, 'The onset of famine: County Clare, 1845–1846', *The Other Clare*, xix (1995), pp. 46–53.

Ó Murchadha, Ciarán, 'One vast abattoir: County Clare, 1848–1849', *The Other Clare*, xxi (1997), pp. 58–67.

Ó Murchadha, Ciarán, *Sable wings over the land: Ennis, County Clare, and its wider community during the great famine.* Ennis, 1998.

O'Rourke, John, *The history of the great Irish famine of 1847, with notices of earlier Irish famines.* 3rd edn. Dublin, 1902.

O'Rourke, John, *The great Irish famine.* New abridged edn. Dublin, 1989.

O'Rourke, K.H., 'Did the great Irish famine matter?', *Journal of Economic History*, li, no. 1 (Mar. 1991), pp. 1–22.

O'Sullivan, Patrick (ed.), *The Irish worldwide: heritage, history, and identity,* vi: *the meaning of the famine.* London, 1996.

Ó Tuathaigh, Gearóid, *Ireland before the famine, 1798–1848.* Dublin, 1972.

Owens, Gary, 'Nationalism without words: symbolism and ritual behaviour in the repeal "monster meetings" of 1843–5' in J.S. Donnelly, Jr, and K.A. Miller (eds), *Irish popular culture, 1650–1850* (Dublin and Portland, Oregon, 1998), pp. 242–69.

Pelly, Patricia, and Andrew Tod (eds), *Elizabeth Grant of Rothiemurchus: the Highland lady in Ireland: journals, 1840–50.* Edinburgh, 1991.

Percival, John, *The great famine: Ireland's potato famine, 1845–51.* New York, 1995.

Póirtéir, Cathal (ed.), *Famine echoes.* Dublin, 1995.

Póirtéir, Cathal (ed.), *The great Irish famine.* Cork and Dublin, 1995.

Post, J.D., *The last great subsistence crisis in the western world.* Baltimore and London, 1977.

Post, J.D., *Food shortage, climatic variability, and epidemic disease in preindustrial Europe: the mortality peak in the early 1740s.* Ithaca and London, 1985.

Potter, George, *To the golden door: the story of the Irish in Ireland and America.* Boston and Toronto, 1960.

Quigley, Michael, 'Grosse Île: Canada's famine memorial', *Éire-Ireland*, xxxii, no. 1 (Spring 1997), pp. 20–40.

Quigley, Michael, 'Grosse Île: "the most important and evocative great famine site outside of Ireland"' in Crawford, *The hungry stream*, pp. 25–40.

Quinlan, Carmel, '"A punishment from God": the famine in the centenary folklore questionnaire', *Irish Review*, no. 19 (Spring/Summer 1996), pp. 68–86.

Scally, R.J., *The end of hidden Ireland: rebellion, famine, and emigration.* New York and Oxford, 1995.

Sen, A.K., *Poverty and famines: an essay on entitlement and deprivation.* Oxford and New York, 1981.

Solar, Peter, 'The great famine was no ordinary subsistence crisis' in Crawford, *Famine*, pp. 112–31.

Somerville, Alexander, *Letters from Ireland during the famine of 1847.* Ed. with intro. by K.D.M. Snell. Dublin and Portland, Oregon, 1994.

Swords, Liam, *In their own words: the famine in north Connacht, 1845–49.* Blackrock, Co. Dublin, 1999.

Thomson, David, with Moira McGusty (eds), *The Irish journals of Elizabeth Smith, 1840–1850.* Oxford, 1980.

Trevelyan, C.E., *The Irish crisis.* London, 1848.

Vaughan, W.E., and A.J. Fitzpatrick (eds), *Irish historical statistics: population, 1821–1971.* Dublin, 1978.

Vaughan, W.E. (ed.), *A new history of Ireland*, v, pt 1, *Ireland under the union, 1801–70.* Oxford and New York, 1989.

Vaughan, W.E., *Landlords and tenants in mid-Victorian Ireland.* Oxford and New York, 1994.

Vincent, Joan, 'A political orchestration of the Irish famine: County Fermanagh, May 1847' in Marilyn Silverman and P.H. Gulliver (eds), *Approaching the past: historical anthropology through Irish case studies* (New York and Oxford, 1992) pp. 75–98.

Whelan, Irene, 'Edward Nangle and the Achill mission, 1834–1852' in Raymond Gillespie and Gerard Moran (eds), *'A various country': essays in Mayo history, 1500–1900* (Westport, Co. Mayo, 1987), pp. 113–34.

Whelan, Irene, 'The stigma of souperism' in Póirtéir, *The great Irish famine*, pp. 135–54.

Whyte, J.H., *The independent Irish party, 1850–9.* London and New York, 1958.

Wilson, C.A., *A new lease on life: landlords, tenants, and immigrants in Ireland and Canada.* Montreal and London, 1994.

Woodham-Smith, Cecil, *The great hunger: Ireland, 1845–1849.* New York and London, 1962.

Yager, Tom, 'Mass eviction in the Mullet peninsula during and after the great famine', *Irish Economic and Social History*, xxiii (1996), pp. 24–44.

Index

Page numbers in italics refer to illustration captions, maps, or tables.